A GUIDE TO CONTEMPORARY HERMENEUTICS

Major Trends in Biblical Interpretation

Edited by
Donald K. McKim

GRAND RAPIDS, MICHIGAN
WILLIAM B. EERDMANS PUBLISHING COMPANY

To Van Hunter

faithful biblical interpreter,
whose insights into Holy Scripture
are matched only by his sensitive, caring friendship

Dedicated with appreciation

Copyright © 1986 by Wm. B. Eerdmans Publishing Co.
255 Jefferson Ave. S.E., Grand Rapids, Mich. 49503
All rights reserved
Printed in the United States of America

Library of Congress Cataloging-in-Publication Data

A Guide to contemporary hermeneutics.

Includes bibliographical references.
1. Bible—Criticism, interpretation, etc.—History—
20th century. I. McKim, Donald K.
BS500.G85 1985   220.6'01   86-16487

ISBN 0-8028-0094-1

CONTENTS

v

PART II: THEOLOGICAL ATTITUDES

PART III: CURRENT ASSESSMENTS

PART IV: CONTEMPORARY APPROACHES

ACKNOWLEDGMENTS

The editor and publisher gratefully acknowledge permission to reprint the following material:

Birch, Bruce C. "Biblical Hermeneutics in Recent Discussion: Old Testament." *Religious Studies Review* 10 (1984): 1-7.

Froehlich, Karlfried. "Biblical Hermeneutics on the Move." *Word and World* 1 (1981): 140-52.

Harrington, Daniel J. "Biblical Hermeneutics in Recent Discussion: New Testament." *Religious Studies Review* 10 (1984): 7-10.

International Council on Biblical Inerrancy. "Articles of Affirmation and Denial." Copyright © 1982 by the International Council on Biblical Inerrancy. Previously appeared in *Hermeneutics, Inerrancy and the Bible*. Edited by Earl D. Radmacher and Robert D. Preus. Grand Rapids: Zondervan, 1984. Pp. 881-87.

Jacobson, Richard, "The Structuralists and the Bible." *Interpretation* 28 (1974): 146-64.

Kaiser, Walter C., Jr. "Legitimate Hermeneutics." In *Inerrancy*. Edited by Norman L. Geisler. Grand Rapids: Zondervan, 1979. Pp. 117-47. Copyright © 1978 by The Zondervan Corporation. Used by permission.

Keifert, Patrick R. "Mind Reader and Maestro: Models for

Understanding Biblical Interpreters." *Word and World* 1 (1980): 153-68.

Kraft, Charles H. "Supracultural Meanings via Cultural Forms." In *Christianity in Culture: A Study in Dynamic Biblical Theologizing in Cross-Cultural Perspective.* Maryknoll, N.Y.: Orbis Books, 1979. Pp. 116-46. Copyright © 1979 by Charles H. Kraft.

LaSor, William Sanford. "The *Sensus Plenior* and Biblical Interpretation." In *Scripture, Tradition, and Interpretation: Essays Presented to Everett F. Harrison by His Students and Colleagues in Honor of His Seventy-fifth Birthday.* Edited by W. Ward Gasque and William Sanford LaSor. Grand Rapids: Eerdmans, 1978. Pp. 260-77.

Macky, Peter W. "The Coming Revolution: The New Literary Approach to New Testament Interpretation." *The Theological Educator* 9 (Spring 1979): 32-46.

Miguez Bonino, José. "Hermeneutics, Truth, and Praxis." In *Doing Theology in a Revolutionary Situation.* Philadelphia: Fortress Press, 1975. Pp. 86-105. Copyright © 1975 by Fortress Press. Used by permission.

Padilla, C. René. "The Interpreted Word: Reflections on Contextual Hermeneutics." *Themelios,* September 1981, pp. 18-23.

Rad, Gerhard von. "Typological Interpretation of the Old Testament." Translated by John Bright. Copyright © 1952, 1963 by Christian Kaiser Verlag. Previously appeared in *Essays on Old Testament Hermeneutics.* Edited by James Luther Mays. Richmond: John Knox Press, 1963. Pp. 17-39.

Schüssler Fiorenza, Elisabeth. "Toward a Feminist Biblical Hermeneutics: Biblical Interpretation and Liberation Theology." In *The Challenge of Liberation Theology: A First World Response.* Edited by Brian Mahan and C. Dale Richesin. Maryknoll, N.Y.: Orbis Books, 1981. Pp. 91-112.

Steinmetz, David C. "Theology and Exegesis: Ten Theses." *Histoire de l'exégèse au XVIe siècle.* Textes Du Colloque International Tenu a Genève en 1976. Genève: Librairie Droz S. A., 1978. P. 382.

Thiselton, Anthony C. "Hermeneutics and Theology: The Legitimacy and Necessity of Hermeneutics." In *The Two Horizons: New Testament Hermeneutics and Philosophical Description.* Copyright © 1980 by Anthony C. Thiselton. First published 1980 by The Paternoster Press. First American edition published through special arrangement with Paternoster by the William B. Eerdmans Publishing Co.

Thiselton, Anthony C. "The New Hermeneutic." In *New Testament Interpretation: Essays on Principles and Methods.* Edited by I. Howard Marshall. Grand Rapids: Eerdmans, 1977. Pp. 308-33. Copyright © 1977 by The Paternoster Press Ltd.

PREFACE

I would like to thank the authors and publishers of the essays in this volume for permission to reprint and in some cases for revising these pieces. The task of finding essays that represent the various dimensions of hermeneutics today and then grouping them in a helpful way has been a challenging one. I have been greatly aided in this work by my friend Jon Pott, editor-in-chief of the William B. Eerdmans Publishing Company, whose wise counsel and advice strengthened the project and made it more comprehensive in scope.

I would also like to thank my student assistants at Dubuque Seminary, Mr. Richard Shaffer and Mr. Thomas E. Smith, for valued help in the final production stages of this book. Thomas Smith also took on major responsibilities for the index. My family, LindaJo, Stephen, and Karl always deserve thanks for the happiness they bring to living.

My hope is that this volume will be useful for those who want a map of the landscape of contemporary hermeneutical thought. Other dimensions than those represented here are certainly present on the current scene, but these major approaches show how far-ranging and at times complicated discussion of hermeneutics can be. The essays have been left in their original forms, which in some cases do not reflect current inclusive language usage.

This volume is dedicated to Dr. A. Vanlier Hunter, who teaches biblical studies at St. Mary's Seminary in Baltimore, Maryland. Van is a sensitive student of holy Scripture whose insights are always stimulating and significant. His friendship has been one of the joys of my life.

Donald K. McKim
University of Dubuque Theological Seminary
Christmas, 1985

INTRODUCTION

To launch into the field of hermeneutics is a major undertaking. There is much literature currently available about the many aspects of how written texts should be understood and interpreted. The task of hermeneutics and interpretation is always before us, and it calls for special insights and skills. Yet to survey the many theories and approaches on the current scene is to face a bewildering array of perspectives and procedures.

The essays collected in this book are meant to serve as a guide to the major hermeneutical approaches and perspectives on interpreting the Bible. Basically, hermeneutics defines the rules one uses when seeking out the meaning of the Scriptures. Since the Bible can be approached in a number of fashions, there are numerous ways in which biblical scholars and theologians come to the task of interpreting its texts. This volume presents samples from a range of approaches representing major trends in biblical interpretation.

Individuals beginning a study of biblical hermeneutics will do well to investigate several related issues, such as the nature of Scripture, the views of the Bible that various theologians and movements have formulated, the ways in which Scripture has been understood to be authoritative for the church and the Christian life, different aspects of biblical hermeneutics involving the various forms of criticism used by biblical scholars, and so on.[1] These kinds of preliminary investigation are important for gaining a broad understanding

---

1. On the nature of Scripture, see *The Authoritative Word: Essays on the Nature of Scripture,* ed. Donald K. McKim (Grand Rapids: Eerdmans, 1983). For Christian perspectives on Scripture, see Donald K. McKim, *What Christians Believe about the Bible* (Nashville: Thomas Nelson, 1985). On the role of the Bible in the life of the church, see Jack B. Rogers and Donald K. McKim, *The Authority and Interpretation of the Bible: An Historical Approach* (San Francisco: Harper & Row, 1979), and Henning Graf Reventlow, *The Authority of the Bible and the Rise of the Modern World,* trans. John W. Bowden (Philadelphia: Fortress Press, 1984); in a broader sense, this topic is also discussed in works on the history of biblical interpretation. Concerning biblical hermeneutics, see Terence J. Keegan's clear and helpful book *Interpreting the Bible: A Popular Introduction to Biblical Hermeneutics* (New York: Paulist Press, 1985), which includes selected bibliographies listing the significant works associated with each approach he discusses. And for more general information, see *The Use of the Bible in Theology: Evangelical Options,* ed. Robert K. Johnston (Atlanta: John Knox Press, 1985), and the articles in the October 1985 issue of *Theology Today* on hermeneutics.

of how the Bible is perceived and studied in the modern world. But this volume focuses more specifically on contemporary hermeneutics itself. Its four major divisions present the many different ways in which biblical interpretation is being conducted today.

Part I, "Biblical Avenues," surveys the basic hermeneutical perspectives of biblical scholars and the ways they propose biblical interpretation should be carried out. One method is to look at the Old and New Testaments respectively and see what particular problems are special to each. For Old Testament theologians, these problems have clustered around issues of Old Testament theology in general and the question of how to find a center, an interpretive key to the diversities of the Old Testament documents. Such major scholars as Gerhard von Rad, Walther Eichrodt, Claus Westermann, and Samuel Terrien have proposed ways of organizing Old Testament data so that individual books and passages might be interpreted in light of the broader context of the Old Testament as a whole. In addition to traditional methods, the discipline of sociology and the perspectives of liberation and feminist theologies have had their effects on the hermeneutics of the Old Testament. Another key question today involves the authority of the biblical canon and the issue of whether critical concern should be with the final form of a biblical text or with its various levels or traditions of growth.

In New Testament studies, continuing debates over how certain texts should be exegeted or explained are overshadowed by a much broader hermeneutical problem — the issue of how a New Testament text, written many centuries ago in an ancient language and culture, can have meaning or significance for twentieth-century people. Reigning methods of biblical criticism known collectively as the "historical-critical method" have been seriously questioned of late. Many critics contend that this method focuses so single-mindedly on the original meaning of the text, on what it meant when it was first written, that it neglects any consideration of what relevance or importance it might have for people today. Another key hermeneutical controversy involves the degree to which present-day interpreters are even able to ascertain any "original meaning" of a text unless they also take into account such matters as their own culture, gender, economic situation, and worldview when engaged in the task of interpretation. The essays by Bruce Birch and Daniel Harrington discuss these problems of biblical hermeneutics with reference to both the Old and New Testaments.

Some groups have found it helpful to spell out their hermeneutical perspectives on biblical interpretation. Selections from two such groups are included here. The International Council on Biblical Inerrancy met in 1978 to draft a series of affirmations and denials defining its understanding of biblical inerrancy. The Council met again in 1982 to put together a similar document, the "Chicago Statement on Biblical Hermeneutics," that outlines the sorts of hermeneutical principles that are compatible with the understanding of biblical inerrancy it had established in its 1978 statement. A second group, with a totally different orientation, met in Geneva in 1976 for the purpose of studying sixteenth-century exegesis and exegetical methods. From that meeting arose "Ten Theses on Theology and Exegesis" prepared by David Steinmetz that give voice to another group of hermeneutical perspectives on the Old and New Testaments.

When it comes to what interpretive procedures students of Scripture can use for studying biblical texts, the essays by Gerhard von Rad, William LaSor, and Anthony Thiselton in this volume describe three prominent options. Von Rad wishes to read the Old Testament with an eye toward "the prefiguration of the Christ-event of the New Testament." Broadly speaking, this is an example of a *typological* interpretation of the Old Testament, in which the Old Testament text is "transcended" as the scholar understands it to be pointing beyond itself to the New Testament.

A similar way of relating the interpretation of the Old Testament to the New Testament (one of the most critical problems for biblical interpreters) involves an understanding of *sensus plenior,* the "fuller meaning" of the biblical text. LaSor argues for a recognition of this "spiritual meaning" of a passage of Scripture, a deeper meaning intended by God but not realized by the human author. He argues that this meaning becomes apparent as the revelation of God in Scripture progresses. This recognition of "levels of meaning" or the "senses of Scripture" has a long history in the church. In an essay entitled "The Superiority of Precritical Exegesis," David Steinmetz also defends this hermeneutical tradition, contending that it is superior to the contemporary historical-critical methodologies that seek only a single meaning from a biblical text.

The approach known as the "new hermeneutic" focuses attention on how a text can be interpreted so it will speak to a modern reader. Central to this interpretive procedure are certain understandings of the nature of language, understanding, the interpreter's worldview, and the relationship between the "horizon" of the human author of the biblical text and the "horizon" of the modern reader. Proponents of the new hermeneutics maintain that these two horizons can be fused in order to create a new world of understanding. Though it is a way of approaching and interpreting the Bible, as Anthony Thiselton points out, the new hermeneutic relies heavily on the philosophical perspectives of Martin Heidegger.

The interplay among biblical scholars, philosophers, and theologians in the area of hermeneutics is the focus of Part II of this volume, "Theological Attitudes." In the first essays of this section, Old Testament scholar Walter Kaiser, Jr., writes from the perspective of an evangelical committed to the inerrancy of the Bible, proposing procedures and methods for hermeneutics that directly reflect his theological attitudes about the nature of Scripture. It is against this background that he proposes ways in which to bridge the gap between what a text meant to its human author and what significance it has for a contemporary reader.

In an essay entitled "Hermeneutics and Theology: The Legitimacy and Necessity of Hermeneutics," Thiselton addresses the theological issue of the role of the Holy Spirit in the process of the interpretation of Scripture. He offers theological responses to objections raised by those who stress the creativity of the Word of God or the importance of the work of the Spirit that hermeneutics is irrelevant. He also goes on to consider the broader issue of the problem of "preunderstanding" and the "self-understanding" of the one who would interpret the text. Our theological attitudes toward these questions significantly shape our perspectives on hermeneutics.

Part III of this volume presents three current assessments of the shape of contemporary hermeneutics. Karlfried Froehlich's "Biblical Hermeneutics on the Move" surveys problems in contemporary hermeneutics, especially those of the language and context of both biblical texts and interpreters. Thomas Gillespie's "Biblical Authority and Interpretation: The Current Debate on Hermeneutics" focuses on definitions of key terms in modern hermeneutical discussion and the ways they are variously used by modern scholars. In his essay "Mind Reader and Maestro Models for Understanding Biblical Interpreters," Patrick Keifert explores the ways in which text and reader are related. Crucial in this regard are the issues of whether the basic nature of biblical texts is construed to be historical or linguistic and how the interpreter's self-understanding plays a part in interpretation. These essays identify major writers on hermeneutics, important definitions in the current debate, and the ways in which significant interpreters can be classified by how they perceive certain key questions.

Part IV presents a number of different contemporary approaches. Essays by prominent scholars offer analyses and examples of methods employed by today's principal hermeneutical movements. Together the pieces provide a broad overview of the approaches that are making a significant impact on the ways in which interpreters come to the biblical texts, the questions they ask of it, and the ways in which they understand themselves in their various contexts as they engage in interpretation.

Karl Barth is a prominent representative of a "theological" approach to hermeneutics — one among many, to be sure. But insofar as Barth represents a major theological voice of the twentieth century with far-reaching influence, his theological approach stands as one of the most powerful and appealing hermeneutical options for modern theologians.[2] Thomas Provence explores Barth's hermeneutics.

Peter Macky describes contemporary literary approaches to New Testament interpretation. Instead of being primarily "objective" or "linear" or "rational" in orientation, a growing body of interpreters is opting for a more imaginative and open-ended approach to Scripture by focusing on the literary action of the biblical account and exploring how they function in human consciousness.

The structuralist movement is growing in the field of hermeneutics. In his essay "The Structuralists and the Bible" Richard Jacobson explains the major elements of this exegetical method, which seeks to dig through the various structural levels of a text to arrive ultimately at the world of meaning and convictions that the text presupposes. This is a highly complex approach involving syntactic and semantic analyses of a text with little concern for the historical context or intention of the author. It seeks to uncover the unconscious narrative program of a text and thus to discover its narrative and mythic structures. Proponents of structuralism maintain that these structures are basic and fundamental to all discourse.

On the other hand, in his essay "The Interpreted Word: Reflections on Contextual Hermeneutics," René Padilla expresses a strong concern for the historical context of both the original biblical authors and the twentieth-century interpreters. Padilla represents those who have learned from contemporary disciplines that "the interpreter is part of the data," that those who interpret must reckon seriously with their own contexts when working at hermeneutics.

This focus on the human context of the interpreter is also evident in the final three essays in this volume. Each represents a particular approach to hermeneutics reflecting a specific context. The anthropological approach is employed by Charles Kraft, who wishes to take the total cultural contexts of interpreters with utmost seriousness. This leads him to speak of "supracultural meanings" that come through Scripture via "cultural forms."

An important movement that begins its theological method with *praxis* and the context in which an interpreter lives is liberation theology. José Miguez Bonino's essay "Hermeneutics, Truth, and Praxis" challenges classical methods of doing theology and perceptions of truth. The temptation to read the Bible only through the

2. For evidence of Barth's continuing influence among contemporary theologians, see *How Karl Barth Changed My Mind*, ed. Donald K. McKim (Grand Rapids: Eerdmans, 1986), a volume commemorating the hundredth anniversary of Barth's birth.

lenses of one's own economic, cultural, and class biases come under fire among the liberation theologians. Although Bonino works and writes out of a Latin American context, he manages to speak for liberation theologians around the world in his calls for new understandings of the hermeneutical tasks.

Further new understandings are also called for in Elisabeth Schüssler Fiorenza's "Toward a Feminist Biblical Hermeneutics: Biblical Interpretation and Liberation Theology." Schüssler Fiorenza speaks for many feminist theologians today in seeking a hermeneutic that will liberate oppressed women. Feminist theologians approach this task in various ways and with various presuppositions and goals.[3] But Schüssler Fiorenza's call for the radical recognition of the sexism in biblical interpretation throughout the history of the Christian church is a first step for all theologians who are developing a feminist hermeneutic.[4]

The sheer variety and complexity of the problems and approaches to hermeneutics means that careful study is necessary. This collection of essays is a guide to many of the current strands of thought. The pieces can be consulted individually as introductions to particular positions or they can be read collectively as a general survey of the larger contours of contemporary hermeneutics. The exchanges taking place among all these positions are raising provocative questions and throwing light on crucial issues for interpreting Scripture in our day. This volume is offered as a resource to help us all to further understandings.

---

3. For examples of various approaches used by feminist theologians, see *Feminist Interpretation of the Bible*, ed. Letty M. Russell (Philadelphia: Westminster Press, 1985).

4. Schüssler Fiorenza presents additional analyses and proposals in her essay "Contemporary Biblical Scholarship: Its Roots, Present Understandings, and Future Directions," in *Modern Biblical Scholarship: Its Impact on Theology and Proclamation*, ed. Francis A. Eigo (Philadelphia: Villanova University Press, 1984), pp. 1-36.

CONTRIBUTORS

Bruce C. Birch	Professor of Old Testament Wesley Theological Seminary Washington, D.C.
José Miguez Bonino	Dean of Graduate Studies Higher Institute of Theological Studies Buenos Aires, Argentina
Elisabeth Schüssler Fiorenza	Talbot Professor of New Testament Episcopal Divinity School Cambridge, Massachusetts
Karlfried Froehlich	Benjamin B. Warfield Professor of Ecclesiastical History Princeton Theological Seminary Princeton, New Jersey
Thomas W. Gillespie	President and Professor of New Testament Princeton Theological Seminary Princeton, New Jersey
Daniel J. Harrington	Professor of New Testament Weston School of Theology Cambridge, Massachusetts
Richard Jacobson	Part-time Lecturer at the University of Wisconsin Law School and Attorney in Madison, Wisconsin
Walter C. Kaiser, Jr.	Professor of Old Testament and Semitic Languages Trinity Evangelical Divinity School Deerfield, Illinois
Patrick R. Keifert	Assistant Professor of Systematic Theology Luther-Northwestern Theological Seminaries St. Paul, Minnesota
Charles H. Kraft	Professor of Anthropology and Intercultural Communication Fuller Theological Seminary Pasadena, California
William Sanford LaSor	Professor Emeritus of Old Testament Fuller Theological Seminary Pasadena, California
Peter W. Macky	Professor of Religion Westminster College New Wilmington, Pennsylvania
C. René Padilla	Director of Ediciones Certeza Buenos Aires Argentina
Thomas Provence	Assistant Pastor Union Presbyterian Church Los Altos, California
Gerhard von Rad	Professor of Old Testament University of Heidelberg Heidelberg, Western Germany

David C. Steinmetz   Professor of Church History and Doctrine
                         Duke Divinity School
                         Durham, North Carolina
Anthony C. Thiselton   Senior Lecturer in Biblical Studies
                         University of Sheffield
                         Sheffield, England

BIBLICAL AVENUES

The essays in Part I present materials related to biblical hermeneutics. In the "Hermeneutical Perspectives" section, Bruce C. Birch surveys current research in Old Testament theology and suggests ways of understanding the hermeneutical principles used today. Daniel J. Harrington discusses the problems faced by those who study New Testament hermeneutics. "The Chicago Statement on Biblical Hermeneutics" was drafted by the International Council on Biblical Inerrancy and conveys a view of how biblical hermeneutics should be approached from the point of view of those who hold to the inerrancy of the Scriptures. David Steinmetz's "Theology and Exegesis: Ten Theses" is derived from discussions at a conference on the history of exegesis in the sixteenth century held in Geneva in 1976.

Biblical scholars use a variety of interpretative procedures in doing exegesis. The essays following in the "Interpretive Procedures" section show some of these methods. The ancient practice of using typology as a tool is discussed by Gerhard von Rad, who applies it to the Old Testament. The "fuller sense" of Scripture, or *sensus plenior,* is explored in William Sanford LaSor's essay as he considers its usefulness for biblical interpretation. In "The Superiority of Precritical Exegesis," church historian David Steinmetz argues that the medieval practice of finding levels of meaning in biblical texts was one valid means for getting at the truth of Scripture and that it may serve as a corrective to some contemporary interpretative presuppositions and practices. In a different vein, Anthony C. Thiselton discusses "The New Hermeneutic" for New Testament study as it has developed particularly through the work of Ernst Fuchs and Gerhard Ebeling.

The variety of perspectives and procedures represented here show the great diversity among those who exegete Scripture, a diversity of both fundamental orientation and methodology. Differing approaches to the nature of Scripture are reflected in this multiplicity and in specific instances can lead to widely disparate interpretations of Scripture.

BIBLICAL HERMENEUTICS IN RECENT DISCUSSION: OLD TESTAMENT

BRUCE C. BIRCH

In an important article appearing in 1979, H. G. Reventlow assessed the current state of Old Testament theology.[1] His judgment (echoed by Brueggemann a year later)[2] was that Old Testament theology had remained largely in an impasse since the publication of the monumental works by von Rad and Eichrodt.[3] Both von Rad's diachronic approach based on tradition-historical methods and Eichrodt's attempt to organize Old Testament theology around a central theme (covenant) were seen as inadequate to deal with the diversity and complexity of the biblical material. For over a decade scholars have described Old Testament theology as in crisis. Gerhard Hasel begins his important monograph chronicling the debate in Old Testament theology with the line "Old Testament theology today is undeniably in crisis" and proceeds to a thorough documentation of the state of the discussion.[4]

After a decade of rather gloomy prospects, the last several years have seen a remarkable flurry of publications which might appropriately be classed as focused on the theology of the Old Testament. They are works concerned with the faith understandings of the biblical communities of the Old Testament and with the claims made by the traditions preserved by those communities on the church which regards them as Scripture.[5] Some of these works are com-

1. Reventlow, "Basic Problems in Old Testament Theology," *Journal for the Study of the Old Testament*, March 1979, pp. 2-22.

2. Walter Brueggemann, "A Convergence in Recent Old Testament Theologies," *Journal for the Study of the Old Testament*, October 1980, pp. 2-18.

3. Gerhard von Rad, *Old Testament Theology*, 2 vols. (New York: Harper & Row, 1962-66); Walther Eichrodt, *Theology of the Old Testament*, 2 vols. (Philadelphia: Westminster Press, 1961-65).

4. Hasel, *Old Testament Theology: Basic Issues in the Current Debate* (Grand Rapids: Eerdmans, 1972), p. 7. The third revised edition of this work, published in 1983, is the most thorough discussion of the debate in Old Testament theology available to date.

5. Biblical theology, if it is not to be merely descriptive, arises out of the claims by confessing communities that they are addressed by the Bible as the Word of God,

Reprinted from *Religious Studies Review* 10 (1984): 1-7.

prehensive and systematic treatments of the whole of Old Testament theology while others treat only a particular issue or problem. Although differences of approach, methodology, and scope separate these works, the creativity and freshness of method reflected in recent work on Old Testament theology suggests renewed vigor in the discipline and the hope of continuing escapes from the impasse of recent years. This article will seek to survey the most promising recent work in Old Testament theology and to suggest ways of understanding the shape of the current discussion.

1

Several recent works have suggested that Old Testament theology should be viewed in terms of a dialectic if it is to do justice to the diversities and tensions in the Hebrew tradition.

In 1978 Claus Westermann published a major systematic presentation which prominently features his thesis that Old Testament theology should be seen in terms of a blessing perspective as well as a deliverance perspective.[6] Although this work draws upon a wide range of Westermann's scholarly interests, especially his creative research on the Psalms, its most distinctive contribution is a full treatment of the deliverance/blessing dialectic already suggested in earlier works such as *Blessing in the Bible and the Life of the Church*.[7]

Westermann sees his work as a corrective to the widespread influence of von Rad, who saw the single mainstream of Old Testament theology in the traditions of the God who saves and the salvation history which preserves Israel's memories of God's deliverance. The emphasis was on history, dramatic events, and the particularity of Israel's election. Westermann does not deny the central importance of this deliverance tradition nor its prominent place in the Old Testament literature. He does believe that this deliverance is balanced in the Hebrew scriptures by a tradition of the God who blesses, which must be seen as of equal importance and has been given too little attention. This blessing tradition is found in the creation material, the Psalms, and the wisdom literature. In the history of Israel it is associated with royal and cultic institutions. Blessing is not mediated in singular events in history. "Blessing is realized in a gradual process, as in the process of growing, maturing, and fading.

Scripture. The works cited in this article reflect recent attempts from a Christian perspective to understand, reflect upon, and appropriate the Old Testament. It lies beyond this reviewer's expertise to assess similar efforts from a Jewish perspective.

6. This work was published in English in 1982 as *Elements of Old Testament Theology* (Richmond: John Knox Press, 1982).

7. Westermann, *Blessing in the Bible and the Life of the Church*, Overtures to Biblical Theology (Philadelphia: Fortress Press, 1978).

The Old Testament does not just report a series of events which consists of the great acts of God. The intervals are also part of it."[8] The blessing traditions are universal rather than particular since they are rooted in the createdness of all things and in the common processes of life and death in all persons. God's activity is not simply to be found in divine historical intervention but in God's creative ordering and ongoing presence through the continuity of life and history.

Of particular interest is Westermann's discussion of the interrelation of these two perspectives, especially in the use of promise as a theme to ground blessing in history.[9] On balance, however, the deliverance perspective seems more highly developed and unified in its theme. As useful as blessing is as an important tradition countering that of deliverance, one wonders if creation, cult, and kingship do not contain some dialectics of their own within the broad sweep of blessing in the Old Testament.

Also appearing in 1978 was Samuel Terrien's monumental work *The Elusive Presence: Toward a New Biblical Theology*. Its central theme is contained in its opening lines: "The reality of the presence of God stands at the center of biblical faith. This presence, however, is always elusive."[10] The scope of Terrien's work is impressive, and many sections of the book constitute important studies in their own right of the discrete themes and literatures of the Old Testament. In fact, although he primarily addresses the work to Old Testament theology, Terrien carries his treatment of the theme of the presence of God into the New Testament in an important effort to shed new light on the relationship between the two Testaments.

Like Westermann, Terrien sees his work as a corrective to overemphasis in Old Testament theology on the historical, covenantal themes. Unlike Westermann, he offers a single category — the presence of God — as a potentially unifying theme, sufficiently flexible to allow for the broad diversity in the Old Testament, yet offering the possibility of understandable interrelationship between diverse traditions. "It is the Hebraic theology of presence, not the covenant ceremonial, that constitutes the field of forces which links . . . the fathers of Israel, the reforming prophets, the priests of Jerusalem, the psalmists of Zion, the Jobian poet, and the bearers of the gospel."[11] One reason Terrien is attracted to the theme of divine presence is that it allows for a fuller appreciation of the creation and

---

8. Westermann, *Elements of Old Testament Theology*, p. 103.
9. Westermann, *Elements of Old Testament Theology*, pp. 104ff.
10. Terrien, *The Elusive Presence: Toward a New Biblical Theology* (Philadelphia: Fortress Press, 1978), p. xxvii.
11. Terrien, *The Elusive Presence*, p. 31.

wisdom traditions, a concern often expressed and demonstrated in his earlier work.

It is precisely at this point that a question must be raised concerning presence as a singular unifying category. Terrien, in speaking of various aspects of divine presence reflected in the Old Testament literature, constantly falls back on the language of dialectic. There is not just one theology of presence in the Hebrew tradition but, rather, a sense of presence as ethical reflected in salvation history themes and the prophets, and a sense of presence as aesthetic reflected in psalms and wisdom and creation materials. The "aesthetics of the mystical eye" must balance the "demands of the ethical ear."[12] Other dialectics relate to this basic ethics/aesthetics tension, including north/south, name/glory, and God's self-disclosure/concealment. Although these do not precisely correlate with one another, they are enough to warn us against reading Terrien's work too quickly as a "centered" biblical theology in the style of Eichrodt (see Hasel, *Old Testament Theology*). The most central dialectic of ethics/aesthetics seems to correlate closely with Westermann's deliverance/blessing tension. On balance it would seem that a careful reading of Terrien would have to characterize his as a dialectic approach, as a number of his reviewers have noted.[13] Terrien, however, warns us that God's presence is elusive, and his suggestion of numerous dialects within the experience of divine presence perhaps points us beyond any single set of polarities in the Old Testament to a more complex pattern of dialectics which might do justice to the material. It is the recent work of Paul Hanson that moves more decisively in this direction.

In 1978 Hanson published *Dynamic Transcendence,* a small book which advanced a dialectic method for understanding divine activity. Hanson is concerned to relate the particular activity of God in history to the universal reality of God which transcends particular moments. He suggests that the Old Testament operates in the tension between a teleological vector and a cosmic vector.[14] His description of these poles of the dialectic are suggestive of similarities with Westermann and Terrien. Brueggeman spoke of this "convergence" of dialectical approaches as a hopeful way out of the impasse in Old Testament theology.[15] The deliverance/ethical/teleological element is balanced and stands in tension with a blessing/aesthetic/cosmic element.

12. Terrien, *The Elusive Presence,* pp. xxviii, 422.
13. See, for instance, Brueggemann, "A Convergence in Recent Old Testament Theologies," and Hasel, "Biblical Theology: Then, Now, and Tomorrow," *Horizons in Biblical Theology* 4 (1982): 61-93.
14. Hanson, *Dynamic Transcendence* (Philadelphia: Fortress Press, 1978), pp. 66ff.
15. See Brueggemann, "A Convergence in Recent Old Testament Theologies."

For Hanson this dialectic of divine relatedness is not adequate to explain the diverse content of Scripture. Already in an earlier work he had suggested a dialectic of visionary/pragmatic operating in the prophets where the sense of God's ultimate purpose is balanced by a reading of the realities of the present world and God's word for it.[16] *The Diversity of Scripture* suggests that the diverse content of Scripture reflects the interplay of two polarities. Added to the visionary/pragmatic is another polarity of form/reform. Form is Scripture's concern for "that ordered sphere within which life can be lived productively and in harmony with others,"[17] whereas reform is concerned for the change demanded by sensitivity to God's ongoing purposes which keeps form from becoming static and oppressive. Form, on the other hand, protects reform from becoming chaos.

For Hanson the diversity of the Old Testament can be seen as expressing balance, imbalance, and interrelationship between these two sets of polarities. Judging from his earlier work (especially *Dynamic Transcendence* and *The Dawn of Apocalyptic*), the teleological and cosmic vectors cut through both sets of polarities and point to a constant dual apprehension of God's particular and universal aspects. On balance, Hanson has given us a more complex set of categories which may be less liable to oversimplification and more capable of doing justice to Scripture's diversity.

2

Hanson's work also illustrates the growing influence of liberation and feminist perspectives on Old Testament theology. Both of his recent works stress the importance of sociological factors in the formation of perspectives within the tradition in the first place, but also in the receptivity to various perspectives on the part of the interpreter.[18] Frequent reference in passing to themes of liberation and the inclusion of an appendix on liberation movements and their impact on hermeneutics in *The Diversity of Scripture* make the influence on Hanson's method clear.[19]

The increasing number of works on feminist and liberation hermeneutics is starting to have an impact on publication in Old Testament theology. These works are interested in the social settings out of which Scripture arose, but are not content simply to study that context with social-scientific tools as an end in itself. There is

16. Hanson, *The Dawn of Apocalyptic* (Philadelphia: Fortress Press, 1974).

17. Hanson, *The Diversity of Scripture*, Overtures to Biblical Theology (Philadelphia: Fortress Press, 1982), p. 17.

18. See Hanson, *Dynamic Transcendence*, p. 68.

19. See Hanson, *The Diversity of Scripture*, pp. 136ff.

concern also for the social setting in which the text is received and
the implications of this dynamic for the claim of scriptural authority.
In contrast to the objectivity often claimed for the historical-critical
method, these works claim that one's own experience and perspective as interpreter not only enter into the hermeneutical process but
should do so in order to make one's context as interpreter visible
and capable of critical interaction with other perspectives. One also,
therefore, approaches the text with what Segundo, following Ricoeur, calls a "hermeneutic of suspicion" in order to discover the
bias of the text.[20] Elisabeth Schüssler Fiorenza has additionally clarified the importance of an advocacy stance as a refusal to enter into
the false objectivity claimed by exegesis that systematically refuses
to see elements of the text that call into question prevailing societal
contexts.[21]

Following the lead of a number of significant articles which discuss or demonstrate a liberation/feminist hermeneutics,[22] some book-
length works representing these perspectives have begun to appear
in the Old Testament field.

 Phyllis Trible's *God and the Rhetoric of Sexuality* is notable for advocating the feminist perspective as a legitimate and important part
of her methodology.

> Within scripture, my topical clue is a text: the image of God male
> and female. To interpret this topic, my methodological clue is rhe-
> torical criticism. Outside scripture, my hermeneutical clue is an issue:
> feminism as a critique of culture. These clues meet now as the Bible
> again wanders through history to merge past and present.[23]

She then proceeds to exegetical studies of themes and narratives in
the Old Testament text which take on strikingly different shape
when viewed through these lenses. In her creative exposure of levels
in biblical texts to which we have been blind, Trible demonstrates
the degree to which historical-critical method has been captive to
its own unexamined cultural presuppositions.

Although recent years have seen increased work relating to the

20. Juan Luis Segundo, *The Liberation of Theology* (Maryknoll, N.Y.: Orbis Books,
1976).
21. Fiorenza, "Toward a Feminist Biblical Hermeneutics: Biblical Interpretation
and Liberation Theology," in *The Challenge of Liberation Theology,* ed. Brian Mahan
and L. Dale Richeson (Maryknoll, N.Y.: Orbis Books, 1981), p. 108.
22. For example, Phyllis Bird, "Images of Women in the Old Testament," in
Religion and Sexism, ed. Rosemary Radford Reuther (New York: Simon & Schuster,
1974); Katharine D. Sakenfield, "The Bible and Women: Bane or Blessing?" *Theology
Today* 32 (1975): 222-33; and Frederick Herzog, "Liberation Hermeneutics as Ideology Critique?" *Interpretation* 28 (1974): 387-403.
23. Trible, *God and the Rhetoric of Sexuality,* Overtures to Biblical Theology (Philadelphia: Fortress Press, 1978), p. 23.

issues of feminist hermeneutic, this has not yet resulted in additional book-length works of Old Testament studies. Some of this work will be available in a future volume of papers from the Feminist Hermeneutics Project of the American Academy of Religion (tentative title: *The Liberated Word*).

One of the key works of liberation hermeneutics in Latin America was translated into English in 1981 — J. Severino Croatto's *Exodus: A Hermeneutics of Freedom*.[24] In many ways Croatto's approach is very like Trible's. He takes a particular topic from the biblical text (Exodus), he brings to bear a methodological approach of his own choice (heavily influenced by Ricoeur, Segundo, and Gadamer), and he makes clear the bias of his particular context for interpretation (liberation in the Latin American context). Although written in a compact, technical style, it is filled with fresh insight into the way texts bridge ancient and modern meanings. It is well worth the effort it takes to mine its riches.

Norman Gottwald has recently edited a revised and expanded edition of *The Bible and Liberation: Political and Social Hermeneutics*.[25] Originally published in 1978 as a special issue of the journal *Radical Religion*, this new edition offers revised versions of many of the original articles as well as reprints of important articles bearing on liberation hermeneutics which appeared elsewhere. One could hardly find a better cross-section of important work representing biblical theology from a liberation perspective.

3

One of the liveliest discussions in Old Testament theology today centers on the question of the canon and its authority. The most recent stage of this discussion has been stimulated by Brevard Childs's monumental work *Introduction to the Old Testament as Scripture*. Childs seeks to describe and demonstrate a "canonical approach" which focuses on the final form of the text because "it alone bears witness to the full history of revelation."[26] Although critical recovery of the prehistory of the text has some value, Childs is insistent that the final form of the text is the only normative basis for biblical theology. On the one hand, this is a welcome corrective to earlier reductionist exegesis which seemed to theologize only on the various levels discernible in texts and seldom on the whole. Childs also discerns cor-

24. Croatto, *Exodus: A Hermeneutics of Freedom* (Maryknoll, N.Y.: Orbis Books, 1981). The original Spanish edition was published in 1978.
25. *The Bible and Liberation: Political and Social Hermeneutics*, ed. Norman K. Gottwald (Maryknoll, N.Y.: Orbis Books, 1983).
26. Childs, *Introduction to the Old Testament as Scripture* (Philadelphia: Fortress Press, 1979), p. 76.

rectly that such reductionist uses of the critical method often left one stranded in the past with a core tradition stripped of its further canonical shaping and therefore incapable of being easily related to the modern context by communities which claim the text as Scripture.

On the other hand, Childs's rather rigid focus on the final form of the text seems unnecessarily restrictive. He has been properly criticized for not allowing Scripture to witness to God's activity in the life of the biblical communities shaping the traditions of the text. His method does not seem to allow enough room for the honoring of God's activity in the community's earlier experience prior to the fixing of the final form, at least to the degree that such experience is left visible in the text and can be discerned by exegetical method.

Over against Childs stands a number of voices which argue in some manner that canonization is but the final stage in the tradition-building process and is not to be viewed as of greater theological value than any discernible stage in that process. *Tradition and Theology in the Old Testament,* a volume of essays edited by Douglas Knight, is still representative of this approach (see especially the essays by Gese and Laurin).[27] This traditio-historical approach is difficult to translate into a usable understanding for modern communities of faith which claim the Bible as Scripture since one can focus on the claims of any level of the tradition without being theologically obligated to measure its claims against the whole of Scripture.

James Sanders seems to occupy a somewhat mediating position in this discussion. In work that preceded Childs's 1979 volume, Sanders stresses the importance of the process whereby communities received and adapted tradition until it achieved its final, fixed form.[28] This process and the discernible evidence in levels of the text can, for Sanders, be the proper focus of theological interpretation; but he also stresses the need to set that reflection in the context of the final canonical form of the tradition. To claim that final form as Scripture is also to claim the witness to God's earlier activity as the tradition was formed, but these levels in the prehistory of the text must be understood in their context within the text's final shape.

Many questions remain to be resolved in the current discussion

---

27. *Tradition and Theology in the Old Testament,* ed. Douglas A. Knight (Philadelphia: Fortress Press, 1977). For a perceptive analysis of this volume, see the review essay by Bernhard Anderson, *Religious Studies Review* 6 (1980): 104-10.

28. See Sanders, *Torah and Canon* (Philadelphia: Fortress Press, 1972), and "Adaptable for Life: The Nature and Function of Canon," in *Magnalia Dei — the Mighty Acts of God: Essays on the Bible and Archeology in Memory of G. Ernest Wright,* ed. Frank Moore Cross, Werner E. Lemke, and Patrick D. Miller, Jr. (Garden City, N.Y.: Doubleday, 1976).

of the nature and function of canon. Questions of "canon within the canon" and the role of canon in the theologies of liberation based in the experience of those often pressed to the margins of the canon as it is now fixed remain important questions for ongoing discussion.

4

Several other recent works in Old Testament theology deserve mention here. *Old Testament Theology: A Fresh Approach*, by R. E. Clements, was published in 1978.[29] As the mature work of a major British scholar, it is rich in insight into the biblical traditions. Clements has been influenced by some of the trends reflected in our earlier discussion. He stresses the importance of attention to the final canonical form of the text. He finds in law and promise a set of categories which set a framework of theological focus within which Old Testament tradition develops. He does not see this as a dialectic nor does he try to relate all of Old Testament tradition to one or the other. In general he seems to treat the material developmentally within thematically defined chapters (faith, God, people of God, law, promise, Israelite religion vis-à-vis ancient Near Eastern religion). He has not intended to produce an exhaustive systematic work, but his command of the material and the insight he brings to it make this an important work.

Two major works of Old Testament theology by evangelical scholars have appeared in recent years. W. C. Kaiser in *Towards an Old Testament Theology* uses the blessing-promise theme to organize the various elements of Old Testament tradition.[30] E. A. Martens in *God's Design: A Focus on Old Testament Theology* uses four themes from a single text (Exod. 5:22 – 6:8) to organize his work: deliverance, community, knowledge of God, and land.[31] Neither this single-text approach nor Kaiser's blessing-promise theme seem capable of doing justice to the diversity of the Old Testament, although they richly present some of its key themes. What is most significant in these works is the degree to which critical method is now at home in evangelical scholarly circles. It is clear that there is a much larger common arena for discussion of biblical theology between evangelical and mainline Christian scholarship.

29. Clements, *Old Testament Theology: A Fresh Approach* (Richmond: John Knox Press, 1978).
30. Kaiser, *Towards an Old Testament Theology* (Grand Rapids: Zondervan, 1978).
31. Martens, *God's Design: A Focus on Old Testament Theology* (Grand Rapids: Baker Book, 1981).

5

A final word must be said concerning the flurry of publications that attempt to bridge the gap between scholarly guild and confessional community. There seems to be a renewed interest in making the work of Old Testament theology available to the life of the modern community of faith in works that go beyond descriptive theology to take up the questions of interpretation and meaning asked by the church.

John Knox Press and the editors of *Interpretation* have reintroduced the tradition of expository writing with the introduction of Interpretation Commentaries. It is referred to as a Bible Commentary for Teaching and Preaching, and the first Old Testament volume, *Genesis,* by Walter Brueggemann, is a first-rate example of excellence in scholarship combined with sensitivity to faith issues in the contemporary church.[32]

Old Testament scholars seem more frequently to focus on the manner in which solid biblical scholarship interacts with various aspects of the life of the confessing community. Donald Gowan has written on preaching,[33] Walter Brueggemann addresses Christian education,[34] a collection of essays by biblical scholars edited by E. E. Shelp and R. Sunderland addresses the theology of ministry,[35] and finally, the excellent book by Phyllis A. Bird *The Bible as the Church's Book* discusses the dynamic relationship of Scripture and church from the canonization process itself to the living qualities of the Word in Christian worship.[36]

Certainly we may not speak of the emergence of any new consensus in Old Testament theology. We can, however, speak of a renewed vitality in the field as evidenced by the numerous works mentioned above. They not only express renewed interest but demonstrate a creative freshness which cannot but stimulate additional constructive discussion and publication.

    32. Brueggemann, *Genesis,* Interpretation: A Bible Commentary for Teaching and Preaching (Philadelphia: Fortress Press, 1982).
    33. Gowan, *Reclaiming the Old Testament for the Christian Pulpit* (Richmond: John Knox Press, 1980).
    34. Brueggemann, *The Creative Word: Canon as a Model for Biblical Education* (Philadelphia: Fortress Press, 1982).
    35. *A Biblical Basis for Ministry,* ed. E. E. Shelp and R. Sunderland (Philadelphia: Westminster Press, 1981).
    36. Bird, *The Bible as the Church's Book* (Philadelphia: Westminster Press, 1982).

BIBLICAL HERMENEUTICS IN RECENT DISCUSSION: NEW TESTAMENT

DANIEL J. HARRINGTON

If we define the hermeneutical problem as the difficulty of getting from there (the world of the New Testament) to here (the world of the late twentieth century), then the most sustained exposition of the problem is Dennis Nineham's *The Use and Abuse of the Bible.* Nineham uses the sociology of knowledge as his major tool. The heart of the hermeneutical problem, he says, is that the Bible expresses "the meaning system of a relatively primitive cultural group,"[1] but at the end of the eighteeneth century a cultural revolution of such vast proportions broke out in Western Europe that it separates our age sharply from all those that preceded it. This means that the fundamental assumption of all traditional understanding of the Bible—the present is like the past—has been brought into question.

Nineham finds the three commonly accepted theological solutions to the hermeneutical problem to be inadequate. The traditional interpreters (fundamentalists, evangelicals, etc.) still assume that the Bible purveys infallible truths. The much-heralded revolution in Roman Catholic biblical study is viewed by Nineham as merely a variant and a continuation of the traditional approach: the point of the Catholic concern with literary forms is that one can find the infallible truth in the Bible if one discovers the literary forms in which it is expressed. The second approach, the historicist, supposes that if the interpreter can get behind the biblical accounts to the history they so inadequately describe, then the events and figures of the Bible will shine forth with persuasive clarity. The biblical-theological approach represented by Karl Barth, Oscar Cullmann, and even Rudolf Bultmann, with its idea of the biblical writers as witnesses and interpreters, is dismissed by Nineham as a clumsy combination of the traditional and historicist approaches, and thus open to the same basic criticisms.

The traditional approach to the hermeneutical problem does not

---

1. Nineham, *The Use and Abuse of the Bible* (New York: Harper & Row, 1977), p. 28.

Reprinted from *Religious Studies Review* 10 (1984): 7-10.

work, according to Nineham, because the biblical events and figures were part of a very different cultural totality. One cannot transfer things from one cultural totality to another in any really adequate way. The historicist approach does not work because the biblical writers did not recognize our modern distinction between history and story. The result is that the historical elements are so embedded in interpretive stories that it is now impossible to disentangle them and write modern scientific history on the basis of the Bible.

What are we to do in such a situation? Nineham's advice is simple: "I should like to see Christians nowadays approach the Bible in an altogether more *relaxed* spirit, not anxiously asking 'What has it to say to me immediately?,' but distancing it, allowing fully for its 'pastness.' "[2]

Bruce Malina draws on theoretical models developed by cultural anthropologists in order to understand better those "foreigners" from the Mediterranean world of the first century who were responsible for producing our New Testament.[3] The foreigners emerge as part of a culture that looked on all interactions outside the family as contests for honor. They needed constantly to compare themselves and interact with others in order to know who they themselves were. As "honorable" people, they derived contentment from preserving their status and living out their inherited obligations instead of competing for the limited supply of available goods. Marriage took place within the group and meant the fusion of the honor of two extended families. The observance of certain purity rules was understood to bring prosperity to the group, while infringement of them would bring danger. The foreignness of the first-century Christians is captured by Malina's contrasting description of twentieth-century North Americans: "achievement-oriented, individualistic, keenly aware of limitless good, competitive and individualistic in marriage strategies, with purity rules focused upon individual rules and individual success."[4]

If Nineham and Malina have highlighted the difficulty of getting from there to here, the Deconstructionists, inspired by Jacques Derrida, cast doubt on whether we in the present can get back to the New Testament world. According to this approach current in literary criticism, the New Testament text is simply the occasion for creating new works of thought or art rather than something having an objective and attainable historical meaning. Herbert Schneidau has summarized the chief contributions of Derrida's deconstruc-

2. Nineham, *The Use and Abuse of the Bible*, p. 196.
3. Malina, *The New Testament World: Insights from Cultural Anthropology* (Richmond: John Knox Press, 1981).
4. Malina, *The New Testament World*, p. 153.

tionist project to biblical interpretation in the following list: the understanding of the self in relation to a historical past, the invitation to see the illusory metaphysics behind phrases like "ordinary language" and "literary meaning" and behind biblical structuralism, sensitivity to heuristic impasses such as those in the Gospel parables, and recognition of the basic "undecidability" of fiction and indeed of all texts.

THE INADEQUACIES OF THE HISTORICAL-CRITICAL METHOD

The most extensive sketches of the history of biblical hermeneutics have been supplied by Peter Stuhlmacher.[5] He concludes that historical-critical exegesis is not in and of itself theological interpretation of Scripture. But it can be such when it is hermeneutically reasoned out as an interpretation of consent to the biblical texts: "Exegesis which serves the church must be hermeneutically equipped to deal with the self-sufficiency of the scriptural word, the horizons of the Christian community's faith and experience, and the truth of God encountering us out of transcendence."[6]

Despite the premature and unlikely claim made by Gerhard Maier that the historical-critical method is at an end,[7] there has been general agreement from practically all religious traditions and academic orientations that the primary task of biblical exegesis is to determine what the biblical authors were saying to people in their own time. There is also general agreement on how to achieve this goal — through the various disciplines (literary, textual, form, source, redaction, etc.). The most controversial point in the whole historical-critical project involves the philosophical and theological assumptions of historical criticism as narrowly conceived by Ernst Troeltsch.[8] This approach to historical criticism asserts (1) that the religious tradition must be subjected to historical criticism, which achieves only probability; (2) that present experiences and occurrences are the criteria of probability in the past; and (3) that all historical phenomena are interrelated as causes and effects. This understanding of historical criticism seems to be the target of Stuhlmacher's plea for an openness to transcendence. It is surely what Maier has

---

5. Stuhlmacher, *Historical Criticism and Theological Interpretation of Scripture: Toward a Hermeneutics of Consent* (Philadelphia: Fortress Press, 1977), and *Vom Verstehen der Neuen Testaments: Eine Hermeneutik* (Göttingen: Vandenhoeck & Ruprecht, 1979).

6. Stuhlmacher, *Historical Criticism and Theological Interpretation of Scripture*, p. 88.

7. See Maier, *The End of the Historical-Critical Method* (St. Louis: Concordia, 1977).

8. On this, see Edgar Krentz, *The Historical-Critical Method* (Philadelphia: Fortress Press, 1975).

in mind when he hopes for the end of historical criticism and complains that historical criticism has led theology up a blind alley.

Besides the charge that the historical-critical method is not open to transcendence and therefore is not adequate to deal with religious texts whose subject is the transcendent, there is also the claim that it does not tell people today what they really want to know or anything that would be useful for them to know. This sense of the irrelevance of much historical-critical study of the Bible led Walter Wink to utter his now famous slogan about the bankruptcy of the biblical critical paradigm and to propose a new paradigm based on models of personal interaction employed in the human sciences, especially in psychotherapy.[9]

Third World biblical scholars such as George M. Soares-Prabhu have also complained that historical criticism is ideologically biased because it has been so closely tied to Western European history.[10] Historical criticism was used originally by the Enlightenment to break the stranglehold of ecclesiastical tradition that was stifling Europe's intellectual development and hindering its political growth. Soares-Prabhu and other non-Westerners suspect that it continues to function (at least by default) as a legitimation of the capitalistic technocracy to which the Enlightenment led.

In summary, most biblical scholars today believe that with the help of the tools of historical criticism they can get back to the world of the New Testament in some meaningful way. But more than a few of them are raising questions about the adequacy of the classic historical-critical method to deal with transcendence, its ability to tell people anything they want to know, and its linkage to Western culture in the past and present.

THE FUSION OF THE TWO HORIZONS

In the most extensive and sophisticated treatment of New Testament hermeneutics in recent years, Anthony C. Thiselton has taken over Hans-Georg Gadamer's phrase "the fusion of horizons." This means the interpreter must recognize that the New Testament writings stand in a given historical context and tradition. It also means that the modern interpreter, no less than the text, stands in a given historical context and tradition. Thus Thiselton's title *The Two Horizons.*[11] For understanding to take place, the two sets of variables —

9. Wink, *The Bible in Human Transformation: Toward a New Paradigm* (Philadelphia: Fortress Press, 1973).

10. Soares-Prabhu, "Toward an Indian Interpretation of the Bible," *Biblebhashyam* 6 (1980): 151-70.

11. Thiselton, *The Two Horizons: New Testament Hermeneutics and Philosophical Description with Special Reference to Heidegger, Bultmann, Gadamer, and Wittgenstein* (Grand Rapids: Eerdmans, 1980).

from the past, and from the present—must be brought into relation with one another. Thus Thiselton's goal of the fusion of the two horizons.

The "given historical context and tradition" of the New Testament writings have been illuminated remarkably well in recent years. For example, Helmut Koester's massive *Introduction to the New Testament* has set the history and literature of early Christianity in the context of the history, culture, and religion of the Hellenistic age.[12] Other scholars have used models developed in the social sciences to enrich our understanding of how the earliest Christians looked at themselves, the world, and God.[13] And, of course, all the individual research done on inscriptions, archeology, ancient texts, and the like aims ultimately to contribute to a more accurate "social description" of early Christianity.[14]

If such research has made us more sensitive to the complexity of the horizon of the New Testament writings, we have also become more aware of the complexity of our own horizons today. I use the word *horizons* because a most important hermeneutical advance in recent years has been the recognition that modern interpreters too live and work in very different historical contexts and traditions. Third World and other minority scholars have made this point most eloquently[15] by reminding us that Africans today can enter the world of the Bible more easily than Westerners can, that the rich tradition of Indian hermeneutics has much to offer, that in Latin America the hermeneutical circle formed by present experiences of oppression and the biblical event of the exodus can produce rich results,[16] and that early Christianity looks very different when viewed from Jewish or feminist perspectives. The "totality" in which Nineham found himself trapped is at least becoming aware of its limitations.

Given our increasing sensitivity to the dimensions of the two horizons, how is the fusion of the horizons to take place? The tra-

12. Koester, *Introduction to the New Testament*, 2 vols. (Philadelphia: Fortress Press, 1982).

13. For example, John J. Gager, *Kingdom and Community: The Social World of Early Christianity* (Englewood Cliffs, N.J.: Prentice-Hall, 1975); Gerd Thiessen, *Sociology of Early Palestinian Christianity* (Philadelphia: Fortress Press, 1978) and *The Social Setting of Pauline Christianity: Essays on Corinth* (Philadelphia: Fortress Press, 1982); and Howard C. Kee, *Christian Origins in Sociological Perspective* (Philadelphia: Westminster Press, 1980).

14. See Abraham J. Malherbe, *Social Aspects of Early Christianity* (Baton Rouge: Louisiana State University Press, 1977), and Wayne A. Meeks, *The First Urban Christians: The Social World of the Apostle Paul* (New Haven: Yale University Press, 1983).

15. See Daniel J. Harrington, "Some New Voices in New Testament Interpretation," *Anglican Theological Review* 64 (1982): 362-70.

16. See J. Severino Croatto, *Exodus: A Hermeneutics of Freedom* (Maryknoll, N.Y.: Orbis Books, 1981).

ditional catalyst facilitating this fusion has been philosophy. The assumption is that the philosopher speaks some truth not only about the present but also about the past. The philosopher is summoned to help us understand better the nature of the hermeneutical task and to shed light on the meaning of certain parts of the New Testament. Of course, the New Testament does not "prove" any philosophy, nor does any philosophy prove the New Testament.

Hans-Georg Gadamer and Paul Ricoeur have certainly helped to elucidate the hermeneutical process for New Testament scholars, and their influence is beginning to make itself felt even in the interpretation of individual texts.[17] Bultmann's creative use of Heidegger's *Being and Time* and the so-called New Hermeneutic's dependence on the writings of the later Heidegger are well known. The 1970s saw the emergence of Marxists philosophy into New Testament interpretation.[18] Among the other surprising entrances, one must include process philosophy as developed by Alfred N. Whitehead,[19] Wittgenstein and the phenomenology of persons,[20] and mathematical logic and the logic theory of meaning.[21]

Since many of the traditional domains of philosophy have been taken over by the social or human sciences, it is not surprising that the search for a hermeneutical catalyst has extended to psychology (Wink), sociology (Gager, Thiessen, Kee), and cultural anthropology (Malina). Structuralism is a spinoff from the cultural anthropology of Claude Lévi-Strauss coupled with the linguistic theory developed by Ferdinand de Saussure.[22] This approach seeks to get beneath the surface structure of a text to its deep structures; that is, to the fundamental assumptions about the world and life that gen-

17. See Gadamer, *Truth and Method* (New York: Seabury Press, 1975). And see Ricoeur, *The Conflict of Interpretations: Essays in Hermeneutics* (Evanston: Northwestern University Press, 1974); "Biblical Hermeneutics," *Semeia* 4 (1975): 27-148; *Interpretation Theory: Discourse and Surplus of Meaning* (Fort Worth: Texas Christian University Press, 1976); and *Essays on Biblical Interpretation* (Philadelphia: Fortress Press, 1980).

18. See Fernanado Belo, *A Materialist Reading of the Gospel of Mark* (Maryknoll, N.Y.: Orbis Books, 1981); and see José P. Miranda, *Marx and the Bible* (Maryknoll, N.Y.: Orbis Books, 1974), and *Communism and the Bible* (Maryknoll, N.Y.: Orbis Books, 1982).

19. On this, see Russell Pregeant, *Christology beyond Dogma: Matthew's Gospel in Process Hermeneutic* (Philadelphia: Fortress Press, 1978).

20. On this, see Thiselton, *The Two Horizons*, and Royce G. Gruenler, *New Approaches to Jesus and the Gospels* (Grand Rapids: Baker Book, 1982).

21. On this, see Arthur Gibson, *Biblical Semantic Logic* (N.Y.: St. Martin's Press, 1981).

22. On this, see Daniel Patte, *What Is Structural Exegesis?* (Philadelphia: Fortress Press, 1976); Robert Detweiler, *Story, Sign, and Self: Phenomenology and Structuralism as Literary Methods* (Philadelphia: Fortress Press, 1978); and Edgar V. McKnight, *Meaning in Texts: The Historical Setting of a Narrative Hermeneutics* (Philadelphia: Fortress Press, 1978).

erated the individual text and its surface structures. A somewhat related approach (minus the jargon) is the concern with the creativity of the religious imagination and its literary expressions. This approach has been explored in great depth for many years by Amos N. Wilder and Northrop Frye.[23]

A third approach to the search for a hermeneutical catalyst has come from the analysis of present-day socio-political experience. J. Emmette Weir has outlined the three basic principles operative in the Latin American liberation theology approach to biblical hermeneutics: (1) the interpretation of Scripture begins with an analysis of contemporary reality rather than an examination of the ancient historical context; (2) creative interpretation involves the adoption of a clear political, sociological, or theological stance; and (3) the meaning of a biblical text is disclosed not only in reflection upon it but also in concrete social action based upon it.[24]

In her insistence on the critical significance of present-day sociopolitical experience, Elisabeth Schüssler Fiorenza's call for a feminist biblical hermeneutics goes even beyond the theologians of liberation in Latin America.[25] Her starting point is the oppression of women today, which she traces in part to oppressive and destructive biblical traditions. The Bible is not only a source of truth and revelation, but also a source of violence and domination. Biblical interpreters must unmask the oppressive patriarchal structures, institutions, and values in the texts they study, and make other scholars and churchpeople admit the existence of oppressive features in the Bible. They must also call attention to the nonsexist and nonandrocentric traditions in the Bible (e.g., coequal discipleship) and use these as resources for developing a critical theology of liberation.

The most significant developments in New Testament hermeneutics in recent years can be summarized under three points. First, the dimension of hermeneutical problems have been sharpened with the help of the social sciences and literary theory. Second, there is general agreement that the exegete's primary task is to determine what the biblical writers were saying to their original audiences; but the classic understanding of the historical-critical method has been attacked as philosophically and theologically inadequate, as irrelevant to people's real concerns, and as too tightly bound to

23. Wilder, *Theopoetic: Theology and the Religious Imagination* (Philadelphia: Fortress Press, 1976); Frye, *The Great Code: The Bible and Literature* (New York: Harcourt Brace Jovanovich, 1982).

24. See Weir, "The Bible and Marx: A Discussion of the Hermeneutics of Liberation Theology," *Scottish Journal of Theology* 35 (1982): 337-50.

25. Fiorenza, *In Memory of Her: A Feminist Theological Reconstruction of Early Christian Beginnings* (New York: Crossroad, 1983).

Western European culture. And third, there is more appreciation
of the rich complexity of the two horizons involved in biblical interpretation; the search for catalysts has focused on hitherto unex-
ploited philosophies, the human sciences, and present-day sociopolitical experiences.

THE CHICAGO STATEMENT ON BIBLICAL HERMENEUTICS

Summit I of the International Council on Biblical Inerrancy took place in Chicago on October 26-28, 1978, for the purpose of affirming afresh the doctrine of the inerrancy of Scripture, making clear the understanding of it and warning against its denial. In the years that have passed since Summit I, God has blessed that effort in ways surpassing most anticipations. A gratifying flow of helpful literature on the doctrine of inerrancy as well as a growing commitment to its value give cause to pour forth praise to our great God.

The work of Summit I had hardly been completed when it became evident that there was yet another major task to be tackled. While we recognize that belief in the inerrancy of Scripture is basic to maintaining its authority, the values of that commitment are only as real as one's understanding of the meaning of Scripture. Thus the need for Summit II. For two years plans were laid and papers were written on themes relating to hermeneutical principles and practices. The culmination of this effort has been a meeting in Chicago on November 10-13, 1982, at which we, the undersigned, have participated.

In similar fashion to the Chicago Statement of 1978, we herewith present these affirmations and denials as an expression of the results of our labors to clarify hermeneutical issues and principles. We do not claim completeness or systematic treatment of the entire subject, but these affirmations and denials represent a consensus of the approximately one hundred participants and observers gathered at this conference. It has been a broadening experience to engage in dialogue, and it is our prayer that God will use the product of our diligent efforts to enable us and others to more correctly handle the word of truth (2 Tim. 2:15).

Reprinted from *Hermeneutics, Inerrancy and the Bible,* ed. Earl D. Radmacher and Robert D. Preus (Grand Rapids: Zondervan, 1984), pp. 881-87.

ARTICLES OF AFFIRMATION AND DENIAL

Article I.   WE AFFIRM that the normative authority of Holy Scripture is the authority of God Himself, and is attested by Jesus Christ, the Lord of the Church.

WE DENY the legitimacy of separating the authority of Christ from the authority of Scripture, or of opposing the one to the other.

Article II.   WE AFFIRM that as Christ is God and Man in one Person, so Scripture is, indivisibly, God's Word in human language.

WE DENY that the humble, human form of Scripture entails errancy any more than the humanity of Christ, even in His humiliation, entails sin.

Article III.   WE AFFIRM that the Person and work of Jesus Christ are the central focus of the entire Bible.

WE DENY that any method of interpretation which rejects or obscures the Christ-centeredness of Scripture is correct.

Article IV.   WE AFFIRM that the Holy Spirit who inspired Scripture acts through it today to work faith in its message.

WE DENY that the Holy Spirit ever teaches to anyone anything which is contrary to the teaching of Scripture.

Article V.   WE AFFIRM that the Holy Spirit enables believers to appropriate and apply Scripture to their lives.

WE DENY that the natural man is able to discern spiritually the biblical message apart from the Holy Spirit.

Article VI.   WE AFFIRM that the Bible expresses God's truth in propositional statements, and we declare that biblical truth is both objective and absolute. We further affirm that a statement is true if it represents matters as they actually are, but is an error if it misrepresents the facts.

WE DENY that, while Scripture is able to make us wise unto salvation, biblical truth should be defined in terms of this function. We further deny that error should be defined as that which willfully deceives.

Article VII.   WE AFFIRM that the meaning expressed in each biblical text is single, definite and fixed.

WE DENY that the recognition of this single meaning eliminates the variety of its application.

Article VIII. WE AFFIRM that the Bible contains teachings and mandates which apply to all cultural and situational contexts and other mandates which the Bible itself shows apply only to particular situations.

WE DENY that the distinction between the universal and particular mandates of Scripture can be determined by cultural and situational factors. We further deny that universal mandates may ever be treated as culturally or situationally relative.

Article IX. WE AFFIRM that the term *hermeneutics*, which historically signified the rules of exegesis, may properly be extended to cover all that is involved in the process of perceiving what the biblical revelation means and how it bears on our lives.

WE DENY that the message of Scripture derives from, or is dictated by, the interpreter's understanding. Thus we deny that the "horizons" of the biblical writer and the interpreter may rightly "fuse" in such a way that what the text communicates to the interpreter is not ultimately controlled by the expressed meaning of the Scripture.

Article X. WE AFFIRM that Scripture communicates God's truth to us verbally through a wide variety of literary forms.

WE DENY that any of the limits of human language render Scripture inadequate to convey God's message.

Article XI. WE AFFIRM that translations of the text of Scripture can communicate knowledge of God across all temporal and cultural boundaries.

WE DENY that the meaning of biblical texts is so tied to the culture out of which they came that understanding of the same meaning in other cultures is impossible.

Article XII. WE AFFIRM that in the task of translating the Bible and teaching it in the context of each culture, only those functional equivalents which are faithful to the content of biblical teaching should be employed.

WE DENY the legitimacy of methods which either are insensitive to the demands of cross-cultural communication or distort biblical meaning in the process.

Article XIII.   WE AFFIRM that awareness of the literary categories, formal and stylistic, of the various parts of
Scripture is essential for proper exegesis, and hence
we value genre criticism as one of the many disciplines of biblical study.

WE DENY that generic categories which negate historicity may rightly be imposed on biblical narratives which present themselves as factual.

Article XIV.   WE AFFIRM that the biblical record of events, dis-
courses and sayings, though presented in a variety
of appropriate literary forms, corresponds to historical fact.

WE DENY that any event, discourse or saying re-
ported in Scripture was invented by the biblical
writers or by the traditions they incorporated.

Article XV.   WE AFFIRM that necessity of interpreting the Bible
according to its literal, or normal, sense. The lit-
eral sense is the grammatical-historical sense, that
is, the meaning which the writer expressed. Interpretation according to the literal sense will take
account of all figures of speech and literary forms
found in the text.

WE DENY the legitimacy of any approach to Scripture that attributes to it meaning which the literal
sense does not support.

Article XVI.   WE AFFIRM that legitimate critical techniques
should be used in determining the canonical text
and its meaning.

WE DENY the legitimacy of allowing any method
of biblical criticism to question the truth or integrity of the writer's expressed meaning, or of any
other scriptural teaching.

Article XVII.   WE AFFIRM the unity, harmony, and consistency
of Scripture and declare that it is its own best
interpreter.

WE DENY that Scripture may be interpreted in
such a way as to suggest that one passage corrects
or militates against another. We deny that later
writers of Scripture misinterpreted earlier passages of Scripture when quoting from or referring
to them.

Article XVIII.   WE AFFIRM that the Bible's own interpretation of
itself is always correct, never deviating from, but
rather elucidating, the single meaning of the inspired text. The single meaning of a prophet's words

includes, but is not restricted to, the understanding of those words by the prophet and necessarily involves the intention of God evidenced in the fulfillment of those words.

WE DENY that the writers of Scripture always understood the full implications of their own words.

Article XIX. WE AFFIRM that any preunderstandings which the interpreter brings to Scripture should be in harmony with scriptural teaching and subject to correction by it.

WE DENY that Scripture should be required to fit alien preunderstandings, inconsistent with itself, such as naturalism, evolutionism, scientism, secular humanism, and relativism.

Article XX. WE AFFIRM that since God is the author of all truth, all truths, biblical and extrabiblical, are consistent and cohere, and that the Bible speaks truth when it touches on matters pertaining to nature, history, or anything else. We further affirm that in some cases extrabiblical data have value for clarifying what Scripture teaches, and for prompting correction of faulty interpretations.

WE DENY that extrabiblical views ever disprove the teaching of Scripture or hold priority over it.

Article XXI. WE AFFIRM the harmony of special with general revelation and therefore of biblical teaching with the facts of nature.

WE DENY that any genuine scientific facts are inconsistent with the true meaning of any passage of Scripture.

Article XXII. WE AFFIRM that Genesis 1–11 is factual, as is the rest of the book.

WE DENY that the teachings of Genesis 1–11 are mythical and that scientific hypotheses about earth history or the origin of humanity may be invoked to overthrow what Scripture teaches about creation.

Article XXIII. WE AFFIRM the clarity of Scripture and specifically of its message about salvation from sin.

WE DENY that all passages of Scripture are equally clear or have equal bearing on the message of redemption.

Article XXIV. WE AFFIRM that a person is not dependent for understanding of Scripture on the expertise of biblical scholars.

WE DENY that a person should ignore the fruits of the technical study of Scripture by biblical scholars.

Article XXV. WE AFFIRM that the only type of preaching which sufficiently conveys the divine revelation and its proper application to life is that which faithfully expounds the text of Scripture as the Word of God.

WE DENY that the preacher has any message from God apart from the text of Scripture.

THEOLOGY AND EXEGESIS: TEN THESES

DAVID C. STEINMETZ

1. The meaning of a biblical text is not exhausted by the original intention of the author.
2. The most primitive layer of biblical tradition is not necessarily the most authoritative.
3. The importance of the Old Testament for the church is predicated upon the continuity of the people of God in history, a continuity which persists in spite of discontinuity between Israel and the church.
4. The Old Testament is the hermeneutical key which unlocks the meaning of the New Testament and apart from which it will be misunderstood.
5. The church and not human experience as such is the middle term between the Christian interpreter and the biblical text.
6. The gospel and not the law is the central message of the biblical text.
7. One cannot lose the tension between the gospel and the law without losing both gospel and law.
8. The church which is restricted in its preaching to the original intention of the author is a church which must reject the Old Testament as an exclusively Jewish book.
9. The church which is restricted in its preaching to the most primitive layer of biblical tradition as the most authoritative is a church which can no longer preach from the New Testament.
10. Knowledge of the exegetical tradition of the church is an indispensable aid for the interpretation of Scripture.

Reprinted from *Histoire de l'exégèse au XVIe siècle*, Textes Du Colloque International Tenu a Genève en 1976 (Genève: Librairie Droz S.A., 1978), p. 382.

TYPOLOGICAL INTERPRETATION OF THE OLD TESTAMENT
GERHARD VON RAD
TRANSLATED BY JOHN BRIGHT

1. It might be well to make it clear at the outset that what we are accustomed to understand under the heading of typology is, in the broad sense, by no means a specifically theological concern or, indeed, a peculiarity of ancient Oriental thought. Rather, typological thinking is an elementary function of all human thought and interpretation. It is, for example, employed in a certain respect in our proverbs, which continually relate a not immediately controllable multiplicity of things to something relatively or absolutely normative, and thus enable us to discern the order that is nevertheless immanent in them. And, above all, without this interpretive, analogical sort of thinking there would be no poetry. The poet goes ceaselessly to and fro; he sees the often insignificant, obvious things and recognizes in them ultimate value. In the movements of the elements, the passing of the years and the days, in the most elementary relationships of man with man, in simple mechanical performances — in everything regularity "reveals" itself, and hints at an order that dwells deep within things, in which the smallest as well as the greatest things participate. Schiller's "Song of the Bell" is an especially beautiful example of this most elementary poetic procedure. It is the world of the mechanical, of the unspiritual, of performances bound by rigid law — yet all of this to the highest degree charged and symbolically powerful and, in any case, related through and through to a Higher, to a final order in the spiritual, which, as has been said, can be seen everywhere delineated, by him who has the vision, in the very mechanical performances which are, in themselves, so difficult to invest with meaning. The theological or pseudo-theological presuppositions of this poetic mode of interpretation ought to be of interest to theologians too, for concern here is continually with revelations, and with the belief that the world that immediately surrounds man possesses transparence. The spiritual

Essays on Old Testament Hermeneutics, ed. Claus Westermann, trans. James Luther Mays (Richmond: John Knox Press, 1963), pp. 17-39.

heritage of the Platonic doctrine of ideas is ever and again to be recognized in this form of interpretation which has become so familiar to us: the soul before its entry into the realm of the corporeal has beheld the ideas—that which is immutable and alone truly exists—and so is able to remember them once more on viewing their images.

2. We encounter quite another form of this analogical thinking in the ancient Orient. There we find the mythological conception of an all-embracing correspondence between the heavenly on the one hand, and the earthly on the other. This "is so of the notion that, in conformity with the law of the correspondence of macrocosm and microcosm, the prototypes of all countries, rivers, cities, and temples exist in heaven in the form of certain astral figures, while those on earth are only copies of them."[1] This notion of correspondence, according to which what is below is only a copy of what is above, perhaps appears in the building inscriptions of the Sidonian kings Bodashtart and Eshmunazar, where *shmm rmm* ("high heaven") and *shmm 'drm* ("magnificent heaven") are used to designate parts of the city. Earthly Sidon is only the copy of its heavenly prototype.[2] So too, the sixth tablet of the Babylonian Epic of Creation points out how the city of Babylon and its sanctuary had first been founded in the world above. The city of Berytos (Beirut) is still called in a late Hellenistic poem *aitheros eikōn*.[3] This sort of mythological-speculative typology remained almost entirely foreign to ancient Israel. Only in the later writings of the Old Testament do certain reminiscences of such conceptions crop up. The clearest example is the *tabnit*, the model of the tabernacle that was shown by God to Moses on Sinai (Exod. 25:9, 40). One might also think of the scroll that was handed to Ezekiel (Ezek. 2:8ff.); his message had thus a preexistence with God as a heavenly book. But what we have here is scarcely more than a rudimentary relic of that all-embracing mythological conceptual world, with which Yahwistic faith plainly could establish no real relationship.

The Old Testament, on the contrary, is dominated by an essentially different form of typological thinking, namely, that of the eschatological correspondence between beginning and end (*Urzeit und Endzeit*). Isaiah and Amos speak of the eschatological return of par-

---

1. B. Meissner, *Babylonien und Assyrien*, 1:110.

2. Lidzbarski, *Altsemitische Texte*, 1:16-20. O. Eissfeldt, *Ras Schamra und Sanchunjaton*, pp. 62ff. My colleague Herr Falkenstein calls my attention to a Sumerian text according to which an earthly temple, in its measurements, takes up half the space of its heavenly prototype. Langdon, *Oxford Editions of Cuneiform Inscriptions*, p. 53, lines 13-14. This may well be the oldest illustration of that impulse toward an increase in the ratio between type and its antitype.

3. O. Eissfeldt, *Ras Schamra und Sanchunjaton*, pp. 109ff.

adise (Isa. 11:6-8; Amos 9:13), Amos of the return of the pristine David ("as in the days of old," Amos 9:11, R.S.V.), Hosea and Deutero-Isaiah of the return of the wilderness days (Hos. 2:16-20; Isa. 52:11-12), and Isaiah of the return of the old Davidic Jerusalem (Isa. 1:21-26). But what is generally known need not be repeated here. To be sure, many distinctions in detail should be made in this connection. One should distinguish between the recapture of a primeval state and the repetition of primeval events whereby the *Urzeit* is at a stroke pushed into the beginning of Israel's *Heilsgeschichte* (Passover, wilderness period, David); and it should be asked whether, and for what reason, the second of these two ideas is the dominant one. And the relationship of the prophetic predictions to this form of typological thinking ought to be generally investigated. Is every messianic prophecy a prophecy of the return of David, as it indeed seems to be in Isaiah 11:1, and certainly is in Jeremiah 30:9 and Ezekiel 34:23-24? Where, and since when, was there the impulse to a heightening in the relationship between type and antitype (cf. Isa. 52:12, "not in anxious haste," with Exod. 12:11)? The night visions of Zechariah (Zech. 1– 6) exhibit a quite unique mixing of mythical-speculative, and historical-eschatological, typological thinking. Zechariah beheld in a single night, compactly yet fully, the final events of *Heilsgeschichte,* and it is thereby made clear that all eschatological benefits are already preexistently present in heaven, although on earth no sign could yet be seen of God's zeal for the completion of his purpose in history (Zech. 1:11).

Whether one must, with Bultmann, connect this sort of typological thinking first of all with the ancient Oriental theory of world-periods is, however, very questionable.[4] Is the linear way from type to antitype really to be designated as a cyclic occurrence? The components of every Old Testament witness, so inalienably historical in character, do not at all permit a consistently developed notion of a repetition. Indeed, one must see the basic ideas of typology less in the notion of *repetition* than in that of *correspondence*. In the one case, the earthly gains its legitimatization through its correspondence with the heavenly; in the other, the relationship of correspondence is a temporal one: the primeval event is a type of the final event.

3. The new thing in the New Testament is the application of this theological thought-form to a book, to the canon of the Old Testament, although this theological-eschatological, analogical way of thinking itself is, as we have seen, prepared for in a far-reaching way by the Old Testament's own self-understanding. It is, in our opinion, the merit of Goppelt's book that it pointed out the prevalence and the variety of this typological way of thinking in the New

4. Bultmann, *ThLZ* 85 (1950): 205.

Testament.[5] The New Testament narrators, often expressly, but often tacitly, parallel Old Testament events, and they presuppose of the reader that he will know of this (as said, often hidden) relationship of correspondence, and will reflect upon it. This referring to the typical in the Old Testament goes far beyond the use of actual citations — just as one often finds himself at the limit to which he may go with the very notion of citations in this connection. (Is "And he gave him to his mother" [Luke 7:15b, R.S.V.] a citation from 1 Kings 17:23, or merely the place at which the narrator in his account moved especially close to the Old Testament model?) It is clear how this theological way of thinking accorded to the Old Testament prototype no less than the character of a source for the portrayal of the final consummating event. In the Passion narrative, as is well known, Psalm 22 is called upon, even to biographical details, as a source for the suffering of the eschatological Anointed One. On the other hand, the New Testament in manifold ways witnesses to the impulse toward a heightening between type and antitype. Everyone knows that in it no impossible attempt is made to set forth the gospel at any price in Old Testament dress. Neither Matthew nor Paul was hindered by the typological way of thinking from expressing what had come to pass with Christ that was different and new.

Allegory, on the other hand, falls strikingly into the background in the New Testament. Hermeneutically, a quite different evaluation is to be placed on allegory, for it is characterized by a much more rigid attachment to the text, indeed to the very letter of it, quite as much as it is by its unbridled freedom in matters of spiritual interpretation. Typology, on the contrary, shows itself to be astoundingly free of attachment to the word or the letter, yet bound to a much greater degree by the historical sense.[6] Indeed, with its much stronger attachment to history, it is concerned with tying onto facts, not with spiritual truths. Allegory is a much more rationalistic phenomenon.[7]

Having thus stressed the great importance of the New Testament's typological way of understanding things, the astounding fact must be pointed out on the other hand that the New Testament — as open as it was toward the Old — nevertheless fails almost entirely

5. L. Goppelt, *Typos: Die typologishe Deutung des Alten Testaments im Neuen* (1939); further, C. T. Fritsch in *Bibliotheca Sacra* (1947), pp. 87ff.

6. Goppelt, *Typos*, p. 8; Cullmann, *Christ and Time*, pp. 131ff.

7. Joh. Gerhard gives the following definitions: "Typus est, cum factum aliquod Vet. Test. ostenditur, praesignificasse seu adumbrasse aliquid gestum vel gerendum in Nov. Test. Allegoria est, cum aliquid ex Vet. vel Nov. Test. exponitur sensu novo atque accomodatur ad spiritualem doctrinam s. vitae institutionem. Typus consistit in factorum collatione. Allegoria occupatur non tam in factis, quam in ipsis concionibus, e quibus doctrinam utilem et reconditam depromit." Loci Theologici (Cotta) Tom. I, p. 69, cited by A. T. Hartmann, *Die enge Verbindung des Alten Testaments mit dem Neuen* (1831), p. 632.

to provide any norm, any handy rule, for its interpretation. The New Testament thus stands as no milepost in the history of hermeneutics, unless it was that it saw in Christ the end of all methodical scribal learning. They who are "in Christ" have themselves already been drawn into this end-time, and they rely only on the Spirit of the Resurrected One, who interprets the Scripture for them with sovereign power.[8]

4. Our present-day theological point of view concerning the Old Testament still exhibits throughout the character imparted to it by the revolution brought about by rationalism. Luther, through his return to the literal sense, inaugurated for those who came after him a new epoch in the typological interpretation of the Old Testament; and Calvin, with his far more methodical exegesis, created a whole tradition of typological interpretation of the Old Testament which, as is well known, reached a particularly high point with Cocceius (1603-1669).[9] But this typologizing, practiced on a broad basis by those of the Lutheran and Reformed traditions alike, came to a sudden end in rationalism, particularly through the work of Michaelis and Semler. From this point on, typology—with which, indeed, the church had even previously found itself no longer happy— was fully discredited. About 1755, to be sure, Michaelis wrote an *Entwurf der typischen Gottesgelahrtheit*; but this very book showed with special clarity the change that had come about, for, while Joh. Gerhard had linked typology with facts, Michaelis is concerned with "the religious truths" symbolically enshrined in the Old Testament.[10] Nothing is more characteristic of this degenerate sort of typology than the relinquishment of the attempt to relate the types to the New Testament (that is, their limitation to the Old), already observable in Michaelis. The spiritual truth contained in this Old Testament symbolism was, without further ado, to be interpreted for itself. And Semler said of typology, "He who assumes no types . . . is deprived of nothing whatever; and even he who is most fond of typology cannot, for all that, place it among the fundamentals of Christianity."[11]

It was at this time that Old Testament interpretation lost all connection with the facts witnessed to in the New Testament, and this

8. G. Ebeling, *Evangelische Evangelienauslegung*, pp. 101-10.

9. On Luther, H. Bornkamm, *Luther und das Alte Testament*, pp. 74ff. On Calvin, H. H. Wolf, *Die Einheit des Bundes: Das Verhältnis von A. und N. T. bei Calvin* (1942). On Cocceius, G. Schrenk, *Gottesreich und Bund im älteren Protestantismus* (1923).

10. J. D. Michaelis, *Entwurf der typischen Gottesgelahrtheit* (1763). At this time a clear distinction had ceased to be made between type, allegory, and symbol. Cf. C. T. Fritsch, *Bibliotheca Sacra* (1947), pp. 216ff.

11. A. H. Sykes, *Paraphrasis des Briefes an die Hebräer*, trans. J. D. Semler (1779), p. 86, n. 96.

it has not won back until today. What was left was a connection with the teachings of the New Testament, with its religious ideas, with the "fundamentals of Christianity."[12] What now comes into play in the interpretation of the Old Testament is another form of analogical thinking — that of historical method. Troeltsch has expressed it with great clarity:

> Historical method, once . . . applied to biblical study, is a leaven that transforms everything, and finally shatters the whole framework of theological method as this has existed hitherto.
>
> Three essential points are in question here: habituation to historical criticism in principle, the significance of analogy, and the correlation that exists between all historical occurrences. . . . The means whereby criticism is possible at all is the employment of analogy. The analogy of what takes place before our eyes . . . is the key to criticism. Delusions . . . the formation of myths, fraud, factions, which we see before our eyes, are the means of recognizing similar things in the traditions. Agreement with normal, customary, or at least repeatedly attested ways of occurrence . . . as we know them, is the mark of likelihood for occurrences which criticism can acknowledge as actually having happened. Observation of analogies between similar occurrences of the past makes it possible to ascribe to them likelihood, and to explain what is unknown from what is not. This almightiness of analogy, however, includes in principle the similarity of all historical events, which is, to be sure, not likeness . . . but presupposes in each instance a kernel of common similarity by virtue of which even the differences can be sympathetically grasped.[13]

For our considerations, the statement about the significance and almighty power of analogy is important. It is superfluous to remark that it was through this method that the picture of Israel, its history and literature, which we consider historically adequate, was first developed. It is superfluous, therefore, to rush to the defense of this historical method. That this "almightiness of analogy" could not stop short of the investigation of inner and spiritual concepts, thus of Israel's religion, was only logical. There is, therefore, no cause for complaint that a more and more methodical science of comparative religion arose, for in this area, too, that new analogical way of thinking has bestowed upon us insights with which we would never be willing to part. The thing became insidious only where there lay at the bottom of this comparative procedure a hidden theological *pathos,* where Israel's religion was placed at "the peak of all ancient

---

12. The great exception, the theology of J. Chr. Karl Hofmann — its closeness to the tasks set for us today and its distance from them — cannot be discussed here in such brief compass.

13. Ernst Troeltsch, *Über historische und dogmatische Methode* (1898); *Gesammelte Schriften,* 2:729ff.

religions" and recognized as "the flower of all ancient religions" which "in the hand of the Master became the tool for shaping the absolute religion."[14] What is odd about such statements, and countless similar ones, is not the comparative method as such, which is everywhere employed; what is odd is rather the change in the object with which theology is now occupied. In order to give an account to Christendom of its belief with regard to the content and significance of the Old Testament, theology now points to Israel's religion. But that is right off to be accounted simply as a quite insidious reduction of the content of the Old Testament as it actually speaks to us. An entire dimension—the fullness of its witness to history—is excluded. Characteristic of this reduction is its seizing upon the spiritual, upon teachings, truths, conceptions of God, the world, man, sin, and the like. But it is nevertheless, as will be shown below, nothing more than a mere reduction.

Now it is our opinion that, in this regard, in spite of numerous changes in the posing of questions, as well as in the results achieved in the area of Old Testament theology, nothing fundamental has been altered even today. L. Köhler says in the first sentence of his *Theologie des Alten Testaments,* in his precise way, "One can call a book a theology of the Old Testament if it offers a compilation, justified by its contents and rightly organized, of those ideas, thoughts, and concepts of the Old Testament which are, or are capable of being, theologically important."[15] Procksch, to be sure, gives the "world of history" considerable space in his large work, but, aside from the fact that one can seriously question the theological relevance of the representation of history as Procksch gives it, he too devotes more space to his second part, which he entitles "The Thought World," than he does to this first part.[16] But, we would ask, is the object of a theology of the Old Testament correctly fixed if we see our task as that of stressing "thoughts, ideas, and concepts," or in describing a "thought world" of the Old Testament? We still stand here under the sway of that notion of religion which stems from rationalism, and which ought to be submitted to a much sharper criticism than it has been; and in such a reorientation the Old Testament is to the highest degree helpful to us.

5. The Old Testament is a history book. It portrays a history brought to pass by God's Word, from creation to the coming of the Son of Man. It may not be superfluous to remark that even the prophetic books are "history books," insofar as they do not seek to

14. R. Kittel, ZAW (1921), pp. 96ff.
15. L. Köhler, *Theologie des Alten Testaments,* p. v.
16. O. Procksch, *Theologie des Alten Testaments* (1950).

transmit teachings, truths, or the like, but rather to portray eschatological events in advance.

We see how the ancestors of Israel were called by the divine Word, and how in obedience to further divine words they wandered thither and yon; we see the promise of great posterity come to fulfillment, and Israel become a people. Then we see this people wandering at God's direction, and we see offices and institutions coming into being within it, founded by God's Word. In other words, we see this people continually driven, moved about, shaped, reshaped, destroyed, and resurrected through the divine Word that ever and again came to it.[17]

This is one thing. The other is that we see prophets who in ever more concentrated fashion predicted the consummation of history; and these predictions, again, are concerned with this same people of God, its institutions and offices, only now in the last and final form in which God will establish them after apocalyptic judgment. This type of prophecy is for Christian theology naturally the principal link between Old Testament and New, since the witness of the New Testament itself designates Christ's appearance in the flesh as the fulfillment of the prophetic predictions. But the question now has to do with the scope that we may accord to the concept of prophecy. Certainly one must begin with the prophetic predictions, that is, those prophetic utterances that are directed toward the future. But Christian belief also asks after the redemptive significance of the Old Testament's witness to past history and present, that is, after the significance of those passages that treat of the numerous facts of history already brought to pass by God's published Word. Indeed, it must ask after these things, for prophetic prediction is related to these witnesses to history in the most intimate way. Prophecy proceeds, in fact, precisely from the creative Word of God, as the sole power that can bring about judgment and redemption; for its own part, it speaks ever and again of those very institutions and offices which God had to begin with founded within the framework of Israel's history. It is therefore merely the connecting link that binds together the witness to God, and to his judgment and redemption (which, as said, had already broken into Israel's history continually), and projects it into the eschatological, in that — constantly basing itself upon what God had already accomplished — it speaks of God's final work with relation to Israel. But since this is the case, can any fundamental theological distinction be made between prophetic prediction on the one hand, and witness to past history on the other? This article, however, aims primarily at posing

---

17. We speak here only of the understanding of her history which Israel herself set down as a witness.

the question of the redemptive significance of the Old Testament witness to past history and present.

6. We begin with a view of the matter which is certainly widely held today, and which Althaus, for instance, has formulated in a programmatic way: "The Old Testament has a pastoral significance for Christendom insofar as it is the deposit of a history of faith, under God's tutelage, which moves away from the bonds of nationalism and particularism, on toward the gospel."[18] Now that is certainly an aspect of the matter, the correctness of which is not to be contested. The Old Testament is indeed the picture book of a history of faith, and one of inexhaustible fullness. But if one asks what it finally and truly is, above all if one questions it regarding its own kerygmatic intention, the concept of a history of faith no longer suffices.

The Old Testament historical work whose theological tendency we can most easily grasp is the Deuteronomistic history. If we question it—especially the two books of Kings—as to its purpose, that is, as to what theological concern this exilic historical school had, the concept of a "history of faith" is at once excluded, while that of a cult—or temple—history is seen to be equally inappropriate. Rather, one sees that what is given here is a history of the creative Word of God, that is, a course of history is described which is determined by a whole pattern of mutually corresponding prophetic promises and divine fulfillments. What interests these historians is the precise functioning in history of the Word as proclaimed by the prophets. In a positively classical manner the concept of *Heilsgeschichte* is here sketched as a course of history which is kept in motion, and guided to its God-ordained goal, by the constantly intruding divine Word.[19] The older historico-theological delineations are to be distinguished from the Deuteronomic only in that the theological-programmatic element is lacking in them, or at least is not explicitly evident. The great history of the "Succession to the Throne of David" (2 Sam. 6– 1 Kings 2) shows the first outworkings of Nathan's prophecy (2 Sam. 7).[20] And it is well known how Yahwist and Elohist trace a history that is set in motion by the promise to the patriarchs and guided on to the conquest of the land. The word to Abr. ham in Genesis 12:3a ("I will bless those who bless you, and him who curses you I will curse," R.S.V.) is of great importance here, for it means to say: God's judgment and redemption have now entered history; judgment and redemption are determined by the attitude adopted toward the historical fact of Israel. According to

18. P. Althaus, *Die christliche Wahrheit*, 1:229, 240.
19. In greater detail, von Rad, *Studies in Deuteronomy*, pp. 52ff.
20. L. Rost, *Die Überlieferung von der Thronnachfolge Davids*, pp. 82ff.

Deutero-Isaiah, too, the peoples confess, "God is with you only, and there is no other" (Isa. 45:14, R.S.V.). So Israel understood the course of her own history; she saw it not as a history of faith, but rather she saw herself snatched up into a divine history in which she was continually led by God's Word from promise to fulfillment.

Before we continue this line of thought, a critical remark must be made regarding the exegesis of historical texts of this sort. The very return from an exegesis based on the history of religions to a theological exegesis has led us in our day into a new danger zone, for exegesis now feels itself under the necessity of drawing from the narrative some "meaning," some "ideology," or whatever you wish to call it, that can be entered on the credit side of the ledger, theologically speaking. An excellent example of this sort of thing is the interpretation of the Genesis narratives by H. Frey (in many respects very useful). This is marked by a very lively theological interpretation of each and every detail; every single situation, every action or failure to act, every turning this way or that, is — with the aid of penetrating interspersed comments based on the psychology of religion — brought into play theologically. Yet, for all that, one has to ask whether the patriarchal narratives do not rather quickly set fixed limits to direct theological interpretation, in that the narrator as a rule refuses with a positively heroic firmness to give us any foothold for a spiritual interpretation, but rather confines himself to portraying the events in a dramatic way. The story of Hagar (Gen. 16), or that of Abram's endangering the life of Sarai, ancestress of the people (Gen. 12:10-20), or that of Jacob's trickery (Gen. 27), and many others of the sort, seem like tightly closed mussels in their lack of any interpretation at all. To be sure, the entire Hexateuch, and especially the traditionary complex of the patriarchal narratives, is organized around quite definite theological themes; but these are anything but an adequate key for the interpretation of the intricate pattern of the stories and happenings in detail. They do suffice to let us see the event as a divine event, but they do not remotely suffice for an understanding of the "How" and the "Why." Did these narrators (with the exception of P) really mean to say anything essentially more than that it happened then just so, for so Yahweh ordained it? That raises the question if we, with our hankering after interpretations that will establish some additional meaning, some truth over and above the facts given, do not overlook something quite essential, namely, the strongly cryptic character that these narratives to such a large degree have. What the Yahwist himself had in mind in these narratives is often impossible to determine. To what degree was he conscious, to what degree was Jacob conscious, of the significance of the events of Genesis 27? And what do we understand of the life of Isaac? We read only a few

stories and then, later, the notice of his death—thus that he who
had been laid by his father on God's altar carried the secret of his
life with him to the grave. Where can any interpretation find firm
footing here? The intelligible factor, the contribution of the narrator
to interpretation, is for the most part minimal. In order to interpret
such deeply cryptic happenings, must one not go much farther,
rather than looking for an interpretation from the Yahwist himself?
The fact that he has clothed the narratives in a dress seemingly so
untheological represents, certainly, a far greater achievement than
if he had charged them with the profoundest of reflections. And so
we are threatened here with a new spiritualizing, not much better
than that old "religious" spiritualizing which we think ourselves
fortunate to have outgrown. Both of Israel's late theologies, the
Priestly Document and the Chronicler's history, could teach us a
lesson here: the way in which they tap about the rock-hard shell of
the tradition might cause us to ponder, and give us a new impression
of how profoundly hidden the divine meaning of this history is. One
likes to talk of ancient Israel's encounter with God. But was the
human partner in this encounter then really conscious of this and
in control of it? Is the gripping narrative of the Yahwist, in spite of
the long history of tradition that lay between him and the event,
much more than a preliminary sketch of God's footprints in the
early history of Israel? What did he know of the cultic theology of
the Priestly Document, or of prophecy, or of the sufferings of Job?
Who, then, in ancient Israel really encountered the God of Israel,
the Father of Jesus Christ?

7. We return now to the words "only in you is God" and to our
rejection of the concept "history of faith" [that is, as a description
of the content of the Old Testament].* Just what does this *'ak bāk
'ēl weēn 'ōd* (Isa. 45:14) embrace, in detail and in particular, if one
would bring out its meaning? If one were to answer this question
as many of our theologies would, one would say that what was
peculiarly Israel's was its "idea of God," or a peculiar form of relationship with God ("God and man"), or a peculiar form of religious and moral sensibility, or the like. In other words, we have
defined this indwelling of God in Israel almost exclusively in terms
of the intellectual and spiritual. But, though such formulations are
not without support in the Old Testament, they nevertheless require
decided supplementation. If one frees himself from the associations
of this spiritual conception of religion, one sees that the Old Testament depicts the peculiar thing vouchsafed by Yahweh to the people Israel in quite another way. It lies in the marvel of the real
indwelling and gracious presence of God (Exod. 29:42ff.; 1 Kings

*Translator's addition.

8:12-13); it lies in the revelation of his righteous will, in the *doxa* of his redemptive dealings in history, in the promise and constant provision of all sorts of redemptive benefits, and the like. It is, in our opinion, precisely of these latter things that Old Testament theology ought to say a great deal more than it has. In the patriarchal narrative of the Yahwist it is the promise of great posterity and possession of the land that runs through the whole like a *cantus firmus* (the "I will be your God," Genesis 17:7, is introduced first in P). In Deuteronomy the gifts promised to Israel are the land, blessing, and rest from all enemies round about (Deut. 12:9; 25:19). Further to be mentioned are gifts conditioned by special historical situations, such as the manna in the wilderness, protection in holy war, and, finally, the eschatological prophecies:

> For behold, I create new heavens
>   and a new earth;
> and the former things shall not be remembered
>   or come into mind.
> but [they will] be glad and rejoice for ever
>   in that which I create;
> for behold, I create Jerusalem a rejoicing,
>   and her people a joy.
> I will rejoice in Jerusalem,
>   and be glad in my people;
> no more shall be heard in it the sound of weeping
>   and the cry of distress.
> No more shall there be in it
>   an infant that lives but a few days,
>   or an old man who does not fill out his days,
> for the child shall die a hundred years old,
>   and the sinner a hundred years old shall be accursed.
> They shall build houses and inhabit them;
>   they shall plant vineyards and eat their fruit.
>   (Isa. 65:17-21, R.S.V.)

The same thing is true of the benefits which the individual expects from Yahweh: life (*hayyim*) and well-being (*shalom*). Nowhere do we encounter the material and this-worldly quality of the Old Testament redemptive benefits in so striking a way as in those accounts that concern the purchase of land.[21] Into the circumstantial realism of such transactions no pious syllable intrudes; and yet everything is supported by an emotion that is sacral through and through. Here are the stable givens, about which the thought and the theological reflection of the earliest as well as the latest periods revolve. In the Old Testament's view of the matter, it is for the sake of these things,

21. Gen. 23; Jer. 32:7ff.; Gen. 33:18-19; 2 Sam. 24:24; Ruth 4:3ff.

that is, for their realization, that the *Heilsgeschichte* itself takes place. Naturally Israel had a religious "thought world" too, that is, a concern to comprehend these redemptive benefits, an effort to understand and appropriate them. And since succeeding generations posed the problem of apprehension afresh, one cannot, for that reason, speak of that thought world as a static thing, but rather as something variable and changeable. Just how is it with all the various complexes of ideas relating to God, man, death, sin, and forgiveness? It cannot fail to strike one how much of this was given Israel only for a fixed term, only until it was once more shattered by perplexing upheavals from the depths. But that is only to say that this thought world was always something secondary as over against what happened to Israel along the way, and as over against the redemptive benefits held out before her. And to all of this there attaches the hermeneutical consideration that we can on the basis of the sources reconstruct a religion of Israel, and her world of piety, for the most part only indirectly, that is, by abstracting from the actual kerygmatic intention of the writings — which, as we have seen, are concerned with emphasizing the acts of God.

8. If one wishes to be fair to the theological thought world of Israel, one must mention its constant reference to the real redemptive benefits. Israel did not, indeed, rest content with a single fixed understanding of these historical gifts. Rather, a continual process of reworking is to be observed, one that was never finished but ever led to new interpretations. The gift of manna was understood in the old tradition as a miracle of physical feeding, and the occurrence has there the gravity of something once-for-all in redemptive history (Exod. 16:1-5, 13b-16a). The source P, on the contrary, sees in the transaction something typical, something that occurred ever and again as God's people received his gifts (that each got his share, that none had too much and none too little, that it could not be stored up, Exod. 16:6-13a, 16b-26). Again, Israel attached to the figure of Samuel almost every office that was in any way adaptable to him: that of seer, of judge, of prophet, and of Levite.[22] Again and yet again she felt impelled to explain this phenomenon within *Heilsgeschichte*, as if what took place in Israel in and through Samuel could be satisfactorily subsumed under none of the offices that stood ready to hand. (Would not the Christian understand and approve of this searching and groping and pondering? But more of that later.)

There is yet another peculiarity having to do with the promised benefits themselves. It is not at all as if such promises only, so to speak, moved on before Israel, and remained till the end something

22. 1 Sam. 9:11ff.; 7:15-16; 3:20; 1 Chron. 6:18ff.

to be hoped for. On the contrary, Israel told of manifold instances of divinely given fulfillment that had already been brought to pass in history. The most outstanding example of all is the fulfillment of the ancient promise of the land, concerning which the book of Joshua asserts in a positively pedantic fashion that everything promised had been fulfilled, and that nothing was lacking (Josh. 21:43ff.; 23:14). Yet this historical fulfillment notably did not diminish the actuality of the promise that had once been given; it did not fall before the law of history. Rather, the promise of land, in spite of its initial fulfillment, remained in force for Israel. In Josiah's day, Israel is addressed by Deuteronomy as if she stood in every respect still prior to the fulfillment of the promise of land, as if "rest from all your enemies round about" (Deut. 12:9; 25:19, R.S.V.) had not yet been given. And Balaam depicts the blessings of Israel's well-watered and fertile land so exuberantly that one might suppose that he was not speaking of the niggardly Palestinian hill country at all, but positively of paradise:

> How fair are your tents, O Jacob, your encampments, O Israel! Like valleys that stretch afar, like gardens beside a river, like "oaks" that the Lord has planted, like cedars beside the waters. Water flows from his buckets; his posterity has plentiful water. (Num. 24:5-7)

It was through the prophets that a division of God's dealings with Israel into an initial and a final phase was then carried out. Thus Deutero-Isaiah prophesied of a second Exodus, which would take place to the accompaniment of yet more marvelous signs than did the first (Isa. 52:11-12). Hosea, too, set the first wilderness sojourn over against a final one: Yahweh would again lead Israel into the wilderness, where his people, once more having been made entirely dependent upon him, would then accept the life-giving benefits from his hands, not from the gods of fertility (Hos. 2:16-20). From such passages as these, and many other similar ones, one sees that already within the Old Testament the dumb facts of history had become prophetic, and had come to be viewed as prototypes to which a new and more complete redemptive act of God would correspond. Thus all is in motion. Things are never used up, but their very fulfillment gives rise, all unexpected, to the promise of yet greater things (for example, so the monarchy founded by God gives rise to the promise of the final Anointed One). Here nothing carries its ultimate meaning in itself, but is ever the earnest of yet greater wonders.

In this connection still another characteristic peculiarity of the portrayal of God's dealings in history, and of the redemptive events, must be mentioned. The narrators are so captivated by the *doxa* of the event that once happened, they see and point out in the event the splendor of the divine gift in so exclusive a way, that they thereby manifestly misdraw the historical picture. There is, therefore, in the portrayal of the facts very frequently something that transcends what actually occurred. The narrator, or better—since it is something that for the most part took place on a far broader basis—the "tradition," is so zealous for God that the event is straightway broadened into the typical. It is precisely sober exegesis that must come across things of this sort and make the effort to understand what has taken place. In the book of Judges, the judges are portrayed as charismatic bearers of a theocratic office that embraced all of Israel—something that went far beyond their actual territorial sphere of influence. Yet the text itself lets it be seen quite clearly how much more limited, in time as well as space, their activity was. In the book of Joshua the entry into the Promised Land under Joshua is so described as if Israel entered Canaan *en bloc* under unified leadership. That contradicts the older portrayal, according to which the conquest was achieved through individual action on the part of separate groups (Judges 1:1ff.). In such cases interpretation must concern itself, perhaps more than heretofore, with what is intended by that later portrayal. Clearly a *credendum* has here been projected into history. That is to say, the redemptive activity of God toward Israel has been portrayed as the unity that it was believed to be; a *doxa* is heaped on the event which reaches far beyond what actually occurred, for what is believed in is placed on view as something already effectuated in history. Conversely, the statements of the Psalms of lament far transcend any individual's personal experience, to the point of drawing a paradigmatic picture of the misery of being utterly forsaken by God. To be sure, an exceeding of the facts aimed at pointing up some glorious act of God that has been made manifest occurs more frequently in the Old Testament. But, one way or the other, such statements tend markedly toward the radical. If one asks what human motives were involved, a certain exuberance, or that natural impulse to magnify or glorify historical events, may assuredly have played a part. But the exegete cannot pass over the fact that these statements are nevertheless now set forth with the claim to witness to a unique action of God in history. And for that reason one must, if one has taken careful cognizance of this entire phenomenon, speak quite precisely of an eschatological impulse in such portrayals, insofar as they introduce a definitive action of God as something already real in history.

9. At this point the question automatically imposes itself: What part have I in the Old Testament as a Christian believer, and what part has the church, if it cannot be that I identify myself, at least partly (it was never a question of more than that!), with the religion of ancient Israel? If I yield myself to the Old Testament's own ker-

ygmatic intention, I must, as we have seen, ask what part I have in its witness to historical facts, and to the redemptive benefits promised to Israel. But I belong to none of the twelve tribes, I do not offer sacrifice in Jerusalem, nor do I hope in terms of Isaiah 2:1-4 for the glorification of the Temple mountain. I am not even a proselyte, and so able to appropriate for myself the greathearted consolation of Trito-Isaiah (Isa. 56:1-8). In other words, I have not "come to a mountain that can be touched" (Heb. 12:18). God's gracious provisions, so lavishly bestowed on Israel, seem to pass me by, because I do not belong to the historical people Israel; and the Old Testament maintains its connection with this historical Israel to its very last word. Is it not possible that a great unease will once more make itself felt in many of our congregations, instructed as they have been for so long, an unease from which this inadequate teaching of the religion of Israel has up till now protected them?

The result of our reflections concerning the Old Testament's various witnesses to past history and present (those that are directly prophetic have concerned us only peripherally) can, therefore, not be that we recognize in them a thought world that is "very nearly that of the New Testament." Rather we see everywhere in this history brought to pass by God's Word, in acts of judgment and acts of redemption alike, the prefiguration of the Christ-event of the New Testament. That is the only analogy—to return to the problem of analogy posed at the beginning—that offers itself for a theological interpretation of these texts. This renewed recognition of types in the Old Testament is no peddling of secret lore, no digging up of miracles, but is simply correspondent to the belief that the same God who revealed himself in Christ has also left his footprints in the history of the Old Testament covenant people—that we have to do with *one* divine discourse, here to the fathers through the prophets, there to us through Christ (Heb. 1:1). We must now, in a few words, define more precisely what this means.

(a) Typological interpretation will thus in a fundamental way leave the historical self-understanding of the Old Testament texts in question behind, and go beyond it. It sees in the Old Testament facts something in preparation, something sketching itself out, of which the Old Testament witness is not itself aware, because it lies quite beyond its purview.

(b) Typological interpretation has to do with the entire Old Testament; any restriction of it to a "high religion," or any blocking out of the "priestly, cultic religion," is impossible. Wherever one of God's dealings with his people, or with an individual, is witnessed to, the possibility exists of seeing in this a shadow of the New Testament revelation of Christ. The number of Old Testament types is unlimited.

(c) But typological interpretation has to do only with the witness to the divine event, not with such correspondences in historical, cultural, or archaeological details as the Old Testament and the New may have in common. It must hold itself to the kerygma that is intended, and not fix upon the narrative details with the aid of which the kerygma is set forth. It is precisely at this point that, as it is used in the church, it frequently runs wild and becomes an overly subtle exhibition of cleverness. Typological interpretation, both in Old Testament and in New, does not fix upon historical or biographical details, but confines itself to the *credenda*. Yet the reference of Old Testament statements to the New is not restricted to the person and life of Christ, but embraces the entire Christ-event as this is witnessed to in the New Testament, including its ecclesiological aspect.

(d) Typological interpretation is aware of the difference between the redemptive benefits of the Old Testament and those of the New; it is aware of the way in which limitations upon salvation are removed in the new covenant; above all, it is aware of the incompleteness of the old covenant, in which God had not yet implanted his precepts in the hearts and wills of men (Jer. 31:31ff.); it is aware both of the lack of complete obedience and of the preponderance of the law in the Old Testament. But it sees in the time-conditioned benefits (land, rest, long life, and the like) foreshadowings of eternal salvation. It sees, too, in the manner in which God provides, in his mysterious leading, in the postponement of his gifts as well as in the marvel of his help, prefigurements of the grace and providence extended to those who are in Christ. Even in details, both the Christian community and individual Christians see in the temptations as well as in the consolations that came to the Old Testament people of God a prefigurement of their own existence in this world.

(e) But though typological interpretation transcends the self-understanding of the Old Testament text, it is not on that account to be divorced in any fundamental way from the process of exegesis. Naturally, it cannot serve as a heuristic principle for the elucidation of particular philological and historical problems. Yet an equally earnest warning must be issued against a sharp separation of typological interpretation from the historico-critical exegetical process, as if the one began only when the other had finished its work. As a matter of fact, both processes — that is, both of these seemingly mutually exclusive forms of analogical thinking — interlock. We face the undeniable fact that so very often even the best "historical" exegesis is achieved from a theological point of view — that is to say, in the final analysis, from the side of the Christian faith. At what other place would Old Testament exegesis reckon with Paul's word about the veil (2 Cor. 3:7ff.)? At what point in its interpretive process does Christian interpretation think itself distinguishable from Jewish?

(f) Typological interpretation frees Old Testament exegesis from the compelling constraint always, in order to be theologically relevant, to bring into the discussion some meaning, some truth beyond that inherent in the event itself. But exegesis not infrequently has to do with texts that describe events but that give little or no interpretative comment. Exegesis must face up to this; and in the very fact that it makes it clear how this phenomenon—that the narrator has offered only a bare event—is to be understood, it shows itself theologically significant.

(g) Regarding the handling of this sort of typological interpretation in the case of individual texts, no pedagogical norm can or may be set up; it cannot be further regulated hermeneutically, but takes place in the freedom of the Holy Spirit.[23]

(h) Typological interpretation confronts today a much more complicated state of affairs, exegetically speaking, than formerly, and must for its part pass on to yet finer theological distinctions. Whether the term "typology" will be retained permanently for what has been outlined in this article, whether the very word is perhaps too heavily burdened with wrong connotations, or has here been so far broadened beyond its established usage as to complicate rather than to further the discussion, is an open question. It has been used here because it seemed the part of candor thus to establish a link with the old hermeneutical tradition, which ever and again shows itself to be more appropriate to the Old Testament witness than our theological spiritualizing. Should the term prove to be intolerable, it will then be equally incumbent on its opponents and on its friends to be prepared to give their precise reasons for this.

One must therefore—at last to use the controversial word—really speak of a witness of the Old Testament to Christ, for our knowledge of Christ is incomplete without the witness of the Old Testament. Christ is given to us only through the double witness of the choir of those who await and those who remember. There is an estimate of, and a verdict with regard to, the "truth contained in" the Old Testament that betrays from the outset a false understanding, for it proceeds from the assumption that Christ is given to us, and known by us, in the New Testament, and that one then needs only to define the worth of the Old Testament and its posture with regard to this Christ. But the Old Testament must first of all be heard in its witness to the creative Word of God in history; and in these dealings of God

<hr>

23. Concerning the only standard that Calvin names in this connection, the *communis lex Dei*, cf. H. H. Wolf, *Die Einheit des Bundes,* pp. 123-24.

in history, in his acts of judgment as well as in his acts of redemption, we may everywhere discern what is already a Christ-event.

The beginning of the road that might lead us out of the confusion and the weakness of our understanding of the Old Testament would appear to look something like this.

THE *SENSUS PLENIOR*
AND BIBLICAL
INTERPRETATION
WILLIAM SANFORD LASOR

In presenting this token of my affection for and appreciation of my beloved colleague, it is fitting that I should deal with some subject that embraces our respective fields, the two Testaments. More and more, scholars have been devoting their attention to the relationship between the Old and the New Testaments — after a long and somewhat sterile period when the two disciplines were handled as having little or no organic relationship. More or less adhering to the position of R. Bultmann, some scholars have found little reason for a New Testament scholar to study the Old Testament.[1] A healthy reaction, sparked by such scholars as, *inter alia,* W. Eichrodt, G. von Rad, G. E. Wright, W. Zimmerli, P. Grelot, and C. Westermann, has set in against this dichotomy of the Christian Bible. R. E. Murphy gives a very good survey of the development of the problem of the interrelationship of the Testaments in recent years up to the time of his writing.[2] But the view that there is a discontinuity between the Testaments continues to attract many scholars. I suppose that the basic worldview of a scholar has something to do with this, for a theist who is a Christian would have relatively little difficulty in accepting a basic continuity in the redemptive and revelatory acts of God in the Old and the New Testaments. On the other hand, one who is basically nontheistic, or who sees the religions of the Hebrews and Christians as simply two of the man-made religions of the world, tends to look upon the concept of progressive revelation as something imposed by man and not originating in the activity of God. But even those of us who hold to the view that the authoritative Scriptures are both Old and New Testaments are not without our

---

1. Cf. R. E. Murphy's comment, "Bultmann's position is one of radical denial of the true relevance of the OT to the Christian" ("The Relationship between the Testaments," *Catholic Biblical Quarterly* 26 [1964]:352).
2. Murphy, "The Relationship between the Testaments."

Reprinted from *Scripture, Tradition, and Interpretation: Essays Presented to Everett F. Harrison by His Students and Colleagues in Honor of His Seventy-fifth Birthday*, ed. W. Ward Gasque and William Sanford LaSor (Grand Rapids: Eerdmans, 1978), pp. 260-77.

own set of problems. What, precisely, is the relationship of Old and New? How are we to perform objective, scholarly, and "scientific" exegesis, particularly on passages which are involved in this inter-relationship? In this essay, I shall attempt to come to grips with one small problem area in the larger discussion, namely, the validity or invalidity of the concept of *sensus plenior* in biblical hermeneutics.

But before entering into my subject, I cannot resist a little humor. Those of us who have known Everett Harrison over the years have come to recognize that his wit is keen and his ability to make a pun is delightful. Therefore, I suggest that to honor my colleague who has been at Fuller Theological Seminary for thirty years (during twenty-eight of which I have enjoyed collegiality with him), a paper on *sensus plenior,* "the fuller sense," is particularly apt.

1. INTERPRETATION OF SCRIPTURE

The art of preaching is the application of Scripture to the present situation. Of course, if Scripture has no application to the present, preaching is nonsense—as indeed it has become in all too many pulpits. For the preacher who believes that the Bible is the author-itative word of God in every generation, his task is to start with the text of Scripture and to derive from it a message that will be in effect the word of God to his audience.[3] But by what process is this done? What are the rules that must be followed, in order that the message will indeed be the word of God and not just the imagina-tions of a human speaker? There are certain well-recognized steps in the process. First, there is the study of the text itself (text criti-cism), in order to establish, as far as is humanly possible with the available means, the inspired text as it came from the biblical author. Then, there is exegesis, by which we attempt to understand as pre-cisely as possible what the author intended to say and what his contemporary hearers or readers understood by his words.[4] Finally, there is the application of this message to our own day—but this is the most difficult, and seemingly the least controllable step of all. The believing community—whether the people of Israel, the church in the New Testament, or the Jews and Christians of post-biblical times—has always attempted this last step, but the methods used

3. What I say about the "preacher" applies equally well, *mutatis mutandis,* to the teacher or author, or to anyone who seeks to proclaim God's word to his or her own day.

4. Some would insert Introduction between Text Criticism and Application; I include it here as part of exegesis, for the problems of date and authorship are elementary parts of identifying the author and his day and place, which in turn are necessary (at least to some extent) for understanding his intention.

have varied from place to place and from time to time. Our present study lies in this area.

The literal meaning. The basic meaning of any text, including the biblical text, is the literal meaning. This is universally admitted, but it is sometimes misunderstood or misinterpreted. In general, it is assumed that the literal meaning can be obtained by adding together the literal meanings of the words, taken in their syntax. Thus, for example, we read the account of Abram's migration from Haran to Canaan:

> Abram was seventy-five years old when he departed from Haran. And Abram took Sarai his wife, and Lot his brother's son, and all their possessions which they had gathered, and the persons that they had gotten in Haran; and they set forth to go to the land of Canaan. (Gen. 12:4b-5a)

This is perfectly clear. The words are familiar, the syntax is quite simple, and about all we need to do to get a clear understanding of the "literal" meaning is fill in definitions of the persons and places named.

But quite often the literal meaning cannot be obtained by this simple process. Take this brief statement:

> Yet it was I who taught Ephraim to walk. . . . (Hos. 11:3)

The simple sum of the words tells us that an unnamed speaker taught someone named "Ephraim" how to walk. But when we read the context, we discover that "Ephraim" is a figure of speech signifying the northern kingdom of Israel,[5] and "I taught Ephraim to walk" is intended to convey the meaning that Israel's religious and national existence was the result of the Lord's tutelage. In fact, "Israel" takes on the larger meaning, in the light of verse 1, and what is said of "Ephraim" is true of all Israel, northern and southern kingdoms. But this is still the literal sense. It is not an interpretation, subject to different viewpoints; it is precisely what the author intended and what his hearers would have understood. Common figures of speech must be understood as such, if we are to get the literal sense of the text.

Poetry not only makes extensive use of figures of speech, but it includes other features, and as a result, the literal meaning is often obscured and sometimes difficult to discover.[6] Take, for example, the following passage:

5. The capital of Israel was Samaria and it was located in the tribal territory of Ephraim.
6. The passage in Hosea 11, which we have just considered, appears to be in poetic structure. My reference here to "poetry," however, is to portions of the Scriptures that are entirely in poetic form, such as the Psalms.

Rebuke the beasts that dwell among the reeds,
   the herd of bulls with the calves of the peoples.
Trample under foot those who lust after tribute;
   scatter the peoples who delight in war.
Let bronze be brought from Egypt;
   let Ethiopia hasten to stretch out her hands to God. (Ps. 68:30-31)

This is a portion of a great psalm concerning the Lord God, his covenant people, and the nations of the world. Hence the figures of speech "beasts" and "bulls" must signify the enemies of God's people. But it is not only a prayer that the enemies might be scattered; it is even a prayer that they might at last be brought to God. Allowing for certain details that may have been and probably were clearer to the people who first united in this song but that now escape us, we may take this as the literal meaning. The *Good News Bible*, which seeks to translate by giving the dynamic equivalent, renders this passage as follows:

Rebuke Egypt, that wild animal in the reeds;
   rebuke the nations, that herd of bulls with their calves,
   until they all bow down and offer you their silver.
Scatter those people who love to make war!
Ambassadors will come from Egypt;
   the Sudanese will raise their hands in prayer to God.
   (Ps. 68:30-31, TEV)[7]

The literal meaning of the text, then, is the basic meaning and the basis for interpretation. When the literal meaning is ignored, all sorts of fanciful interpretations and applications result, as can be seen in the homilies of medieval Christians and in sectarian writings of modern times. Without the literal sense we have no control of any other sense.[8]

Grammatico-historical exegesis. Since the Reformation, biblical exegetes have generally applied a method that includes, among other things, the grammatical elements of the text and its historical setting. In the passages of Scripture which we have previously considered, we have seen the need for both of these elements. Now, let us take them up in a bit more detail.

---

7. Some may object that the TEV at times moves from dynamic translation to interpretation. This is a very fine line, and the TEV translators might reply that the original worshipers had *Egypt* in mind when they spoke of "the beasts that dwell among the reeds," and *ambassadors*, when they mentioned the bringing of bronze. In my mind, the TEV often adds interpretation, sometimes with great value, and sometimes with questionable result.

8. See further my remarks on the literal interpretation in my article on "Interpretation of Prophecy," in *Baker's Dictionary of Practical Theology* (*BDPT*), ed. Frank G. Turnbull (1967), pp. 129-30. The encyclical *Divino afflante Spiritu* defines the literal meaning as follows: "litteralem, ut aiunt, verborum significationem, quam hagiographus intenderit atque expresserit," — that is, what the hagiographer intended and expressed (see *Enchiridion Biblicum* [2nd ed., 1954], p. 552.

In grammatical exegesis, the basic unit is generally taken to be the *word*. Students in the process of learning how to exegete usually begin with word studies. Unfortunately, they often stop there as well. It does not take much exegetical experience to recognize that words rarely exist alone. In some cases they cannot exist alone and convey any meaning. To study a word, the context is essential. The word "Sit!" conveys meaning, but only in the context of a person (or a pet dog) who is standing, whereas "through" is meaningful only when in the context of another word or word-group.[9] The study of the word is nevertheless of primary importance, for communication in written form (and usually in spoken form) is composed of words, and unless we know the meaning(s) of each word, the communication is nonsense.[10]

A few words of caution may be called for at this point. For one thing, any given word rarely has precisely the same meaning in every context. Therefore, if we are working from a Hebrew or Greek lexicon, we need to make use of one that gives contexts as well as meanings, and further, we need to study several of these contexts.[11] There simply is no such thing as a "word-for-word" translation. A second factor to be noted is the type of literature (or genre) in which the word occurs. We have already seen that poetry and other figurative language requires special study of words, but this same principle extends to other literary types. A third word of caution concerns the use of etymological word-studies.[12] While there is considerable value in tracing the cognates of a word in various related languages, it is undeniably true that each language has its own peculiar semantic development for the word under investigation.[13] A fourth caution concerns special usage of words, such as paronomasia, al-

---

9. With rising inflection in certain contexts, "Through?" may mean "Are you finished (yet/already)?" and with falling inflection, "Through!" may mean "I've finished." In any case, the context is required for the conveying of meaning, even if the context is a situation and not a text.

10. A splendid example is the poem "Jabberwocky" in Lewis Carroll's *Through the Looking Glass*. For a very clever analysis of the grammatical structure of this poem, see E. A. Nida and C. R. Taber, *The Theory and Practice of Translation* (1974), pp. 34-35. But though we may know from such a study that *toves* can *gyre and gimble* and that such activity takes place *in the wabe,* or that *borogroves* are *mimsy* whereas *raths* are *mome,* we haven't the foggiest idea of what is being said—because we don't know the meaning of the significant words.

11. The biblical student who cannot work in Hebrew or Greek can still accomplish such contextual study by the use of a good concordance, such as Young's or Strong's, where the Hebrew and Greek words are given and contexts using the same word can be examined.

12. The best-known of such works is Kittel's *Theological Dictionary of the New Testament,* 10 vols. (1964-76).

13. This was the strong point of criticism of Kittel's *TWNT* (the German original of *TDNT*) made by James Barr in *The Semantics of Biblical Language* (1961).

literation, assonance, and the like, where the author, in order to make a point, may make an unusual use of a word, use a word that is uncommon, or even coin a word for the occasion.

As we have already seen, meaning is conveyed by words in context, and the study of *syntax* is an essential part of obtaining the literal meaning. Since all grammatical study, and especially syntax, is in a sad state today, particularly in the United States of America, most students have a terrifying experience trying to learn Greek or Hebrew syntax. Students who have worked under Daniel Fuller or me know that we seek to get into the study of the text through the use of sentence diagrams. Diagramming is simply an attempt to visualize the rules of syntax. This deals with the "surface structure" of language. There is another approach through semantics, which goes beneath the surface structure. There are four basic semantic categories which "include exhaustively all the semantic subcategories of all languages."[14] These are:

(O)   Object: things or entities which normally participate in events (i.e., nouns, pronouns, and other substantives);

(E)   Event: actions, processes, happenings (i.e., verbs and verb phrases);

(A)   Abstract: expressions which set forth qualities, quantities, and degrees of objects, events, and other abstracts (i.e., adjectives and adverbs);

(R)   Relations: expressions of the meaningful connections between the other kinds of terms (i.e., prepositions, conjunctions, and the like).

It is possible to analyze any statement and restructure it in a way that is clear and unambiguous. This analytic process of reducing the surface structure to its underlying kernels is called back-transformation.[15] By whatever method we approach the problem, we must ultimately have a clear idea of how the words of the text are interrelated so as to convey the meaning.

It is well known that language undergoes changes as we move from place to place and from time to time. Therefore, if we would know precisely what the author meant and what his hearers/readers understood, we should know precisely where and when that text was composed. This is the *historical* element of grammatico-historical exegesis. History and geography are integral parts of the biblical Scriptures. The number of personal and place names in the Bible

14. Nida and Taber, *The Theory and Practice of Translation*, pp. 37-38.
15. For a clear discussion with good illustrations, see Nida and Taber, *The Theory and Practice of Translation*, chapter 3, "Grammatical Analysis."

far exceeds that of any other religious literature. We of the believing community like to use expressions such as, "God is active in history." Especially when we turn to the Old Testament prophets we realize how much we need to know the historical situation in order to comprehend the basic message.[16] The historical context is as important as the textual context.

The failure of the grammatico-historical method. During the past century-and-a-half, exegetical scholars have refined grammatico-historical exegesis in many ways, creating in the process many tools of great value for understanding the Scriptures. But along the way, some scholars seemed to lose sight of the truth that the Scriptures are the Word of God — of the living God, whose Word is alive and active. Exegesis was firmly anchored in history, but it was not the history of God's redemptive revelation; rather, it was the secular history of the past, and had only antiquarian interest for the present. The literal meaning of the biblical text is the basic meaning, but if it is the only meaning, then God is not speaking to us; he spoke to men of old — or so they believed — and that was that.

Part of the reason for this failure of the method must be traced to the dominance of the "scientific" worldview. The theistic system, according to which God is everywhere and always greater than the universe he created and active in the laws which he himself ordained, was replaced by a worldview that completely ruled out anything that could not be accounted for by the scientific process. The "god" of Israel was no different from the gods of the Canaanites or the Babylonians. When the prophet said, "Thus saith the Lord," he was simply expressing his own insights and attributing them to his particular deity. In fact, the god of Abraham, the god of Isaac, and the god of Jacob were different deities which the ancient figures worshiped. To talk of a "covenant," a "covenant people," a "progressive revelation," or indeed any kind of "revelation" is simply to impose upon the religious and mythological recollections of the people the concept of a later, but still prescientific, age. To discover the historical situation — which was now specified as the *Sitz im Leben* — was a circular process whereby it was first determined what the situation must have been at any particular time and then the scriptural data were reworked to fit that situation. The exegetical commentaries that resulted gave the preacher little if any help in his

16. Failure to recognize the importance of this fact has led to two different results: on the one hand, there are those who see nothing significant in the prophets because they do not understand the situation that called forth the prophetic message; on the other hand, the prophetic messages have been cut up into predictions of things to come that have no relationship whatever to the basic prophetic message.

effort to discover what God wanted him to say to his congregation on the following Sunday.

It is not my intention to cast aside the grammatico-historical method. Quite the contrary, I use it and I try to teach it to my students. It is simply my purpose to show that this method brings us only to the end of the first stage of biblical preaching, namely, the literal meaning. B. L. Ramm has expressed it well: "Exegesis without application is academic; exposition that is not grounded in exegesis is either superficial or misleading or even both."[17]

The spiritual meaning(s). Starting from the premise that the Bible is the Word of God to the people of his covenant, it follows that this Word is applicable according to his will to all generations. Since he is a spiritual being and since his purpose is redemptive, it follows that his Word is spiritual and redemptive. There is therefore a spiritual meaning — or possibly more than one spiritual meaning — implicit in his Word. Discovering the spiritual message in, rather than imposing it on, the Scripture is a serious task, and the believing community has attempted various methods.

A full discussion of the history of interpretation can be found in the well-known work by Dean Farrar.[18] A useful summary is given by Ramm in his work on interpretation.[19] We need only take time here to remember some of the more striking methods. Jewish exegesis is often illustrated by the use of gematria, whereby the numerical values of the letters of a word unlock the secret of the meaning. Thus, "Shiloh shall come" in Genesis 49:10 gives the value of 358, which is the number of "Messiah."[20] It is sometimes overlooked that the Jews also produced Philo of Alexandria (ca. 20 B.C.– ca. A.D. 54), and that his allegorical method largely influenced Origen (ca. A.D. 185-254) and subsequent Christian exegetes. Using the trichotomous theory of the human being as a pattern, Origen held that all Scripture had three meanings, the sense of the words which was for the simple, the moral sense which is like the soul, and the spiritual sense which is the highest. John Cassian (died ca. 435) held to a fourfold method of interpretation involving the historical, the allegorical, the tropological, and the anagogical. His best-known illustration is the city of Jerusalem, historically a Jewish city, allegorically the church of Christ, tropologically the soul of man, and

---

17. *BDPT,* p. 101.

18. F. W. Farrar, *The History of Interpretation* (1886; reprint 1961).

19. B. Ramm, *Protestant Biblical Interpretation* (rev. ed., 1956), chapters 2, 3.

20. The numerical value of the consonants YB' ŠYLH is 358 (10+2+1+ 300+10+30+5), which is the same as the value of the letters of MŠYH (40+300+10+8). This method is not entirely dead. Several years ago I attended a meeting where a learned Jewish scholar used gematria as the basis for deriving his message from a passage in the prophets.

anagogically the heavenly city.[21] This fourfold method was adopted by Thomas Aquinas (ca. 1225-1274) and used widely by Catholic exegetes.[22] Martin Luther started out using the allegorical method and later claimed to have abandoned it—but a study of his commentaries, particularly those on the Old Testament, shows that he still reverted to it in order to find Christ everywhere in the Old Testament. Thus, for example, in his comments on Genesis 28:12-14 (Jacob's ladder), he says: "The ladder is the wonderful union of the divinity with our flesh. On it the angels ascend and descend, and they can never wonder at this enough. This is the historical, simple, and literal sense." In the next paragraph, Luther gives the allegorical meaning of the ladder, "a union between us and Christ."[23] It is obvious that what Luther considered to be the "historical, simple, and literal sense" is rather the allegorical, and his "allegorical" is more like the tropological.

It was the Reformation, without doubt, that started the trend toward using the grammatico-historical exegetical method as the basis for developing the spiritual message from the text. In my opinion, John Calvin was the greatest of exegetes in this effort. If in some of his commentaries he seems to be a child of his day,[24] this does not greatly detract from his stature as an exegete. The test of the preacher is not whether he seems to relate the text overmuch to the situation of his own day, but whether indeed he draws this message from the text.

The spiritual meaning of a text, as I see it, is the timeless truth inherent in a passage of Scripture as it is applied to the preacher's day and its spiritual needs. This spiritual meaning may be drawn in different ways, by twisting or accommodating the text, by allegorizing it, by the use of typology (to be discussed below), or by strict application of the grammatico-historical method. We reject accommodation and most allegory as having no objective controls,

---

21. *Collationes* xiv.8, in J. Migne, *Patrologia Latina* 49, 964A; see also Philip Schaff and Henry Wace, eds., *Nicene and Post-Nicene Fathers*; Second Series (1894), 11, pp. 437-38. The formula, *Littera gesta docet, quid credas allegoria, moralis quid agas, quo tendas anagogia*, attributed to Thomas (*Quaestiones quodlibetales duodecim* 7, Q.6, and *Summa Theologica* I.i.10), appears in a footnote to Cassian in *NPNF* 11, p. 438.

22. Thomas groups the allegorical, anagogical, and moral senses under the spiritual sense, and points out that all the senses are founded on the literal, insisting that only from the literal can any argument be drawn. *Summa* I.i.10 (see Anton C. Pegis, *Basic Writings of St. Thomas Aquinas* [1945], 1, p. 17) See also *Commentary on Epistle to Galatians*, IV, 7, in Mary T. Clark, ed., *An Aquinas Reader* (1972), pp. 412-13.

23. *Luther's Works*, ed. Jaroslav Pelikan, vol. 5, *Lectures on Genesis, Chaps. 26-30* (1968), p. 223.

24. On Jacob's Ladder, for example, Calvin rejects the interpretation that "the ladder is a figure of Divine Providence" and says, "If, then, we say that the ladder is a figure of Christ, the exposition will not be forced" (John Calvin, *Commentaries on . . . Genesis*, trans. John King [reprinted 1948], 2, pp. 112-13).

thereby leaving the preacher free to find whatever message he will in any text that suits his fancy. The grammatico-historical method, we have seen, has sometimes failed to yield a spiritual meaning. Where does this leave us in our quest for meaning in the Word of God?

2. THE THEORY AND PRACTICE OF
SENSUS PLENIOR

The spiritual meaning of a passage of Scripture, derived by using grammatico-historical exegesis, is completely valid and provides objective controls; but it often leaves us with a basic gap between the Old and the New Testaments. Take, for example, the account of the Davidic covenant in 2 Samuel 7:

> When your days are fulfilled and you lie down with your fathers, I will raise up your son after you, who shall come forth from your body, . . . and I will establish the throne of his kingdom forever. (2 Sam. 7:12-13)

The literal meaning is clear enough: The Lord is promising David, through the prophet Nathan (see v. 4), an eternal dynasty. Saul had been the first king of Israel, but he established no dynasty; David had supplanted Saul's son. The Lord was assuring David that his son would succeed him and the Davidic line would continue for future generations. We could add more details from the immediate context, such as the promise that David's son would build the "house" (temple) which David himself had longed to build for the Lord (7:13); that even though this son sinned, he would be chastened but not supplanted (7:14, 15); and that Israel would have a permanent and peaceful dwelling place (7:10). The spiritual truth is also clear: the Lord is faithful to keep the promises which he made to Abraham and the patriarchs concerning the people of his covenant in providing for them not only the land but also a dynastic succession that would give them rest from their enemies, hence we may trust him to keep other promises to us who are also people of his covenant.

But there are obvious flaws in a methodology that stops here. For one thing, the Davidic covenant, if we understand it only literally, was not kept; it was broken. Israel did not continue to live "in their own place, and be disturbed no more" (7:10); the Assyrians and the Babylonians uprooted them and demolished their holy temple. The throne of David was not "made sure for ever" (7:16); it vanished in 586 B.C., and no king of the Davidic line has ruled since then. A second fact must be faced, namely, the New Testament writers considered Jesus Christ to be the "son of David" and applied to Christ the promises that had been made to David. How can this be derived from the Old Testament text if we adhere strictly to the literal mean-

ing and its spiritual truth? It becomes obvious that, for the New
Testament writers (and for Jesus), at least, the Old Testament passage must have some deeper meaning.

Symbol, Allegory, and Type. There is a great deal of confusion in the
terms that are used. According to some writers, "allegory" and
"type" are the same, and others would even include *sensus plenior* in
this category. Therefore, I shall first attempt to specify the terms
that I shall use.

All language is symbolic, for words and clauses are merely symbolic ways of communicating. The proof of this can be seen when
we translate, for the purpose of translation is to convert one set of
symbols to another while conveying the same meaning. In a large
sense, then, the entire Bible, like all spoken or written language, is
symbolic. Obviously, this is too broad a definition to be useful.
There are certain concepts which are capable of immediate visual-
ization, for example, "chair," "red," "she smiled," and so on. There
are other concepts that cannot be visualized, such as "God," "transcendence," "the age to come," and so on. To communicate such
ideas, we use symbols, making use of some visualizable word or
expression. The Bible is full of such symbols, and these must be
recognized and treated as such in order to understand the message
that is intended. For example, the account of the garden of Eden
includes a tree identified as "the tree of the knowledge of good and
evil" (Gen. 2:17). We are not told what kind of tree it was—and
that is unimportant. The symbolic meaning of the tree is most important, for it symbolized the right of the Creator to impose a sanction on the Adamic creature, to say, "This is a no-no," while at the
same time it symbolized the free choice of Adam in his God-given
ability to disobey the divine command. The serpent, likewise, is
symbolic of the satanic. I use the word *satanic* here in its literal sense,
to mean that which is adverse, specifically opposed, to God's will.
The suggestion to disobey God's command did not originate in the
Adamic pair; it came from outside. Therefore, Adam cannot blame
God for making him satanic. At the same time, Adam and his wife
are culpable, for they had a clear revelation of the will of God and
they knowingly disobeyed. So far, we are dealing with the literal
meaning by seeking to understand the significance of the symbols.
This is clearly to be distinguished from allegory, as I use the word.

In some instances, the symbol is later replaced by a reality, or
will be replaced by a reality in a future age. In this case, the symbol
may properly be called a "type." The reality may be called the
"antitype" of the symbol that it replaces. One of the best illustrations
of this is the tabernacle which the Israelites constructed and carried
with them during the wilderness period. The tabernacle was a port-
able building, an elaborate tent with decorations and furnishings.

But it was more importantly a symbol, symbolizing the presence of the Lord. This is indicated by the names which it bore, namely, "tent of meeting," and *miškān*, "dwelling place." It was also indicated as such by another symbolic act, namely, the visible descent of the cloud upon the completed tabernacle (Exod. 40:34-38). The tabernacle, however, was later replaced by the reality, when God became incarnate in the virgin-born child, Emmanuel (which means "God with us"). John puts this truth in clear language, "The word became flesh and tabernacled among us" (John 1:14, lit.).[25] It is even possible to carry the symbolism further, and see the Incarnation itself as a symbol of a greater reality; for in the Holy City of Revelation, the "tabernacle" of God is with men, and God himself, the ultimate reality, makes any further symbolic representation of himself unnecessary (Rev. 21:2-3). Since the tabernacle was a symbol that was later replaced by the reality it symbolized, it is entirely proper to speak of the tabernacle as a *type* of Christ, and the earthly incarnation of Christ as a *type* of the presence of God himself in the new Jerusalem.

This use of the word *type* is clearly to be distinguished from allegory. An allegorical interpretation of the tabernacle goes into fanciful explanations of every color, every type of material, every piece of furniture, and sometimes results in a portrayal of Jesus Christ in such detail that the Incarnation would seem to be unnecessary. It is certainly true that some of the items used in the tabernacle cultus were in themselves symbolic of spiritual truth, and even types of realities to come. The sacrifices of bulls and goats, which (as the author of Hebrews reminds us) were not able to take away sin, were typical of the sacrifice of Christ which does take away sin. Other items may profitably be studied in similar fashion. As long as we begin with the reality that is symbolized in the text and proceed to the reality that replaces the symbol, we have controllable interpretation of the text. It avoids the criticism leveled against allegorizing the text, often deserved, and yields the spiritual meaning of the scriptural passage.

To speak of certain biblical persons as "types" (such as "David is a type of Christ") seems to me to be incorrect. David did symbolize something, but he was not a symbol. What he symbolized was later replaced by the reality when the Messiah appeared, but David himself was not replaced; and we believe that he shall continue to exist forever in the age to come. I would prefer to say that

25. Even the verb in John, *skēnoō*, is reminiscent of the word for "tabernacle," which in Greek is *skēnē*.

the Davidic office or throne was the type, and the messianic reign the antitype.[26]

Sensus plenior. The term *sensus plenior* ("the fuller meaning") is attributed to Andrea Fernández in an article written in 1925. The subject has been treated most fully by the Catholic scholar Raymond E. Brown.[27] Brown defines *sensus plenior* as follows:

> The *sensus plenior* is that additional, deeper meaning, intended by God but not clearly intended by the human author, which is seen to exist in the words of a Biblical text (or group of texts, or even a whole book) when they are studied in the light of further revelation or development in the understanding of revelation.[28]

Brown's earlier presentations of the concept called forth considerable reaction, almost entirely limited to Catholic scholars, and a study of this material is most helpful—but it lies beyond our present purpose.[29] Some of the objections and clarifications will be considered here; those that deal principally with implications that concern Roman Catholic but not Protestant dogma we shall disregard.

The definition raises a particularly difficult problem by its statement "intended by God, but not clearly intended by the human author." This concept, it would seem at first glance, lies beyond grammatico-historical exegesis and therefore opens the door for subjective interpretation. In fact, it seems clear from the discussion that ensued that some Catholic scholars were making use of *sensus plenior* and the magisterial teaching of the Church to support certain Marian dogmas which Protestant scholars would disclaim as nonbiblical. At the same time, other Catholic scholars were raising the objection that if the biblical authors did not intend to teach something, it was not allowable to read that teaching into the passage.

There are a number of Old Testament passages which are used by New Testament authors in a way that seems to support the concept of *sensus plenior*. We may mention two that cause difficulty, namely, the "virgin shall conceive" passage in Isaiah (Isa. 7:14), and the "out of Egypt" passage in Hosea (Hos. 11:1). In neither case is there any indication that the author had some distant future event in mind, hence it is most difficult to conclude that the authors were speaking of Jesus Christ or even an unnamed Messiah. Isa-

26. I have dealt with this matter more fully in my article in *BDPT,* pp. 130-32.

27. Brown, "The History and Development of the Theory of a *Sensus Plenior,*" *Catholic Biblical Quarterly* 15 (1953): 141-62; *The Sensus Plenior of Sacred Scripture* (S.T.D. dissertation; Baltimore: St. Mary's University, 1955); "The *Sensus Plenior* in the Last Ten Years," *Catholic Biblical Quarterly* 25 (1963): 262-85. Fr. Brown gives extensive bibliography for further study, and his words deserve careful reading.

28. Brown, *The Sensus Plenior of Sacred Scripture,* p. 92.

29. Brown's article "The *Sensus Plenior* in the Last Ten Years" will refer the reader to the most significant reactions.

iah 7 deals with Ahaz, king of Judah, and the Syro-Ephramite coalition of Rezin of Syria and Pekah of Israel. The point does not
seem to be a virgin birth, but rather it lies in the sequence of events:
a young woman is pregnant and will bear a son, and before this
child is old enough to know good and evil, the Lord will deal with
the enemy kings (Isa. 7:1-17).[30] The prophecy is dated ca. 735 B.C.,
and the fulfillment occurred in 732 and 722 B.C. Hosea 11:1 ("out
of Egypt I called my son") clearly deals with the deliverance of
Israel from Egypt at the time of the exodus, and the words of verse 2
obviously cannot be applied to Jesus. The author is using the re-
deeming love of the Lord in contrast with the stubborn sinfulness
of Israel to get across his lesson. Yet both of these passages are cited
as "fulfilled" in Jesus Christ (see Matt. 1:22-23 and 2:14-15). There
are other passages in the New Testament that raise similar problems
concerning the use of the Old Testament.

To say that "God intended" the Old Testament passages to refer
to a later fulfillment in Christ raises as many problems as it solves.
If God intended to foretell the virgin birth of Jesus, why did he do
it in just this way? Until Matthew quoted Isaiah 7:14, would any
Jew who carefully read Isaiah 7 have thought of the Messiah at all,
much less have understood it to teach his virgin birth? It seems that
it would have made more sense for God to have included the virgin-
birth prophecy in Isaiah 9 or 11, both of which are more obviously
passages dealing with a future period that could be associated with
the Messiah. But any attempt to suggest what God should have
done or what he intended to do is presumptuous, and I am reluctant
to deal with his Word in such manner.

It is more common to find modern scholars suggesting that New
Testament writers, notably Matthew and Paul, were simply using
methods of their day, either "rabbinic exegesis," or simply searching
for proof-texts. I find this effort no better solution, and so I return
to *sensus plenior,* but with some concern that the definition may need
to be reworded slightly.

There are passages of Scripture where there is indeed something
"deeper" or "fuller" than the literal and the spiritual meanings as
they appear on the surface. This has been obvious to the people of
God through the centuries, and it occurs in the Old Testament,
without the need of using New Testament illustrations. There is a
deep sense of the organic nature of the elect people. The call of
Abram was likewise a call to all of God's people to forsake everything and follow him (a spiritual sense), and the promise of blessing

---

30. This is in no way to be taken as a denial of the virgin-birth of Jesus, which
I cordially receive, believe, and teach, since it is clearly stated in Matthew 1:18-20
and Luke 1:31, 34-35.

to all the nations of the earth through Abraham and his descendants was indeed to be fulfilled by those descendants. Yet, when Isaiah considered the glories of the future, he saw Israel (the descendants of Abraham through Isaac and Jacob) and himself as in need of redemption (see Isa. 53).[31] Israel is portrayed in the Old Testament both as a redemptive agent (and hence a type of the Redeemer) and as a redeemed community (hence either a type of the church or the earlier organic portion of which the church is a later portion). At the same time, the completion of the redemptive activity of the Lord always lies beyond the Old Testament. Thus there is a *fullness* which is never achieved in the Old Testament but which is required. There is a *fuller* meaning of the promises of the Lord than is ever realized in the Old Testament.

Take, for example, the "protevangelium" of Genesis 3:15. This is part of the curse which God pronounced on the serpent after the Adamic couple yielded to the temptation:

> I will put enmity between you and the woman,
> and between your seed and her seed;
> he shall bruise your head,
> and you shall bruise his heel.

To suggest that this story was first told to explain why women don't like snakes is ridiculous. But to suggest that the surface meaning, namely, that descendants (or some one descendant) of the woman would deal a mortal wound to one of the serpent's descendants, certainly does not exhaust the implicit purpose of the story. The entire account (Gen. 3:14-19) contains two interwoven strands, one of which speaks of defeat, suffering, toil, and death, while the other speaks of future generations, provision of food and sustenance of life, and triumph over the satanic tempter. To suggest that the "seed" of the "woman" who would bruise the serpent's head is a prophecy of Mary, the Virgin Birth, and Jesus, is to get more from the text than can be gotten by grammatico-historical exegesis, spiritual interpretation, and the objective processes of scriptural scholarship. But to see a *fullness* in the story, in precisely the way it is told, that can be understood when (and only when) that fullness is revealed, seems to me to be reasonable. In the seed are all the elements that will ultimately develop into the tree, its leaves, and its fruit. Yet careful analysis of that seed, even under the highest-powered microscope, will not reveal those elements. So it is, I believe, with Scripture.

Or again, take the Davidic covenant, which we discussed previously. It is clearly implied that the Lord is speaking of something

---

31. See my book *Israel: A Biblical View* (1976), pp. 26-28.

more than the successor of David on the throne, for the Lord declares a particular, personal relationship with the "son" of David: "I will be his father, and he shall be my son" (2 Sam. 7:14). This, of course, was the same terminology used in Israel's relationship to the Lord, and we should not press it to mean that the successor is to be the "son of God"—but it can involve such a concept, and indeed this concept appears with reference to the king of Israel in the Psalms (e.g., Ps. 2:7; 45:6). David wanted to build a "house" for the Lord, and in denying him this privilege, the Lord promised that David's "son" would make him a "house." But as we read the passage more carefully, we find that the term "house" means something more than a building (cf. 7:2, 6, 11, 13, 16). It is something that David's "son" would build (7:13), and something that the Lord himself would build (7:11). Like the throne, the house was to be permanent, and the Lord closed the promise with the words, "Your house and your kingdom shall be made sure for ever before me" (7:16). Certainly this demands a fuller meaning than Solomon, the Davidic dynasty, and Solomon's temple! It requires something more than a spiritual meaning. Even the people of the Old Testament came to realize that fact, for "son of David" came to be a term for the ruler who would inaugurate the age of justice and peace. They had more difficulty with the concept of the temple, but at least Jeremiah seems to have realized that the temple's continual existence was not guaranteed (see Jer. 7:3-15). The early church saw the fulfillment in Jesus Christ, the "son of David," in his kingship, even though he had been crucified (see Acts 2:22-36; 4:25-28), and in something other than Solomon's temple (see Acts 7:44-50).

To take one more example out of many that might be chosen,[32] let's look at Micah 5:2,

> But you, O Bethlehem Ephrathah,
>   who are little to be among the clans of Judah,
> from you shall come forth for me
>   one who is to be ruler in Israel,
> whose origin is from of old,
>   from ancient days. (Mic. 5:2 [MT 5:1])

The prophecy was spoken prior to the Assyrian invasion (see 5:5). The scattering of Israel is in view (5:7). The people are filled with fear (4:9). The prophet not only deals with their sins, but he offers some promise of deliverance (4:10), and he offers assurance that the Davidic line will again rule Israel. Of course, he does not mention the Davidic dynasty, but the ruler comes from Bethlehem, David's ancestral home; and the "ruler" is one "whose origin is from of old,

---

32. I have dealt with several others in my article in *BDPT*, pp. 133-35.

from ancient days" (5:2), not one from a new dynasty. Spiritually, this verse could be applied to any time of insecurity. But in the redemptive activity of God, an ultimate defeat of the enemies of God's people is required, along with a ruler who shall provide security and sufficiency for his people (5:3-4); and this *fullness* of meaning is present in the prophecy.

3. CONCLUSION AND IMPLICATIONS

Something like a *fuller meaning*, a *sensus plenior*, is required by many portions of Scripture, possibly by all of Scripture. By the very nature of God's redemptive and revelatory activity, the ultimate purpose of God is contained in this process; and as the redemptive activity proceeds ever to its fullness, so the revelatory activity at last is complete—full. The concept of "fulfillment" is not to be looked upon as discrete events which "fulfill" discrete predictions. There are predictions of coming events in the Bible, to be sure; but the proper juxtaposition is not "prediction and fulfillment" but rather "purpose and fulfillment." Prediction is something that is associated with clairvoyants and wizards, who have no power to bring about the events that they predict. If one of their predictions is "fulfilled," it is a matter of chance, or at most of prescience. With God, fulfillment is the accomplishment of his purpose. What God revealed to the prophets and through them to his people, he fulfilled by his own power, for he is able to fulfill his own Word.

The quest for a *sensus plenior* is part of the process of discovering the fullness of his purpose in his revelation. It is the recognition that at any moment in God's revelatory activity, he has the end in view and he has his people of future generations in mind. When he delivered the Israelites from Egypt, he was delivering all of his people from bondage—in a literal sense, for if Israel had not been delivered from Egypt there would have been no Israel; and in a fuller sense, for if there had been no Israel, there would have been no Davidic king, no prophets, no Scriptures, no Messiah, and no redemptive fulfillment. It was therefore true, in this fuller sense, that God did call his Son out of Egypt. In a similar manner we can trace the fullness of God's purpose in establishing the throne of David; for, as Isaiah saw so clearly (see Isa. 9:1-7; 11:1-10, etc.), the ultimate hope of a world of peace and security was to be found in that throne.

There are guidelines to be observed. *Sensus plenior*, like typology, must always begin with the literal meaning of the text. It is not a substitute for grammatico-historical exegesis, but a development from such exegesis. It is not a reading into the text of theological doctrines and theories, but a reading from the text of the fullness of meaning required by God's complete revelation. The *sensus plenior* is derived from total context, usually including what has already been revealed of God's redemptive activity, and always including the ultimate purpose of that activity. In this sense, it is correct to say that the human author did not intend to say all that can be found in *sensus plenior*. On the other hand, it seems clear from our study of prophetic passages that the prophets were led by the Spirit, who inspired them to express their prophecies in such ways that the fuller meaning was not lost. In some cases, we can see in the words of the prophets only the general trend of God's redemptive work; but in other instances even the words are capable of conveying a fuller meaning. We must guard equally against reading into a text more than is there and failing to find the deepest meaning of the text.

Finally, we must reject any notion that the *sensus plenior* comes from any mystical, spiritual, or other source than the Scriptures. A person who is spiritually minded may find deeper meanings in the Bible, simply because he enjoys putting more effort into the task and because he is sensitive to the Spirit's leadings. But that does not mean that he has a special line of revelation direct from God. The Scriptures of the Old and New Testament are the *only* infallible rule of faith and practice. It is from the Word alone that we have this revelation, and from the Word alone that we find any fuller meaning. The Scriptures are full of wonderful revelations from God. We admit that "we see through a glass darkly" — but that is no reason to shut our eyes. The concept of *sensus plenior* opens our eyes to see more of God's revealed truth.

THE SUPERIORITY OF PRECRITICAL EXEGESIS

DAVID C. STEINMETZ

In 1859 Benjamin Jowett, then Regius Professor of Greek in the University of Oxford, published a justly famous essay on the interpretation of Scripture.[1] Jowett argued that "Scripture has one meaning — the meaning which it had in the mind of the Prophet or Evangelist who first uttered or wrote, to the hearers or readers who first received it."[2] Scripture should be interpreted like any other book and the later accretions and venerated traditions surrounding its interpretation should, for the most part, either be brushed aside or severely discounted. "The true use of interpretation is to get rid of interpretation, and leave us alone in company with the author."[3]

Jowett did not foresee great difficulties in the way of the recovery of the original meaning of the text. Proper interpretation requires imagination, the ability to put oneself into an alien cultural situation, and knowledge of the language and history of the ancient people whose literature one sets out to interpret. In the case of the Bible, one has also to bear in mind the progressive nature of revelation and the superiority of certain later religious insights to certain earlier ones. But the interpreter, armed with the proper linguistic tools, will find that "universal truth easily breaks through the accidents of time and place"[4] and that such truth still speaks to the condition of the unchanging human heart.

Of course, critical biblical studies have made enormous strides since the time of Jowett. No reputable biblical scholar would agree today with Jowett's reconstruction of the gospels in which Jesus appears as a "teacher . . . speaking to a group of serious, but not highly educated, working men, attempting to inculcate in them a loftier and sweeter morality."[5] Still, the quarrel between modern biblical scholarship and Benjamin Jowett is less a quarrel over his

---

1. Jowett, "On the Interpretation of Scripture," in *Essays and Reviews*, 7th ed. (London: Longman, Green, Longman and Roberts, 1861), pp. 330-433.

2. Jowett, "On the Interpretation of Sripture," p. 378.

3. Jowett, "On the Interpretation of Scripture," p. 384.

4. Jowett, "On the Interpretation of Scripture," p. 412.

5. Helen Gardner, *The Business of Criticism* (London: Oxford University Press, 1959), p. 83.

Reprinted from *Theology Today*, April 1980, pp. 27-38.

hermeneutical theory than it is a disagreement with him over the application of that theory in his exegetical practice. Biblical scholarship still hopes to recover the original intention of the author of a biblical text and still regards the precritical exegetical tradition as an obstacle to the proper understanding of the true meaning of that text. The most primitive meaning of the text is its only valid meaning, and the historical-critical method is the only key which can unlock it.

But is that hermeneutical theory true?

I think it is demonstrably false. In what follows I want to examine the precritical exegetical tradition at exactly the point at which Jowett regarded it to be most vulnerable—namely, in its refusal to bind the meaning of any pericope to the intention, whether explicit or merely half-formed, of its human author. Medieval theologians defended the proposition, so alien to modern biblical studies, that the meaning of Scripture in the mind of the prophet who first uttered it is only one of its possible meanings and may not, in certain circumstances, even be its primary or most important meaning. I want to show that this theory (in at least that respect) was superior to the theories which replaced it. When biblical scholarship shifted from the hermeneutical position of Origen to the hermeneutical position of Jowett, it gained something important and valuable. But it lost something as well, and it is the painful duty of critical scholarship to assess its losses as well as its gains.

I

Medieval hermeneutical theory took as its point of departure the words of St. Paul: "The letter kills but the spirit makes alive" (2 Cor. 3:6). Augustine suggested that this text could be understood in either one of two ways. On the one hand, the distinction between letter and spirit could be a distinction between law and gospel, between demand and grace. The letter kills because it demands an obedience of the sinner which the sinner is powerless to render. The Spirit makes alive because it infuses the forgiven sinner with new power to meet the rigorous requirements of the law.

But Paul could also have in mind a distinction between what William Tyndale later called the "story-book" or narrative level of the Bible and the deeper theological meaning or spiritual significance implicit within it. This distinction was important for at least three reasons. Origen stated the first reason with unforgettable clarity:

> Now what man of intelligence will believe that the first and the second and the third day, and the evening and the morning existed

without the sun and moon and stars? And that the first day, if we may so call it, was even without a heaven? And who is so silly as to believe that God, after the manner of a farmer, "planted a paradise eastward in Eden," and set in it a visible and palpable "tree of life," of such a sort that anyone who tasted its fruit with his bodily teeth would gain life; and again that one could partake of "good and evil" by masticating the fruit taken from the tree of that name? And when God is said to "walk in the paradise in the cool of the day" and Adam to hide himself behind a tree, I do not think anyone will doubt that these are figurative expressions which indicate certain mysteries through a semblance of history and not through actual event.[6]

Simply because a story purports to be a straightforward historical narrative does not mean that it is in fact what it claims to be. What appears to be history may be metaphor or figure instead and the interpreter who confuses metaphor with literal fact is an interpreter who is simply incompetent. Every biblical story means something, even if the narrative taken at face value contains absurdities or contradictions. The interpreter must demythologize the text in order to grasp the sacred mystery cloaked in the language of actual events.

The second reason for distinguishing between letter and spirit was the thorny question of the relationship between Israel and the church, between the Greek Testament and the Hebrew Bible. The church regarded itself as both continuous and discontinuous with ancient Israel. Because it claimed to be continuous, it felt an unavoidable obligation to interpret the Torah, the prophets, and the writings. But it was precisely this claim of continuity, absolutely essential to Christian identity, which created fresh hermeneutical problems for the church.

How was a French parish priest in 1150 to understand Psalm 137, which bemoans captivity in Babylon, makes rude remarks about Edomites, expresses an ineradicable longing for a glimpse of Jerusalem, and pronounces a blessing on anyone who avenges the destruction of the temple by dashing Babylonian children against a rock? The priest lives in Concale, not Babylon, has no personal quarrel with Edomites, cherishes no ambitions to visit Jerusalem (though he might fancy a holiday in Paris), and is expressly forbidden by Jesus to avenge himself on his enemies. Unless Psalm 137 has more than one possible meaning, it cannot be used as a prayer by the church and must be rejected as a lament belonging exclusively to the piety of ancient Israel.

A third reason for distinguishing letter from spirit was the conviction, expressed by Augustine, that while all Scripture was given

---

6. Origen, *On First Principles*, ed. G. W. Butterworth (New York: Harper & Row, 1966), p. 288.

for the edification of the church and the nurture of the three theological virtues of faith, hope, and love, not all the stories in the Bible
are edifying as they stand. What is the spiritual point of the story
of the drunkenness of Noah, the murder of Sisera, or the oxgoad of
Shamgar, son of Anath? If it cannot be found on the level of narrative, then it must be found on the level of allegory, metaphor, and
type.

That is not to say that patristic and medieval interpreters approved of arbitrary and undisciplined exegesis, which gave free rein
to the imagination of the exegete. Augustine argued, for example,
that the more obscure parts of Scripture should be interpreted in
the light of its less difficult sections and that no allegorical interpretation could be accepted which was not supported by the "manifest testimonies" of other less ambiguous portions of the Bible. The
literal sense of Scripture is basic to the spiritual and limits the range
of possible allegorical meanings in those instances in which the literal meaning of a particular passage is absurd, undercuts the living
relationship of the church to the Old Testament, or is spiritually
barren.

II

From the time of John Cassian, the church subscribed to a theory
of the fourfold sense of Scripture.[7] The literal sense of Scripture
could and usually did nurture the three theological virtues, but when
it did not, the exegete could appeal to three additional spiritual
senses, each sense corresponding to one of the virtues. The allegorical sense taught about the church and what it should believe, and
so it corresponded to the virtue of faith. The tropological sense
taught about individuals and what they should do, and so it corresponded to the virtue of love. The anagogical sense pointed to the
future and wakened expectation, and so it corresponded to the virtue
of hope. In the fourteenth century Nicholas of Lyra summarized
this hermeneutical theory in a much quoted little rhyme:

> Littera gesta docet,
> Quid credas allegoria,
> Moralis quid agas,
> Quo tendas anagogia.

This hermeneutical device made it possible for the church to pray
directly and without qualification even a troubling Psalm like 137.

7. For a brief survey of medieval hermeneutical theory which takes into account
recent historical research, see James S. Preus, *From Shadow to Promise* (Cambridge:
Harvard University Press, 1969), pp. 9-149; see also the useful bibliography, pp. 287-93.

After all, Jerusalem was not merely a city in the Middle East; it was, according to the allegorical sense, the church; according to the tropological sense, the faithful soul; and according to the anagogical sense, the center of God's new creation. The Psalm became a lament of those who long for the establishment of God's future kingdom and who are trapped in this disordered and troubled world, which with all its delights is still not their home. They seek an abiding city elsewhere. The imprecations against the Edomites and the Babylonians are transmuted into condemnations of the world, the flesh, and the devil. If you grant the fourfold sense of Scripture, David sings like a Christian.

III

Thomas Aquinas wanted to ground the spiritual sense of Scripture even more securely in the literal sense than it had been grounded in Patristic thought. Returning to the distinction between "things" and "signs" made by Augustine in *De doctrina christiana* (though Thomas preferred to use the Aristotelian terminology of "things" and "words"), Thomas argued that while words are the signs of things, things designated by words can themselves be the signs of other things. In all merely human sciences, words alone have a sign-character. But in Holy Scripture, the things designated by words can themselves have the character of a sign. The literal sense of Scripture has to do with the sign-character of words; the spiritual sense of Scripture has to do with the sign-character of things. By arguing this way, Thomas was able to show that the spiritual sense of Scripture is always based on the literal sense and derived from it.

Thomas also redefined the literal sense of Scripture as "the meaning of the text which the author intends." Lest Thomas be confused with Jowett, I should hasten to point out that for Thomas the author was God, not the human prophet or apostle. In the fourteenth century, Nicholas of Lyra, a Franciscan exegete and one of the most impressive biblical scholars produced by the Christian church, built a new hermeneutical argument on the aphorism of Thomas. If the literal sense of Scripture is the meaning which the author intended (presupposing that the author whose intention finally matters is God), then is it possible to argue that Scripture contains a double literal sense? Is there a literal-historical sense (the original meaning of the words as spoken in their first historical setting) which includes and implies a literal-prophetic sense (the larger meaning of the words as perceived in later and changed circumstances)?

Nicholas not only embraced a theory of the double literal sense of Scripture, but he was even willing to argue that in certain contexts

the literal-prophetic sense takes precedence over the literal-historical. Commenting on Psalm 117, Lyra wrote, "The literal sense in
this Psalm concerns Christ; for the literal sense is the sense primarily
intended by the author." Of the promise to Solomon in 1 Chronicles
17:13, Lyra observed: "The aforementioned authority was literally
fulfilled in Solomon; however, it was fulfilled less perfectly, because
Solomon was a son of God only by grace; but it was fulfilled more
perfectly in Christ, who is the Son of God by nature."

For most exegetes, the theory of Nicholas of Lyra bound the interpreter to the dual task of explaining the historical meaning of a
text while elucidating its larger and later spiritual significance. The
great French humanist, Jacques Lefèvre d'Etaples, however, pushed
the theory to absurd limits. He argued that the only possible meaning of a text was its literal-prophetic sense and that the literal-historical sense was a product of human fancy and idle imagination.
The literal-historical sense is the "letter which kills." It is advocated
as the true meaning of Scripture only by carnal persons who have
not been regenerated by the life-giving Spirit of God. The problem
of the proper exegesis of Scripture is, when all is said and done, the
problem of the regeneration of its interpreters.

IV

In this brief survey of medieval hermeneutical theory, there are
certain dominant themes which recur with dogged persistence. Medieval exegetes admit that the words of Scripture had a meaning in
the historical situation in which they were first uttered or written,
but they deny that the meaning of those words is restricted to what
the human author thought he said or what his first audience thought
they heard. The stories and sayings of Scripture bear an implicit
meaning only understood by a later audience. In some cases that
implicit meaning is far more important than the restricted meaning
intended by the author in his particular cultural setting.

Yet the text cannot mean anything a later audience wants it to
mean. The language of the Bible opens up a field of possible meanings. Any interpretation which falls within that field is valid exegesis
of the text, even though that interpretation was not intended by the
author. Any interpretation which falls outside the limits of that field
of possible meanings is probably eisegesis and should be rejected as
unacceptable. Only by confessing the multiple sense of Scripture is
it possible for the church to make use of the Hebrew Bible at all or
to recapture the various levels of significance in the unfolding story
of creation and redemption. The notion that Scripture has only one
meaning is a fantastic idea and is certainly not advocated by the
biblical writers themselves.

V

Having elucidated medieval hermeneutical theory, I should like to take some time to look at medieval exegetical practice. One could get the impression from Jowett that because medieval exegetes rejected the theory of the single meaning of Scripture so dear to Jowett's heart, they let their exegetical imaginations run amok and exercised no discipline at all in clarifying the field of possible meanings opened by the biblical text. In fact, medieval interpreters, once you grant the presuppositions on which they operate, are as conservative and restrained in their approach to the Bible as any comparable group of modern scholars.

In order to test medieval exegetical practice I have chosen a terribly difficult passage from the Gospel of Matthew, the parable of the Good Employer, or, as it is more frequently known, the parable of the Workers in the Vineyard (Matt. 20:1-16). The story is a familiar one. An employer hired day laborers to work in his vineyard at dawn and promised them the standard wage of a denarius. Because he needed more workers, he returned to the marketplace at nine, noon, three, and five o'clock and hired any laborers he could find. He promised to pay the workers hired at nine, noon, and three what was fair. But the workers hired at the eleventh hour or five o'clock were sent into the vineyard without any particular promise concerning remuneration. The employer instructed his foreman to pay off the workers beginning with the laborers hired at five o'clock. These workers expected only one-twelfth of a denarius, but were given the full day's wage instead. Indeed, all the workers who had worked part of the day were given one denarius. The workers who had been in the vineyard since dawn accordingly expected a bonus beyond the denarius, but they were disappointed to receive the same wage which had been given to the other, less deserving workers. When they grumbled, they were told by the employer that they had not been defrauded but had been paid according to an agreed contract. If the employer chose to be generous to the workers who had only worked part of the day, that was, in effect, none of their business. They should collect the denarius that was due them and go home like good fellows.

Jesus said the kingdom of God was like this story. What on earth could he have meant?

VI

The church was puzzled over this parable ever since it was included in Matthew's Gospel. St. Thomas Aquinas in his *Lectura super Evangelium Sancti Matthaei* offered two interpretations of the parable, one going back in its lineage to Irenaeus and the other to Origen. The "day" mentioned in the parable can either refer to the life span of an individual (the tradition of Origen), in which case the parable is a comment on the various ages at which one may be converted to Christ, or it is a reference to the history of salvation (the tradition of Irenaeus), in which case it is a comment on the relationship of Jew and Gentile.

If the story refers to the life span of a man or woman, then it is intended as an encouragement to people who are converted to Christ late in life. The workers in the story who begin at dawn are people who have served Christ and have devoted themselves to the love of God and neighbor since childhood. The other hours mentioned by Jesus refer to the various stages of human development from youth to old age. Whether one has served Christ for a long time or for a brief moment, one will still receive the gift of eternal life. Thomas qualifies this somewhat in order to allow for proportional rewards and a hierarchy in heaven. But he does not surrender the main point: eternal life is given to late converts with the same generosity it is given to early converts.

On the other hand, the story may refer to the history of salvation. Quite frankly, this is the interpretation which interests Thomas most. The hours mentioned in the parable are not stages in individual human development but epochs in the history of the world from Adam to Noah, from Noah to Abraham, from Abraham to David, and from David to Christ. The owner of the vineyard is the whole Trinity, the foreman is Christ, and the moment of reckoning is the resurrection from the dead. The workers who are hired at the eleventh hour are the Gentiles, whose complaint that no one has offered them work can be interpreted to mean that they had no prophets as the Jews have had. The workers who have borne the heat of the day are the Jews, who grumble about the favoritism shown to latecomers, but who are still given the denarius of eternal life. As a comment on the history of salvation, the parable means that the generosity of God undercuts any advantage which the Jews might have had over the Gentiles with respect to participation in the gifts and graces of God.

Not everyone read the text as a gloss on Jewish-Christian relations or as a discussion of late conversion. In the fourteenth century the anonymous author of the *Pearl*, an elegy on the death of a young girl, applied the parable to infancy rather than to old age. What is important about the parable is not the chronological age at which one enters the vineyard, but the fact that some workers are only in the vineyard for the briefest possible moment. A child who dies at the age of two years is, in a sense, a worker who arrives at the eleventh hour. The parable is intended as a consolation for bereaved parents. A parent who has lost a small child can be comforted by the knowledge that God, who does not despise the service of persons converted in extreme old age, does not withhold his mercy from boys and girls whose eleventh hour came at dawn.

Probably the most original interpretation of the parable was offered by John Pupper of Goch, a Flemish theologian of the fifteenth century, who used the parable to attack the doctrine of proportionality, particularly as that doctrine had been stated and defended by Thomas Aquinas. No one had ever argued that God gives rewards which match in exact quantity the weight of the good works done by a Christian. That is arithmetic equality and is simply not applicable to a relationship in which people perform temporal acts and receive eternal rewards. But most theologians did hold to a doctrine of proportionality; while there is a disproportion between the good works which Christians do and the rewards which they receive, there is a proportion as well. The reward is always much larger than the work which is rewarded, but the greater the work, the greater the reward.

As far as Goch is concerned, that doctrine is sheer nonsense. No one can take the message of the parable of the vineyard seriously and still hold to the doctrine of proportionality. Indeed, the only people in the vineyard who hold to the doctrine of proportionality are the first workers in the vineyard. They argue that twelve times the work should receive twelve times the payment. All they receive for their argument is a rebuke and a curt dismissal.

Martin Luther, in an early sermon preached before the Reformation in 1517, agreed with Goch that God gives equal reward for great and small works. It is not by the herculean size of our exertions but by the goodness of God that we receive any reward at all.

But Luther, unfortunately, spoiled this point by elaborating a thoroughly unconvincing argument in which he tried to show that the last workers in the vineyard were more humble than the first and therefore that one hour of their service was worth twelve hours of the mercenary service of the grumblers.

The parable, however, seems to make exactly the opposite point. The workers who began early were not more slothful or more selfish than the workers who began later in the day. Indeed, they were fairly representative of the kind of worker to be found hanging around the marketplace at any hour. They were angry, not because they had shirked their responsibilities, but because they had discharged them conscientiously.

In 1525 Luther offered a fresh interpretation of the parable, which attacked it from a slightly different angle. The parable has essentially one point: to celebrate the goodness of God which makes nonsense of a religion based on law-keeping and good works. God pays no attention to the proportionately greater efforts of the first workers in the vineyard, but to their consternation, God puts them on exactly the same level as the last and least productive workers. The parable shows that everyone in the vineyard is unworthy, though not always for the same reason. The workers who arrived after nine o'clock are unworthy because they are paid a salary incommensurate with their achievement in picking grapes. The workers who spent the entire day in the vineyard are unworthy because they are dissatisfied with what God has promised, think that their efforts deserve special consideration, and are jealous of their employer's goodness to workers who accomplished less than they did. The parable teaches that salvation is not grounded in human merit and that there is no system of bookkeeping which can keep track of the relationship between God and humanity. Salvation depends utterly and absolutely on the goodness of God.

VII

The four medieval theologians I have mentioned—Thomas Aquinas, the author of the *Pearl*, the Flemish chaplain Goch, and the young Martin Luther—did not exhaust in their writings all the possible interpretations of the parable of the Workers in the Vineyard. But they did see with considerable clarity that the parable is an assertion of God's generosity and mercy to people who do not deserve it. It is only against the background of the generosity of God that one can understand the relationship of Jew and Gentile, the problem of late conversion, the meaning of the death of a young child, the question of proportional rewards, even the very definition of grace itself. Every question is qualified by the severe mercy of God, by the strange generosity of the owner of the vineyard who pays the nonproductive latecomer the same wage as his oldest and most productive employees.

If you were to ask me which of these interpretations is valid, I should have to respond that they all are. They all fall within the field of possible meanings created by the story itself. How many of those meanings were in the conscious intention of Jesus or of the author of the Gospel of Matthew, I do not profess to know. I am inclined to agree with C. S. Lewis, who commented on his own book *Till We Have Faces*, "An author doesn't necessarily understand the meaning of his own story better than anyone else."[8] The act of creation confers no special privileges on authors when it comes to the distinctly different if lesser task of interpretation. Wordsworth

8. Lewis, in *Letters of C. S. Lewis*, ed. W. H. Lewis (New York: Harcourt, Brace and World, 1966), p. 273.

the critic is not in the same league with Wordsworth the poet, while Samuel Johnson the critic towers over Johnson the creative artist. Authors obviously have something in mind when they write, but a work of historical or theological or aesthetic imagination has a life of its own.

VIII

Which brings us back to Benjamin Jowett. Jowett rejected medieval exegesis and insisted that the Bible should be read like any other book.[9] I agree with Jowett that the Bible should be read like any other book. The question is: How does one read other books?

Take, for example, my own field of Reformation studies. Almost no historian that I know would answer the question of the meaning of the writings of Martin Luther by focusing solely on Luther's explicit and conscious intention. Marxist interpreters of Luther from Friedrich Engels to Max Steinmetz have been interested in Luther's writings as an expression of class interests, while psychological interpreters from Grisar to Erikson have focused on the theological writings as clues to the inner psychic tensions in the personality of Martin Luther. Even historians who reject Marxist and psychological interpretations of Luther find themselves asking how Luther was understood in the free imperial cities, by the German knights, by the landed aristocracy, by the various subgroups of German peasants, by the Catholic hierarchy, by lawyers, by university faculties — to name only a few of the more obvious groups who responded to Luther and left a written record of their response. Meaning involves a listener as well as a speaker, and when one asks the question of the relationship of Luther to his various audiences in early modern Europe, it becomes clear that there was not one Luther in the sixteenth century, but a battalion of Luthers.

Nor can the question of the meaning of Luther's writings be answered by focusing solely on Luther's contemporaries. Luther's works were read and pondered in a variety of historical and cultural settings from his death in 1546 to the present. Those readings of Luther have had measurable historical effects on succeeding generations, whose particular situation in time and space could scarcely have been anticipated by Luther. Yet the social, political, economic, cultural, and religious history of those people belongs intrinsically and inseparably to the question of the meaning of the theology of Martin Luther. The meaning of historical texts cannot be separated from the complex problem of their reception; the notion that a text means only what its author intends it to mean is historically naive.

9. Jowett, "On the Interpretation of Scripture," p. 377.

Even to talk of the original setting in which words were spoken and heard is to talk of meanings rather than meaning. To attempt to understand those original meanings is the first step in the exegetical process, not the last and final step.

Modern literary criticism has challenged the notion that a text means only what its author intends it to mean far more radically than medieval exegetes ever dreamed of doing. Indeed, contemporary debunking of the author and the author's explicit intentions has proceeded at such a pace that it seems at times as if literary criticism has become a jolly game of ripping out an author's shirt-tail and setting fire to it. The reader and the literary work to the exclusion of the author have become the central preoccupation of the literary critic. Literary relativists of a fairly moderate sort insist that every generation has its own Shakespeare and Milton, and extreme relativists loudly proclaim that no reader reads the same work twice. Every change in the reader, however slight, is a change in the meaning of the text. Imagine what Thomas Aquinas or Nicholas of Lyra would have made of the famous statement of Northrop Frye:

> It has been said of Boehme that his books are like a picnic to which the author brings the words and the reader the meaning. The remark may have been intended as a sneer at Boehme, but it is an exact description of all works of literary art without exception.[10]

Medieval exegetes held to the sober middle way, the position that the text (any literary text, but especially the Bible) contains both letter and spirit. The text is not all letter, as Jowett with others maintained, or all spirit, as the rather more enthusiastic literary critics in our own time are apt to argue. The original text as spoken and heard limits a field of possible meanings. Those possible meanings are not dragged by the hair, willy-nilly, into the text, but belong to the life of the Bible in the encounter between author and reader as they belong to the life of any act of the human imagination. Such a hermeneutical theory is capable of sober and disciplined application and avoids the Scylla of extreme subjectivism on the one hand and the Charybdis of historical positivism on the other. To be sure, medieval exegetes made bad mistakes in the application of their theory, but they also scored notable and brilliant triumphs. Even at their worst they recognized that the intention of the author is only one element — and not always the most important element at that — in the complex phenomenon of the meaning of a text.

10. Frye, cited by E. D. Hirsch, Jr., in *Validity in Interpretation* (New Haven: Yale University Press, 1967), p. 1, at the beginning of a chapter which sets out to elaborate an alternative theory.

IX

The defenders of the single-meaning theory usually concede that the medieval approach to the Bible met the religious needs of the Christian community, but that it did so at the unacceptable price of doing violence to the biblical text. The fact that the historical-critical method after two hundred years is still struggling for more than a precarious foothold in that same religious community is generally blamed on the ignorance and conservatism of the Christian laity and the sloth or moral cowardice of its pastors.

I should like to suggest an alternative hypothesis. The medieval theory of levels of meaning in the biblical text, with all its undoubted defects, flourished because it is true, while the modern theory of a single meaning, with all its demonstrable virtues, is false. Until the historical-critical method becomes critical of its own theoretical foundations and develops a hermeneutical theory adequate to the nature of the text which it is interpreting, it will remain restricted — as it deserves to be — to the guild and the academy, where the question of truth can endlessly be deferred.

THE NEW HERMENEUTIC

ANTHONY C. THISELTON

I. AIMS AND CONCERNS: HOW MAY THE TEXT SPEAK ANEW?

(1) The approach to the New Testament which has come to be known as the new hermeneutic is associated most closely with the work of Ernst Fuchs and Gerhard Ebeling.[1] Both of these writers insist on its practical relevance to the world of today. How does language, especially the language of the Bible, strike home (*treffen*) to the modern hearer?[2] How may its words so reach through into his own understanding that when he repeats them they will be *his* words? How may the word of God become a living word which is heard anew?

This emphasis on present application rather than simply antiquarian biblical research stems partly from connections between the new hermeneutic and the thought of Rudolf Bultmann,[3] but also from a pastor's deep and consistent concern on the part of Fuchs and Ebeling, both of whom served as pastors for some years, about the relevance and effectiveness of Christian preaching. Central to Fuchs's work is the question "What do we have to do at our desks, if we want later to set the text in front of us in the pulpit?"[4]

It would be a mistake to conclude that this interest in preaching, however, is narrowly ecclesiastical or merely homiletical. Both writers share an intense concern about the position of the unbeliever.

---

1. For objections to the customary use of the term, see C. E. Braaten, "How New Is the New Hermeneutic?" *Theology Today* 22 (1965): 218-35, and J. D. Smart, *The Strange Silence of the Bible in the Church* (London: SCM Press, 1970), pp. 37-38. On the other side, see James M. Robinson, "Braaten's Polemic: A Reply," *Theology Today* 22 (1965): 277-82.

2. See E. Fuchs, "Zur Frage nach dem historischen Jesus," in *Gesammelte Aufsätze*, 2 vols. (Tübingen: J. C. B. Mohr, 1959-60), 2: 411-14, 418; cf. his *Studies of the Historical Jesus* (London: SCM Press, 1964), pp. 196-98, 202.

3. See Fuchs, *Hermeneutik*, 4th ed. (Tübingen: J. C. B. Mohr, 1970), p. 281; cf. R. Bultmann, *Essays Philosophical and Theological* (London: SCM Press, 1955), p. 14. Cf. further Fuchs, *Hermeneutik*, p. 182, and Bultmann, *Faith and Understanding* (London: SCM Press, 1969), pp. 286-312.

4. Fuchs, *Studies of the Historical Jesus*, p. 8.

Reprinted from *New Testament Interpretation: Essays on Principles and Methods*, ed. I. Howard Marshall (Grand Rapids: Eerdmans, 1977), pp. 308-33.

If the word of God is capable of *creating* faith, its intelligibility cannot be said to *presuppose* faith. Thus Fuchs warns us, "the proclamation loses its character when it anticipates (i.e. presupposes) confession,"[5] while Ebeling boldly asserts, "the criterion of the understandability of our preaching is not the believer but the non-believer. For the proclaimed word seeks to effect faith, but does not presuppose faith as a necessary preliminary."[6]

Nevertheless the problem goes even deeper than this. The modern hearer, or interpreter, stands at the end of a long tradition of biblical interpretation, a tradition which, in turn, moulds his own understanding of the biblical text and his own attitude towards it. His attitude may be either positive or negative, and his controlling assumptions may well be unconscious ones.[7] The New Testament is thus interpreted today within a particular frame of reference which may differ radically from that within which the text first addressed its hearers. Hence simply to *repeat* the actual words of the New Testament today may well be, in effect, to say something different from what the text itself originally said. Even if it does not positively alter what was once said, it may be to utter "nothing more than just a tradition, a mere form of speech, a dead relic of the language of the past."[8] For never before, Ebeling believes, was there so great a gulf between the linguistic tradition of the Bible and language that is actually spoken today.[9]

Two undue criticisms must be forestalled at this point. First, some may believe that this problem is solved simply by an appeal to the work of the Holy Spirit. Fuchs and Ebeling are fully aware of the role of the Holy Spirit in communicating the word of God, but they rightly see that problems of understanding and intelligibility cannot be short-circuited by a premature appeal of this kind.[10] The New Testament requires hermeneutical translation no less than it obviously requires linguistic translation. This point will become clearer as we proceed.

Second, Fuchs and Ebeling do not in any way underestimate the power of the New Testament to interpret itself and to create room for its understanding. Ebeling insists that hermeneutics "only consist in removing hindrances in order to let the word perform its own

5. Fuchs, *Studies of the Historical Jesus*, p. 30; cf. his essay, "Zum hermeneutischen Problem in der Theologie," in *Gesammelte Aufsätze*, 1: 9-10.

6. Ebeling, *Word and Faith* (Philadelphia: Fortress Press, 1963), p. 125.

7. See Ebeling, *The Word of God and Tradition* (London: Collins, 1968), pp. 11-31, especially 26 and 28.

8. Ebeling, *God and Word* (Philadelphia: Fortress Press, 1967), p. 3; cf. pp. 8-9.

9. Ebeling, *God and Word*, p. 4.

10. See Fuchs, "Proclamation and Speech-Event," *Theology Today* 19 (1962): 354; and Ebeling, *Theology and Proclamation: A Discussion with Rudolf Bultmann* (London: Collins, 1966), pp. 42, 100-102.

hermeneutic function."[11] "Holy Scripture, as Luther puts it, is *sui ipsius interpres.*"[12] The "one bridge" to the present is "the Word alone."[13] Similarly Fuchs stresses the importance of Hebrews 4:12-13 ("The word of God is living and active, sharper than any two-edged sword") even in the present moment.[14] Indeed it is crucial to Fuchs's position, as we shall see, that the New Testament itself effects changes in situations, and changes in men's preconscious standpoints. The language of Jesus "singles out the individual and grasps him deep down."[15] "The text is itself meant to live."[16]

The key question in the new hermeneutic, then, is how the New Testament may speak to us *anew.* A literalistic repetition of the text cannot *guarantee* that it will "speak" to the modern hearer. He may understand all of its individual words, and yet fail to understand what is being said. In Wolfhart Pannenberg's words, "in a changed situation the traditional phrases, even when recited literally, do not mean what they did at the time of their original formulation."[17] Thus Ebeling asserts, "the *same word* can be said to another time only by being said differently."[18]

In assessing the validity of this point, we may well wish to make some proviso about the uniquely normative significance of the original formulation in *theology.* The problem is recognized by Fuchs and Ebeling perhaps more clearly than by Bultmann when parallel questions arise in his program of demythologizing.[19] It is partly in connection with this problem that both writers insist on the necessity of historical-critical research on the New Testament.[20] At the same time, at least two considerations reinforce their contentions about the inadequacy of mere repetition of the text from the stand-

11. Ebeling, *Word and Faith,* pp. 318-19.

12. Ebeling, *Word and Faith,* p. 306.

13. Ebeling, *Word and Faith,* p. 36.

14. Fuchs, *Hermeneutik,* p. 92.

15. Fuchs, *Studies of the Historical Jesus,* p. 35.

16. Fuchs, *Studies of the Historical Jesus,* p. 193.

17. Pannenburg, *Basic Questions in Theology,* vol. 1 (London: SCM Press, 1970), p. 9.

18. Ebeling, "Time and Word," in *The Future of Our Religious Past: Essays in Honour of Rudolf Bultmann,* ed. J. M. Robinson (London: SCM Press, 1971), p. 265; italics mine. Cf. W. G. Doty, *Contemporary New Testament Interpretation* (Englewood Cliffs, N.J.: Prentice-Hall, 1972), pp. 34-37.

19. See James D. G. Dunn, "Demythologizing—The Problem of Myth in the New Testament," in *New Testament Interpretation: Essays on Principles and Methods,* ed. I. Howard Marshall (Grand Rapids: Eerdmans, 1977), pp. 285-307; Ian Henderson, *Myth in the New Testament* (London: SCM Press, 1952), p. 31; and my "Myth, Mythology," in *The Zondervan Pictorial Encyclopedia of the Bible,* vol. 4 (Grand Rapids: Zondervan, 1975), pp. 333-43.

20. See Ebeling, *Word and Faith,* pp. 17-61. See also Fuchs, *Hermeneutik,* pp. 159-66; and *Studies in the Historical Jesus,* pp. 95-108.

point of *hermeneutics*. First, we already recognize the fact that in translation from one language to another, literalism can be the enemy of faithful communication. "To put it into another language means to think it through afresh."[21] Second, we already have given tacit recognition to this principle whenever we stress the importance of preaching. The preacher "translates" the text by placing it at the point of encounter with the hearer, from which it speaks anew into his own world in his own language.[22] But this hermeneutical procedure is demanded in *all* interpretation which is faithful to the New Testament. For "God's revelation consisted simply in God's letting men state God's own problems *in their language*, in grace and judgment."[23]

(2) How, then, may the text of the New Testament speak anew? Four sets of considerations are relevant to a positive answer, each of which turns on a given point of contrast.

(a) First, Fuchs and Ebeling draw *a contrast between problems about words (plural) and the problem of the word (singular)*. Ebeling laments the fact that too often preaching today sounds like a foreign language.[24] But he adds, "We need not emphasize that the problem lies too deep to be tackled by cheap borrowing of transient modern jargon for the preacher's stock of words. It is not a matter of understanding single words, but of understanding the word itself; not a matter of new means of speech, but of a new coming to speech."[25] Mere modern paraphrase of the New Testament does not answer the problem. The concern is, rather, that the word of God itself should "come to speech" (*das Zur-Sprache-kommen der Sache selbst*), in the technical sense which this phrase has come to bear in the philosophical writings of Martin Heidegger and Hans-Georg Gadamer.[26]

(b) Second, hermeneutics in the writings of Fuchs and Ebeling concerns "the theory of understanding" and *must not be reduced "to a*

21. Ebeling, *The Nature of Faith* (London: SCM Press, 1961), p. 188.

22. See Fuchs, *Studies of the Historical Jesus*, pp. 191-206; cf. his *Hermeneutik*, pp. 249-56, and *Marburger Hermeneutik* (Tübingen: J. C. B. Mohr, 1968), pp. 2-4. Fuchs's approach is related to that of Manfred Mezger. Mezger, "Preparation for Preaching: The Route from Exegesis to Proclamation," *Journal for Theology and the Church* (= *Translating Theology into the Modern Age*) 2 (1965): 159-79, especially p. 166.

23. Fuchs, "The New Testament and the Hermeneutical Problem," in *New Frontiers in Theology, II: The New Hermeneutic*, ed. James M. Robinson and J. B. Cobb, Jr. (New York: Harper & Row, 1964), pp. 135-36. (Fuchs has almost the whole sentence in italics.)

24. Ebeling, *The Nature of Faith*, p. 15; cf. his *Introduction to a Theological Theory of Language* (London: Collins, 1973), pp. 15-80.

25. Ebeling, *The Nature of Faith*, p. 16; cf. *God and Word*, pp. 2-3. See also Fuchs, "The New Testament and the Hermeneutical Problem," p. 125.

26. Gadamer, *Wahrheit und Methode: Grundzüge einer philosophischen Hermeneutik*, 2d ed. (Tübingen: J. C. B. Mohr, 1965), p. 360 (ET: *Truth and Method* [London: Sheed & Ward, 1975], p. 350).

collection of rules."[27] Indeed, because it concerns the whole question
of how a man comes to *understand*, Ebeling asserts: "Hermeneutics
now takes the place of the classical epistemological theory."[28] This
is why hermeneutics cannot be separated from philosophy. Because
it concerns "a general theory of understanding," hermeneutics is
"becoming the place of meeting with philosophy."[29] Similarly for
Fuchs the central question of hermeneutics is "How do I come to
understand?"[30] Yet both writers are concerned not simply with the
theory, but with the *practice* of setting understanding in motion.
Fuchs suggests an analogy. It is possible, on the one hand, to theo-
rize about an understanding of "cat" by cognitive reflection. On the
other hand, a practical and preconceptual understanding of "cat"
emerges when we actually place a mouse in front of a particular cat.
The mouse is the "hermeneutical principle" that causes the cat to
show itself for what it is.[31] In this sense biblical criticism and even
the traditional hermeneutical "rules" do "not *produce* understanding,
but only the preconditions for it."[32]

Admittedly it would not be wholly incorrect to argue that this
distinction goes back in principle to Schleiermacher. An illuminating comment comes from the philosopher Heinz Kimmerle, whose
research on the earlier writings of Schleiermacher is so important
for the new hermeneutic. He writes, "the work of Schleiermacher
constitutes a turning point in the history of hermeneutics. Till then
hermeneutics was supposed to support, secure, and clarify an *already
accepted* understanding [of the Bible as theological hermeneutics; of
classical antiquity as philological hermeneutics]. In the thinking of
Schleiermacher, hermeneutics achieves the qualitatively different
function of first of all *making understanding possible*, and deliberately
initiating understanding in each individual case."[33] This touches on yet
another central and cardinal feature of the new hermeneutic. The
concern is not simply to support and corroborate an *existing* understanding of the New Testament text, but to lead the hearer or the
interpreter onward *beyond* his own existing horizons, so that the text
addresses and judges him *anew*. This fundamental principle will
emerge most clearly in connection with Hans-Georg Gadamer and
the wider philosophical background.

27. Ebeling, *Word and Faith*, p. 313.
28. Ebeling, *Word and Faith*, p. 317.
29. Ebeling, *Word and Faith*, p. 317; cf. *The Word of God and Tradition*, p. 9.
30. Fuchs, "The New Testament and the Hermeneutical Problem," p. 136.
31. See Fuchs, *Hermeneutik*, pp. 109-10 ("die Maus das hermeneutische Prinzip
für das Verständnis der Katze zu sein . . .").
32. Ebeling, *The Word of God and Tradition*, p. 17.
33. Kimmerle, "Hermeneutical Theory or Ontological Hermeneutics," *Journal for
Theology and the Church* (= *History and Hermeneutic*) 4 (1967): 107; italics mine. See
pp. 107-21.

(c) The problem of initiating understanding brings us to another concept which is also central in the thinking of Fuchs, namely, that of *das Einverständnis*.[34] This is often translated as "common understanding," "mutual understanding," or "agreement," and in one essay as "empathy." Fuchs illustrates this category with reference to the language of the home. Members of a close-knit family who live together in one home share a common world of assumptions, attitudes, and experiences, and therefore share a common language. A single word or gesture may set in motion a train of events, because communication functions on the basis of a common understanding. Fuchs explains, "at home one does not speak so that people may understand, but because people understand."[35] The problem of understanding a language, in the sense of "appropriating" its subject matter, "does not consist in learning new words—languages are learned from mothers."[36] So important is this category of *Einverständnis* for Fuchs that in the preface to the fourth edition of *Hermeneutik* he stresses that "all understanding is grounded in *Einverständnis*," and in a later essay he sums up the thrust of his *Hermeneutik* by saying that it is "an attempt to bring the hermeneutical problem back into the dimension of language with the aid of the phenomenon of 'empathy' [*des Phänomens des Einverständnisses*] as the foundation of all understanding."[37]

Jesus, Fuchs maintains, established a common understanding with his hearers, especially in the language of the parables. Or more accurately, the parables communicated reality effectively because they operated on the basis of this common understanding, which they then extended and reshaped.[38] The hermeneutical task today is to recreate that common world of understanding which is the necessary basis of effective communication of language and appropriation of its truth. Such a task, however, stands in sharp contrast to a merely cognitive and conscious exchange of language. Like Heidegger's category of "world," it is preconceptual. "It is neither a subjective nor an objective phenomenon but both together, for world is prior to and encompasses both."[39] It is therefore, for Fuchs

---

34. Fuchs, *Marburger Hermeneutik*, pp. 171-81, 239-43.

35. Fuchs, "The New Testament and the Hermeneutical Problem," p. 124; cf. *Marburger Hermeneutik*, p. 176.

36. Fuchs, "The Hermeneutical Problem," in *The Future of Our Religious Past*, pp. 267-68.

37. Fuchs, "The Hermeneutical Problem," p. 270.

38. See Fuchs, "The New Testament and the Hermeneutical Problem," p. 126; "Proclamation and Speech-Event," pp. 347-51; *Hermeneutik*, pp. 219-30; *Studies of the Historical Jesus*, pp. 97-99, 130-66; and *Marburger Hermeneutik*, pp. 231-32. The parables are discussed further below.

39. Richard E. Palmer, *Hermeneutics: Interpretation Theory in Schleiermacher, Dilthey, Heidegger, and Gadamer* (Evanston, Ill.: Northwestern University Press, 1969), p. 139.

as for Gadamer, primarily a "linguistic" phenomenon, reflecting ways in which men have come to terms with themselves and with their world.[40]

(d) Both Fuchs and Ebeling view language as much more than merely a means of information. Ebeling writes, "we do not get at the nature of words by asking what they contain, but by asking what they effect, what they set going."[41] In the terminology of J. L. Austin, Fuchs and Ebeling are most interested in the *performative* functions of language, in which "the issuing of the utterance is the performing of an action."[42] The word of God, Ebeling believes, enacts "an event in which God himself is communicated. . . . With God word and deed are one: his speaking is the way of his acting."[43] Thus the word of Jesus in the New Testament does not simply provide information about states of affairs. His language constitutes a call or a pledge.[44] He promises, demands or gives.[45] Actually to *make* a promise, or to *convey* a gift is very different from talking *about* promises or gifts. The one is action; the other is mere talk.

In the terminology used by Fuchs, language which actually conveys reality constitutes a "language-event" (*Sprachereignis*); Ebeling uses the term "word-event" (*Wortgeschehen*) in much the same way.[46] Fuchs comments, "The true language-event, for example an offer, shows that, though it sets our thoughts in motion, it is not itself thought. The immediate harmony between what is said and what is grasped is not the result of a process of thought; it takes place at

40. This point is elucidated below, but for a simple introduction to this aspect of Fuchs's thought, see Paul J. Achtemeier, *An Introduction to the New Hermeneutic* (Philadelphia: Westminster Press, 1969), pp. 91-100.

41. Ebeling, *The Nature of Faith*, p. 187.

42. See Austin, *How to Do Things with Words* (Oxford, Clarendon Press, 1962), p. 6; cf. his *Philosophical Papers* (Oxford: Clarendon Press, 1961), pp. 220-39. See further my essay "The Parables as Language-Event: Some Comments on Fuchs's Hermeneutics in the Light of Linguistic Philosophy," *Scottish Journal of Theology* 23 (1970): 437-68, especially 438-39; R. W. Funk, *Language, Hermeneutic and Word of God: The Problem of Language in the New Testament and Contemporary Theology* (New York: Harper & Row, 1966), pp. 26-28; J. M. Robinson, "The Parables as God Happening," in *Jesus and the Historian*, ed. F. T. Trotter (Philadelphia: Westminster Press, 1968), p. 142; and Doty, *Contemporary New Testament Interpretation*, pp. 39-43.

43. Ebeling, *The Nature of Faith*, pp. 87, 90

44. Fuchs, *Zur Frange nach dem historischen Jesus*, pp. 291, 293.

45. Fuchs, *Zur Frage nach dem historischen Jesus*, pp. 288, 291, 224, 226, and 347.

46. See Fuchs, *Zum hermeneutischen Problem in der Theologie*, pp. 281-305; *Marburger Hermeneutik*, pp. 243-45; and *Studies of the Historical Jesus*, pp. 196-212. See Ebeling, *Word and Faith*, pp. 325-32; and *Theology and Proclamation*, pp. 28-31. Concerning the different terminology used by Fuchs and Ebeling, James Robinson states that "*Sprachereignis* and *Wortgeschehen* are synonyms. . . . The choice depends on which Bultmannian term serves as the point of departure, *Heilsereignis* or *Heilsgeschehen*" (*New Frontiers in Theology II*, p. 57).

an earlier stage, as event. . . . The word 'gets home.' "[47] For example, to name a man "brother" performatively is thereby to admit
him into a brotherly relationship within the community.[48] In this
sense, when the word of God addresses the hearers anew, it is no
longer merely an object of investigation at the hands of the interpreter. Fuchs concludes, "the text is therefore not just the servant
that transmits kerygmatic formulations, but rather a master that
directs us into the language-context of our existence."[49] It has become a language-event.

II. SUBJECT AND OBJECT: UNDERSTANDING AS EXPERIENCE

Two further principles now emerge from all that has been said. The
first concerns the interpreter's experience of life, or subjectivity.
Ebeling writes, "Words produce understanding only by appealing
to experience and leading to experience. Only where word has already taken place can word take place. Only where there is already
previous understanding can understanding take place. Only a man
who is already concerned with the matter in question can be claimed
for it."[50] This is certainly true of a text which concerns history: "It
is impossible to understand history without a standpoint and a perspective."[51] Thus there are connections between the new hermeneutic and Bultmann's discussion about *preunderstanding*.

The second principle concerns the direction of the relation between the interpreter and the text. In traditional hermeneutics, the
interpreter, as knowing subject, scrutinizes and investigates the text
as the object of his knowledge. The interpreter is active subject; the
text is passive object. This kind of approach is encouraged by a
notion of theology as "queen of the sciences." But it rests upon, or
presupposes, a particular model in epistemology, a model which is
exemplified in the philosophy of Descartes. If understanding is viewed
in terms of experience rather than knowledge, a different perspective
may also be suggested. James Robinson offers an illuminating comment. In the new hermeneutic, he explains, "the flow of the traditional relation between subject and object, in which the subject
interrogates the object . . . has been significantly reversed. For it is
now the object—which should henceforth be called the subject-matter—that puts the subject in question."[52] Thus Fuchs asserts, "*The*

---

47. Fuchs, *Studies of the Historical Jesus*, p. 196.
48. Fuchs, *Studies of the Historical Jesus*, p. 196.
49. Fuchs, *Studies of the Historical Jesus*, p. 211.
50. Ebeling, *Word and Faith*, p. 320.
51. Ebeling, *The Word of God and Tradition*, p. 18.; cf. Fuchs, *Hermeneutik*, pp. 103-26.
52. Robinson, *New Frontiers in Theology II*, pp. 23-24.

truth has us ourselves as its object."[53] Or even more strikingly, "The texts must translate us before we can translate them."[54]

A. Language and Preunderstanding

It is well known that Rudolf Bultmann, among others, has repudiated the idea that an interpreter can "understand" the New Testament independently of his own prior questions. One cannot, for example, understand a text about economic history unless one already has some concept of what a society and an economy is.[55] In this sense Bultmann rightly insists, *"There cannot be any such thing as presuppositionless exegesis. . . .* Historical understanding always presupposes a relation of the interpreter to the subject-matter that is . . . expressed in the texts."[56] "The demand that the interpreter must silence his subjectivity . . . in order to attain an objective knowledge is therefore the most absurd one that can be imagined."[57] "Preunderstanding," or a prior life-relation to the subject matter of the text, implies "not a prejudice, but a way of raising questions."[58]

This principle must not be rejected merely because it has particular connections with other assumptions made by Bultmann in his program of demythologizing. Other more moderate scholars including, for example, Bernard Lonergan and James D. Smart, have made similar points.[59] Lonergan rightly asserts, "the principle of the empty head rests on a naive intuitionism. . . . The principle . . . bids the interpreter forget his own views, look at what is out there, and let the author interpret himself. In fact, what is out there? There is just a series of signs. Anything over and above a re-issue of the same signs in the same order will be mediated by the experience, intelligence, and judgment of the interpreter. The less that experience, the less cultivated that intelligence, the less formed that

53. Fuchs, "The New Testament and the Hermeneutical Problem," p. 143; italics his.

54. Fuchs, "The Hermeneutical Problem," p. 277. (The phrase reads "die Texte zuvor uns übersetzen müssen bevor wir sie übersetzen können" in the original German edition, *Zeit und Geschichte: Dankesgabe an Rudolf Bultmann zum 80. Geburtstag*, ed. E. Dinkler [Tübingen: J. C. B. Mohr, 1964], p. 365). Cf. Ebeling, *Word and Faith*, p. 331.

55. See Bultmann, "Is Exegesis without Presuppositions Possible?" in *Existence and Faith: Shorter Writings of Rudolf Bultmann* (London: Collins, 1964), p. 347; and "The Problem of Hermeneutics," in *Essays Philosophical and Theological*, pp. 242-43; see pp. 234-61.

56. Bultmann, *Existence and Faith*, pp. 343-44, 347; italics his.

57. Bultmann, "The Problem of Hermeneutics," p. 255.

58. Bultmann, *Existence and Faith*, p. 346.

59. See Lonergan, *Method in Theology* (London: Darton, Longman & Todd, 1972), pp. 156-58; see pp. 153-266; and see Smart, *The Interpretation of Scripture* (London: SCM Press, 1961), pp. 37-64.

judgment, the greater will be the likelihood that the interpreter will impute to the author an opinion that the author never entertained."[60]

In this connection both Bultmann and the new hermeneutic look back to Wilhelm Dilthey, and even beyond to Friedrich Schleiermacher.[61] Both the later thinking of Schleiermacher after 1819 and also the earlier thinking as rediscovered by Heinz Kimmerle are relevant in different ways to the new hermeneutic. At first sight, Fuchs's central concept of *Einverständnis* seems to relate to the later Schleiermacher's insistence that the modern interpreter must make himself contemporary with the author of a text by attempting imaginatively to relive his experiences. Especially if we follow the translator who rendered *Einverständnis* as "empathy," this looks like Schleiermacher's procedure of entering into the hopes and fears, desires and aims of the author through artistic imagination and rapport.

We have seen, however, that "mutual understanding" in Fuchs operates at a preconscious level. It is not primarily, if at all, a matter of psychology, as it was in the later thought of Schleiermacher. With Manfred Mezger, Fuchs believes that this psychological approach founders on the existential individuality of the "I" who is each particular interpreter.[62] Thus Mezger asserts that we must find "the new place at which this text, without detriment to its historical individuality, meets us. The short cut by which I picture myself as listener in the skin of Moses or of Paul is certainly popular, but it is not satisfactory, for I am neither the one nor the other" (i.e., neither Moses nor Paul).[63] Mezger adds that the way to overcome this problem is "not by treating the particular details with indifference, thus effacing the personal profile of the text, but by becoming aware of the involvement (*Betroffenheit*) which is the same for them as for me, but which is described in a particular way in each instance."[64] He then quotes Fuchs's redoubled warning that the modern listeners "are not the same men to whom the gospel was first proclaimed"; although their concrete situation can nevertheless be "appropriated" today, when the text is accurately translated.[65]

In the earlier writings of Schleiermacher, however, as Kimmerle has shown, hermeneutics is more language-centered and less orien-

---

60. Lonergan, *Method in Theology*, p. 157. Cf. my article "The Use of Philosophical Categories in New Testament Hermeneutics," *The Churchman* 87 (1973): 87-100.

61. See Palmer, *Hermeneutics*, pp. 94, 96; and see Schleiermacher, *Hermeneutik und Kritik*, ed. F. Lucke, p. 29.

62. Fuchs, *Hermeneutik*, p. 281; italics mine.

63. Mezger, "Preparation for Preaching," p. 166; cf. Robinson, *New Frontiers in Theology II*, p. 59.

64. Mezger, "Preparation for Preaching," p. 166.

65. Mezger, "Preparation for Preaching," pp. 166-67.

tated towards psychology. Understanding is an *art*, for the particular utterance of a particular author must be understood "in the light of the larger, more universal, linguistic community in which the individual . . . finds himself."[66] "Rules" perform only the negative function of preventing false interpretation. Even on a purely linguistic level the subjectivity of the interpreter has a positive role to play. What we understand forms itself into unities made up of parts. In understanding a stretch of language, we need to understand words in order to understand the sentence; nevertheless our understanding of the force of individual words depends on our understanding of the whole sentence. But this principle must be extended. Our understanding of the sentence contributes to our understanding of the paragraph, of the chapter, of the author as a whole; but this understanding of the whole work in turn qualifies and modifies our understanding of the sentence.

This principle prepares the way for hermeneutics in Heidegger and Gadamer, as well as in Fuchs and Ebeling, and is in fact tantamount to a preliminary formulation of the theory of the hermeneutical circle.[67] It shatters the illusion, as Dilthey later stressed, that understanding a text could be purely "scientific." As Richard Palmer puts it, "somehow a kind of 'leap' into the hermeneutical circle occurs and we understand the whole and the parts together. Schleiermacher left room for such a factor when he saw understanding as partly a comparative and partly an intuitive and divinatory matter."[68] Still commenting on Schleiermacher but with obvious relevance to Fuchs's notion of *Einverständnis*, Palmer adds, "the hermeneutical circle suggests an area of shared understanding. Since communication is a dialogical relation, there is assumed at the outset a community of meaning shared by the speaker and the hearer. This seems to involve another contradiction: what is to be understood must already be known. But is this not the case? Is it not vain to speak of love to one who has not known love . . . ?"[69] Thus we return to Ebeling's comment that "words produce understanding by appealing to experience and leading to experience. Only where word has already taken place can word take place. Only where there is already previous understanding can understanding take place."[70]

This helps to explain why the new hermeneutic inevitably involves problems of philosophy.[71] But it also raises theological ques-

---

66. Kimmerle, "Hermeneutical Theory or Ontological Hermeneutics," p. 109.

67. See Heidegger, *An Introduction to Metaphysics* (New Haven: Yale University Press, 1959), pp. 123-38.

68. Palmer, *Hermeneutics,* p. 87.

69. Palmer, *Hermeneutics,* p. 87.

70. Ebeling, *Word and Faith*, p. 320.

71. See Ebeling, *Word and Faith*, p. 317.

tions. In one direction, the New Testament cannot be understood without reference to the interpreter's own experiences of life. Thus Fuchs insists, *"in the interaction of the text with daily life we experience the truth of the New Testament."* [72] In another direction, it raises questions about the relation between exegesis and systematic theology. For the *total* context of any theological utterance is hardly less than Scripture and the history of its interpretation through tradition. In Heinrich Ott's words on the subject, Scripture as a whole constitutes "the 'linguistic room,' the universe of discourse, the linguistic net of co-ordinates in which the church has always resided. . . . Heidegger says, 'Every poet composed from only a single poem. . . . None of the individual poems, not even the total of them, says it all. Nevertheless, each poem speaks from the whole of the one poem and each time speaks it.' " [73]

B. *The Interpreter and the Text*

All that has been said about the subjectivity of the interpreter, however, must now be radically qualified by the second of the two major principles at present under discussion. We have already noted Fuchs's assertions that the texts must translate us before we can translate them, and that the truth has "ourselves" as its object. It is not simply the case that the interpreter, as active subject, scrutinizes the text as passive object. It is not simply that the present experience throws light on the text, but that the text illuminates present experience. Ebeling insists, *"the text . . . becomes a hermeneutic aid in the understanding of present experience."* [74] In an important and often-quoted sentence in the same essay he declares, *"the primary phenomenon in the realm of understanding is not understanding OF language, but understanding THROUGH language."* [75]

Both Ebeling and especially Gadamer call attention to the parallel between theological and juridical hermeneutics in this respect. [76] The interpretation of legal texts, Gadamer insists, is not simply a "special case" of general hermeneutics, but, rather, reveals the full dimensions of the general hermeneutical problem. In law the interpreter does not examine the text purely as an "object" of

---

72. Fuchs, "The New Testament and the Hermeneutical Problem," p. 142; italics his.

73. Ott, "What Is Systematic Theology?" in *New Frontiers in Theology, I: The Later Heidegger and Theology*, ed. J. M. Robinson and J. B. Cobb, Jr. (New York: Harper & Row, 1963), pp. 86-87; cf. Heidegger, *Unterwegs zur Sprache*, 2d ed. (Pfulligen: Naske, 1960), pp. 37-38.

74. Ebeling, *Word and Faith*, p. 33; italics his.

75. Ebeling, *Word and Faith*, p. 318; italics his.

76. Gadamer, *Wahrheit und Methode*, pp. 307-24, especially p. 311; Ebeling, *Word and Faith*, p. 330.

antiquarian investigation. The text "speaks" to the present situation in the courtroom, and the interpreter adjusts his own thinking to that of the text. Each of our two principles, in fact, remains equally relevant. On the one hand, the interpreter's own understanding of law and of life guides him in his understanding of the ancient legal texts; on the other hand, that preliminary understanding is modified and moulded, in turn, as the texts themselves deliver their verdicts on the present situation. Even outside the courtroom itself, Ebeling believes that "the man who has no interest in giving legal decisions will be a poor legal historian."[77] Similarly Gadamer asserts, "understanding the text is always already applying it."[78]

These two principles operate together in Gadamer's version of the hermeneutical circle. We have already noted the idea in Schleiermacher and in Heidegger that we can understand a whole only in the light of its parts, but also that we can understand the parts only in the light of the whole. But Heidegger and especially Gadamer take us a step further.[79] The "circle" of the hermeneutical process begins when the interpreter takes his own preliminary questions to the text. But because his questions may not be the best or most appropriate ones, his understanding of the subject matter of the text may at first remain limited, provisional, and even liable to distortion. Nevertheless the text, in turn, speaks back to the hearer: it begins to interpret him; it sheds light on his own situation and on his own questions. His initial questions now undergo revision in the light of the text itself, and in response to more adequate questioning, the text itself now speaks more clearly and intelligibly. The process continues, while the interpreter achieves a progressively deeper understanding of the text.

In his book *The Bible in Human Transformation*, the American scholar Walter Wink develops his own particular version of this kind of approach. He criticizes New Testament scholars for failing to interpret the New Testament in accordance with its own purpose, namely "so to interpret the scriptures that the past becomes alive and illumines our present with new possibilities for personal and social transformation."[80] Because of a deliberate suspension of participational involvement, "the outcome of biblical studies in the academy is a trained incapacity to deal with the real problems of actual living persons in their daily lives."[81] The kind of *questions* asked by the

---

77. Ebeling, *Word and Faith*, p. 330.
78. Gadamer, *Wahrheit und Methode*, p. 291; see pp. 290-95.
79. See Gadamer, *Wahrheit und Methode*, pp. 250-90, especially pp. 250-61, 275-90; cf. Heidegger, *Being and Time* (London: Blackwell, 1962), pp. 188-95.
80. Wink, *The Bible in Human Transformation: Towards a New Paradigm for Biblical Study* (Philadelphia: Fortress Press, 1973), p. 2.
81. Wink, *The Bible in Human Transformation*, p. 6.

New Testament scholar are not those raised by the text, but those
most likely to win a hearing from the professional guild of academ-
ics.[82] Scholars seek to silence their own subjectivity, striving for the
kind of objective neutrality which is not only an illusion, but which
also requires "a sacrifice of the very questions the Bible seeks to
answer."[83]

Nevertheless, Wink is not advocating, any more than Fuchs, a
suspension of critical studies. In order to hear the New Testament
speak for itself, and not merely reflect back the interpreter's own ideas
or the theology of the modern church, the interpreter must allow
critical enquiry first to *distance* him from the way in which the text
has become embedded in the church's tradition. The text must be
heard as "that which stands over against us."[84] Only after this "distance" has first been achieved can there then occur "a communion
of horizons" between the interpreter and the text.[85] Thus while
Wink acknowledges the necessity for "rigorous use of biblical criticism," his primary concern, like that of Fuchs, is "for the rights of
the text."[86]

Hans-Georg Gadamer makes some parallel points. Descartes's
theory of knowledge, in which man as active subject looks out on
the world as passive object, provides only *one* possible model for the
apprehension of truth. This model is more appropriate to the
"method" of the sciences than to the art of understanding in hermeneutics. There has always been a tradition in philosophy which
stressed the connection between understanding and *experience.* For
example, Vico, with his sensitivity for history, rejected the narrow
intellectualism of Descartes's notion of truth, even in the latter's
own lifetime. In ancient times the Greek idea of "wisdom" included
practical understanding of life as well as intellectual theory.[87] Later,
Shaftesbury stressed the role of wit, Reid stressed the role of common sense, and Bergson stressed the role of intuitive insight as valid
ways through which truth could be revealed.[88] It is not simply a
matter of discovering theoretical "methods" by which man can arrive at truth. In true understanding, man is grasped *by* truth through
modes of experience.[89] A more adequate model than that provided
by Descartes is the experience of truth in a work of art, in which

82. Wink, *The Bible in Human Transformation,* p. 10.
83. Wink, *The Bible in Human Transformation,* p. 3.
84. Wink, *The Bible in Human Transformation,* p. 32.
85. Wink, *The Bible in Human Transformation,* p. 66.
86. Wink, *The Bible in Human Transformation,* p. 62.
87. See Gadamer, *Wahrheit und Methode,* pp. 17-18.
88. See Gadamer, *Wahrheit und Methode,* pp. 21-24.
89. See Gadamer, *Wahrheit und Methode,* pp. xxvi, 77-105.

something real and *creative* takes place. We shall refer to Gadamer's comments on this in our third section.

One reason why hermeneutics, according to Gadamer, must take account of something more than cognitive "knowledge" (*Erkenntnis*) is that every interpreter already stands within a historical tradition, which provides him with certain presuppositions or prejudgments (*Vorurteile*).[90] Gadamer insists that "an individual's prejudgments, much more than his judgments, are the reality of his being [*die geschichtliche Wirklichkeit seines Seins*]."[91] To bring these prejudgments to conscious awareness is a major goal of hermeneutics, and corresponds to what Walter Wink describes as "distancing." For Gadamer believes that the very existence of a temporal and cultural *distance* between the interpreter and the text can be used to jog him into an awareness of the differences between their respective horizons. The interpreter must cultivate a "hermeneutically trained" awareness, in which he allows the distinctive message of the text to reshape his own questions and concepts.[92]

Once this has been done, the interpreter is free to move beyond his own original horizons, or better, to *enlarge* his own horizons until they come to *merge* or *fuse* with those of the text. His goal is to reach the place at which a merging of horizons (*Horizontverschmelzung*), or fusion of "worlds," occurs.[93] This comes about only through sustained dialogue with the text, in which the interpreter allows his own subjectivity to be challenged and involved. Only in the to-and-fro of question and answer on both sides can the text come to speech (*zur-Sprache-kommen*).[94] Thus in Gadamer's notion of the merging of horizons we find a parallel to Wink's ideas about "fusion" and "communion," and to Fuchs's central category of *Einverständnis*. But this is achieved, as we have seen, only when, first, the interpreter's subjectivity is fully engaged at a more-than-cognitive level; and when, second, the text, and the truth of the text, *actively* grasps *him* as its object.

III. THE ESTABLISHING OF NEW "WORLDS" IN LANGUAGE: HEIDEGGER AND THE PARABLES

To achieve a merging of horizons or an area of shared understanding amounting to *Einverständnis* involves, in effect, the creation of a new "world." In common with Heidegger's philosophy in both the earlier

90. Gadamer, *Wahrheit und Methode*, pp. 250-61.
91. Gadamer, *Wahrheit und Methode*, p. 261.
92. Gadamer, *Wahrheit und Methode*, pp. 282-83.
93. Gadamer, *Wahrheit und Methode*, pp. 288-90.
94. Gadamer, *Wahrheit und Methode*, p. 345.

and later periods, Fuchs believes that man stands within a linguistic world which is decisively shaped by his own place in history, that is, by his "historicality." But with the later Heidegger, Fuchs also looks for a *new* coming-to-speech in which the confines and conventions of the old everyday "world" will be set aside and broken through. The language-event, especially the language-event of the parables of Jesus, corresponds to the establishment of a new world through language.

It is difficult to summarize Heidegger's view in a few paragraphs, but we may note the following major themes.

(1) One consequence of man's historicality (his being radically conditioned by his place within history) is that he views objects from the man-centered perspective of his own world. He sees things from the point of view of this relation to his own purposes, seeing them through a kind of grid of egocentric functionalism. A hammer, for example, is not merely a neutral "object" of wood and metal but a tool which can be used for certain jobs. Thus a hammer is something very different from a broken hammer; although in "neutral" terms of their physical properties the difference would not be very great.[95] Man's language reveals, creates, and sustains this perspective. Thus in everyday language, "time," for example, "has ceased to be anything other than velocity, instantaneousness. . . . Time as history has vanished from the lives of all peoples."[96]

(2) Man has lost touch with genuine reality still further by accepting in his intellectual orientation the legacy of Plato's dualism. In Heidegger's words, Western philosophy since Plato has "fallen out of Being."[97] It embodies a split perspective, in which subject becomes separated from object. "Appearance was declared to be mere appearance and thus degraded. At the same time, Being as *idea* was exalted to a suprasensory realm. A chasm . . . was created."[98] Man thus looks out, in the fashion of Plato and Descartes, onto a merely *conceptualized* world, a reality of his own making. He himself, by seeing "reality" through the grid of his own split perspective, becomes the measure of his own knowledge.[99] An example of the evil consequences of this can be seen in the realm of art. Art is divided off into one of the two realms, so that it is *either* a merely "material" thing, in which case it cannot reveal truth; *or* it is conceptualized into "aesthetics," in which case it becomes tamed and emasculated and, once again, unable to reveal truth. By contrast,

95. Heidegger, *Being and Time*, pp. 95-102.
96. Heidegger, *An Introduction to Metaphysics*, p. 31.
97. Heidegger, *An Introduction to Metaphysics*, p. 30.
98. Heidegger, *An Introduction to Metaphysics*, pp. 89-90.
99. Heidegger, *Nietzsche*, vol. 2 (Pfulligen: Neske, 1961), pp. 148-49, especially on Descartes.

"on the strength of a recaptured, pristine, relation to Being, we must provide the word 'art' with a new content."[100]

(3) The combined effect of these two factors is to lead to circularity and fragmentation in the use of *language*. The truth of language now depends on an artificial correspondence between man's concepts and what he supposes to be "reality" but which is in fact another set of his own concepts.[101] For everything which he thinks and sees, he thinks and sees through the medium of his own "linguisticality" or language-conditionedness. Thus, Heidegger concludes, "he is always thrown back on the paths that he himself has laid out; he becomes mired in his paths, caught in the beaten track. . . . He turns round and round in his own circle."[102]

Fuchs and Ebeling accept the linguistic and hermeneutical problems which Heidegger's diagnosis lays down. Ebeling believes that language has become loosed from its anchorage in reality, to disintegrate into "atoms of speech. . . . Everything seemed to me to fall into fragments."[103] This has precipitated "a profound crisis of language . . . a complete collapse of language."[104] Today "we threaten to die of language poisoning. . . . With the dawn of the modern age . . . the path was clear for an unrestricted development of the mere sign-function of language. . . . Words are reduced to ciphers . . . and syntax to a question of calculus."[105] Language has wrongly become a mere "technical instrument."[106] Yet, Fuchs argues, language and reality are bound so closely together that there can be no "reality" *for us* outside this language.[107]

The solution, if it is a solution, offered by Heidegger, and indirectly by Fuchs, is to put oneself in the place at which language may, once again, give voice not to a fragmented set of human concepts, but to undivided "Being." First, this "Being" is not the substantial "beingness" (*Seiendheit*) of human thought but the verbal, eventful, temporal Being-which-happens (*Sein* or better, *Anwesen*). Echoing Heidegger, Fuchs declares, "Language . . . makes Being into an event."[108] Second, when language is once again pure and

100. Heidegger, *An Introduction to Metaphysics*, p. 111; cf. *Unterwegs zur Sprache* (Pfulligen: Neske, 1959), pp. 83-155, especially 86-87; *Holzwege*, 4th ed. (Frankfurt: Klostermann, 1963) pp. 7-68; and "The Origion of a Work of Art," in *Philosophies of Art and Beauty*, ed. A. Hofstadter and R. Kuhns (New York: Modern Library, 1964).

101. See Heidegger, *Vom Wesen der Wahrheit*, 4th ed. (Frankfurt: Klostermann, 1961), pp. 6-13.

102. Heidegger, *An Introduction to Metaphysics*, p. 132.

103. Ebeling, *Introduction to a Theological Theory of Language* (London, 1973), p. 71.

104. Ebeling, *Introduction to a Theological Theory of Language*, p. 76.

105. Ebeling, *God and Word*, pp. 2, 17.

106. Ebeling, *Introduction to a Theological Theory of Language*, p. 127.

107. Fuchs, *Hermeneutik*, pp. 126-34; and *Marburger Hermeneutik*, pp. 228-32.

108. Fuchs, *Studies of the Historical Jesus*, p. 207.

creative, Heidegger believes, "the essence of language is found in the act of gathering."[109] Before the advent of Plato's dualism, the word (*logos*) was "the primal gathering principle."[110] Where modern Western culture and its idle talk merely divides and fragments, the pure language of Being integrates and brings together. Thus Fuchs writes, "the proclamation gathers (i.e., into a community) . . . and this community has its being, its 'togetherness,' in the possibility of its being able to speak the kind of language in which the event of its community is fulfilled. . . . *The language of faith brings into language the gathering of faith.*"[111]

Once again this notion of "gathering" approaches the idea of sharing a common "world," or achieving *Einverständnis*. But Heidegger, followed by Fuchs, insists that language can achieve this "gathering" only when man accepts the role of *listener* rather than that of subject scrutinizing "object." For Heidegger, this means a silent, receptive waiting upon Being. Language is the "house" or "custodian" of Being (*das Haus des Seins . . . des Anwesens*).[112] Man's task is to find the "place" (*Ort*) at which Being may come to speech.[113] As listeners, whose task is to cultivate a wakeful and receptive openness to Being, Heidegger urges that "we should *do* nothing, but rather wait."[114] The listener must not impose his own concepts of reality onto Being, but should "know how to wait, even for a whole life-time."[115]

Although in principle he is concerned with the word of God rather than the voice of Being, Fuchs does at times seem to identify the two. The word of God relates to "the meaning of Being" (*der "Sinn" des Seins*) and comes as the "call of Being" (*der Ruf zum Sein*).[116] But above all man "listens" in receptive silence and openness to the text of the New Testament. To be sure, critical analysis, as in Wink's and Gadamer's "distancing," is first necessary as a preliminary. In this way, by active critical scrutiny, the interpreter "must in the *first instance* strike the text dead."[117] But *after* this he must wait for God, or Being, to speak: "in the tranquillity of faith, where noise is reduced to silence, a *voice* is heard. . . . It sings out in Phil. 2:6-11."[118]

109. Heidegger, *An Introduction to Metaphysics*, p. 145.
110. Heidegger, *An Introduction to Metaphysics*, p. 108.
111. Fuchs, *Studies of the Historical Jesus*, pp. 208-9; italics his.
112. Heidegger, *Unterwegs zur Sprache*, p. 267.
113. Heidegger, *Unterwegs zur Sprache*, p. 19.
114. Heidegger, *Gelassenheit* (Pfulligen, 1959), p. 37.
115. Heidegger, *An Introduction to Metaphysics*, p. 172.
116. Fuchs, *Hermeneutik*, p. 71.
117. Fuchs, *Studies of the Historical Jesus*, p. 194; italics his.
118. Fuchs, *Studies of the Historical Jesus*, p. 192; italics his. Cf. his *Hermeneutik*, pp. 103-7.

All these principles about language and "world" apply in particular to Fuchs's handling of the parables of Jesus. By means of the
image part or picture-half (*Bildhälfte*) of the parable, Jesus creates
and enters a "world" which, in the first place, is shared by the
hearer. He stands within the hearer's horizons. But everyday conventions and everyday assumptions are then challenged and shattered by the actual message or content-half (*Sachhälfte*). The hearer
is challenged at a deep and preconceptual level. It is not simply a
matter of his assessing certain "ideas" presented to him by Jesus.
Rather, "he is drawn over on to God's side and learns to see everything with God's eyes."[119] The parable is both a creative work of
art, and also a *calling* of love, in contrast to flat cognitive discourse.
Thus "Jesus draws the hearer over to his side by means of the artistic
medium, so that the hearer may think together with Jesus. Is this
not the way of true love? Love does not just blurt out. Instead, it
provides in advance the sphere in which meeting takes place."[120]

The difference between entering a "world" and merely assessing
ideas is further clarified by Gadamer in his comments on the nature
of games and the nature of art. A game creates a special "world" of
experience. The player participates in this world, rather than simply
observing it, by accepting its rules, its values, and its presuppositions. He yields himself to them, and *acts* on them. It is not a matter
of his consciously carrying them in his mind. Hence the *reality* of a
game is something shared by the players in the play itself.[121] Such
"real-life" experience (*Wirklichkeitserfahrung*) is also involved when
one is grasped by a true work of art.[122] It is not a mere set of
concepts to be manipulated by a spectator, but a "world" which
takes hold of a man as someone who *enters into it*. It is not something
presented as a mere object of scrutiny or source of theoretical
concepts.[123]

In his treatment of specific parables, therefore, Fuchs insists that
the main point is not simply to convey a conscious "idea." In this
sense, he steps away from Jülicher's "one-point" approach. For the
"point" or verdict of a parable may come differently to different
people. Thus in his work on the Parable of the Unmerciful Servant,
Fuchs declares, first, that "the parable is not intended to exemplify
general ethics."[124] Second, the verdict for Israel is "God is harder

119. Fuchs, *Studies of the Historical Jesus*, p. 155.
120. Fuchs, *Studies of the Historical Jesus*, p. 129.
121. Gadamer, *Wahrheit und Methode*, p. 100; see pp. 97-115.
122. Gadamer, *Wahrheit und Methode*, pp. 66-96.
123. Gadamer, *Wahrheit und Methode*, p. 98; cf. my essay "The Parables as Language-Event," pp. 442-45.
124. Fuchs, "The Parable of the Unmerciful Servant," in *Studia Evangelica, I,* ed.
K. Aland et al. (Berlin: Akademie, 1959), p. 487 (= *Texte und Untersuchungen* 73
[1959]).

than you are," while the verdict for the church is "God insists upon his indulgence."[125] If these verdicts, however, are turned into merely conceptual generalizations, the result is only a self-contradiction: God is hard and indulgent.

Three principles are especially important for understanding Fuchs's approach to the parables.

(1) The image-part of picture-half of the parable is not merely an illustrative or homiletical device to make a lesson more vivid or memorable. It is a means of creating a common world in which Jesus and the hearer stand together. When Jesus speaks "of provincial and family life as it takes place in normal times," of the farmer, of the housewife, of the rich and poor or the happy and sad, he is not simply establishing a "point of contact" but standing with the hearer in *his* "world."[126] "We find *existentialia* wherever an understanding between men is disclosed through their having a common world."[127]

(2) Conventional everyday presuppositions about life and "reality" may then be challenged and shattered. This is where Fuchs's approach relates closely to Heidegger's verdict about the circularity and "fallenness" of man's everyday concepts and everyday talk. Something new and creative must break in to rescue him—in this case, the creative word and person of Jesus. Thus in the parable of the laborers in the vineyard (Matt. 20:1-16) at first "we too share the inevitable reaction of the first. The first see that the last receive a whole day's wage, and naturally they hope for a higher rate for themselves."[128] But then comes the shock. "in fact they receive the same. . . . It seems to them that the lord's action is unjust." Finally comes the verdict on the assumption which has been brought to light: "Is your eye evil because I am kind?" The word of Jesus thus "singles out the individual and grasps him deep down." For the hearer, by entering the world of the parable, has been drawn into an *engagement* with the verdict of Jesus. "The parable effects and demands our decision." It is *not* simply "the pallid requirement that sinful man should believe in God's kindness. Instead it contains, in a concrete way . . . Jesus' *pledge*." Jesus pledges himself to "those who, in face of a cry of 'guilty,' nevertheless found their hope on an act of God's kindnesss."[129]

The creative language event, therefore, shatters the mold imposed by man's "linguisticality." Even ordinary life, Fuchs suggests, can provide a model of this occurrence: "A new observation can throw

125. Fuchs, "The Parable of the Unmerciful Servant," p. 493; see pp. 487-94. And see his *Studies of the Historical Jesus,* pp. 152-53.

126. Fuchs, "The New Testament and the Hermeneutical Problem," p. 126.

127. Fuchs, *Studies of the Historical Jesus,* p. 97; cf. *Marburger Hermeneutik,* pp. 171-81.

128. Fuchs, *Studies of the Historical Jesus,* p. 33; see pp. 32-38, 154-56.

129. Fuchs, *Studies of the Historical Jesus,* pp. 33-37.

all our previous mental images into confusion. . . . What has already been observed and preserved in mental images comes into conflict with what is newly observed."[130] This conflict, this clash, demands a decision and reorientation. Robert Funk illustrates this principle with reference to the parable of the Prodigal Son (Luke 15:11-32). The "righteous" find themselves in the "world" of the elder brother, endorsing his conventional ideas of justice and obligation. "Sinners" participate in the "world" experienced by the prodigal son. Funk writes, "The word of grace and the deed of grace divide the audience into younger sons and elder sons—into sinners and Pharisees. This is what Ernst Fuchs means when he says that one does not interpret the parables; the parables interpret him. *The Pharisees are those who insist on interpreting the word of grace, rather than letting themselves be interpreted by it.*"[131] The judges find themselves judged. Sinners find themselves welcomed. "It is man and not God who is on trial."[132] The same principle operates in the parable of the Great Supper (Matt. 22:2-10; cf. Luke 14:16-24). One group is excluded; the other, embraced. "Each hearer is drawn into the tale as he wills."[133]

Walter Wink applies this approach to the interpretation of the parable of the Pharisee and the Publican (Luke 18:9-14). Most of Jesus' own hearers would at first identify themselves with the Pharisee as the bearer of religious and social status; but "then suffer shock and consternation at the wholly unexpected justification of the publican."[134] This of course raises a major hermeneutical problem, to which both Fuchs and Wink are eager to call attention. The *modern* reader already knows that it is the *Pharisee* who will be condemned. Hence nowadays "a simple descriptive approach wrecks the parable."[135] It must come to speech anew, and not merely be "repeated." For the ending of the parable has now in turn become embedded in the conventional judgments of "religious" man, from which the language-event is meant to free us!

(3) There is not sufficient space to comment adequately on the importance of Christology for Fuchs's understanding of the parables. We must note, however, that he stresses this aspect with special reference to the oneness of word and deed in the ministry of Jesus, and also to the status and role of Jesus as one who pronounces God's word in God's stead. God is present in the word of Jesus. Moreover, since Jesus enters the common world of understanding experienced by the hearer, the hearer makes his response to God's word "together

130. Fuchs, "Proclamation and Speech-Event," p. 349.
131. Funk, *Language, Hermeneutic and Word of God,* pp. 16-17; italics his.
132. Funk, *Language, Hermeneutic and Word of God,* p. 17.
133. Funk, *Language, Hermeneutic and Word of God,* p. 192; see pp. 124-222.
134. Wink, *The Bible in Human Transformation,* p. 42.
135. Wink, *The Bible in Human Transformation,* p. 43.

with" Jesus. Thus in the parable of the laborers in the vineyard "Jesus acted in a very real way as God's representative," especially in "his conduct . . . and proclamation." Jesus gives us "to understand his conduct as God's conduct." "Jesus' proclamation . . . went along with his conduct." Finally, if I respond in faith," I am not only near to Jesus; in faith I await the occurrence of God's kindness together with Jesus."[136] Similarly, in the parable of the Unmerciful Servant, "God accepted the conduct of Jesus as a valid expression of his will." The hearer "lets Jesus guide him to the mercy of God. . . . Jesus does not give a new law, but substitutes himself for the law."[137]

This means that as Jesus stands "together with" the hearer, he becomes in some sense a model for faith. For as the hearer, through the language-event, enters the "world" of Jesus, he finds a new vision of God and of the world which he shares with Jesus. For Fuchs this means especially the abandonment of self-assertion, even to the point of death, which is the repetition of Jesus' own decision to go the way of the cross and way of love.[138] "To have faith in Jesus now means essentially to repeat Jesus' decision."[139] This is why the new hermeneutic has definite connections with the new quest of the historical Jesus. Fuchs writes, "in the proclamation of the resurrection the historical Jesus himself *has* come to us. The so-called Christ of faith is none other than the historical Jesus. . . . God himself, *wants to be encountered* by us in the historical Jesus."[140] For the message of Jesus to come-to-speech creatively and liberatingly as language-event presupposes some kind of continuity between his words and his life. Thus Ebeling also concludes, "The kerygma . . . is not merely speech about man's existence. It is also a testimony to that which has happened."[141]

IV. SOME CONCLUSIONS

(1) While the new hermeneutic rightly faces the problem of how the interpreter may understand the text of the New Testament more *deeply* and more *creatively*, Fuchs and Ebeling are less concerned about how he may understand it *correctly*. Admittedly they insist on the need for historical-critical study, but rightly or wrongly we receive the impression that this is mainly a preliminary to the real

136. Fuchs, *Studies of the Historical Jesus*, pp. 36-38; italics his.
137. Fuchs, "The Parable of the Unmerciful Servant," pp. 491-92.
138. Fuchs, *Studies of the Historical Jesus*, pp. 80-82.
139. Fuchs, *Studies of the Historical Jesus*, p. 28.
140. Fuchs, *Studies of the Historical Jesus*, pp. 30-31; italics his.
141. Ebeling, *Theology and Proclamation*, p. 38; see pp. 32-81 for his response to Bultmann.

task of hermeneutics. Fuchs and Ebeling are looking at *one* side, albeit a neglected and yet important side, of a two-sided problem. Rather than simply "first" using critical methods, is it not possible *both* to "listen" to the text as subject, and also *alongside this* critically to test one's understanding of it? May not both attitudes be called into play successively and repeatedly as if in dialogue?

It will be suggested, by way of reply, that this is necessarily to surrender a vision of wholeness in exchange for a split conceptualizing perspective in which the text becomes once again a mere "object" of scrutiny. But while we may accept the warning of Heidegger and Gadamer that the subject-object "method" of Descartes is not always adequate, nevertheless conceptualizing thinking must be given *some* place in hermeneutics. Commenting on Heidegger's notion of openness to the call of Being, Hans Jonas points out that thinking "is precisely an effort not to be at the mercy of fate."[142] To surrender one's own initiative in thinking in exchange for a mere "listening" is precisely *not* to escape from one's own conditionedness by history and language, but is to make everything "a matter of the chance factor of the historical generation I was born into."[143] Theologians, Jonas concludes, have been too easily seduced by the pseudo-humility of Heidegger's orientation. The Christian has been delivered from the power of fate, and must use his mind to distinguish the true from the false.

We have already seen that Heidegger, and presumably Fuchs, would regard this as a misunderstanding and short-circuiting of the whole problem of man's "linguisticality." Subject-object thinking, they believe, as well as distancing man from reality also sets in motion a vicious circularity by evaluating one set of human concepts in terms of another. But the New Testament itself, especially Paul, seems to be less pessimistic than Heidegger about the use of reason or "mind" (*nous*). In this respect Heidegger stands nearer to the sheer irrationality of Zen Buddhism. For it is noteworthy that after reading a work of Suzuki's, Heidegger declared "this is what I have been trying to say in all my writings."[144] Moreover, the actual practical difficulties of trying to distinguish between the true and the false in "non-objectifying" language are insuperable. They have been exposed, for example, by Paul van Buren in his discussion of Heinrich Ott.[145] Thus, in spite of its emphatic character, there is some

142. Jonas, in *The Review of Metaphysics* 18 (1964): 216; see pp. 207-33.

143. Jonas, in *The Review of Metaphysics*, p. 216.

144. Heidegger, quoted by W. Barrett in "Zen for the West," in *The World of Zen: An East-West Anthology*, ed. N. W. Ross (London: Collins, 1962), p. 344; cf. p. 284, and also in that volume, see D. T. Suzuki, "Satori, or Acquiring a New Viewpoint," pp. 41-47.

145. Van Buren, *Theological Explorations* (London, 1968), pp. 81-105.

justice in the verdict of J. C. Weber when he insists that in Fuchs's thought "there can be no basis for distinguishing the language of the word of God and the language of Being. . . . In what way can we know that language does not bring to expression illusion, falsehood, or even chaos? If the criterion of truth is only in the language-event itself, how can the language-event be safeguarded against delusion, mockery, or utter triviality? Why cannot the language-event be a disguised event of nothingness? . . . Fuchs's ontology is in danger of dissolving into a psychological illusionism."[146]

(2) *The new hermeneutic is also one-sided in its use of the New Testament and in its relation to the New Testament message.* To begin with, there are large areas of the New Testament which are explicitly concerned with rational argumentation and with the elucidation of theological concepts. Bornkamm, among others, has drawn attention to the role of reasoned argument in Paul, and Hebrews also invites consideration in this respect.[147] However, the approach of Fuchs and Ebeling better fits such language-categories as hymns, poems, metaphors, and parables. It is no accident that Fuchs tends to concentrate his attention on the parables, and also on such passages as 1 Corinthians 13 and Philippians 2:5-11. This seems to confirm our claim that the new hermeneutic is one-sided. It is tempting to wonder whether if Fuchs were still pastor to a congregation, they would find themselves confronted regularly by the same kinds of passages. This is partly, too, because Fuchs tends to see the "translated" message of the New Testament itself in narrowly selective terms. In the end, almost everything in the New Testament can be translated into a call to love; into a call to abandon self-assertion.

The problem for the new hermeneutic, however, is not only that certain parts of the New Testament take the form of cognitive discourse; it is also that it is frequently addressed to those who *already believe,* and often spoken out of an already existing theological *tradition* in the context of the historical community of the church. But tradition, even *within* the New Testament, is for Fuchs a factor that tends to obscure rather than clarify the original proclamation of Jesus, which was to *un*believers. Just as Heidegger wishes to step back "behind" the conceptualizing tradition of Western philosophy, so Fuchs wishes to step back "behind" the tradition of the primitive church.

The consequences of such a move can be seen most clearly in Fuchs's handling of the resurrection of Christ. This may never be

146. Weber, "Language-Event and Christian Faith," *Theology Today* 21 (1965): 455; see pp. 448-57.

147. See Bornkamm, "Faith and Reason in Paul," in *Early Christian Experience* (London: SCM Press, 1969), pp. 29-46.

seen as a past historical event known on the basis of apostolic testimony. Like Bultmann, Fuchs sees it simply as expressing the positive value of the cross, as expressing exhaustively and without
historical remainder Jesus' abandonment of self-assertion in the
death of the cross. In his attempt to support such a view, Fuchs
even claims that Paul made a mistake in 1 Corinthians 15:5-8, being
driven to ground the resurrection in history only by the exigency of
a polemic against the Corinthians.[148] Fuchs can find no room in his
hermeneutic for tradition, the church, or history after the event of
the cross. The issue is put sharply by P. J. Achtemeier: "The church
itself could, and did, become a historical 'security' for faith, thus
robbing faith of its announcement of the danger of all such security.
. . . In this way . . . the new hermeneutic attempts to defend a view
of faith based on some portions of the New Testament from a view
of faith based on other portions."[149]

Once again, however, these difficulties should not blind us to the
positive insights of the new hermeneutic where they occur. Fuchs
does make some valid comments on the hermeneutics of the epistles;
and from this kind of viewpoint Robert Funk offers some very valuable insights on 1 Corinthians 2:2-16 and especially on "Second
Corinthians as Hermeneutic." He sees this epistle as "a re-presen-
tation of the kerygma in language that speaks to the controversy in
which [Paul] is engaged."[150] The main contribution of the new hermeneutic, however, concerns the parables of Jesus, and here, although many criticisms about exegetical details could be made, the
suggestiveness and value of the general approach is clear.

(3) Just as it represents a one-sided approach to the hermeneutical task and also a one-sided use of the New Testament, *the new
hermeneutic further embodies a one-sided view of the nature of language.* This
shows itself in two ways.

First, like Heidegger, whom they follow here, Fuchs and Ebeling
fail to grasp that language functions on the basis of convention and
is not in fact "reality" or Being itself. While language admittedly
determines, or at least shapes, the way in which reality is perceived
and organized in relation to a language-community, effective lan-
guage-activity presupposes "rules" or conventions accepted by that
community. It is an established principle not only of Korzybski's
"general semantics" but also of general linguistics since Saussure
that the word is not the thing. Saussure himself described *"l'arbitraire
du signe"* as the first principle of language study, and the point is

148. See Fuchs, *Marburger Hermeneutik,* pp. 123-24, and *Glauben und Erfahrung,*
p. 216.
149. Achtemeier, *An Introduction to the New Hermeneutic,* pp. 156-57, 162.
150. Funk, in *New Frontiers in Theology II,* p. 168; see pp. 164-97. See also his
Language, Hermeneutic and Word of God, pp. 275-305.

discussed in the chapter on semantics.[151] Opaqueness in vocabulary, polysemy or multiple meaning, change in language, and the use of different words for the same object in different languages, all underline the conventionality of language. But the attitude of Fuchs and Ebeling, by contrast, is close to that which has been described as the belief in "word-magic." Their view is sometimes found especially among primitive peoples. Malinowski comments, "the word . . . has a power of its own; it is a means of bringing things about; it is a handle to acts and objects, not a definition of them. . . . The word gives power."[152] Heidegger, of course, would not be embarrassed that such an outlook is primitive; he is concerned with "primal" language.[153] But this does not avoid the problem when Ebeling writes that a language-event is not "mere speech" but "an event in which *God himself is communicated.*"[154]

This is *not* to say that we should reject Ebeling's contrast between a word which speaks *about* reconciliation and a word which actually *reconciles,* between speaking *about* a call and actually *calling.* But in two articles I have tried to show that the sense in which "saying makes it so" is best explained in terms of performative language, not in terms of word-magic.[155] Furthermore, it should be stressed that, in spite of any appearances to the contrary, Fuchs and Ebeling base their approach on a particular view of language, not on some affirmation of faith about the "power" of God's word.

Second, the new hermeneutic has a one-sided concern with imperatival, conative, directive language as over against the language of description or information. Ebeling writes, "we do not get at the nature of words by asking what they contain, but by asking what they effect, what they set going."[156] "The basic structure of word is therefore not statement . . . but appraisal, certainly not in the colourless sense of information, but in the pregnant sense of participation and communication."[157] Here it is important to see exactly

151. Saussure, *Cours de linguistique générale* (Wiesbaden: Harrassowitz, 1967), pp. 146-57. Cf. J. Lyons, *Introduction to Theoretical Linguistics* (Cambridge: Cambridge University Press, 1968), pp. 4-8, 38, 59-70, 74-75, 272, and 403; S. Ullmann, *Semantics: An Introduction to the Science of Meaning,* 2d ed. (Oxford: Blackwell, 1958), pp. 80-115; and my essay "The Supposed Power of Words in the Biblical Writings," *Journal of Theological Studies* 25 (1974): 283-99.

152. B. Malinowski, "The Problem of Meaning in Primitive Languages," in *The Meaning of Meaning,* ed. C. K. Ogden and I. A. Richards, 8th ed. (London: Routledge & Kegan Paul, 1946), pp. 489-90.

153. See Heidegger, *Existence and Being,* 3d ed. (London: Vision Press, 1968), pp. 291-315; *Wegmarken,* pp. 74-82; and *Unterwegs zur Sprache, passim.*

154. Ebeling, *The Nature of Faith,* pp. 87, 183; italics mine.

155. See my essays "The Supposed Power of Words in the Biblical Writings" and "The Parables as Language-Event."

156. Ebeling, *The Nature of Faith,* p. 187.

157. Ebeling, *Word and Faith,* p. 326.

what we are criticizing. We are *not* criticizing his concern with function, with communication, with self-involvement. We welcome this. But it is false to make two exclusive *alternatives* out of this, as if description somehow undermined other functions of language. Indeed, in my article on the parables as language-event, I have argued in detail first that not all descriptive propositions function in the same way (some may be open-ended) and second that, in Austin's words, "for a certain performative utterance to be happy, certain statements have to be *true*."[158] Amos Wilder presses this kind of point in a different way. He writes, "Fuchs refuses to define the content of faith. . . . He is afraid of the word as convention or as a means of conveying information. . . . Fuchs carries this so far that revelation, as it were, reveals nothing. . . . Jesus calls, indeed, for decisions. . . . But surely his words, deeds, presence, person, and message rested . . . upon dogma, eschatological and theocratic."[159]

(4) There is some force in the criticism that the new hermeneutic lets "what is true *for me*" become the criterion of "what is true" and that *its orientation towards the interpreter's subjectivity transposes theology too often into a doctrine of man.* We have noted Fuchs's comment that he proposes "a more radical existential interpretation" than even Bultmann. The hermeneutical task, he writes, is "the interpretation of *our own existence*. . . . We should accept as *true* only that which we acknowledge *as valid for our own person*."[160] At the same time, we should also note that there is another qualifying emphasis in Fuchs. He insists, "Christian faith means to speak of God's act, not of . . . acts of man."[161]

Some conservative theologians believe that we are drawn into a man-centered relativism if we accept either the notion of the hermeneutical circle, or Fuchs's idea of "self-understanding" (*Selbstverständnis*). Thus J. W. Montgomery calls for "the rejection of contemporary theology's so-called hermeneutical circle."[162] He writes, "the preacher must not make the appalling mistake of thinking, as do followers of Bultmann and post-Bultmann new hermeneutic, that the text and one's own experience enter into a relationship of mutuality. . . . To bind text and exegete into a circle is not only to put all theology and preaching into the orbit of anthropocentric sinful-

158. J. L. Austin, *How to Do Things with Words* (Oxford: Clarendon Press, 1962), p. 45; italics his. Cf. my essay "The Parables as Language-Event," p. 438.

159. Wilder, "The World as Address and Meaning," in *New Frontiers in Theology II*, p. 213.

160. Fuchs, "The New Testament and the Hermeneutical Problem," p. 117; italics mine.

161. Fuchs, "The New Testament and the Hermeneutical Problem," p. 114.

162. Montgomery, "An Exhortation to Exhorters," *Christianity Today* 17 (1973): 606; cf. "Toward a Christian Philosophy of History," in *Jesus of Nazareth: Saviour and Lord,* ed. C. F. H. Henry (Grand Rapids: Eerdmans, 1966), pp. 231-36.

ness, but also to remove the very possibility of a 'more sure word of prophecy' than the vagueness of men."[163]

The problem formulated by Montgomery, however, turns on epistemology, or the theory of understanding, and not upon theological considerations alone. To begin with, there are some areas of discussion in which it is possible to distinguish between "Scripture" and "interpretation of Scripture," and others in which it is not. We can and must distinguish between the two, for example, when we are discussing questions about theological method *in principle* and at a formal level. As Ebeling points out, this was important in the Reformation and for Luther. But as soon as we begin to consider a *particular text,* every way of understanding it constitutes an act of interpretation which is related to the experience of the interpreter. This is clear, for example, when we look back on Luther's handling of specific texts. On this level, it is simply philosophically naive to imply that some interpreters can have access to a self-evidently "true" meaning as over against their interpretation of it. Moreover, the interpreter's understanding, as Gadamer rightly insists, is a *progressive* one. In the words of Heinrich Ott, "there is no final black-and-white distinction between 'having understood' and 'not having understood.' . . . Understanding by its very nature takes place at different levels."[164] Thus the interpreter is in the position of a student confronted with a new textbook on a new subject. At first his preliminary understanding of the subject matter is disjointed and fragmentary, not least because he does not yet know how to question the text appropriately. Gradually, however, the text itself suggests appropriate questions, and his more mature approach to it brings greater understanding. At the same time, the parts and the whole begin to illuminate one another. But in all this the interpreter is not merely active subject scrutinizing passive object. The text "speaks" to him as its object, molding his own questions. The notion of the hermeneutical circle is not, then, a sellout to man-centered relativism, but a way of describing the *process of understanding* in the interpretation of a text.

The problem of "self-understanding" is often misunderstood. It does not simply mean man's conscious understanding of himself, but his grasp of the possibilities of being, in the context of his "world." It concerns, therefore, his *way of reacting* to life or to reality or to God and not merely his opinions about himself.[165] In one sense, therefore, it is less man-centered than is often supposed. In Ebeling's words, "when God speaks, *the whole of reality as it concerns*

163. Montgomery, "An Exhortation to Exhorters," p. 606.
164. Ott, "What Is Systematic Theology?" p. 80.
165. Fuchs, *Marburger Hermeneutik,* pp. 20, 41-47.

us enters language anew."[166] In another sense, however, it is true that a preoccupation with self-understanding may narrow and restrict the attention of the interpreter away from a wider theological and cosmic perspective. Indeed this underlines precisely the problem of one-sidedness which we have noted in connection with the task of hermeneutics, with the scope of the New Testament, and with language. We saw, for example, that Fuchs fails to do full justice to the resurrection of Christ.

(5) *The new hermeneutic is concerned above all with the "rights" of the text,* as over against concepts which the interpreter himself may try to bring with him and impose on it. A "subject-object" scrutiny of the text which takes no account of man's linguisticality tends to tame and to domesticate the word of God, so that it merely echoes the interpreter's own perspectives. By contrast, the text should challenge him, judge him and "speak" to him in its otherness. But in order that this word may be understood and "strike home," there must also be a common "world," an *Einverständnis,* in which the horizons of the text become fused with those of the interpreter.

Some further strengths and weaknesses of this rejection of mere "knowledge" and "analysis" can be seen when the new hermeneutic is set in the wider context of literary interpretation, of art, and even of educational theory. In the world of literature for example, Susan Sontag argues that interpretation impoverishes, tames, and distorts a literary creation. "Interpretation makes it manageable, comfortable." Instead of interpreting literature we ought simply "to show *how* it is what it is."[167] Similarly, R. E. Palmer sees a further attempt "to transcend the subject-object schema" in the French phenomenological literary criticism of Blanchot, Richard or Bachelard, and in the phenomenological philosophy of Ricoeur or Merleau-Ponty."[168] In the realm of art one could cite the work of Adolph Gottlieb. In education theory it is possible to see both gains and losses in the move away from concerns about "knowledge" and "information" toward an emphasis on participation, engagement, and "experience." The pupil will gain from attempts to help him to understand in terms of his own life experiences, but he may well lose as less stress is laid on the "content" part of instruction.

It is our claim that *both* aspects are important for New Testament interpretation, but that at present there is more danger of neglecting the new hermeneutic than of pressing its claims too far. Although it would be wrong to reduce its lessons simply to a few maxims for

166. Ebeling, *The Nature of Faith,* p. 190.
167. Sontag, "Against Interpretation," in *Twentieth Century Literary Criticism: A Reader,* ed. D. Lodge (London: Longman, 1972), pp. 656, 660; see pp. 652-59.
168. Palmer, *Hermeneutics,* p. 246.

preachers, nevertheless it does have something to say about preaching and basic Bible study. For example, it calls attention to the difference between talking about the *concept* of reconciliation or the *concept* of joy on the one hand, and so proclaiming the word of Christ that a man *experiences* joy or reconciliation on the other, even if these concepts are never mentioned. The preacher must concern himself with what his words effect and bring about rather than simply with what concepts they convey. The gospel must not merely be spoken and repeated; it must also be *communicated*. Similarly, in Bible study the student is not only concerned with "facts" and information but with verdicts on himself. Moreover, as he "listens" to the text he will not be content only to use stereotyped sets of questions composed by others but will engage in a *continuous* dialogue of question and answer until his own original horizons are creatively enlarged.

The otherness of the New Testament must not be tamed and domesticated in such a way that its message becomes merely a set of predictable religious "truths." Through the text of the New Testament, the word of God is to be encountered as an attack, a judgment, on any way of seeing the world which, in Fuchs's phrase, is not "seeing with God's eyes." The hermeneutical task is genuine and valid. Two sets of horizons must be brought together — those of the text and those of the modern interpreter — and this must be done at a more than merely conceptual level. Few questions can be more important than that asked by Fuchs, namely, how the text of the New Testtament, written in the ancient world, can come alive in such a way as to *strike home* in the present.

PART II

THEOLOGICAL ATTITUDES

Hermeneutical theories may be based upon or express themselves in theological attitudes. Philosophically, the study of hermeneutics relates to the rules by which a document should be interpreted. Theologically, when the document is the Bible, which is both an ancient historical collection of writings and, according to the confession of the Christian churches, in some sense "the Word of God," the hermeneutical problems are compounded. The theological factors relating to this confession of faith have given to many interpreters a special concern for developing sound hermeneutical procedures.

Two discussions of such theological attitudes and how they relate to the hermeneutical task are given in the following essays. Walter Kaiser in "Legitimate Hermeneutics" presents his views of the relation of general hermeneutics to the special hermeneutics of interpreting the biblical texts. His focus is specifically on a distinction between "meaning" and "significance." "Hermeneutics and Theology: The Legitimacy and Necessity of Hermeneutics," by Anthony Thiselton, examines the theological issue of the relationship between the Word of God and the Holy Spirit with emphasis on various theological objections to the relevance of hermeneutical inquiry. This leads to a focus on the concept of "preunderstanding" and how it may affect biblical interpretation.

In these theological attitudes we see appraisals of how the character of the Bible (from a Christian perspective) may affect one's hermeneutical stance. The theological implications of certain hermeneutical decisions can be far-reaching according to these authors. One's general hermeneutical principles, on the other hand, may need to be modified or applied to some degree in a special way when one approaches the Bible.

LEGITIMATE HERMENEUTICS

Walter C. Kaiser, Jr.

Much of the current debate over the Scriptures among believing Christians is, at its core, a result of failure on the part of evangelicals to come to terms with the issue of hermeneutics. Because we who are living in this century have been occupied with many other battles, usually not of our choosing, one issue that should have claimed our attention was neglected. Consequently, while many evangelicals may find a large amount of agreement on the doctrines of revelation, inspiration, and even canonicity, something close to a Babel of voices is heard on methods of interpreting the Scriptures.

Evangelicals are now being pressed on several sides, however, to attend to this missing part of theological curriculum. The hermeneutical debate outside our circles has grown so prolific and vigorous that at times it threatens to be, for some, the only issue. Yet the discussion may be "not less serious than that of the Reformation" itself.[1] Indeed, we believe something comparable to a hermeneutical reformation is needed in our day.

As one of the contributions that arose outside evangelical circles, the new hermeneutic of some existentialist theologians focused on the problem of transcending the historical particularity and the antique address of Scripture by stressing the words *now* and *today* and the need to recapitulate scriptural stories in the believer's present existence.[2] Meanwhile, two other offerings arose as a partial rebuke to the sterility of the liberal historical-critical approach:[3] new crit-

1. The phrase is that of Bernard Ramm, *Protestant Biblical Interpretation*, 3d rev. ed. (Grand Rapids: Baker, 1970), p. vii.
2. Especially in Kornelis Miskotte's *Zur biblischen Hermeneutik* (Zollikon: Evangelischer Verlag, 1959), pp. 42-46; and J. M. Robinson's "Hermeneutic since Barth," in *New Frontiers in Theology, II: The New Hermeneutic,* ed. J. M. Robinson and J. B. Cobb (New York: Harper & Row, 1964), pp. 1-77.
3. See E. F. Scott, "The Limitations of the Historical Method," in *Studies in Early Christianity,* ed. Shirley Jackson Case (New York: Century, 1928), p. 5; O. C. Edwards, Jr., "Historical-Critical Method's Failure of Nerve and a Prescription for a Tonic: A Review of Some Recent Literature," *Anglican Theological Review* 59 (1977): 116-17; and my essay "The Current Crisis in Exegesis and the Apostolic Use of Deuteronomy 25:4 in 1 Corinthians 9:8-10," *Journal of the Evangelical Theological Society* 21 (1978): 3-11.

Reprinted from *Inerrancy,* ed. Norman Geisler (Grand Rapids: Zondervan, 1979), pp. 117-47.

icism[4] and canon criticism.[5] In both approaches the focus of attention was on the text itself rather than on the alleged literary sources
and the reigning historical situation. As a redress to the previous
imbalances and sterility of historical-critical exegesis, these solutions would have the interpreter now concentrate on repeated phrases,
patterns, larger sense units, and the canon as a whole rather than
on individual words, tenses, and literary sources. The literature and
varieties of positions thus grew bulkier by the day, as more and
more solutions were set forth.[6]

But what of evangelicals? The time was long past for our entry
into this field once again. Already we were faced with problems
arising from an accelerated culture, not to mention our own needs
and the challenges of numerous novel hermeneutical systems. Where
was one to begin?

In our judgment, we must first return to the basics and then
make a frontal assault on the most difficult questions of interpretation faced today.

GENERAL HEMENEUTICS

No definition of interpretation could be more fundamental than this:
*To interpret we must in every case reproduce the sense the scriptural writer
intended for his own words.* The first step in the interpretive process is
to link only those ideas with the author's language that he connected
with them. The second step is to express these ideas understandably.

Yet at no point has modern society, including many evangelicals,
resisted hermeneutical rules more strenuously than at the point of
this definition. In our post-Kantian relativism, most interpreters
have concluded, as E. D. Hirsch correctly analyzes,[7] that "all
'knowledge' is relative"[8] and a return to the author's own meanings
is considered both unnecessary and wrong. Instead, meaning has
often become a personal, subjective, and changing thing. "What
speaks to me," "what turns me on," "what I get out of a text" are

4. Major exponents of the school of new criticism include R. S. Crane, Northrup
Frye, I. A. Richards, Oscar Walzel, and W. K. Wimsatt. For a definition and criti-
cism, see E. D. Hirsch, *The Aims of Interpretation* (Chicago: University of Chicago
Press, 1976), pp. 124-30.

5. On this, see Brevard S. Childs, *Biblical Theology in Crisis* (Philadelphia: Westminster, 1970), pp. 97-114; and Gerald T. Sheppard, "Canon Criticism: The Proposal
of Brevard Childs and an Assessment for Evangelical Hermeneutics," *Studia Biblica
et Theologica* 6 (1976): 3-17.

6. A fairly recent review article is Robert Lapointe's "Hermeneutics Today,"
Biblical Theology Bulletin 2 (1972): 107-54.

7. Hirsch, *Validity in Interpretation* (New Haven: Yale University Press, 1967), and
The Aims of Interpretation.

8. Hirsch, *The Aims of Interpretation,* p. 4.

the significant concerns, not what an author intended by his use of words.

But in our view, such "cognitive atheists"[9] subvert the goal of objective knowledge and threaten the very possibility of learning. All knowledge is reduced to the horizon of one's own prejudices and personal predilections. This is true whether it is done for "spiritual" or for philosophical reasons; both approaches usurp the author's revelatory stance and insert one's own authority for his. Our generation will be delivered from this kind of outrageous interpretive solipsism only if we adopt the earlier distinction of E. D. Hirsch between meaning and significance:

> *Meaning* is that which is represented by a text; it is what the author meant by his use of a particular sign sequence; it is what the signs represent. *Significance,* on the other hand, names a relationship between that meaning and a person, or a conception or a situation.[10]

Only by maintaining these definitions and distinctions will Scripture be delivered from the hands of its enemies — and its friends. All our own notions of truth and principle must be set aside in favor of those the sacred writers taught if we are to be valid interpreters. In fact, the basic teaching of all of sacred theology is inseparably connected with the results of our hermeneutics; for what is that theology except what Scripture teaches? And the way to ascertain what Scripture teaches is to apply the rules and principles of interpretation. Therefore it is imperative that these rules be properly grounded and that their application be skillfully and faithfully applied. If the foundation itself is conjecture, imagination, or error, what more can be hoped for what is built on it?

The Bible Is to Be Interpreted by the Same Rules as Other Books

Now it may be laid down as a first rule that the Bible is to be interpreted in the same manner and with the same principles as all other books. Of course, we mean by this the manner they were interpreted before the literary revolution that came in 1946, which autocratically announced the autonomy of a work, that is, its freedom from its author, and which reversal E. D. Hirsch sought to rectify in his *Validity in Interpretation.*

But some will object that the Bible is not a common or profane book. It deals with supernatural things; therefore it ought to be treated separately from other books. While it is a fact that it is a unique revelation containing supernatural things that no human

---

9. Hirsch, *The Aims of Interpretation,* pp. 4, 36, and 49.

10. Hirsch, *Validity in Interpretation,* p. 8. Unfortunately, even Hirsch undermines his own judgments in his later work *The Aims of Interpretation*; see my essay "The Current Crisis in Exegesis . . . ," pp. 3-4.

may aspire to know on his own, yet the above conclusion, often drawn from this agreed-on fact, is not necessary. After all, it is a *revelation* to us that God deliberately designed to communicate to human beings what they themselves could not or would not know unless they received it from him. To deny this is to say that God gave a revelation in which nothing is revealed or that the disclosure of God is also a concealment! It reverses the meaning of words and of reality itself.

More recently, another objection has been voiced. To insist that Scripture is to be read like any other book, some maintain, cuts at the heart of understanding Scripture's unique status and how it continues to function as a norm in a religious community. The rules must be loose enough to allow altogether new "meanings" to be attached to the ancient words if they are to function for people removed from the original audience by several thousand years.[11] But this is to confuse the very distinction Hirsch makes between *meaning* and *significance*. Past particularity must not be transcended by substituting present significance as the new meaning of the text, for then the chasm between the "then" and "now" of the text is jumped too facilely and at terrible cost. One must sacrifice all objectivism and divine authority. The price is too high.

The point remains. God has deliberately decided to accommodate mankind by disclosing himself in our language and according to the mode to which we are accustomed in other literary productions. While the content is vastly different, the medium of language is identical.

The Principles of Interpretation Are as Native and Universal to Man as Is Speech Itself[12]

A second rule is that man's basic ability to interpret is not derived from some science, technical skill, or exotic course open only to the more gifted intellects of a society. The general principles of interpreting are not learned, invented, or discovered by people. They are part and parcel of the nature of man as a being made in the image of God. Given the gift of communication and speech itself, man already began to practice the the principles of hermeneutics. The art has been in use from the moment God spoke to Adam in the Garden, and from the time Adam addressed Eve, until the present. In human conversation, the speaker is always the author; the person

---

11. Sheppard, "Canon Criticism," p. 17.

12. I am indebted for many of my ideas in these rules to Moses Stuart; see his "Remarks on Hahn's Definition of Interpretation and Some Topics Connected with It," *The Biblical Repository* 1 (1831): 139-59; and "Are the Same Principles of Interpretation to Be Applied to the Scripture as to Other Books?" *The Biblical Repository* 2 (1832): 124-37.

spoken to is always the interpreter. Correct understanding must always begin with the meanings the speaker attaches to his own words.

It is agreed that proper interpretation is more than a native art. The science of hermeneutics collects these observed rules as already practiced by native speakers and arranges them in an orderly way for the purpose of study and reflection. But such a science does not alter the fact that the rules were in operation before they were codified and examined. The situation here is exactly as it is with grammars and dictionaries: they do not prescribe what a language must do; they only describe how its best speakers and writers use it. So it is with hermeneutics.

But all this sounds too facile to match the experience of many who have wrestled with the Greek, Hebrew, and Aramaic of the original text of Scripture. How can the art of interpretation be of such a common-sense variety when it seems to be so dependent on great learning and dedicated study, placing the interpreter, as it does, back into the government, climate, society, and religious conditions of biblical times? How can we accurately hear the prophets and apostles without possessing a good command of Hebrew and Greek? Is not the object of language study to place the interpreter as close as possible to the times and thought of the sacred writers? But does not such study then contradict our second rule stated above?

On the contrary, this study is only preparatory, an antecedent for the task of hermeneutics, which still must follow. Never can any or all of this learning and study be substituted for actual interpretation or by itself constitute the science of hermeneutics. If birth and providence has so favored us that we were part of the culture and language when one or another of the prophets or apostles spoke, we could dispense with all background and language study. We would understand these areas as immediately as we now understand speakers and writers in our own day, basically without the aid of encyclopedias, grammars, dictionaries, and geographies. It is only the passing of time that has rendered these additional steps necessary for those who must not only declare what is transparently clear on the surface of Scripture with regard to our salvation (the perspicuity of Scripture, about which more later) but must also teach the full counsel of God.

True, scholars have occasionally in the science of general hermeneutics laid down rules that depart from the principles known to us by virtue of the image of God and the gift of communication. Fortunately, however, their recognition has been short-lived, and more reliable leaders have arisen to call for a return to rules that do not violate what God-given *nature* has taught, *art* has practiced, and *science* has collected and arranged in systems.

A good deal of learning is sometimes necessary to understand words that we do not ordinarily know from daily experience. We must study those words until they become as much a part of us as our native vocabulary. But the principles for interpreting these foreign Hebrew and Greek words is not different from the principles for interpreting those of our normal conversations.

It would be wrong, of course, to argue that everyone is automatically and totally successful in the *practice* of hermeneutical art just because it is an integral part of the gift of communication. Surely there are conversations and books that are difficult for some persons to understand because the words and general subject are not "part of the person" as yet. Here again learning is necessary. Yet the basic rules remain the same, whether the language is Isaiah's Hebrew, Virgil's Latin, Paul's Greek, or Shakespeare's English.

My Personal Reception and Application of an Author's Words Is a Distinct and Secondary Act from the Need First to Understand His Words

The "significance" of a literary work indicates a *relationship* between the "meaning" intended by the author in his use of a certain sequence of words and some person, idea, or situation — as Hirsch so aptly contends in the definition already given. It is wrong, therefore, to confuse meaning and significance.

But some will contend that it is God who speaks in the Bible and not men; the men who wrote the Scriptures were the mere receptacles of what God wanted to say through them. Revelation, in this view, perhaps concealed as much from the authors as it made known to them. Therefore the normal rules of interpretation do not apply.

The answer to this charge is easy. What God spoke, he spoke in human, not heavenly, language! Moreover, he spoke through the vocabularies, idioms, circumstances, and personalities of each of the chosen writers. Try translating each of the writers of Scripture, and this difference will be immediately apparent. You will wear out a lexicon looking up new Hebrew words in Job and Hosea, but you will read Genesis and Haggai with delightful speed and ease. The Greek grammar of the book of Hebrews slows down even experienced translators to a snail's pace, but John's Gospel poses few grammatical problems. No, the superiority of the Scriptures over other books does not come in the *manner* we interpret it but in its *matter* and grand source.

Still, it will be argued that "the man without the Spirit does not accept the things that comes from the Spirit of God . . . and he cannot understand them, because they are spiritually discerned" (1 Cor. 2:14). Surely, it is contended, the Bible calls for a different set of rules. A person must be spiritually enlightened before he can understand Scripture.

The case is overstated, however. It is not as if there were two logics and two hermeneutics in the world, one natural and the other spiritual. Paul's point (in 1 Cor. 2:14) has to do with the personal application and significance of the understood and basic meaning of his words. It is also true, of course, that a person must be in a sympathetic state of mind and in a proper mental condition to begin to understand subjects toward which he is not naturally inclined — whether those subjects are astrophysics, mathematics, poetry, or the Bible. Consequently, Paul's word cannot be used to claim that people without the Spirit do not understand any part of the Bible until they become spiritual. Such a claim plainly contradicts both our own experience and the teachings of Scripture that man will also be judged for rejecting that which Scripture itself declares should be abundantly clear to them, because they refuse to receive it. A professor at the university I attended gave one of the best explanations of Romans 1–6 I have ever heard, but when he was asked by a skeptical student if he "believed that stuff," he scoffed and mockingly replied, "Who said anything about personally believing it? I just said that's what Paul said, and you better remember that's what he said!" He understood Romans well enough to teach it, but he didn't "buy" it. He did not accept it because he refused to see any relationship between the text and himself. We believe it is the special work of the Holy Spirit to convict people so that they see that relationship and believe and act accordingly. But it does not contradict the fact that God means for his revelation to be understood.

One more attempt is made to break this third rule of general hermeneutics. It suggests that the prophets confessed that they themselves sometimes did not understand the words they wrote. Why then should we attempt to return to the human author's meanings when they confessed their own ignorance (e.g., 1 Pet. 1:10-12)?

I have examined this problem and the text of 1 Peter 1:10-12 in two other works.[13] I strongly affirm that the prophets claimed ignorance only on the matter of *time*. They decisively affirm that they knew five rather precise components of salvation. They knew they were writing about (1) the Messiah, (2) his sufferings, (3) his glorified state yet to come, (4) the precedence of his suffering to his glory, and (5) the application of the salvation they announced in pre-Christian days as being not only to themselves but also to those

13. See my essays "The Eschatological Hermeneutics of Evangelicalism: Promise Theology," *Journal of the Evangelical Theological Society* 13 (1970): 94-96, and "The Single Intent of Scripture," in *Evangelical Roots: A Tribute to Wilbur Smith*, ed. Kenneth Kantzer (Nashville: Nelson, 1978), pp. 125-26.

in the Christian era! Scholars err badly when they translate the Greek phrase *eis tina ē poion kairon* ("what [time] or what manner of time") as if it meant "what [person]!" The Revised Standard Version, the New American Standard Bible, the Modern Language Bible, and the New English Bible (footnote) are definitely incorrect here. It is a grammatical impossibility! The passage teaches that these men were most aware of what they were writing.

The same arguments can be raised against the attempt to use Daniel 12:6-8 to prove that Daniel had no idea what he was predicting there, using Caiaphas's prediction that "one man must die for the nation" (John 11:49-52) to prove that men can make unconscious predictions and extreme interpretations of Peter's claim that "no prophecy of Scripture is of any private loosing" (2 Pet. 1:10-21).[14]

Some will cite the promises of our Lord that the Holy Spirit will "teach *you* all things" (John 14:26), "take from what is mine and make it known to *you*" (John 16:15), and "will guide *you* into all truth" (John 16:13).[15] These verses, however, were spoken only to the Lord's disciples and they specifically constitute the promise regarding the New Testament canon. If some should complain that this so severely restricts the "you" of this text that other instructions, such as the Great Commission, would thereby be similarly restricted, I reply, as did William Carey to his generation (who preferred to leave the work of discipling all nations to the first disciples of Jesus), by saying that the divine intention in Matthew 28 is a universal "you." The text continues, "And surely I will be with you [i.e., *all* believers] always, to the very end of the age." Where such extension is made, we must make it also. But where a command or promise is restricted to others (as in John 14:25-26; 15:2-27; and 16:12-15), we must not expropriate it and arrogantly declare that, by a miracle of the Spirit's special revelation of the meaning of biblical passages, we are spared the difficult work of exegesis and interpretation!

ALLEGED EXCEPTIONS TO GENERAL HERMENEUTICAL PRINCIPLES

Some five principal bypasses have been used by various interpreters of Scripture to escape the three basic rules and the key distinction between meaning and significance already set forth in this essay: (1) allegorical interpretation, (2) overdependence on the principle of the "perspicuity of Scripture," (3) improper use of the principle of "progressive revelation," (4) unfair appropriation of the alleged free-

14. See my essay "The Single Intent of Scripture," pp. 126-33.
15. See my essay "The Single Intent of Scripture," pp. 133-34.

dom with which the New Testament writers cite the Old Testament, and (5) appeal to the implied presence of a dual sense in the messianic predictions of the Old Testament. Each of these claims must be examined, especially with a view to determining if divine revelation does indeed give some "hints" that qualify as a restriction of interpretation to the single intention of the author. Unfortunately, many hope that such procedures will protect their Bibles from errors and allow them to claim the doctrine of inerrancy with good conscience, while others are left only with what they call the mere letter of the text.[16]

Allegorical Interpretation

This method of explaining Scripture adopts as its ruling idea the principle that certain words have another meaning besides their natural one. Those who hold this view say either (1) that many passages of Scripture have, in addition to the literal (grammatical-historical) sense, a hidden (deeper, higher spiritual) sense or (2) that Scripture has, besides the simple literal meaning, another deeper sense *under* the literal one, a *hypomoia*. Both views produce the same results, except that the second is a little more sophisticated in its approach.

The source for this pattern of thinking is not Scripture. It is built mostly on a so-called doctrine of correspondences, in which there is said to be a correspondence between the earthly or natural world and the heavenly or spiritual realm. The former produces correct and perfect analogies of the latter. This concept, of course, is clearly seen in ancient Platonic thought, where things of the visible world are only shadows of invisible and higher images. The Greeks adopted the view out of expediency and desperation as a tactic to conceal, excuse, and even venerate the mythological exploits of their gods and men, which were no longer accepted as literal. Likewise some Jewish philosophers, theosophists, and Pharisees found the method useful for deriving their own opinions and patterns of thinking from texts that otherwise would have resisted the boldest hermeneutical assaults.

No less vulnerable is much present-day evangelical preaching and teaching, which is often superficial and frothy because of failure to spend enough time with the text and patiently hear what it is

16. This brings us the infamous interpretation of the dichotomy between the "letter" and the "spirit" of Scripture attributed to 2 Corinthians 3:6 and Romans 2:29 and 7:6. We reject this interpretation, however, as failing to understand at all what Paul meant in these passages. See my essays "The Single Intent of Scripture," pp. 134-36, and "The Weightier and Lighter Matters of the Law," in *Current Issues in Biblical and Patristic Interpretation*, ed. Gerald Hawthorne (Grand Rapids: Eerdmans, 1975), pp. 187-88.

saying first—rather than out of any overt embarrassment about the literal claims of an allegedly defunct Scripture. This method of sermonizing opens up an easy path—particularly for quick, adroit, fanciful, but lazy minds who, under pretense of truth and righteousness, teach *what* they will from *where* they will in Scripture. Fortunately for the church, little immediate harm is done in most cases (other than teaching poor methodology and starving God's people of the full counsel of God). Most evangelical practitioners of this method merely "gather wool" from various passages and then import the ideas into unnatural biblical contexts.

However, there is a serious wing of conservative interpreters who claim that the dual meaning of Scripture can in principle be argued from the fact that there is a dual set of authors for every text—namely, God and the writer. Still others allege that Scripture itself recommends this method by giving us two examples of "mild allegory" in Galatians 4:19-26 and 1 Corinthians 9:8-10.[17]

The first argument for dual authorship we have already dealt with, and we have examined at length 1 Corinthians 9:8-10 elsewhere.[18] But Galatians 4:22-26 appears at first blush to support the case. Two rejoinders may be made. First, in Galatians 4:20 Paul confesses that he is somewhat hesitant as to just how he should address the Galatians but that he will now explain his point to them in their own way (*allaxai tēn phōnēn mou*),[19] using the Genesis story

17. Among those arguing for the existence of such "mild allegory" is Richard Longenecker in his *Biblical Exegesis in the Apostolic Period* (Grand Rapids: Eerdmans, 1975), p. 126. In fairness to Longenecker, I should say, however, that he explicitly wants to limit such allegorical privileges to the apostles due to their "revelatory stance." Whether he can convince others to do so is another problem.

For a good discussion of the Galatians passage, see Robert J. Kepple, "An Analysis of Antiochene Exegesis of Galatians 4:24-26," *Westminster Theological Journal* 39 (1977): 239-49.

18. See my essay "The Current Crisis in Exegesis . . . ," pp. 11-18.

19. This phrase is generally translated "and to change my voice tone." Yet Augustus Hahn has argued that the change was from argument to accommodating the Galatians in their own allegories so they could see Paul's preceding point (see Hahn, "On the Grammatico-Historical Interpretation of the Scriptures," *The Biblical Repository* 1 [1831]: 133). This suggestion should not be dismissed, as is almost universally done by commentators. "My little children," urges Paul, "I could wish indeed that I were present now with you, but to change my tone (let me put it to you this way) . . . all these classes of things can be allegorized (as follows)." In other words, his tone may well indicate his substance as well as his manner. Hahn's full quote is, *"Gladly were I now with you, my children, and would speak with each of you in particular, according to his special wants, consequently, with each one differently,* in order to convince each of you after his own opinions and prejudices, that his union of Judaism with Christianity is to be rejected. . . . For I am hesitating in respect to you; i.e., doubtful how I shall rightly address you. But ye now, who would gladly retain the yoke of Judaism (and how the Judaizing teachers and their Rabbins allegorized is well known), tell me, do you understand the law? I will explain it then to you—*allaxai ten phonen*—in your own way; in order thus to convince you. . . ."

of Sarah and Hagar as an illustration to suit better their rabbinical tastes. Second, as Ellicott observed, Galatians 4:24 warns that Paul merely borrowed the Old Testament account as an illustration; he was not exegeting it. He clearly says *"all which class of things"* (*hatina*) viewed in the most general way "may be put into an allegory" (*estin allēgoroumena*).[20] Paul supplies no comfort, either in this text or in 1 Corinthians 9:8-10, for an allegorical practice.

Surprisingly enough, what some interpreters label as the spiritual, deeper, or higher sense is often nothing more than the real and proper sense that the writer intended. For example, when Paul, in 1 Corinthians 10, mentions that Christ led the Israelites in the desert and gave them food and water, he is only pointing out that Christ was the angel of God in whom God had placed his name (Exod. 23:20-21; cf. 17:6). In fact even the theophoric name *Rock* of 1 Corinthians 10 is Mosaic (Deut. 32:4, 15, 18; 32:31). Our problem often is that we do not know the Old Testament well enough to recognize it in the New.

Another problem is that the word *literal* too frequently is automatically linked with features of the text that deal solely with the physical and the material. This practice is unjustifiable. No meaning of a text is complete until the interpreter has heard the *total single* intention of the author, who stood in the presence of God. Thus the command "Thou shalt not murder" does not simply forbid the overt act itself but also forbids every thought and emotion that may lead to murder. It likewise encourages every positive act whereby one seeks to promote and enhance the lives of one's fellow beings, as seen in subsequent examples given in the "Covenant Code" of Exodus 21–23. These are not double or triple senses of the literal meaning but together give the full sense included in the author's *single* meaning. This truth can be demonstrated from the antecedent revelations of God against which background new words are given. The portion of Scripture available to writers at a given time acted as an informing theology.

We conclude, therefore, that the so-called "literal" interpretation must include the same *depth* of meaning as the writer himself included. The interpretation is controlled by the words the writer uses, by the range of meaning he gives to those words as judged by his usage elsewhere, by the total context of his thought, and by the preceding revealed theology in existence when he wrote and to which

20. Not only Ellicott but also John Eadie makes the point that this text does not say "which things have been allegorized" already, but that the whole class of these things in Genesis may be group and allegorized now (present participle) for the present purposes (*Epistle to the Galatians* [Edinburgh: T. & T. Clark, 1884], p. 359).

he explicitly refers or clearly alludes by his use of phrases, concepts, or terms that were then generally known and accepted.

Another species of allegorical argument views the Old Testament as containing the New Testament "under a *veil*." We will deal with this argument in more detail shortly, but for the present, we conclude that the allegorical method cannot be established as a legitimate means for interpreting Scripture. While Scripture itself sometimes uses allegory (e.g., Prov. 5:15-19), such uses are clearly marked by the writer's intention and not the interpreter's wish, however sincere. Only in these instances may the interpreter employ the rules for interpreting allegory.

The Principle of the Perspicuity of Scripture

The principle of perspicuity means simply that the Bible is sufficiently clear in and of itself for believers to understand it. As J. Stafford Wright has stated, the principle implies three things: (1) "Scripture is clear enough for the simplest person to live by it," (2) "Scripture is deep enough to form an inexhaustible mine for readers of the highest intellectual capacity," and (3) the perspicuity of the Scriptures resides in the fact that God "intend[ed] all Scripture to be revelation of Himself to man."[21] Thus, just as the natural order is sufficiently simple for the ordinary person to live in it without being aware of all that the physical and natural scientist knows, so the spiritual order is sufficiently clear. The comparison is more than accidental.

But this principle may be overextended if it is used as an excuse against further investigation and strenuous study by believers who were not contemporaries of the prophets and apostles who first spoke the Word of God. Scripture, in any faithful translation, is sufficiently perspicuous (clear) to show us our sinfulness, the basic facts of the gospel, what we must do if we are to be part of the family of God, and how to live for Christ. This does not mean, however, that in seeing (and even understanding) these truths we have exhausted the teaching of Scripture. Neither does it imply that the solution to every difficult question in Scripture or life is simple, much less simplistic. It only affirms that, despite the difficulties we find in Scripture, there is more than enough that is plainly taught to keep all believers well nourished.[22]

21. Wright, "The Perspicuity of Scripture," *Theological Students Fellowship Letter*, Summer 1959, p. 6.

22. Bishop Herbert Marsh explains: "When [the Reformers] argued for the perspicuity of the Bible, they intended not to argue against the application of *learning*, but against the application of *tradition* to the exposition of Scripture. . . . In rejecting *tradition* as necessary to make the Bible perspicuous, they never meant to declare that the Bible was alike perspicuous [in its total message] to the *learned* and unlearned" (*A Course of Letters . . . in Theological Learning* [Boston: Cummings & Hilliard, 1815], p. 18; italics his).

A story attributed to Dwight L. Moody related that he was once accosted by a woman who asked in a complaining tone, "Mr. Moody, what shall I do about the hard things I can't understand in the Bible?" He replied, "Madam, have you ever eaten chicken?" Somewhat upset by this *non sequitur,* she hesitantly replied, "Ye-es." "What did you do with the bones?" interrupted Moody. "I put them on the side of my plate," she responded. "Then put the difficult verses there also," advised Moody; "there's more than enough food to digest in the rest that you *can* understand." This is the principle of perspicuity.

Two related problems, however, must be raised: (1) How can the principle of perspicuity be squared with the wide divergence of scriptural interpretations in Christendom, even among equally committed believers? and (2) Why should so much emphasis be placed on advanced training of teachers, preachers, and other interpreters in Christ's church when all believers have an anointing from the Holy Spirit, by which they know the truth (1 John 2:20)? In both of these instances, if perspicuity is pressed beyond what is intended in its proper definition, it becomes a magic wand that gives the interpreter not just sufficient and adequate answers for salvation and living but a kind of total knowledge of Scripture.

To answer the first question more specifically, we must point out that the amount of agreement in Christendom is really large and impressive—and it exists precisely in those areas and in those church councils where patient listening to large blocks of biblical texts has been uppermost. When, however, tradition or certain patterns of thinking were required as prior commitments to the hearing of the Word of God itself, the Word became bound. It was forced to serve these systems, traditions, and hermeneutics. More subtle differences between believers may be caused by overemphasis of certain truths or parts of Scripture. God may certainly raise up a person or group to emphasize a neglected truth. But once this truth is generally recognized, continued special emphasis tends to produce imbalance. What was formerly underemphasized is now overemphasized. Sometimes lack of candor prevents us from distinguishing truths from those that are primarily descriptive and are especially cherished for personal and historical reasons.

The second question is more serious. First John 2:20 was not meant to deny the need for explaining some texts. If it did, then this very letter of John would violate its own teaching. The teaching of 1 John about the anointing of the Holy Spirit is similar to that of 1 Corinthians 2 about the spiritual person's reception of the Word. Ideally, a believer should not need to be urged by teachers to make personal application of clear scriptural teachings or be urged to see their wider and fuller significance. But application and comprehension should not be confused with interpretation. Furthermore, is it not true that the more removed a reader is from the original languages and from the times in which the biblical authors wrote, the greater will be his need for specially trained teachers and various other kinds of assistance?

We need to recall the system of checks and balances used by the Reformers to grapple with the very problem we face here. They argued for the priesthood of believers (for it was taught in Scripture and embodied the truth of the perspicuity of Scripture), but they also insisted that the final court of appeal was the original languages in which Scripture was written. It was the prophets and apostles, not we, who stood in the counsel of God and received his precise Word. Our generation must reflect the same balance or we will suffer for our recklessness.

The Principle of Progressive Revelation

One of the chief areas of concern for interpreters of Scripture is that of the progressiveness of revelation, especially as it bears on certain moral issues. Unfortunately, despite the popularity of the term, not all are agreed on exactly what is meant by progressive revelation.

C. H. Dodd devoted a key chapter in his book *The Authority of the Bible* to showing that Jesus Christ was "the climax to a whole complex process which we have traced in the Bible," and since this process was "of the highest spiritual worth, . . . we must recognize it in the fullest sense as a revelation of God."[23] For liberal Protestants, the phrase "progressive revelation" is important for three reasons. (1) From a critical standpoint, the idea tends to downgrade, and label as late or unauthentic, those elements scholars are most skeptical about, while it elevates the "highest" truths of Scripture. Thus, liberal scholars have a standard by which to correct or negate the "baser elements" of Scripture. (2) Similarly, from an apologetic standpoint the term gives a rationale by which one can excuse and justify the more "primitive" morality of the Bible by means of later revelation that allegedly corrects it. (3) From a theological standpoint, progressive revelation often becomes a slogan for the arbitrary and inconsistent process of selecting a favored few teachings out of the total history of biblical revelation and drawing the doctrines of the Bible from these.[24]

Yet, when all is said and done, the implied and explicit claims in

23. Dodd, *The Authority of the Bible* (London: Fontana, 1960), p. 263. This volume was originally published in 1928, with revised editions appearing in 1938 and 1960. In those days "progressive revelation" was "a current phrase" (p. 248; for Dodd's whole discussion, see pp. 248-63).

24. This analysis is dependent on James Barr's discussion in *The Bible in the Modern World* (New York: Harper & Row, 1973), pp. 144-46. I am also indebted to J. I. Packer for almost the same analysis in "An Evangelical View of Progressive Revelation," in *Evangelical Roots*, pp. 143-58, especially 146-48.

the liberal's use of the phrase do not answer our problem. Certainly everyone agrees that a revelation that has been mediated throughout an expanse of history must necessarily have been progressive in some sense. But this then raises the key question: How much accommodation of the *message* was involved? Even if we are convinced, as we should be, that the revelation of God was, from the very inception of the Old Testament, of the loftiest type, a serious difficulty still remains. What about those teachings or records that appear to involve God himself in a practice that later revelation decries? Abraham is commanded by God to sacrifice his son Isaac; Deborah, a prophetess, pronounces Jael blessed when she literally nails Sisera down; Moses' teaching includes provisions for slavery and divorce; Joshua is commanded to totally wipe out all Canaanites; and David, "the sweet psalmist of Israel," invokes curses on his enemies and prays for their destruction.[25] The problems are well known. The answers are not!

It is not enough, nor is it an adequate response, to note that a good deal of the morality described in that earlier age fell under the judgment of God. It is a fact that Jesus did not regard the Mosaic law on divorce as superseding the earlier statements in Genesis but declared that it was given because of the hardness of men's hearts. It is also true that, though polygamy and unchastity are plainly described, they are only that—descriptions of the sins of mankind.[26]

Neither is it proper to accept the critical solution, with its out-

25. Those who believe there was direct or implied permission for polygamy in the Old Testament usually point to three passages—Exodus 21:7-11; Deuteronomy 21:15-17; and 2 Samuel 12:7-8. The first passage is cleared up in modern versions that follow the Hebrew text with its "not" in verse 8 instead of following the LXX as some earlier English versions did; by omitting "wife" in verse 10, since there is no Hebrew word for it there; and by properly rendering the Hebrew of the rest of verse 10 as "her food, clothing, and lodging," *not* "her food, clothing, and marital rights." In Deuteronomy 21:16-17 the problem is again a translation problem as can be seen from the identical translation of the various versions of the Polyglot and the identical tense in the Hebrew in the compound clause "If a man *has* two wives . . . and they *have* borne him sons. . . ." Thus Moses rules not on a man who currently has two wives, but on one who has had two. Finally, 2 Samuel 12:7-8: Saul's wives Ahinoam (mother of David's wife Michal) and Rizpah are never listed as David's wives. In fact, had God authorized David to marry Ahinoam, it would have violated the prohibition against incest specifically stated in Levitical law and backed with a threat of burning for its violation; thus the phrase in 2 Samuel means nothing more than the fact that God delivered everything Saul had into David's hands, yet he stole from Uriah! See the very perceptive work by S. E. Dwight, *The Hebrew Wife: or, The Law of Marriage Examined in Relation to the Lawfulness of Polygamy and to the Extent of the Law of Incest* (New York: Leavitt, 1836), pp. 14-24.

26. The list of sins is a modified version of the list provided by James Orr in *The Problem of the Old Testament* (London: Nisbet, 1909), p. 466. See also H. S. Curr, "Progressive Revelation," *Journal of the Transactions of the Victorian Institute* 83 (1951): 1-23, especially p. 7.

right denial of the revelation of God, that limits these so-called mistaken notions to the human writers, who speculated according to the best light they possessed. Nor can we allegorize all problem passages and attempt to overlook their plain statements. There are enough problems without adding to them.

A whole treatise on the ethics of the Old Testament would be necessary to deal adequately with the issues raised here, but for now let it be suggested that the best response still is given in the 1929 Princeton lectures on ethics given by William Brenton Greene, Jr.[27]

Nevertheless, we will deal with the issues presented by the progress of revelation insofar as they bear on the subject of scriptural interpretation. It seems in order to make the following observations:

1. Whenever the charge is leveled that *God* is depicted in the Old Testament as vengeful, hateful, partial to a few favorites, and even vindictive, let the interpreter beware. He must strive all the more to understand both the words used and the concepts appealed to by the biblical writers. For example, the common depiction of Yahweh as a vengeful and wrathful God is relieved by a fair understanding of the meaning and use of the Hebrew *naqam*. When George Mendenhall studied this term, he concluded that "if we analyze the actual word uses that have supported the ideas of blood vengeance held by many modern scholars, the results are simply incompatible both with the ideas of primitive tribal organization and the concept of God that have long been considered to be self-evident."[28] According to Mendenhall's studies, God's vengeance is no more than the exercise of responsible sovereignty. So it is with the wrath and hate of God. Abraham Heschel devotes a large segment of his book *The Prophets* to the problem of divine wrath and concludes that it is a problem for us because of the associations we now have with the word *anger* or *wrath* and not because of the meanings of the biblical writers.[29]

2. The interpreter must distinguish what the Bible teaches and approves from what it merely reports or records. The lies of Shiphrah, Puah, and Rahab are just that: lies. Nevertheless, the women themselves are approved on other grounds — for heroic acts of faith. We must be aware that approval of *one* act or characteristic is not an endorsement of a biblical individual in *all* that he does or is. Abraham and David are guilty of great lapses of faith, yet they are nonetheless used, and even especially commended. by God.

27. Greene, "The Ethics of the Old Testament," *Princeton Theological Review* 27 (1929): 153-92, 313-66.

28. Mendenhall, "The 'Vengeance' of Yahweh," in *The Tenth Generation* (Baltimore: The Johns Hopkins University Press, 1973), p. 70.

29. Heschel, *The Prophets* (New York: Harper & Row, 1962), pp. 279-306.

3. The Scriptures' own assessment of a thing must be preferred to our own offhand impressions. Thievery is not approved in the Israelites' massive "borrowing" from the Egyptians. The word ša'al means they "asked" for jewels and precious ornaments from the Egyptians. God then gave his people favor in their oppressors' eyes. Likewise believers must not try to plead the case for the condemned Canaanites and Amalekites (Gen. 9:25-27; Exod. 17:14-16) without first understanding how long the righteous patience of God has endured the sinful outrages and continuation of their eponymous hero's own sexual perversions (Gen. 9:22) and their barbaric form of attack on the sick, elderly, and defenseless. Here again the solution is not in evolutionary arrangement of revelation and morality but in letting the text itself speak clearly and fully.

4. The prayers of imprecation in the Old Testament (and New Testament!—2 Tim. 4:14; Gal. 5:12; Rev. 6:10) must be understood as couched in any inbred hatred for sin and wickedness wherever it occurs. They should also be interpreted in the light of the writer's earnest wish that all attacks on the kingdom of God receive such public and stinging rebuke that they will not impede God's imminent triumph over all evil. And again, hardly a single curse in one of the sixty-five verses of imprecation in the whole Psalter cannot be found elsewhere in the Bible as a declarative sentence or a simple statement of fact as to what the fate of the cause and persons of wickedness will be![30]

Progressive revelation, rightly understood, does not open the door to the idea that inferior revelations were a prelude to more satisfactory and less embarrassing later revelations. This concept of progress and accommodation derives from philosophic ideas imported from our culture. As James Orr concludes (in a better part of his essay),

> Revelation can be held responsible only for *the new element which it introduces*. . . . Revelation . . . implants a truth, constitutes a relation, establishes a principle, which may have a whole rich content implicit in it, but it cannot convey to the recipient from the first a full, all-around apprehension of everything that principle involves.[31]

---

30. See the exceptionally fine article by Chalmers Martin, "Imprecations in the Psalms," *Princeton Theological Review* 1 (1903): 537-53. On the most offensive of all Psalms (137), we see Howard Osgood's "Dashing the Little Ones against the Rock," *Princeton Theological Review* 1 (1903): 23-37.

31. Orr, *The Problem of the Old Testament*, p. 473; italics his.

Surely, in every case the total subject to which a revelation belongs is greater by far than any single revelation that contributes to that subject!

The Precedent of New Testament Quotations of the Old Testament

A widespread school of thought today emphasizes the point that New Testament authors were often extremely free in their use of Old Testament texts. This school generally follows the thought that leading rabbinical practice in New Testament times allowed pesher, midrashic, or multiple senses in interpreting biblical passages. Some modern evangelical scholars affirm, on shaky hermeneutical grounds, that the rather free New Testament quotation of the Old Testament sets for us a precedent that allows for a "fuller sense" (the Catholic contribution of *sensus plenior*) of the Old Testament text than what the original Old Testament human authors intended or understood. Some, knowing what a Pandora's box this opens up for hermeneutics, have tried to insist that this privilege be restricted to the New Testament writers alone, since they had a "revelatory stance."[32] The problem, however, is that many who hold the "fuller sense" point of view often do not heed this qualification and argue that what was good enough for the apostles will certainly also produce good results for them as teachers and preachers of the Word. The issue must be faced.

To be fair, we must limit our discussion solely to those passages where the New Testament writers were in debate with the Jews or where they invoked the authority of the Old Testament. If in these passages we claim some fuller or secondary sense as an authoritative interpretation of the text, it becomes clear that our wish is parent to the thought. This hermeneutical principle must then be acknowledged to be a priori, as it is in Richard Longenecker's masterful presentation:

> The Jewish roots of Christianity make it *a priori* likely that the exegetical procedures of the New Testament would resemble to some extent those of then [sic] contemporary Judaism. This has long been established with regard to the hermeneutics of Paul and the Talmud, and it is becoming increasingly evident with respect to the Qumran texts as well.[33]

---

32. See Richard N. Longenecker, *Biblical Exegesis in the Apostolic Period* (Grand Rapids: Eerdmans, 1975), p. 218. See also the similar but less cautious approach of Donald A. Hagner in his essay "The Old Testament in the New Testament," in *Interpreting the Word of God*, ed. Samuel Schultz and Morris Inch (Chicago: Moody, 1976), pp. 78-104. As an example of one who takes his cue from this principle and asserts that "the necessity of recognizing the mystical sense is quite evident from the way in which the New Testament interprets the Old," see Louis Berkhof, *Principles of Biblical Interpretation* (Grand Rapids: Baker, 1952), pp. 140ff.

33. Longenecker, *Biblical Exegesis in the Apostolic Period*, p. 203.

It must follow, then, as Donald Hagner states, that "the true value of the arguments from the *sensus plenior* of the Old Testament is for those who are already in the household of faith."[34] Then the real problem emerges. Of what use would that "value" be to the new, struggling New Testament faith that was trying to establish its credibility, appeal, and direct continuity with the ancient predictions given through the Jews? "In-house" words were the last thing needed. As long ago as 1885, Frederic Gardiner announced,

> in all quotations which are used argumentatively, or to establish any fact or doctrine, it is obviously necessary that the passage in question should be fairly cited according to its real intent and meaning in order that the argument drawn from it may be valid. There has been much rash criticism of some of these passages, and the assertion has been unthinkingly made that the apostles, and especially St. Paul, brought up in rabbinical schools of thought, quoted the Scriptures after a rabbinical and inconsequential fashion. A patient and careful examination of the passages themselves will remove such misapprehensions.[35]

A full examination of every relevant passage cannot be attempted here, though we have elsewhere demonstrated solutions to some of these passages.[36] We can, however, list some errors that should be avoided in this area. They include (1) using the New Testament as a proving ground to identify possible predictions in earlier texts, (2) using the New Testament to set the meaning that an Old Testament text may have, (3) allowing New Testament argumentative quotation of the Old Testament to reinterpret or to supersede the original meaning and sense of the Old Testament writer, and (4) separating the doctrinal sense of a New Testament argumentative use of the Old Testament from the doctrinal sense of the Old Testament writer and thereby breaking continuity in the progress of God's revelation.

One of the chief confusions in this area results from the argument by analogy and, on top of that, the use of subsequent revelation as an exegetical tool to unlock God's Word to earlier generations. While we acknowledge that the analogy of faith has its place in the summary and conclusion of the exegetical procedure, it is totally out of place methodologically when used as a type of "divining rod" to unlock previous revelations. Words, clauses, and sentences must

34. Hagner, "The Old Testament in the New Testament," p. 103.

35. Gardiner, "The New Testament Use of the Old," in *The Old and New Testaments in Their Mutual Relations* (New York: James Pott, 1885), pp. 317-18.

36. See my essay "The Davidic Promise and the Inclusion of the Gentiles (Amos 9:9-15 and Acts 15:13-18): A Test Passage for Theological Systems," *Journal of the Evangelical Theological Society* 20 (1977): 97-111.

first be understood as the writer's own usage indicates before theological comparisons are added.

We certainly recognize that a passage may have a fuller *significance* than what was realized by the writer. We also wholeheartedly agree that the *subject* to which the Old Testament prophets made individual contributions was wider by miles than what they ever dreamed of. But the whole revelation of God as revelation hangs in jeopardy if we, an apostle, or an angel from heaven try to add to, delete, rearrange, or reassign the sense or meaning that a prophet himself received. In so doing, the friends of Scripture imperil the Scriptures as much as do her enemies. We beg the church to take another look at this area as well.

The Alleged Dual Sense of Messianic Prophecies

Closely related to the preceding topic is the question of the predictions of the Messiah in the Old Testament and their fulfillment in the New. The issue is the same as we have seen above. Milton S. Terry states it best when he affirms that "the moment we admit the principle that portions of Scripture contain an occult or double sense, we introduce an element of uncertainty in the Sacred Volume, and unsettle all scientific interpretation."[37]

In this situation, not as in some of those already examined, I suspect that the problem is one of terminology, definition, and adequate explanation that fits all the biblical data. The trouble begins when terms such as "double fulfillment" and "double reference" are used synonymously with "double sense" or "double meaning" and interpreters begin talking about an early versus a later meaning. Specific terms used in regard to this practice include "gap prophecy," "foreshortening of prophetic perspective," "generic prophecy," "corporate solidarity," and several others. Not all of these terms are bad, but they are often undefined and present the possibility for misunderstanding and misuse.

Earlier expositors tended to separate the *literal* sense in the immediate context of the prophecy and a secondary *mystical* sense in its New Testament fulfillment.[38] Our response to this practice is the same as that given above regarding the New Testament argumentative use of the Old Testament. Other expositors have included additional distinctions that need not concern us here. All who take

37. Terry, *Biblical Hermeneutics* (New York: Easton & Mains, 1883), p. 383. He there cites Owen and Ryle as supporting his view to the effect that "if Scripture has more than one meaning, it has no meaning at all." He says, "I hold that the words of Scripture were intended to have one definite sense and that our first objective should be to discover that sense, and adhere rigidly to it."

38. For example, Thomas Hartwell Horne, *Introduction to the Critical Study and Knowledge of the Holy Scriptures*, vol. 1 (New York: Robert Carter, 1859), p. 643.

this general approach focus on several specific issues: Scripture did address the generation living at the time of the original prophecy, but it also speaks of a distant fulfillment; indeed, it often includes several intermediate fulfillments, which line up with the climactic conclusion. In this lies the issue for hermeneutics.

Let us be clear about the biblical facts. When Scripture predicts a victorious "seed" for Eve and repeats that word to each of the patriarchs and each Davidite before the prophecy is fulfilled in Christ, that is a single idea with a single meaning and single sense, which also has multiple fulfillments. Moreover, that "seed" is deliberately given as a collective or corporate term. The divinely authorized meaning, as communicated by the Old Testament writers, is that believers were to share in an identity with the coming "Seed," who would be their representative. Accordingly, when Paul insisted that the "seed" in Genesis was singular and not plural (Gal. 3:16) and added that if we belong to Christ then we too are part of Abraham's "seed" (Gal. 3:29), he was neither pulling a rabbinical trick of exegesis nor giving a "fuller sense" to the text than Moses had intended in Genesis 12:3. That was the original scope of the word *seed* and also was the single intent of the Old Testament writer, even though the fulfillments were multiple and lasted over many generations. Similar single meanings with multiple fulfillments relate to other biblical terms: "firstborn," "my son" (Exod. 4:22), "servant of the Lord" (thirty-two times in Isaiah, beginning in 42:1), "your Holy One" (e.g., Ps. 16:10), and many others.

In regard to the examples given thus far, the "law of double reference" errs only when it slips in the idea of double *meaning* or when it implies that there were *only* two foci involved: the moment of the predicted word and the moment of its fulfillment in the New Testament. Nevertheless, we believe Christ's church would be better served if some other term, such as Willis J. Beecher's *generic prophecy*, were adopted. He defines a generic prophecy as

> one which regards an event as occurring in a series of parts, separated by intervals, and expresses itself in language that may apply indifferently to the nearest part, or to the remoter parts, or to the whole — in other words, a prediction which, in applying to the whole of a complex event also applies to . . . its parts.[39]

Beecher sounded an important note when he stressed that interpreters should study the historical *means* (as recorded in Scripture) that God uses to fulfill his purposes as well as the predictive word

---

39. Beecher, *The Prophets and the Promise* (Grand Rapids: Baker, 1975), p. 130.

itself and its climactic fulfillment.[40] The whole complex had a single meaning in the intention of prophet. Therefore, it would be wrong to speak of a literal sense of the ancient historic word, which was contemporaneous with its announcement, and of a deeper, mystical, or double sense that became clear when the "prediction" (?) was fulfilled. Patient and careful examination of every Old Testament prediction that we are aware of will bear out this claim.

The teaching of the *nearness* of the day of the Lord may serve as a good example. Five prophets, who spanned about four centuries, each proclaimed the day of the Lord was "near," was "at hand," and had been fulfilled at least in part—the locust plague of Joel, the destruction of Jerusalem in 586 in Isaiah and Zephaniah (Obad. 15; Joel 1:15; 2:1; Isa. 13:6; Zeph. 1:7, 14; Ezek. 30:3). They also spoke of fulfillment yet to come, when our Lord returns a second time (Joel 3:14; Zech. 14:1; cf. 2 Pet. 3:10). Thus the Day of the Lord is a generic, collective term wherein the prophet saw the near event, some of the intervening events, and the final climactic fulfillment all in a single literal sense. The case is absolutely no different whether the text is James's use of Amos 9:11 at the Jerusalem council (Acts 15:16), Isaiah's prediction of a virgin conceiving and bearing a son (Isa. 7:14), Matthew's appeal (2:15) to Hosea 11:1 ("Out of Egypt I called my son"), or Peter's appeal to Psalm 16:8-11 on the Day of Pentecost—in which, incidentally, Peter affirmed under inspiration that David, "seeing what was ahead, . . . spoke of the resurrection of the Christ" as well as of the final triumphant enthronement of his own seed when he wrote that Psalm (Acts 2:29-31). That should settle the argument for evangelicals!

SPECIAL HERMENEUTICS

If the key hermeneutical question is, as we have argued thus far, "What was the biblical author's meaning when he wrote a particular text?" then we must address ourselves to another question, which has also become troublesome for twentieth-century believers: "What are the implications of that single meaning for those who live and read that text in a different time and culture?"

One of the most distinguishing features of God's revelation is its historical element. Does not Hebrews 1:1-2 clearly declare the same? "In the past God spoke to our forefathers through the prophets at many times and in various ways, but in these last days he has spoken to us by his Son." This raises another question for contem-

40. See Beecher, *The Prophets and the Promise*, p. 361. See also my essay "Messianic Prophecies in the Old Testament," in *Dreams, Visions, and Oracles*, ed. Carl E. Amerding and W. Ward Gasque (Grand Rapids: Baker, 1977), pp. 75-88.

porary men and women: "To what extent is the relevance of the Bible limited or conditioned by the history, culture, customs, and modes of expression of the era in which the text was written?" In fact, would there not be an equation of inverse proportionality here: the more suited the text was for the original listeners and readers the less apparent and relevant its message is for subsequent readers like ourselves?

Nonevangelicals in particular have repeatedly argued that the cultures of the writers of Scripture so conditioned and bound the Word of God that it often reflects no more than the ancient views of life, history, culture, customs, religion, and the world that were current in those days. But most of this modern attitude can be attributed to a predisposed denial of revelation and supernaturalism, or to personal dislike for many of the concepts of Scripture. Accordingly, Rudolf Bultmann's program for "demythologizing" the Bible is more accurately a program for dividing Scripture into a dualism of a this-world view and an upper-world view—with the upper-world view being firmly rejected. This is no reliable solution. It is solving the issue by determining our own philosophical grid and imposing it over Scripture. The real hermeneutical work is still to be done. The author's abiding and transcultural message must be identified along with his so-called dated information. Indeed, the biblical Word did come to specific people in a specific setting during a specific time and with specific idioms. Why then should these very characteristics of revelation, which were so helpful to the people in their first reception of the message, now be used as an argument against its trustworthiness by a later generation—a generation that boasts of a knowledge superior to that of the ancients?

What are the primary areas of tension that have been generated concerning historical particularities of the text? They are (1) divine commands that are directed to special persons or isolated situations, (2) practices or customs that may merely reflect the cultural norm of the day but that nevertheless cause consternation for subsequent readers who are puzzled over the problem of whether these descriptions are really prescriptions and are still normative, and (3) use of language dealing with factual matters outside the spiritual and moral realms, such as allusions to biology, geography, and cosmology.

The most disputed section of Scripture is, of course, Genesis 1–11. Can a consistent, legitimate hermeneutic piece together the puzzles found here? Can it sustain the view of inerrancy that affirms that the *extent* of divine activity in revelation and inspiration included provision for the writer's ability both to *adequately select* and to *accurately use* words in such a way that they would in every instance reflect God's estimate, evaluation, interpretation, and point of view for mortal beings? That position will receive strenuous examination in the areas now before us.

Direct Divine Commands to Specific Individuals in Specific Situations

Frequently Scripture addresses individuals with commands such as "Take off your sandals, for the place where you are standing is holy ground" (Exod. 3:5), "Put out into deep water and let down the nets for a catch" (Luke 5:4), "Untie [the donkey and her colt] and bring them to me" (Matt. 21:2-3), and "Do not take a purse or bag or sandals; and do not greet anyone on the road" (Luke 10:4). These, obviously are commands directed to no one other than those to whom they were originally given. It must be readily acknowledged that our Lord addressed a significant number of commands and promises to his twelve disciples that do not apply (except perhaps coincidentally) to any others — as his calling certain of them to leave their occupations and follow him.

There is much in Scripture that involves the local and the temporary, but such things should not raise a barrier between ourselves and the text, much less between us and the mind of God. The best statement on this problem came from Patrick Fairbairn in 1869:

> The principle is . . . that the *particular* features in revelation, derived from its historical accompaniments, were meant to be, not to the prejudice or the subversion, but rather for the sake of its *general* interest and application. They but served to give more point to its meaning, and render more secure its presentation in the world [much as illustrations serve to clarify the truth of sermons!]. So that, instead of saying, . . . I find therein a word of God to such a person, or at such a period in the past, therefore not strictly for me; I should rather, according to the method of Scripture, say, here, at such a time to such a party, was a revelation in the mind and will of Him who is Lord of heaven and earth, made to persons of like nature and calling with myself — made indeed *to* them, but only that it might *through* them be conveyed and certified to others; and coming as it does to me, a component part of the Word, which reveals the character of the Most High.[41]

Thus what was special in person, time, or place in the letters to the churches, the Gospels, the psalmists, the prophets, or the Law, possesses special *significance* for later generations, even if the *meaning* is not directed to them. The call to remember detailed individual items relating to previous times is heard constantly from biblical writers themselves. A striking illustration is Hosea's (12:4) finding

41. Fairbairn, "The Historical Element in God's Revelation," in *Classical Evangelical Essays,* ed. Walter C. Kaiser, Jr. (Grand Rapids: Baker, 1972), pp. 74-75.

special significance for his generation, though removed by a millennium, in the Jacob-Esau birth struggle (Gen. 25:26) and in Jacob's contest with the angel of God (Gen. 32:24ff.). Hosea declared, "[Jacob] met him at Bethel and there he spoke with *us*" (Hos. 12:4 NASB). Some modern translators are so surprised by this pronoun that they arbitrarily emend it to "him," but the tactic is rebuked by numerous other biblical examples.[42] The first-person plural pronoun is also used in Hebrews 6:18, in declaring that God gave a promise (Gen. 12, 15, 17) and an oath (Gen. 22) to Abraham so that "we" might have a strong consolation! Similarly, in 1 Corinthians 9:8-10 Paul affirms that the Mosaic instruction prohibiting the muzzling of oxen when they are threshing was also addressed to the Corinthians, for it was spoken especially (*pantos*) for "our" sakes! There was no hermeneutical trickery in this type of teaching, as we have argued in detail elsewhere,[43] but it was another affirmation of the principle that past particularity (sometimes called the doctrine of *particularisms*) is no obstruction to present significance. The distinction between *meaning* and *significance*, however, must be rigidly followed. There can be little doubt, according to both biblical example and declaration, that, while not at all Scripture is addressed directly to us personally, all Scripture is given for our instruction.

Customs, Cultures, and Biblical Norms

Our concern for the abiding message of the Bible must not run roughshod over the cultural vehicles in which it was originally conveyed. Neither must the cultural vehicle become an excuse for considering certain truths of God to be ancient but now defunct advice. The presence of a multiplicity of historical cultural details — involving politics, economics, society, foods, clothing, institutions, and so forth — must be accounted for in a valid and legitimate hermeneutic. But how?[44]

It would appear that we are presented with the following options when handling the real cultural items in Scripture:

1. One hermeneutical procedure dictates that we retain, in some cases, both the theology taught (i.e., the principle affirmed or contextually implied) and the cultural-historical expression of the principle. For example, some would claim that 1 Corinthians 11:2-5 argues that the principle of divinely authorized lines of responsibility

42. For additional examples, see Matthew 15:7 and 22:31; Mark 7:6; Acts 4:11; Romans 4:23ff. and 15:4; 1 Corinthians 10:11; and Hebrews 10:15 and 12:15-17.

43. See my essay "The Current Crisis in Exegesis . . . ," pp. 11-18.

44. For additional background, see Robert C. Sproul, "Controversy at Culture Gap," *Eternity* 27 (1976): 12-13; Alan Johnson, "History and Culture in New Testament Interpretation," in *Interpreting the Word of God*, pp. 128-61; and Edwin M. Yamauchi, "Christianity and Cultural Differences," *Christianity Today* 16 (1971): 901-4.

within the Godhead and the husband-wife relationship should be reflected in a certain coiffure for women when they pray or prophesy in public meetings.[45] Yet the matter of hair style was not intended by Scripture to be the abiding emphasis of this passage; the basic exhortation is that proper demeanor be evidenced by women who are prominently in the public eye. But the debate must be denied by the meaning of the text, not by our wishes or reactions. In 1 Corinthians 11:16 Paul affirms that neither he nor the churches of God have any such rule regarding women's coiffure (compare the Greek text to many translations).

2. In some cases, only the theology of a passage (i.e., the principle) is observed, but the behavioral expression is replaced with one that is more recent but equally meaningful. Thus the injunction to "greet the brethren with a holy kiss" will usually be best observed in the West by a hearty handshake. The scriptural precedent for such cultural replacements is seen in the New Testament use of the ceremonial and civil aspects of the moral law of God. Often the principle that undergirded these laws remains, while the illustration or sanction (i.e., the penalty) of it, or both, change because the culture has changed. Thus Paul urged that the mother and son guilty of incest be excommunicated (1 Cor. 5) rather than stoned to death as the Old Testament required (Lev. 20:11; cf. 18:7). Behind both the Old Testament and the New Testament rules against incest stand the holy character of God and the sanctity of marriage. Hence the principle also stands, though the means for enforcing it have changed.

Let it again be noted, however, that regardless of the position an interpreter assumes, if he desires to teach with the authority of Scripture, he needs to observe the clues that the writer has left in the text in order to validate the option chosen. No interpreter may, with the mere wave of the hand, consign recognized principles of God's Word to a mere cultural level in the text or vice versa.

The following list of guidelines should aid us in the job of arriving at the single meaning of the author in those places he includes cultural-historical elements.

1. In every case, the *reason* for the cultural command, custom, or historical practice must first be sought in the context. If the *reason* for a questioned practice or custom has its basis in God's unchanging nature, then the practice is of permanent relevance for all believers in all times. Genesis 9:6 commands that all who shed man's blood shall suffer capital punishment "for in the image of God has God made man." Consequently, because men are still in the image

45. See my essay "Paul, Women and the Church," *Worldwide Challenge* 3 (1976): 9-12.

of God, they continue to have such worth, value, and esteem in God's eyes that the state owes the life of the murderer to *God* — not to the grieving family of the victim as a revenge nor to society as a warning to potential criminals!

2. The cultural *form* of a command may be modified even though the principle of that form remains unchanged for all subsequent readers. The principle of humility, for example, abides, though the form of washing one another's feet (John 13:12-16; cf. Mark 10:42-45) has changed, due to changes in culture, geography, types of roads, and footwear. James urged believers to be nonpartial. The teaching is still valid, though we have never compelled the poor to sit on the floor in our church services.

3. When *practices* that are identified as integral parts of pagan culture and yet also concern God's moral nature are forbidden in the Old or New Testament, they are forbidden in our culture as well. In this category may be placed the strong biblical condemnation of bestiality, homosexuality, transvestitism, and public nudity. Each of these offends one aspect or another of God's moral nature, his attributes, his image in us, or his provision and plan for sexuality, the family, and marriage.

4. A practice or cultural command is permanent when it is grounded in the nature of God or in the ordinances of creation. The issues, therefore, of divorce and remarriage, obedience to parents, and the legitimate respect owed to human government are unchanged and nonnegotiable. Thus the command "What God has joined together, let man not separate" (Matt. 19:6) is still valid, in accordance with God's directive in creation.

Interestingly enough, the moral responsibility for deciding whether or not a believer should pay his taxes or give tolls to a government that he has come to believe is in opposition to accepted moral law, is lifted from his shoulders. Romans 13:7 puts these taxes in the same category as debts paid for services rendered by men who are in service professions. We pay plumbers, electricians, or others for their services to us, but do not thereby aid and abet any false beliefs or immoral practices they may be guilty of.

5. The last guideline I will mention is the biblical precedent for saying that circumstances sometimes alter the application of those laws of God that rest not on his nature (i.e., the moral law of God) but on his will for particular men and women in particular contexts. An example of such a change in the application of God's command can be seen in that given to Aaron and his sons. They alone were to eat of the sacred "bread of the Presence" (Lev. 24:8-9; cf. Exod. 25:30); yet our Lord not only approved of Ahimelech's offering that untouchable food to hungry David and his famished men (1 Sam. 21:1-6), but he used this example to reinforce his own practice of

performing emergency deeds of mercy on the Sabbath (Matt. 12:1-5; Mark 2:23-25; Luke 6:1-4). What appears, at first blush, to allow no exception, actually has a condition of *ceteris paribus* ("other things being equal") understood.[46]

There is an absolute loyalty in Scripture to the principles founded in the nature of God or in the ordinances of creation; yet there is flexibility in applying other commands, such as those regarding sanitary laws, dietary laws (see Mark 7:19 and Acts 10:15, where all foods are declared clean), and ceremonial regulations. Because the brazen altar was too small for the occasion, Solomon used the middle of the temple court to sacrifice the numerous animals during the dedication ceremony (1 Kings 8:64; cf. 2 Chron. 4:1). The principle of worship was identical with that prescribed, though the means of observing it was changed for this occasion. A similar instance is Hezekiah's observance of Passover in the second month rather than the first, since there was not sufficient time for the people to prepare after first learning of it (2 Chron. 30:2-4).

The Alleged Inadequate Language of Scripture in Factual Matters

Under the heavy pressure of the prestigious scholarship of the late nineteenth and the twentieth centuries, one view of this issue has become all but unanimous: Genesis 1– 11 is primeval history, reflecting its ancient Near Eastern origins (mainly Babylonian). Furthermore, it is alleged, wherever Scripture becomes involved in such factual matters as cosmology, natural history, the sciences, historiography, botany, astronomy, or a dozen other such subjects, chances are that it reflects the level of cultural and intellectual achievement of that day, and its statements, therefore, cannot be squared with reality. Among various exponents the wording may vary, but the criticisim usually reaches the same conclusion: Scripture may not be trusted in these details no matter how much we may trust it and even depend on it with our lives in regard to spiritual matters. In fact, goes the argument, it is unfair to ask Scripture to serve this subordinate function.

How may legitimate hermeneutics be employed to decide such problems? After all, has not this essay stressed the fact that meaning must terminate on that which the author himself intended? How then could the author possibly be expected to have spoken beyond his time and learning? Does not progressive revelation correct such past excesses (or primitiveness)?

But such questions exhibit an inadequate view of the type of revelation these writers claimed. To have stood in the counsel of

46. See J. Oliver Buswell, *A Systematic Theology of the Christian Religion*, vol. 1 (Grand Rapids: Zondervan, 1962), pp. 368-73.

God, as these men insist they did, and to have come up deficient in any area, does not square with their claim. And while *meaning* is restricted to the writer's own meanings, these meanings were received from God. One may not force a wedge between God and the writer—unless one cares nothing for the writer's own claims. Likewise, the suggested "help" from progressive revelation is also deficient, for the reasons stated previously.

The problems faced here may be best resolved by noting the following set of guidelines for interpreting scriptural language that points to facts outside the spiritual realm:

1. Determine the literary form to which the section under examination belongs. What textual (or contextual) clues does the writer offer that will aid us in deciding to what literary genre his statements belong? When the literary type is found, we may proceed with an interpretation according to the rules of that literary type.

As an example, let us compare the organization of Genesis 1 – 11 with that of Genesis 12 – 50. The writer used the rubric "These are the generations [i.e., histories] of . . ." (KJV) ten times throughout the book, six times in the first eleven chapters and four times in the remainder of the book. Since the historical nature of the patriarchal narratives of Genesis 12 – 50 is usually conceded to be "substantially accurate" even by many nonevangelical scholars, we believe it is fair to argue that the writer wanted to indicate that the prepatriarchal material is of similar nature.

2. Examine individual words and phrases to see if they have Near Eastern or classical backgrounds and then determine the type of similarity and the use made of them in Scripture.

For example, Psalm 74:13-14 declares that God crushed the heads of Leviathan, and Isaiah 27:1 speaks of the day when God will "punish . . . Leviathan the coiling serpent" and "slay the monster of the sea." It is a fairly easy task to show the parallels of these passages with the Ugaritic text 67:I:1-3 and the Anat text III:38-39. However, to insist that the biblical writers adopted Canaanite mythology as well as terminology is to go beyond the facts. These same writers clearly scorned pagan idols and myths. In these comparisons, therefore, we see borrowed imagery but not borrowed mythology.[47] The conclusion of Father John McKenzie is correct: "In no sense can it be said that the Hebrews incorporated mythopoeic thought . . . into their own religious conceptions; they did, however,

---

47. See Bruce Waltke, *Creation and Chaos* (Portland: Western Conservative Baptist Seminary, 1974), pp. 1-17. See also John N. Oswalt, "The Myth of the Dragon and Old Testament Faith," *Evangelical Quarterly* 49 (1977): 163-72. He concludes that Isaiah 51, Job 40, and Psalm 72 used the myth material of the Near East for nonmythical purposes and never once shared its mythical outlook, contrary to various assurances of B. S. Childs and Mary Wakeman.

assimilate mythopoeic imagery and language."[48] Thus the mention of Leviathan and other names in common with mythology was merely poetic garb that offered no more than convenient similes and metaphors for the theological claims of the writers. It should be noted that often facile comparisons produce totally negative results, as in regard to the alleged connection between the Babylonian goddess Tiamat and the Hebrew *tehom*, "deep" (Gen. 1:2).[49] It turns out that there is no connection between the two. Likewise the case for a biblical triple-decked universe, patterned after pagan models, is also falsely constructed, since the Hebrew text gives no credence to a hard dome complete with windows to serve as the sky or to a flat earth or to literal pillars to support this earth. Every step of the construction is faulty and without biblical support, as we and others have argued elsewhere.[50]

3. Note all figures of speech and determine the part they play in the total statement of the author. This exegetical step is as exacting and as subject to hermeneutical controls as any other. A figure of speech must be named, the definition given, the case for its presence in the verse noted and the function and meaning of the figure in its broader context explained.

E. W. Bullinger lists approximately 150 different examples of figurative language in Genesis 1–11 alone![51] But if one argues that the mere presence of figures of speech consigns the whole section to myth, parable, or apocalyptic-type literature, the response is clear: it does not. Genesis 1–11, for example, is prose, and narrative prose at that. Its description of sequential acts with a special form of the Hebrew verb, its use of the Hebrew direct object sign, its use of the so-called relative pronoun, its stress on definitions and sequence make it more than evident that this section is not poetic. Similar arguments can be pressed in regard to every other disputed text. While Scripture often uses phenomenological language (even as we now do in weather reports and daily conversation) to communicate factual data, this in no way commits the human author or God to distorted science any more than do our references to the sun's rising and to the four "corners" of the earth.

4. Whenever Scripture touches on factual matters, note the way the author uses the data. Too frequently the interpreter either prematurely dismisses such matters (e.g., it is often wrongly stated that Genesis 1 tells us *who* created the universe but not *how* it was done — an obvious slighting of the phrase repeated ten times, "and God

48. McKenzie, "A Note on Psalm 73 [74]:13-15," *Theological Studies* 2 (1950): 281.

49. See my essay "The Literary Form of Genesis 1–11," in *New Perspectives on the Old Testament*, ed. J. Barton Payne (Waco, Tex.: Word Books, 1970), pp. 52-54.

50. See my essay "The Literary Form of Genesis 1–11," pp. 57-58.

51. Bullinger, *Figures of Speech* (1898; rpt., Grand Rapids: Baker, 1968), pp. 1032-33.

said") or overenthusiastically embraces what is *described* as being part of what is also being *prescribed* by God—as in adopting on the basis of Genesis 30, a view of human or environmental prenatal influence on birthmarks, when, in fact, the birthmarks mentioned here were due to God's blessing, as Jacob himself later grudgingly concedes.

In conclusion, I affirm, with all the forcefulness I can muster, that our generation needs a whole new hermeneutical reformation. The current crisis regarding the doctrine of Scripture is directly linked to poor procedures and methods of handling Scripture. This crisis has shown little regard for traditional ecclesiastical or theological categories, for it has spread like the plague among liberal and evangelical scholars alike. As a partial corrective for this astonishing situation, I urge that talk *about* the Bible be modified to this extent: that evangelicals in particular get equally busy identifying the *meaning* of the text itself—the meaning the original writer of Scripture intended—before we go on to name the relationships between that meaning and ourselves, our country, our day, and our conception of things; that is, before we consider the *significance* of the text for us.

When liberalism excused itself from this demand, it turned its back on the revelation of God. If evangelicalism continues to dabble in the text as we have been doing for several decades, substituting Bible surveys and "what do you get out of it" types of pooled-ignorance sessions for the hard work of exegesis, we will also pay the supreme price—there will be no answer from God (Mic. 3:7). It is possible that a strong confessional stand on Scripture and its inerrancy could remain orthodox, even long after the practice and method of interpreting Scripture had turned neoorthodox or liberal. Is this not a good enough reason to issue a call for legitimate hermeneutics?

HERMENEUTICS AND THEOLOGY: THE LEGITIMACY AND NECESSITY OF HERMENEUTICS

ANTHONY C. THISELTON

THE WORD OF GOD AND THE HOLY SPIRIT

In Germany and America, more frequently than in England, questions about New Testament hermeneutics may be related to an explicitly theological doctrine of the Word of God. This has two opposite effects on conclusions about the urgency, value, and legitimacy of hermeneutics. In the majority of cases it leads to a positive assessment of the relevance of hermeneutics to thought and life. The work of Rudolf Bultmann, Ernst Fuchs, Robert Funk, and Walter Wink illustrates this positive approach. However, a minority of writers use theological considerations as a point of departure for criticizing the relevance and legitimacy of hermeneutics. Such writers sometimes invoke a doctrine of the Holy Spirit to argue that hermeneutics is unnecessary and even wrong, since it represents an attempt on the part of man to do the work of God. Other arguments in the same direction appeal to the distinctive role of faith in appropriating the Word of God, to the notion that the truth of God is supposedly "timeless," to the intrinsic power of the Word of God to hammer home its own message, and to the supposedly anthropocentric perspective necessitated by accepting the problem of preunderstanding. We shall consider these negative arguments shortly.

Meanwhile, it is worth noting in the first place now, for most writers, theological factors serve to indicate only the relevance and urgency of the hermeneutical task. Ernst Fuchs explicitly relates his New Testament work to the needs of Christian proclamation. He asks, "What do we have to do at our desks if we want later to set the text in front of us in the pulpit?"[1] Elsewhere he declares, "the

---

1. Fuchs, *Studies of the Historical Jesus* (London: SCM Press, 1964), p. 8.

Reprinted from *The Two Horizons: New Testament Hermeneutics and Philosophical Description* (Grand Rapids: Eerdmans, 1980), pp. 85-114.

text is interpreted when God is proclaimed."[2] On the last page of his *Hermeneutik* he concludes a discussion of Bultmann's work with the words "what is theory in all this should now be brought to an end. . . . Let us leave theory."[3] It is not surprising to find the theologian Gerhard Ebeling, who is often closely associated with Fuchs, expressing a similar viewpoint in this respect. He criticizes all theories of hermeneutics which are formulated "without an eye to proclamation."[4]

In his recent small book *The Bible in Human Transformation* the American New Testament scholar Walter Wink is sharply critical of what he regards as the professionalism of many New Testament scholars, which, he believes, leads them to avoid the most important issues of hermeneutics. The community of reference in New Testament interpretation, he complains, has become a professional guild of scholars rather than the men and women of the living church.[5] The Bible was written by ordinary men, he insists, for ordinary people who face practical problems in their daily lives. But the scholar is too often "insulated . . . from the Bible's own concerns." In a style reminiscent of Kierkegaard, Wink declares, "he examines the Bible, but he himself is not examined—except by his colleagues in the guild."[6] Some reviewers have been hostile to Wink not least because he often overstates his case. For example, he writes, "the outcome of biblical studies in the academy is a trained incapacity to deal with the real problems of actual living persons in their daily lives."[7] It should be stressed, however, that Wink is by no means writing from a narrow or fundamentalist theological base. Indeed, he carefully argues for the positive role of biblical criticism in its proper place. Wink is concerned to make a particular point, which he does with all the force he can muster. Taken as a whole, his book makes a valuable contribution to New Testament hermeneutics.

Robert Funk, who writes as a New Testament scholar of worldwide reputation, also relates New Testament hermeneutics to Christian theology, as well as to broader questions about language and understanding. The problem of hermeneutics, he argues, has to do partly with a crisis of language. In this respect he shares Ebeling's concern, although less exclusively from a standpoint informed by

2. Fuchs, "The New Testament and the Hermeneutical Problem," in *New Frontiers in Theology, II: The New Hermeneutic*, ed. J. M. Robinson and J. B. Cobb, Jr. (New York: Harper & Row, 1964), p. 141.

3. Fuchs, *Hermeneutik*, 4th ed. (Tübingen: J. C. B. Mohr, 1970), p. 281.

4. Ebeling, *Word and Faith* (London: SCM Press, 1963), p. 312.

5. Wink, *The Bible in Human Transformation: Toward a New Paradigm for Biblical Study* (Philadelphia: Fortress Press, 1973), pp. 8-11; see pp. 1-15.

6. Wink, *The Bible in Human Transformation*, p. 4.

7. Wink, *The Bible in Human Transformation*, p. 6.

Heidegger. He also discusses the approaches of Van Buren and Ogden. Another part of the problem which is equally important for Funk is that the critical historical method as used in New Testament studies "failed to take into account the limitations and biases of the interpreter."[8] But the most serious part of his diagnosis of the problem is a theological one. Negatively, New Testament hermeneutics is frequently vitiated by the mistaken assumption that the word of God is merely a "thing" which is "accessible to the exegete as an object for scrutiny."[9] This is part of "the assumption, endemic to the modern period, that man is the subject to which all things, including the word of God, must give account." "The word of God . . . is not on trial."[10]

This relates at once to philosophical questions about epistemology. It calls in question whether the hermeneutical process of understanding the New Testament text is compatible with the epistemological model suggested by Descartes that the ego, as active subject, looks out on the world, as passive object, and scrutinizes everything in terms of the subject-object schema.[11] From a theological point of view, it can also be said that the subject matter of the text is not merely passive object but speaks back, as subject, to the interpreter, as object. This forms one of the themes to be discussed in relation to the work of Gadamer, and especially Fuchs and Ebeling, and also has connections with Karl Barth's theology of the Word of God. The point we are making here, however, is that an established New Testament scholar raises such questions because his approach to the biblical writings is not isolated from broader theological questions about a doctrine of the Word of God.

It will become clear from our discussion on the hermeneutics of Rudolf Bultmann that his approach to this subject is decisively shaped by his own theological convictions about the nature of revelation and faith, and concerning talk of God. One writer, David Cairns, examines Bultmann's proposals about demythologizing not only in relation to Heidegger's philosophy but also in terms of its challenge for the Christian preacher. His book contains chapters entitled "Preaching, Theology and Philosophy," "Mythical Think-

8. Funk, *Language, Hermeneutic and Word of God: The Problem of Language in the New Testament and Contemporary Theology* (New York: Harper & Row, 1966), p. 10.

9. Funk, *Language, Hermeneutic and Word of God,* p. 11.

10. Funk, *Language, Hermeneutic and Word of God,* p. 11.

11. Funk, *Language, Hermeneutic and Word of God,* p. 11. Funk comments, "with this startling insight the direction of the flow between interpreter and text that has dominated modern biblical criticism from its inception is reversed, and hermeneutics in its traditional sense becomes hermeneutic, now understood as the effort to allow God to address man through the medium of the text." Cf. J. M. Robinson, "Hermeneutics since Barth," in *New Frontiers in Theology II,* pp. 23-24, 55-58.

ing and the Preacher," and "Will This Preach?"[12] He pays special attention to Bultmann's sermons and asks only whether the radical nature of Bultmann's program "really justifies the evangelical warmth of the language used."[13] In spite of his negative criticisms of Bultmann's use of Heidegger's thought, he does not question that his hermeneutics is basically motivated by his concern for Christian proclamation.

It would be possible to mention other scholars whose approach to biblical interpretation from the standpoint of Christian theology, indeed from the standpoint of a doctrine of the Word of God, leads them to a positive appraisal of the legitimacy of hermeneutics. We might mention, for example, James Smart's book *The Strange Silence of the Bible in the Church* as well as his earlier book on biblical interpretation. In his second book Smart is concerned about the relation between hermeneutics and preaching.[14] However, we must now turn to the negative arguments which are sometimes put forward in order to question the legitimacy of hermeneutics on the basis of theological considerations.

In the first place, it is sometimes argued that no natural point of contact already exists between men and the Word of God, and that this discontinuity, therefore, can and must be bridged not by hermeneutics but by the work of the Holy Spirit. One of the classic expositions of this principle of discontinuity comes in the pages of Karl Barth's early book translated under the title *The Word of God and the Word of Man*. In the essay entitled "The Strange New World within the Bible," Barth describes this world as a new life, and comments, "one cannot learn or imitate this life . . . one can only let it live, grow, ripen, within him. One can only believe . . . or not believe. There is no third way."[15] The gulf between the Bible and human understanding is no less than the gulf between human understanding and God himself, for "it is not the right human thoughts about God which form the content of the Bible, but the right divine thoughts about men."[16]

Barth stresses this principle of discontinuity in his *Church Dogmatics*, especially in the volume on the doctrine of the Word of God. Arguing on the basis of such passages as 2 Corinthians 3:14-18 and 1 Corinthians 2:6-16, he concludes that the subject matter of Scrip-

12. Cairns, *A Gospel without Myth? Bultmann's Challenge to the Preacher* (London: SCM Press, 1960), pp. 15-33, 81-93, and 164-95.

13. Cairns, *A Gospel without Myth?* p. 180.

14. Smart, *The Strange Silence of the Bible in the Church: A Study in Hermeneutics* (London: SCM Press, 1970), pp. 28-38.

15. Barth, *The Word of God and the Word of Man* (London: Hodder & Stoughton, 1928), p. 41.

16. Barth, *The Word of God and the Word of Man*, p. 43.

ture can be known "only spiritually, i.e. on the basis of the work of the . . . Spirit."[17] Barth also appeals to Luther and the Reformers for the doctrine that "the word of Scripture given by the Spirit can be recognized as God's Word only because the work of the Spirit . . . becomes an event for its hearer or reader. How else will God be recognized except by God Himself?"[18] Hence, "we cannot possibly understand the Word of God . . . except as the act of God" even though "the event of the Word of God is not continuation, but the end of all other events that we know."[19] Not only does the event of the Word of God stand in discontinuity with all human thought and experiences, it also stands altogether apart from them. Thus, "the presence of the Word of God is not an experience, precisely because and as it is the divine decision concerning us."[20]

Barth's starting point is in accord with the outlook of Pauline and Johannine theology. The Holy Spirit is active in interpreting the Word of God to men. However, Barth's opposition to the emphasis of Schleiermacher and Ritschl on religious experience, together with his stress on the sovereign transcendence of God, has led him beyond this starting point, so that at times it seems to be implied that the Spirit's communication of the Word of God is somehow independent of all ordinary processes of human understanding. It is not surprising, therefore, to find a head-on collision between Barth and Bultmann in the former's well-known essay "Rudolf Bultmann—An Attempt to Understand Him."[21] Barth declares, "this Word of God can only confront and illuminate man as truth and reality if it is seen to run *counter to his whole natural capacity to understand.*"[22] He himself, Barth claims, tried to emancipate the Bible from its Egyptian bondage to "one philosophy after another," which tried to "teach us what the Holy Spirit was allowed to say as the Word of God." But "Bultmann has forsaken our road and gone back to the old one again."[23]

Although we used the phrase "head-on collision," in point of fact it is doubtful whether Barth and Bultmann are actually addressing themselves to the same issue. H.-W. Bartsch hepfully pinpoints G. Gloege's verdict that the misunderstanding which lies at the cen-

17. Barth, *Church Dogmatics,* 5 vols., ed. Geoffrey W. Bromiley and Thomas F. Torrance, trans. Geoffrey W. Bromiley et al. (Edinburgh: T. & T. Clark, 1955-57), 1/2: 516.

18. Barth, *Church Dogmatics,* 1/2: 521.

19. Barth, *Church Dogmatics,* 1/2: 527, 528.

20. Barth, *Church Dogmatics,* 1/2: 532.

21. Barth, "Rudolf Bultmann—An Attempt to Understand Him" in vol. 2 of *Kerygma and Myth,* ed. H.-W. Bartsch, 2d ed. (London: S.P.C.K., 1964), pp. 83-132.

22. Barth, "Rudolf Bultmann—An Attempt to Understand Him," p. 123, italics mine.

23. Barth, "Rudolf Bultmann—An Attempt to Understand Him," p. 127.

ter of Barth's criticisms against Bultmann "arises from the confusion between the ontic and noetic approaches, and the respective points of view they imply."[24] The point that Gloege is making is so important that his words may be quoted in full. He writes, "there is no question that Bultmann is right: the problem of understanding (i.e., hermeneutics), the question of knowledge, comes before the question of the object known. That, however, does not rule out—in fact it assumes—that the question of the object known provides the basis and structures of the question of knowledge."[25] We sympathize with the theological values which Barth is seeking to preserve, but he has paid an unnecessary price to do it. Many scholars, including some who are otherwise supporters of Barth's own general position, see that it in no way diminishes the crucial importance of the role of the Holy Spirit to say that the Spirit works *through* the normal processes of human understanding, and neither independently of them nor contrary to them.

John Macquarrie looks carefully at this particular theological criticism of hermeneutics with reference not only to Barth, but also to Helmut Thielicke.[26] This kind of thinking about the role of the Holy Spirit, Macquarrie urges, tends to make the Spirit into a mysterious *tertium quid* which stands over against both God and man. However, "the Holy Spirit is the God who addresses us, not an intermediary between us."[27] When the biblical writers or Christian theologians speak of the testimony of the Spirit, this is not to invoke some *additional* means of communicating the Word of God but is to claim that a message which is communicated in human language to human understanding addresses man *as* the Word of God.[28] It would not invalidate Macquarrie's argument to point out that in Pauline theology the Spirit is sometimes portrayed as standing over against God, as, for example, when the Spirit calls forth from the Christian the response of "Abba, Father" (Rom. 8:15-16). For this has nothing to do with any suggestion that, as Prosper Grech expresses it, in the context of hermeneutics the Spirit operates on the principle of *deus ex machina*.[29]

Heinrich Ott and Wolfhart Pannenberg also reject this view of the work of the Holy Spirit. Ott examines the objection that "one should not concern oneself so much about the problem of under-

---

24. Bartsch, in *Kerygma and Myth*, 2: 31.

25. Gloege, quoted by Bartsch in *Kerygma and Myth*, 2: 31.

26. See Macquarrie, *The Scope of Demythologizing: Bultmann and His Critics* (London: SCM Press, 1960), pp. 48-53.

27. Macquarrie, *The Scope of Demythologizing*, p. 50.

28. Macquarrie, *The Scope of Demythologizing*, p. 50.

29. Grech, "The 'Testimonia' and Modern Hermeneutics," *New Testament Studies* 19 (1972-73): 324.

standing, since the Holy Spirit surely sees to it that the message is
understood. This 'pious' objection, designed to make light of the
hermeneutical problem, is quite popular."[30] The objection, Ott replies, rests on a kind of "inferior orthodoxy" that fails to see the
issue: "One should not degrade God to a *deus ex machina*. Actually
. . . the witness of the Spirit is taken fully into account in the concept
of understanding, when the concept is itself correctly understood."[31]

Wolfhart Pannenberg makes a similar point about a doctrine of
the Holy Spirit in the context of wider questions about truth and
the role of argument. He writes, "an otherwise unconvincing message cannot attain the power to convince simply by appealing to the
Holy Spirit."[32] "Argument and the operation of the Spirit are not in
competition with each other. In trusting in the Spirit, Paul in no
way spared himself thinking and arguing."[33] In other words, the
Spirit is conceived of as working *through* these means, not independently of them.

In addition to these arguments about the role of a doctrine of the
Holy Spirit, we may note that in practice many authors who do
take the hermeneutical problem seriously also have a doctrine of the
Spirit. Gerhard Ebeling, for example, warns us against short-circuiting hermeneutics by a premature appeal to the Spirit, but he
also states that "the Holy Spirit, which is the Spirit of the Word, is
concerned with everything which has to do with the word-event."[34]
Conversely, Helmut Thielicke, who repeats in *The Evangelical Faith*
his earlier criticism that "the final secret or difficulty of Bultmann's
theology is that he has no doctrine of the Spirit," devotes considerable attention to hermeneutics as the problem of understanding
in this same volume.[35]

The argument that the Holy Spirit works *through* human understanding, and does not therefore short-circuit the problem of hermeneutics, may be confirmed still more clearly with reference to two
chapters in T. F. Torrance's book *God and Rationality*. The two chapters are entitled "The Word of God and the Response of Man" and

30. Ott, "What Is Systematic Theology?" in *New Frontiers in Theology, I: The Later
Heidegger and Theology*, ed. J. M. Robinson and J. B. Cobb, Jr. (New York: Harper
& Row, 1963), p. 81.
31. Ott, "What Is Systematic Theology?" p. 81.
32. Pannenberg, *Basic Questions in Theology*, 3 vols. (London: SCM Press, 1970-73),
2: 34.
33. Pannenberg, *Basic Questions in Theology*, 2: 35; cf. p. 43.
34. Ebeling, *Theology and Proclamation: A Discussion with Rudolf Bultmann* (London:
Collins, 1966), p. 102; cf. p. 42.
35. Thielicke, *The Evangelical Faith*, vol. 1: *Prolegomena: The Relation of Theology to
Modern Thought-Forms*, trans. Geoffrey W. Bromiley (Grand Rapids: Eerdmans, 1974),
p. 60; cf. his "Reflections on Bultmann's Hermeneutic," *Expository Times* 67 (1956):
157, where he uses the phrase "final embarrassment" (see pp. 154-57).

"The Epistemological Relevance of the Spirit," and both come under the general heading of "Word and Spirit."[36] Torrance points out that to speak of the epistemological relevance of the Spirit does not mean that the problem of knowledge becomes Spirit-centered in the more obvious and superficial sense of the term. "By His very mode of being as Spirit He hides Himself from us so that we do not know Him directly in His own hypostasis, and in His mode of activity as transparent Light He effaces Himself that the one Triune God may shine through Him to us."[37] This reminds us of John Macquarrie's warnings against theologies which make the Spirit a *tertium quid.* This means also that the Holy Spirit does not bypass human rationality, or make questions about the nature of human language irrelevant.[38] The parables of Jesus, Torrance points out, illustrate the interaction between the Word of God and methods of communication through concrete human language.[39] Because man is still man in his ordinary humanity, it is still relevant to take account of "this sign-world which God has appointed and uses."[40] The epistemological relevance of the Holy Spirit lies not in some esoteric gnostic route to knowledge, but "in the dynamic and transformal aspects of this knowledge."[41]

We may conclude, then, that the Holy Spirit may be said to work *through* human understanding, and not usually, if ever, through processes which bypass the considerations discussed under the heading of hermeneutics. Indeed from the point of view of Christian theology, the more concerned the New Testament interpreter is about a doctrine of the Word of God and the work of the Spirit, the more concerned he should be to approach hermeneutical issues seriously and responsibly as problems which require thought but are nevertheless capable of some solution. Moreover, an emphasis on the Holy Spirit is by no means incompatible with Schleiermacher's insight that understanding constitutes an art rather than a mechanistic science, since the Spirit is thought of in Christian theology as acting in and through men creatively. This emphasis also harmonizes well with the hermeneutical conclusions of Fuchs and Funk that the interpreter does not simply pass judgment on the Word, but also places himself under the judgment of the Word. To pronounce judgment on man is an activity of the Spirit. In the end, then, far from suggesting that the problem of hermeneutics can be

36. Torrance, *God and Rationality* (London: Oxford University Press, 1971), pp. 137-92.
37. Torrance, *God and Rationality*, p. 167.
38. Torrance, *God and Rationality*, pp. 146-51, 183-92.
39. Torrance, *God and Rationality*, p. 150.
40. Torrance, *God and Rationality*, p. 184.
41. Torrance, *God and Rationality*, p. 166.

bypassed, considerations about the Holy Spirit serve to underline
the legitimacy and importance of this subject.

FAITH, "TIMELESS TRUTH," TIME, AND THE WORD

The second theological argument against the legitimacy of hermeneutics concerns the role of faith. It is sometimes argued that since
without faith the New Testament will necessarily remain a closed
book, considerations about hermeneutics will fail to solve the problem of understanding. Conversely, it is argued that if an interpreter
already has faith, the New Testament is *already* intelligible, and hence
hermeneutics remains unnecessary.

To some extent the standard passages cited in the New Testament
for supposed support for this outlook raise the very same issues as
those outlined in the previous section about the Holy Spirit. We
have seen, for example, that Barth's appeal to such passages as
1 Corinthians 2:6-16 fails to call in question the relevance of hermeneutics, provided that it is accepted that the Spirit works through
human means. The same point may be made about faith. As Pannenberg and Ebeling insist, faith does not constitute some alternative or additional avenue of knowledge or understanding which
operates alongside, and independently of, the normal processes of
human understanding.[42] However, the really decisive argument
against this sort of criticism comes from Fuchs, as well as Ebeling.
If the intelligibility of the New Testament, he argues, is said to
presuppose faith, *how can it be said that the message of the New Testament
serves to create faith*?

Ernst Fuchs insists that, on the basis of this principle, when it is
said to presuppose faith, the message of the New Testament "loses
its character."[43] In his work on the parables of Jesus, which we shall
discuss later, he argues that it is precisely the way of grace and love,
manifested in Jesus, to create and establish, through language, a
"place of meeting" with the unbeliever. He writes, "Jesus draws the
hearer over to his side . . . so that the hearer may think together
with Jesus. Is this not the way of true love? Love . . . provides in
advance the sphere in which meeting takes place."[44] In much the
same way, Gerhard Ebeling asserts that "the proclaimed word seeks
to effect faith, but does not presuppose faith as a necessary prelim-

42. Note Ebeling's comment about "a misunderstanding of what faith means.
Faith is seen as an organ that competes with reason or supplements it, as a kind of
reason projected into the superrational" (*Word and Faith*, p. 116).

43. Fuchs, *Studies of the Historical Jesus*, p. 30; cf. *Zum hermeneutischen Problem in der
Theologie* (Tübingen: J. C. B. Mohr, 1959), pp. 9-10.

44. Fuchs, *Studies of the Historical Jesus*, p. 129.

inary."[45] This conviction provides the linchpin not only for his discussions about Bonhoeffer's comments on the "non-religious interpretation of Biblical concepts," but also for all his work on hermeneutics.[46]

This perspective may perhaps also shed light on one or two of the passages which are cited in supposed support of the objection which we are considering. James Smart makes much of Paul's words in 2 Corinthians 3:14-16: "for to this day, when they read the old covenant that same veil remains unlifted, because only through Christ is it taken away. Yes, to this day, whenever Moses is read a veil lies over their minds; but when a man turns to the Lord the veil is removed." Smart points out that "the testimony of Paul, once a rabbi himself, is that the rabbis, with all their diligent searching of the Scriptures, were not able to see what was there for them."[47] While we have no wish to drive any unnecessary wedge between the theological status of the Old and New Testaments, the arguments of Fuchs and Ebeling remind us that Paul is not speaking so much about whether Scripture, as such, can be "understood," as whether the Old Testament alone is capable of producing Christian faith when the interpreter's preunderstanding remains isolated from questions and concerns about Christ.

In terms of the capacity to create *Christian* faith, the Old Testament, even as the Scripture of Paul and Judaism, cannot simply be equated with the kerygma of the New Testament. This, emphatically, is *not* to surrender to Bultmann's notorious statement that "the Old Testament, in so far as it is Law, need not address us as direct Word of God and as a matter of fact does not do it."[48] But it is to accept Bultmann's statement in the same essay that "characteristic of the New Testament, in distinction from the Old, is the idea that man's relation to God is bound to the person of Jesus."[49] Hence, given Paul's christocentric view of the Old Testament, he can only say that it is unable to effect its proper purpose in the hearts of men unless or until they approach it with a preunderstanding colored by concerns about Christ and the Christian gospel. Once again, therefore, this kind of passage in no way calls in question the relevance of hermeneutics. Indeed James Smart himself, who appeals to this passage in order to argue for a theologically informed preunder-

45. Ebeling, *Word and Faith*, p. 125.

46. See Ebeling, *Word and Faith*, pp. 98-161, 282-87.

47. Smart, *The Interpretation of Scripture* (London: SCM Press, 1961), p. 13.

48. Bultmann, "The Significance of the Old Testament for the Christian Faith," in *The Old Testament and Christian Faith*, ed. B. W. Anderson (London: SCM Press, 1964), p. 17; see pp. 8-35.

49. Bultmann, "The Significance of the Old Testament for the Christian Faith," p. 11.

standing, is one of those very writers who argues for the importance of hermeneutics. He comments, "hermeneutics is a basic concern of all of us who are interested in letting the message of the Scripture be heard in our time."[50] Hermeneutics brings together the "two worlds" of the interpreter and the text, so that *through* the text the interpreter can see himself and the world as if it were "a magic glass."[51] Appeals to specific New Testament passages, then, in no way weaken the force of the point made by Fuchs and Ebeling that the New Testament message serves to *create* faith, and that in so doing it does not bypass the normal processes of understanding.

The *positive* point behind appeals to the need for faith in biblical interpretation relates to the question of theological preunderstanding. There are different levels at which the biblical text engages with the interpreter's horizons, and certainly at one level faith is created rather than presupposed by the Word. Nevertheless, at a different level the Church Fathers from Irenaeus onward had to cope with the problem that unbelievers and heretics attempted to use the Bible in such a way as to defend views which were plainly contrary to the witness of Scripture as a whole. Irenaeus constantly accuses the Gnostics, for example, of garbling and twisting biblical passages in order to defend their heterodox opinions. In this context Irenaeus and many of the Church Fathers insisted on two principles: first, that Scripture is to be interpreted in the light of its own witness as a whole; and second, that valid interpretation depends on Christian faith, in the sense of accepting the tradition accepted by the believing community. This particular point in no way invalidates the task of hermeneutics, however. Indeed, the reverse is the case.

This positive point may also be expressed in broader and more general terms. R. P. C. Hanson rightly asserts, "the Bible . . . was written from faith to faith. It was intended for the use of a worshipping community, and outside the context of a worshipping community it is inevitably . . . misapplied. It is intended for the use of a living Church. . . ."[52] This claim cannot be said to contradict what we have already said about the Bible's capacity to *create* faith, for both principles are equally true to the experience of the Christian community down the centuries. The point in question in no way challenges the legitimacy or necessity of hermeneutics, even though it may well call in question some of the claims for a purely "historical" approach, as over against a "faith" interpretation (e.g., of the causes of the Exile) which we have noted in D. E. Nineham's writings.

50. Smart, *The Strange Silence of the Bible in the Church*, pp. 37-38.

51. *The Strange Silence of the Bible in the Church*, p. 163.

52. Hanson, *The Bible as a Norm of Faith* (Durham: Durham University Press, 1963), p. 11.

We come now to a third objection to the relevance of hermeneutics which is often put forward on supposedly theological grounds. We shall see that the issues it raises point in the end rather to the validity and relevance of hermeneutical discussions. However, it is sometimes argued that the truth of God conveyed through the New Testament is changeless, and therefore "timeless." Hence, questions about understanding the Bible cannot be said to vary from generation to generation. It is perhaps implied that the truth of the New Testament, because it is the truth of God, stands apart from historical and cultural change in much the same way as may be claimed for the truth of mathematics. The angles of a triangle add up to 180° independently of what particular triangles a mathematician actually draws. In the language of philosophical logic, such truths are said to be necessary truths rather than contingent truths.

If this is what is meant by claiming that the Bible conveys "timeless" truth, quite clearly this would not be the view of the biblical writers themselves. Such a view of truth can be described as theological only if Christianity is built on Platonist metaphysics. In practice, this point need not detain us, for it is generally accepted today that this view of truth is drawn from Greek philosophy and not from the Bible, and that, in any case, a God of "necessary" truth would be unrelated to human life and experience. The point is expressed admirably by Wolfhart Pannenberg in his essay "What is Truth?" He writes, "for Greek thought . . . truth excluded all change. . . . It belongs to the essence of truth to be unchangeable and, thus, to be one and the same, without beginning or end."[53] *Necessary* truth depends not on the actual occurrence of particular events, but on whether a proposition is true by definition, on whether, for example, it is part of the very concept of triangularity that the sum of the angles of a triangle should amount to 180°. By contrast, contingent truth depends on circumstances which may change from time to time, such as in the case of the statement "It is raining." Pannenberg insists that in the Bible truth is contingent rather than necessary because it is related to historical events. It is "not the result of logical necessity. . . . The truth of God must prove itself anew."[54] "The Greek dualism between true being and changing sense-appearance is superseded in the biblical understanding of truth. Here, true being is thought of not as timeless, but instead as historical, and it proves its stability through a history whose future is always open."[55]

Quite clearly statements such as "God was in Christ reconciling the world to himself" (2 Cor. 5:19) and "Christ died for our sins

---

53. Pannenberg, *Basic Questions in Theology,* 2: 19; see pp. 1-27.
54. Pannenberg, *Basic Questions in Theology,* 2: 8.
55. Pannenberg, *Basic Questions in Theology,* 2: 9.

according to the scriptures" (1 Cor. 15:3) would have been false if uttered before a certain date in history. In this sense they are not timeless. But are there not other types of statements which occur in the New Testament of which this cannot be said?

The wide range of meanings which might be conveyed by the term "timeless truth" has been discussed from a philosophical point of view by Friedrich Waismann, and more recently by Paul Helm.[56] Waismann, for example, considers such questions as "Is a statement about the future true now?" and indeed "What is *meant* by saying that a statement about the future is true now?" The statement "*p* is true," he argues, is *not a description of* "*p*" which can be completed by adding a time specification. To say that truth is timeless is only to say that it is logically confusing and inappropriate to add a time specification to the words "It is true that. . . ." It would be logically puzzling, for example, to say: "It is true at 4 o'clock on Tuesday that God is good." To quote Waismann's own words, "one is misled by the external form of the expression. It seems as if the adjective 'true' stands for a quality of propositions of which it can be asked: 'When does *p* have this quality?' It is quite right to say, 'Truth is timeless,' provided this means no more than: 'There is a rule . . . which forbids the addition of a time-specification to the words 'It is true that.' "[57]

Waismann, then, allows the use of the term "timeless truth" merely to safeguard a negative point about logic. If the term is used in this "weak" sense, *some* New Testament statements may be described as timeless, but this is not in a sense which has any relevance to the discussion about hermeneutics. Paul Helm, whose article is also taken up by James Barr, shows that there are confusions about the ways in which the term "timeless truth" is applied to the biblical writings.[58] For example, some claim that the New Testament cannot be said to contain "revealed propositions" on the ground that such propositions would then be timeless. Some claim that Bultmann reduces the New Testament to "timeless truths" on the grounds that history is swallowed up in eschatology. Bultmann himself insists that "the kerygma does not proclaim universal truths, or a timeless idea . . . but historical fact."[59] It is doubtful whether the word "timeless" is being used in exactly the same way in each statement. How-

---

56. Waismann, *The Principles of Linguistic Philosophy* (London: Macmillan, 1965), pp. 27-34; and Helm, "Revealed Proposition and Timeless Truths," *Religious Studies* 8 (1972): 127-36.

57. Waismann, *The Principles of Linguistic Philosophy*, p. 29 (italics his), p. 32 (italics mine).

58. Helm, "Revealed Propositions and Timeless Truths," pp. 132-35: cf. J. Barr, *The Bible in the Modern World* (London: SCM Press, 1973), pp. 123-24.

59. Bultmann, *Faith and Understanding*, vol. 1 (London: SCM Press, 1969), p. 241.

ever, it is the responsibility of those who appeal to the timeless nature of New Testament truth as an argument against the necessity for hermeneutics to show both in what sense they use the term, and how this sense substantiates their argument. I am not aware of a carefully argued attempt to achieve this, let alone of one that is successful.

It might perhaps be argued that one particular type of passage in the New Testament constitutes a special case and comes very near to being "timeless." This is the symbolism and imagery, which draws on archetypal patterns, to which writers such as Austin Farrer and L. S. Thornton have often drawn attention. What could be, in a sense, more timeless than the symbolism of "the river of the water of life" (Rev. 22:1) and the tree of life, the leaves of which are "for the healing of the nations" (Rev. 22:2)? Every child from every age who knows the meaning of a party can share in the meaning of the words "Blessed are those who are invited to the marriage supper" (Rev. 19:9), just as anyone who has ever had a door shut in his face and locked knows something of the meaning of the words "and the door was shut" (Matt. 25:10). Thomas Fawcett has gathered together many examples of biblical symbolism that reach back to man's primeval and primordial existence, as may be suggested by their occurrence throughout mythology.[60] We may cite, for example, the symbolism of light shining in darkness (Matt. 24:27; John 1:4-9 and 9:5); the symbol of the serpent or dragon (Gen. 3:1-15; Rev. 12:3 and 20:2); or the imagery of inaccessible Eden (Gen. 3:23-24; 1 Enoch 32:1, 3 and 61:1).

Even so, Paul Tillich's warnings about symbols remind us that even though, archetypally, they "grow out of the . . . unconscious," nevertheless, "like living beings they grow and die."[61] For example, water may seem to be a perennial symbol of refreshment and purity. But this dimension may be eclipsed in a culture or at a time when what is most significant about water is the destructive potential of floods. In ancient Israel the vine may have stood as a symbol of prosperity, but in many cultures vines are unknown. Even kingship no longer conveys what it might in cultures which regard the monarch as the enemy of the proletariat or of democracy. Even symbolism, then, does not necessarily escape the ravages of time. Even though in the majority of cases biblical symbols still strike responsive chords because of their archetypal or primordial character, it cannot be assumed that they will function "timelessly" in the sense of requiring no hermeneutical explanation or translation.

In point of fact, the more closely we examine claims about "time-

60. Fawcett, *Hebrew Myth and Christian Gospel* (London: SCM Press, 1973).
61. Tillich, *Dynamics of Faith* (New York: Harper & Row, 1956), p. 43.

less truth," the clearer it becomes that the biblical material itself
points in the other direction. The point is well expressed in a careful
statement by Helmut Thielicke. Christian truth, he declares, "has
nothing whatever to do with timeless truth.... Every word, including God's Word, implies a recipient, present-day man, contemporaries. This Word is historical not merely in the sense of being
grounded in history, but also as it is addressed to historical situations. Both the authors and the recipients of verbal messages are
subject to the process of history." He adds, by way of warning, "the
message, then, cannot be detached at either point. If an effort is
made in this direction there arises the false notion of perennial
theology characterized by an abstract conceptual system. Scholas-
ticism and seventeenth-century orthodoxy are classical examples."[62]
Thielicke does not deny that, again in some kind of "weak" sense,
the truths of the New Testament and of Christian theology are eternal in the sense that they are capable of application to men of all
generations, *given* hermeneutical reflection. In one sense, he acknowledges, the experience of trial and temptation expressed in
Psalm 73 speaks to man's experience of temptation down the ages.
But in another sense, he adds, we cannot say that the trials of Luther
or Jerome were the same as those of Jacobsen or Camus or other
men of the modern world. They are "historically variable . . . they
change with each new present."[63] Hence, "the history of theology
is fundamentally no other than the history of its various attempts
at address."[64] Thielicke concludes that it is not necessarily to "accommodate" theological truth to attempt to "actualize" it through
readdress and reinterpretation from generation to generation.[65]

The part played by nearly two thousand years of intervening
tradition and history also affects the nature of the discussion. Pannenberg, Fuchs, and especially Gerhard Ebeling strongly emphasize
this point. Each of these three writers argues that on the basis of
this historical situation merely to abstract certain words from the
New Testament and to repeat them mechanically would be *un*faithful
to the intention of the New Testament writers. Pannenberg asserts,
"in a changed situation the traditional phrases, even when recited
literally, do not mean what they did at the time of their original
formulation."[66] He adds, "an external assimilating of Christian language to the thoughts and manner of speaking of the biblical writings is always an infallible sign that theology has sidestepped its
own present problems, and thus has failed to accomplish what Paul

62. Thielicke, *The Evangelical Faith*, 1: 23.
63. Thielicke, *The Evangelical Faith*, 1: 25.
64. Thielicke, *The Evangelical Faith*, 1: 25.
65. Thielicke, *The Evangelical Faith*, 1: 27-29.
66. Pannenberg, *Basic Questions in Theology*, 1: 9.

or John, or, in his own way, even Luther, each accomplished for his own time."[67] Theology, Pannenberg concludes, comes closest to agreement with the biblical witnesses when it seriously engages with the problems and thought-forms of its own time. At this point in his argument he explicitly appeals to the contribution of modern hermeneutics, making special reference to Gadamer's concept of a fusion of horizons.

In his essay "Time and Word" Gerhard Ebeling also asserts, "the same word can be said to another time only by being said differently."[68] In addition to the discussions in *Word and Faith* to which we have already referred, the issue emerges, as perhaps the titles suggest, in Ebeling's books *The Word of God and Tradition* and *The Problem of Historicity*. In this last work Ebeling considers concrete examples where the text of the Bible seems already to speak, as it were, timelessly, without any expository interpretation from the Christian preacher. For instance, he recalls how at the end of the war, when he heard of Hitler's death, he read to his fellow-soldiers Isaiah 14, the song of triumph at the overthrow of the king of Babylon. The impact of the passage was effective in its own right, after many centuries of historical change. However, Ebeling argues, "it would not be right to want to adduce such an example as evidence for the opinion that in certain cases proclamation may consist in mere repetition of the word of the Scriptures and need not have the structure of interpretation, or that this might even be the ideal way to test the Scriptures."[69] This is because, he claims, something like interpretation did indeed take place. Everything hinged on a parallel in the mind of the hearers between the historical situation behind the text and that of the hearers themselves. Ebeling adds, "however, no situation is identical with another. Therefore every interpretation of the scriptural word which rests its case on the similarity of the past and present situations already rests on a translation (*Übertragung*) and thus on a fully unconscious exegetical operation which, on reflection, is seen to touch upon difficult hermeneutical questions."[70] Every understanding, he concludes, even if it is not explicitly arrived at by a conscious process of hermeneutics, still tacitly includes interpretation.

Ebeling turns at this point to consider the theological question of whether Luther and the Reformers do not in fact draw a sharp contrast between "interpretation" as the changing word of man and

---

67. Pannenberg, *Basic Questions in Theology*, 1: 9.

68. Ebeling, "Time and Word," in *The Future of Our Religious Past: Essays in Honour of Rudolf Bultmann*, ed. J. M. Robinson (London: SCM Press, 1971), p. 265.

69. Ebeling, *The Problem of Historicity in the Church and Its Proclamation* (Philadelphia: Fortress Press, 1967), p. 11.

70. Ebeling, *The Problem of Historicity in the Church and Its Proclamation*, p. 11.

"Scripture" as the Word of God. He concludes, "Luther is concerned with setting forth and affirming the necessity of an interpretation which is always carried through anew in repeated listening to the word of Scripture, as opposed to a persistence in a normative interpretation previously established and now placed above the Scriptures."[71] The recognition of the necessary place of interpretation, Ebeling argues, accords with Luther's conviction that Scripture is not merely a written word belonging to the past, but a *viva vox evangelii*, a word of God which encounters us here and now. In accordance with this understanding of Luther's thought, Ebeling declares, "interpretation does not jeopardize but actually establishes the claim of the Scriptures to be the Word of God."[72]

Ebeling brings us back, in the end, to the considerations which we outlined in the first chapter of this study. The history of interpretation, he argues, begins in the Bible itself, for example when the Old Testament is expressed through the medium of the Septuagint. Even the supposedly straightforward matter of Bible translation, he points out, involves interpretation, and this cannot be done "timelessly," but is achieved in different ways from age to age and culture to culture.[73] Indeed, most of the many arguments about the need for interpretation put forward by Ebeling and Fuchs appeal, at some point, to the dual activities of Bible translation and Christian preaching. If the New Testament does not need to be articulated anew, why do we need translations which "speak" to a given language, culture, and community? If the New Testament already speaks in a "timeless" way, why do we believe that sermons are still necessary as a means of expounding the meaning of Scripture for today? Fuchs declares, "although preaching may say the same thing as the text, it in no case says the identical thing."[74] The task of the preacher, he urges, is so to "translate" the text that it speaks anew to his own time.[75] In one of Fuchs's typically aphoristic utterances he writes, "God's revelation consisted simply in God's letting men state *God's own problems in their language.*"[76]

What began as a consideration of a theological objection to hermeneutics on the basis of language about "timeless truth" has become, instead, the exposition of an argument for the urgency of hermeneutics on the ground of considerations about time and temporal change. We shall see in due course that Fuchs and Ebeling

71. Ebeling, *The Problem of Historicity in the Church and Its Proclamation*, p. 14.
72. Ebeling, *The Problem of Historicity in the Church and Its Proclamation*, p. 15.
73. Ebeling, *The Problem of Historicity in the Church and Its Proclamation*, p. 16.
74. Fuchs, *Zum hermeneutischen Problem in der Theologie*, p. 95.
75. Fuchs, *Hermeneutik*, pp. 249-56; and *Marburger Hermeneutik* (Tübingen: J. C. B. Mohr, 1968), pp. 2-4.
76. Fuchs, "The New Testament and the Hermeneutical Problem," pp. 135-36.

are admittedly influenced by Heidegger's thought about the relation between time and being. However, the validity of the comments about interpretation which we have noted are by no means dependent on any particular philosophical theory about time.

The fourth theological objection to the relevance of hermeneutical inquiry is based on the theory that, according to the outlook of many of the biblical writers, the Word of God encounters man with utterly compelling force. Appeals are made, for example, to such passages as Hebrews 4:12-13: "the word of God is living and active, sharper than any two-edged sword, piercing to the division of soul and spirit, of joints and marrow, and discerning the intentions of the heart." The Word of God is spoken of as "the power of God" for believers (1 Cor. 1:18) and as the sword of the Spirit (Eph. 6:17). Old Testament passages are cited still more frequently in this connection. The Word of God is as efficacious as the snow and rain which nourish the earth: "it shall not return to me empty" (Isa. 55:10-11). The Word of God has power to pluck up and to break down and is like a hammer that breaks in pieces, or like a fire (Jer. 1:9-10; 5:14; 23:29). If the Word of God is said to be like this, can there (from an admittedly *theological* viewpoint) be any room or need for hermeneutics?

This question need not detain us long at this point. In an article entitled "The Supposed Power of Words in the Biblical Writings" I have considered the issue in detail and conclude that allusions to the power of the word of God in the Old and New Testaments depend not on a particular supposedly ancient or "Hebraic" view of language but on the fact that the word in question is spoken with the authority of *God*.[77] Once this point is accepted, however, it only remains to ask what *kind* of authority or power God is said to exert in the communication of the Word. If this is conceived of quasi-physically or mechanically, it would certainly short-circuit discussions about hermeneutics. However, most traditions in Christian theology conceive of this "power" as being exercised in moral and above all personal terms. If this is the case, the points which we made in our discussion about the work of the Holy Spirit provide an adequate answer already to the question under consideration.

It is noteworthy that Helmut Thielicke finds no incompatibility between stressing, on the one hand, the creative power of the Word of God and the Holy Spirit to give birth to new capacities and orientations in man, and stressing, on the other hand, that God respects the personhood of the addressee in such a way that he does not impose upon him an external heteronomy. On the one hand he

---

77. See my essay "The Supposed Power of Words in the Biblical Writings," *Journal of Theological Studies*, n.s. 25 (1974): 283-99.

writes, "the creative Spirit of God . . . cannot be integrated into the structure of the 'old' existence. . . . Who God is and what he does to me cuts right across my theories about him."[78] The communication of the Word of God, Thielicke urges, involves new creation by the Spirit.[79] Nevertheless, he also writes that "as Kant pointed out, God's dignity is also at stake. For God does not want to force us as a heteronomous tyrant. He does not want servile obedience. He wants filial obedience. He wants us to turn to him spontaneously. We can do this, however, only if we are vanquished or inwardly persuaded by the claim of the message. . . . It is unavoidable, then, that the *autos* should become a theme of theological importance, that the anthropological question should be given a new stress. The question is now relevant what points of contact the message finds in our prior understanding . . . what concepts, e.g., in contemporary philosophy, are at our disposal in putting the message into another schema."[80] This perspective, Thielicke allows, although he believes that it contains many dangers, "does not have to be an enemy of theological tradition. . . . The question of understanding thus becomes more and more central until finally hermeneutics becomes a theological discipline of its own."[81]

Theological considerations about the creative power of the Word of God, then, no more call hermeneutics in question than parallel considerations about the work of the Holy Spirit, the need for faith, or claims about so-called timeless truth. On the contrary, each of these four sets of considerations serve in the end only to underline the importance of the hermeneutical task. We must now turn, however, to a broader issue, namely the questions raised by the problem of preunderstanding.

UNDERSTANDING AND PREUNDERSTANDING: SCHLEIERMACHER

Before we can try to evaluate the force of theological criticisms brought against the notion of preunderstanding, we must first outline what it is that is often under attack. We have already argued that theological considerations do not short-circuit the relevance of hermeneutics as the problem of human understanding. Further, in the first chapter we argued that understanding takes place when two sets of horizons are brought into relation to each other, namely those of the text and those of the interpreter. On this basis under-

78. Thielicke, *The Evangelical Faith*, 1: 145.
79. Thielicke, *The Evangelical Faith*, 1: 138-211.
80. Thielicke, *The Evangelical Faith*, 1: 38-39: see also p. 51.
81. Thielicke, *The Evangelical Faith*, 1: 39.

standing presupposes a shared area of common perspectives, concepts, or even judgments. Fuchs describes this common perspective as the phenomenon of "common understanding" (*Einverständnis*). But if understanding, as it were, presupposes understanding, how can it begin?

Friedrich Schleiermacher was one of the first major thinkers to wrestle with this problem. His early aphorisms on hermeneutics in 1805 and 1806 were sparked off by his critical dialogue with Friedrich Ast (1778-1841) and Friedrich August Wolf (1759-1824). Schleiermacher frequently alludes to these two writers, especially in his comments on their approach written in August 1829.[82] Schleiermacher saw that what is to be understood must, in a sense, be already known. If this seems to involve a circularity or even a contradiction, it can only be said that this very account of understanding is true to the facts of everyday experience. Schleiermacher drew attention to this when he wrote, "every child arrives at the meaning of a word only through hermeneutics [*Jedes Kind kommt nur durch Hermeneutik zur Wortbedeutung*]."[83] On the one side, the child attempts to relate a new word to what he already knows. If he cannot achieve this, the new word remains meaningless. On the other side (as Gadamer phrases it in his comment on Schleiermacher's aphorism), the child has to assimilate "something alien, universal, which always signifies a resistance for the original vitality. To that extent it is an accomplishment of hermeneutic."[84] Schleiermacher adds that since understanding new subject matter still depends on a positive relation to the interpreter's own horizons, "lack of understanding is never wholly removed."[85] It constitutes a progressive experience or process, not simply an act that can be definitively completed.

Richard Palmer defends Schleiermacher's approach. He writes, "is it not vain to speak of love to one who has not known love, or of the joys of learning to those who reject it? One must already have, in some measure, a knowledge of the matter being discussed. This may be termed the minimal pre-knowledge necessary for understanding, without which one cannot leap into the hermeneutical circle."[86]

82. Schleiermacher, *Hermeneutik: Nach den Handschriften neu herausgegeben und eingeleitet von Heinz Kimmerle* (Heidelberg: Carl Winter, 1959), pp. 123, 125-26, 128-29, 133, and 152-55.
83. Schleiermacher, *Hermeneutik*, p. 40.
84. Gadamer, "The Problem of Language in Schleiermacher's Hermeneutic," *Journal for Theology and the Church* 7 (1970): 72; see pp. 68-95.
85. Schleiermacher, *Hermeneutik*, p. 141.
86. Palmer, *Hermeneutics: Interpretation Theory in Schleiermacher, Dilthey, Heidegger, and Gadamer*, Studies in Phenomenology and Existential Philosophy (Evanston: Northwestern University Press, 1969), pp. 87-88.

Although it has now become a fixed and unalterable technical term in hermeneutics, the phrase "hermeneutical circle" is in one respect an unfortunate one. For although the center of gravity moves back and forth between the two poles of the interpreter and the text, there is also an ongoing movement and progressive understanding which might have been better conveyed by some such image as that of the spiral. There is also the additional problem that the phrase "hermeneutical circle" is used in two distinct ways. Often it is used in connection with the process of putting questions to the text, which are in turn reshaped by the text itself. Here, however, we are concerned with the principle that understanding a whole stretch of language or literature depends on an understanding of its component parts, while an understanding of these smaller units depends, in turn, on an understanding of the total import of the whole. For example, in attempting to grapple with the meaning of a difficult philosophical text such as Heidegger's *Being and Time,* we understand paragraphs and sentences only if we understand individual words within them. Yet the words cannot be understood by looking up their separate meanings in a dictionary. They depend for this meaning on their role within the sentence, paragraph, or chapter. Even the use of a technical glossary to explain individual terms depends on the understanding of the work as a whole arrived at in this case vicariously through the compiler of the glossary. In principle, the truth of the hermeneutical circle holds good. This is why a really difficult text which deals with new or seemingly strange subject matter may require a second or even a third reading if satisfactory understanding is to be achieved. This way of describing the issue, of course, only scratches the surface of Schleiermacher's hermeneutics, and we shall return to his approach again.

Meanwhile, in effect we have been exploring the category of preunderstanding (*Vorverständnis*). John Macquarrie helpfully expounds this concept in a way which takes up the approach which we have been observing in the writings of Schleiermacher. He comments, "we could never enter into any understanding of it [a text] unless there were at least some minimum of common ground between ourselves and the text."[87] "If it . . . did not link up at any point with our experience, we could make nothing of it."[88] This link is a matter of the interpreter's preunderstanding: "he already has certain categories of understanding under which the meaning of the text can be grasped, and these constitute the pre-understanding which he brings to the text."[89]

87. Mcquarrie, *The Scope of Demythologizing,* p. 45.
88. Macquarrie, *The Scope of Demythologizing,* p. 45.
89. Macquarrie, *The Scope of Demythologizing,* pp. 45-46.

We shall see in due course how the principle is taken up by both Bultmann and Heidegger. Heidegger writes, "in every case this interpretation is grounded in *something we have in advance* — in a *fore-having [Vorhabe]*." Understanding depends always on having a particular "point of view"; it is grounded in a "fore-sight" [*Vorsicht*]. It entails a given way of conceiving something; therefore, "it is grounded in . . . a *fore-conception (Vorgriff)*."[90] Heidegger continues, "an interpretation is never a presuppositionless apprehending of something presented to us."[91] Everything is understood in a given context and from a given point of view. Man's "world" and man's existence are bound up together. Hence, "in every understanding of the world, existence is understood with it and vice versa. . . . Any interpretation which is to contribute understanding must already have understood what is to be interpreted."[92] To be sure, the process seems to be circular. *"But if we see this circle as a vicious one and look out for ways of avoiding it . . . then the act of understanding has been misunderstood from the ground up."*[93]

Schleiermacher distinguished between the linguistic or "grammatical" aspects of hermeneutics and the "psychological" aspects of the subject. Heinz Kimmerle traces his shift in emphasis in his earlier and later writings in his introduction to Schleiermacher's *Hermeneutik*, and the volume is arranged in such a way that it is easy to note the chronological development of Schleiermacher's thought.[94] After twenty pages of aphorisms composed in the period between 1805 and 1809, the work is divided into five further sections covering the periods 1810-19 and 1820-29 as well as material specifically from the years 1819 and 1829.[95] Grammatical hermeneutics, Schleiermacher writes, requires the use of objective linguistic resources. Psychological hermeneutics involves penetration into the *inner* connections of thought that characterize an author's own consciousness. The linguistic and psychological aspects, therefore, correspond to the two poles of outward and "inner" reality, as Schleiermacher saw them. The interpreter must strive to enter into the mind of the author of the text that is to be understood, in an act of imaginative and sympathetic understanding. Just as on the grammatical level an understanding of individual words demands an

90. Heidegger, *Being and Time* (Oxford: Blackwell, 1962), p. 191.

91. Heidegger, *Being and Time*, pp. 191-92.

92. Heidegger, *Being and Time*, p. 194.

93. Heidegger, *Being and Time*, p. 194.

94. In addition to his introduction, see his essay "Hermeneutical Theory or Ontological Hermeneutics," *Journal for Theology and the Church* (=*History and Hermeneutics*) 4 (1967): 107.

95. Schleiermacher, *Hermeneutik*, pp. 31-50 (1805-09), 55-76 (1810-19), 79-109 (1819), 113-20 (1820-29), 123-56 (1829), and 159-66 (1832-33).

understanding of the whole, and vice versa, so on the psychological level each individual "thought" that lies behind single linguistic articulations must be understood in the whole context of the author's life. But the hermeneutical circle does not end even here. For an understanding of the author's life and consciousness depends on an understanding of human life and existence as a whole.

How this psychological aspect of hermeneutics relates to the preunderstanding of the interpreter himself is admirably expressed by T. F. Torrance in his article on Schleiermacher's hermeneutics.[96] The interpreter's understanding, he writes,

> depends upon his own ability or art to recreate in himself the basic determination of consciousness he finds in the author. This is the principal element in Schleiermacher's hermeneutics which was taken over and developed by Dilthey in his notion of hermeneutics as the rediscovery of the I in the Thou through a transposition by the interpreter of his own self into the other and a reliving of his experience in himself. From these views of Schleiermacher and Dilthey no extension is needed to the theory that *the key to the interpretation of a text,* whether of Plato or of St. Paul, *is self-understanding.*[97]

Three comments may be suggested at this point. First of all, Schleiermacher's attempt to relate hermeneutics to preunderstanding and to self-understanding rings true to the facts of everyday experience both in religious and secular life. We have only to compare our own "understanding" of such literature as the Psalms or even Shakespeare in childhood, youth, early adulthood, and later life, to see how this understanding is profoundly conditioned by our own experience. Can someone who has never suffered the pangs of guilt before God know what it is to appropriate the glad assurance of the psalmist, "though he fall, he shall not be utterly cast down" (Ps. 37:24)? Can someone who has never experienced the ups and downs of life enter into the hopes and fears of some of Shakespeare's more profound characters?

Second, however, Schleiermacher's emphasis on self-understanding also raises serious problems. James B. Torrance calls attention to these problems in his article "Interpretation and Understanding in Schleiermacher's Theology: Some Critical Questions."[98] Schleiermacher shares with romanticism the emphasis on feeling and subjective experience. But when he turns to questions about Christian

---

96. Torrance, "Hermeneutics according to F. D. E. Schleiermacher," *Scottish Journal of Theology* 21 (1968): 257-67.

97. Torrance, "Hermeneutics according to F. D. E. Schleiermacher," p. 261; italics mine.

98. Torrance, "Interpretation and Understanding in Schleiermacher's Theology: Some Critical Questions," *Scottish Journal of Theology* 21 (1968): 268-82.

faith, does he not go too near to translating Christian doctrine into descriptions of human states? J. B. Torrance allows that Schleiermacher does not reduce all theological content to human consciousness without qualification, but questions whether he pays adequate attention to "the 'objective' 'factual' reference of theological statements."[99] The weakness of this type of approach from the standpoint of Christian theology is that "it becomes so pre-occupied with the self-understanding of the human subject, that it fails to yield any positive affirmation about the Being of God as He is in Himself."[100] This is a recurring difficulty in the application of hermeneutics to theological texts. While as a hermeneutical starting point Bultmann rightly begins with the problem of preunderstanding, many writers have argued that in the end he reduces theology to anthropology. The question of whether this criticism is justified with reference to Bultmann begins to emerge with Schleiermacher, as soon as we have a sensitive awareness of the problem of preunderstanding.

Third, we may also note that Schleiermacher's recognition of the importance of understanding the whole as well as the parts, together with his emphasis on the role of sympathetic imagination, finds further expression in his notion of "divination." Divination entails a "leap" into fresh understanding. Schleiermacher writes, "the divinatory is that in which one transforms oneself into the other person in order to grasp his individuality directly."[101] Once again, this is connected with the hermeneutical circle. For Schleiermacher states that one must have an understanding of man himself in order to understand what he speaks, and yet one comes to know what man is from his speech.[102] Thus, understanding, once again, is not merely a matter of scientific "rules," but is a creative act.

PREUNDERSTANDING AND THEOLOGY

Regarding Bultmann's use of the category of preunderstanding, one or two preliminary comments are in order, since it is most frequently in the context of Bultmann's thought that the concept of preunderstanding is attacked. Bultmann is heavily indebted to Dilthey for the belief that understanding of a text depends on a prior relation to "life." Thus Bultmann writes, "Can one understand economic history without having a concept of what economy and society in general mean? Can one understand the history of religion and phi-

99. Torrance, "Interpretation and Understanding in Schleiermacher's Theology," p. 272; cf. p. 274.
100. Torrance, "Interpretation and Understanding in Schleiermacher's Theology," p. 278.
101. Schleiermacher, *Hermeneutik*, p. 109.
102. Schleiermacher, *Hermeneutik*, p. 44.

losophy without knowing what religion and philosophy are? . . . One cannot understand the Communist Manifesto of 1848 without understanding the principles of capitalism and socialism."[103] Bultmann concludes, "a specific understanding of the subject-matter of the text, on the basis of a 'life-relation' to it, is always presupposed by exegesis."[104]

Two elements in Bultmann's hermeneutics are attacked on the basis of their alleged dependence on his view of preunderstanding. First of all, he is attacked for laying down the principle that, in his own words, "the interpretation of the biblical writings is not subject to conditions different from those applying to all other kinds of literature."[105] Second, Bultmann also insists that for the interpreter to begin with questions about his own existence (*Existenz*) is thereby to ask questions about God. In *Jesus Christ and Mythology*, for example, he asks, What is the "life-relation" which the interpreter already has in advance to the theological subject matter of the New Testament? He is moved, he answers, "by the question about his personal existence." He then adds, "The question of God and the question of myself are identical."[106] Similarly, in his essay on hermeneutics Bultmann writes, "in human existence an *existentiell* knowledge about God is alive in the form of the inquiry about 'happiness,' 'salvation,' the meaning of the world, and . . . the real nature of each person's particular 'being.' "[107]

We should not draw far-reaching conclusions about Bultmann's hermeneutics solely on the basis of these two principles, however. For instance, it would be unwise to jump to conclusions about any supposed naturalism or immanentism implied by the second principle until we have first noted how strongly Bultmann is influenced by dialectical theology and by a recognition of the limitations of theological liberalism. His thought on this subject is complex, not least because he is attempting to do justice to a variety of theological perspectives, not all of which are clearly compatible with one another. However, our immediate purpose is simply to note that a number of writers, including Karl Barth, James Smart, and Carl Braaten, among others, explain these principles on the basis of Bult-

103. Bultmann, "Is Exegesis without Presuppositions Possible?" in *Existence and Faith* (London: Collins-Fontana, 1964), p. 347; see pp. 342-51.
104. Bultmann, "Is Exegesis without Presuppositions Possible?" p. 347.
105. Bultmann, *Essays Philosophical and Theological* (London: SCM Press, 1955), p. 256.
106. Bultmann, *Jesus Christ and Mythology* (London: SCM Press, 1960), p. 53; see pp. 52-56.
107. Bultmann, *Essays Philosophical and Theological*, p. 257.

mann's view of preunderstanding.[108] Carl Braaten writes, "the Achilles' heel of Bultmann's hermeneutical proposal is his narrow conception of the pre-understanding appropriate in Biblical interpretation."[109]

In practice, however, other theologians invoke the category of preunderstanding without accepting the two principles which are so often attacked in Bultmann's hermeneutics, and certainly without accepting an existentialist analysis of human existence. We shall illustrate this point by selecting for consideration the hermeneutics of some theologians who write from the standpoint of very different theological traditions. We shall refer briefly to some statements made by two Catholic theologians, Edward Schillebeeckx and Bernard Lonergan. We shall then compare the approach to New Testament hermeneutics represented by Latin American theologians such as Gustavo Gutiérrez and José Porfirio Miranda. After this we shall turn, finally, to the work of the philosopher Paul Ricoeur, in order to show that the category of preunderstanding is fruitfully employed by a thinker who cannot be accused of having any particular theological ax to grind.

We begin with a brief reference to the hermeneutics of Edward Schillebeeckx and Bernard Lonergan. Both stress that the truth of the New Testament is communicated through ordinary human language and appropriated by the normal processes of human understanding. In his wide-ranging book *The Understanding of Faith* Schillebeeckx gives more than adequate weight to distinctively theological considerations about faith.[110] However, he also emphatically asserts, a relationship with "lived experience" is an indispensable criterion for the meaning of theological interpretation.[111] He writes, "language only communicates meaning when it expresses an experience that is shared."[112] That is to say, he advocates what he calls "hermeneutics of experience."[113] He points out that he is not claiming that it is possible to deduce from ordinary human experiences the meaning of, say, the resurrection of Jesus Christ. He goes on to say, "What I am saying, however, is that the Christian meaning of the resurrection ... will be *a priori* unintelligible to us ... if the universally intelligible content of this concept does not include hu-

108. See Barth, "Rudolf Bultmann—An Attempt to Understand Him," pp. 83-132; Smart, *The Interpretation of Scripture*, p. 48; and Braaten, *History and Hermeneutics*, New Directions in Theology Today, no. 2 (London: Lutterworth Press, 1968), p. 35.

109. Braaten, *History and Hermeneutics*, p. 135.

110. Schillebeeckx, *The Understanding of Faith, Interpretation and Criticism* (London: Sheed & Ward, 1974), e.g., pp. 5-19, 135-55.

111. Schillebeeckx, *The Understanding of Faith, Interpretation and Criticism*, pp. 14-17.

112. Schillebeeckx, *The Understanding of Faith, Interpretation and Criticism*, p. 15.

113. Schillebeeckx, *The Understanding of Faith, Interpretation and Criticism*, p. 16.

man experience."[114] The criterion of intelligibility is "the relationship with lived human experience."[115] In effect this is a defense of
the category of preunderstanding as a necessary hermeneutical tool
and as grounded in human life.

Bernard Lonergan also argues for the importance of preunderstanding simply as a given fact of life by virtue of the nature of
language and understanding. We cannot claim to find meaning in
a biblical text, he argues, if we approach it on the basis of "the
principle of the empty head."[116] This approach is merely "naive."
We see that it is naive, he argues, as soon as we pause to think what
the "empty head" will in practice see. "There is just a series of
signs. Anything over and above a re-issue of the same signs in the
same order will be mediated by the experience, intelligence and
judgment of the interpreter. The less that experience, the less cultivated that intelligence, the less formed that judgment, the greater
will be the likelihood that the interpreter will impute to the author
an opinion that the author never entertained."[117]

This conclusion, which Lonergan states in his book *Method in
Theology*, also echoes his more general comments in his earlier work
Insight: A Study of Human Understanding. In this earlier work he writes,
"if a correct interpretation is possible, it has to be possible . . . for
interpreters to proceed from their own experience, understanding,
and judgment, to the range of possible meanings of documents."[118]
Lonergan does not seem to suggest in his later book on theology
that when the subject matter to be understood is theological, more
general theories of understanding become irrelevant.

Hermeneutics and especially theological questions about the significance of preunderstanding have been given a new turn in the last
few years by the emergence of the theology of liberation in Latin
America. In a survey article about this movement published in 1976,
José Miguez Bonino of Buenos Aires writes that biblical studies
constitute a challenge for the theology of liberation not least because
"we have, in the first place, the question of hermeneutics: Is it legitimate to start Biblical interpretation from a contemporary historical interpretation? . . . How can the freedom of the text be
maintained?"[119] Bonino gives a fuller description of the hermeneu-

---

114. Schillebeeckx, *The Understanding of Faith, Interpretation and Criticism*, p. 17.

115. Schillebeeckx, *The Understanding of Faith, Interpretation and Criticism*, p. 17.

116. Lonergan, *Method in Theology* (London: Darton, Longman & Todd, 1972),
p. 157.

117. Lonergan, *Method in Theology*, pp. 153-266.

118. Lonergan, *Insight: A Study of Human Understanding*, 2d ed. (London: Long-
mans, Green, 1958), p. 578.

119. Miguez Bonino, "Theology and Theologians of the New World, II: Latin
America," *Expository Times* 87 (1976): 199; see pp. 196-200.

tics of the movement in his book *Revolutionary Theology Comes of Age*, and the hermeneutics can be seen in action in such works as José Porfirio Miranda's *Marx and the Bible*.[120] The hermeneutics of the movement is also critically discussed in a recent doctoral thesis by J. Andrew Kirk.[121]

These writers, together with others such as Gustavo Gutiérrez, Juan Luis Segundo, and Hugo Assmann, stress that biblical hermeneutics turns on a preunderstanding which is shaped, in turn, by *praxis*. Theoretical knowledge, it is argued, especially the philosophical values associated with the Western bourgeoisie, distort the message of the Bible and obscure the rights of the text. There is no such thing as purely neutral knowledge. Bonino asserts, "the sociology of knowledge makes abundantly clear that we think out of a definite context . . . , *out of a given praxis*. What Bultmann has so convincingly argued concerning a *preunderstanding* which every man brings to his interpretation of the text *must be deepened and made more concrete*."[122] Preunderstanding, Bonino continues, relates to such concrete considerations as a man's social class and nationhood. Freud and Marx, he argues, were correct in their suspicions about hidden factors which control man's conscious accounts of life and literature. The Latin American theologians are especially suspicious of approaches to the Bible undertaken from bourgeois or non-Marxist perspectives. "Why is it, for instance, that the obvious political motifs and undertones in the life of Jesus have remained so hidden to liberal interpreters until very recently?"[123] Juan Luis Segundo argues that theologians have managed to draw from the Bible and Christian tradition the image of a timeless and impersonal God only because their interpretations were shaped by a prior view of life in which God was relegated to an "inner" or "private" zone. "Hermeneutics in this new context means also an identification of the ideological framework of interpretation implicit in a given religious praxis."[124]

Many of the Latin American theologians themselves quite explicitly and consciously interpret the New Testament in terms of a

120. See Miranda, *Marx and the Bible: A Critique of the Philosophy of Oppression* (Maryknoll, N.Y.: Orbis Books, 1974); Gutiérrez, *A Theology of Liberation* (Maryknoll, N.Y.: Orbis Books, 1973); and other writers discussed by Miguez Bonino in *Revolutionary Theology Comes of Age* (London: S.P.C.K., 1975), especially the selection entitled "Hermeneutics, Truth, and Praxis" (pp. 86-105); see pp. 344-57 herein.

121. Kirk, "The Theology of Liberation in the Latin American Roman Catholic Church since 1965: An Examination of Its Biblical Basis" (Ph.D. Diss., University of London, 1975). Part II concerns especially preunderstanding and hermeneutics. See also Kirk's *Liberation Theology: An Evangelical View from the Third World* (London: Marshall, Morgan & Scott, 1979).

122. Miguez Bonino, *Revolutionary Theology Comes of Age*, p. 90.

123. Miguez Bonino, *Revolutionary Theology Comes of Age*, p. 91.

124. Miguez Bonino, *Revolutionary Theology Comes of Age*, p. 94.

preunderstanding oriented towards Marxist perspectives. Thus Bonino asks, "Is it altogether absurd to re-read the resurrection today as a death of the monopolies, the liberation from hunger, or a solidary form of ownership?"[125] José Porfirio Miranda's *Marx and the Bible* provides a more detailed example. Too often, he complains, the biblical interpreter has approached the text with a preunderstanding of man as an abstraction, "a Platonic essence valid *semper et pro semper,* not real flesh-and-blood humanity, a humanity of blood and tears and slavery and humiliations and jail and hunger and untold sufferings."[126] Miranda also stresses that preunderstanding must be oriented to *praxis*. Otherwise the interpreter becomes sidetracked into merely dealing in "concepts" *about* God. The God of the Bible, he declares, is the one "to objectify whom is to break off the imperative relationship."[127]

Yet Miranda and Bonino do not wish to open the door to subjectivism (as against subjectivity). Miranda asserts, "I am not reducing the Bible to Marx. . . . I only wish to understand what the Bible says. . . . We want to take the Bible seriously."[128] Indeed, he argues that his own approach is motivated by an attempt to read the Bible on its own terms. It is precisely *not* simply all "a matter of the mind of the interpreter." It is only the defeatist and cynical belief that "Scripture has various 'meanings' " that (in Miranda's view) allows conservative theologians of the West "to prevent the Bible from revealing *its* own subversive message. Without a recourse to this belief, how could the West, a civilization of injustice, continue to say that the Bible is its sacred book? Once we have established the possibility of different 'meanings' each as acceptable as any other, then Scripture cannot challenge the West."[129] Bonino also insists that critical appraisal must take place to insure that "reading" the New Testament does not become a matter of "only arbitrary inventions."[130] Andrew Kirk sums up the perspective as follows: "The Marxist interpretation provides an ideological mechanism which is capable of exposing the intentions of any exegesis seeking, through the employment of preunderstanding tied to conservative philosophical systems, to use the Biblical text . . . to defend the status-quo of a pre-revolutionary situation."[131]

The effect of this approach is first of all to stress the importance

125. Miguez Bonino, *Revolutionary Theology Comes of Age,* p. 101.
126. Miranda, *Marx and the Bible,* p. 31.
127. Miranda, *Marx and the Bible,* p. 41.
128. Miranda, *Marx and the Bible,* pp. 35, 36.
129. Miranda, *Marx and the Bible,* p. 36.
130. Miguez Bonino, *Revolutionary Theology Comes of Age,* p. 100.
131. Kirk, "The Theology of Liberation in the Latin American Roman Catholic Church since 1965," Part II, sect. 2-1.

of questions about preunderstanding, and second to show that the use of this category in New Testament hermeneutics does not belong exclusively to those who start from the standpoint of Heidegger and existentialist philosophy, nor even from the philosophical tradition of Schleiermacher and Dilthey. But thereby they provide two warnings which we must heed when we look at Bultmann's thought more closely. First of all, the fact that Marxist interpreters do in fact tend to arrive at Marxist interpretations of the Bible even when they are aware of their own preunderstanding sharpens the problem of objectivity in biblical hermeneutics. A mere awareness of the problem of preunderstanding is not enough to solve the problems to which this phenomenon gives rise. We have arrived at the point where the problem is less "the pastness of the past" than that of evaporating past meaning in the horizons of the present. Second, if such different preunderstandings seem to lead on to such different ways of interpreting the New Testament, we must beware of the claim of any one New Testament interpreter to start from the "right" preunderstanding. This is sometimes urged as a criticism of Bultmann, and we shall see in due course that it is not entirely without some truth. On the one hand, Bultmann sets too high a value on the *one* starting point of the earlier Heidegger's view of existence; but on the other hand he does also stress that any preunderstanding is provisional and open to later correction.

As a final comment on the subject of preunderstanding in general we may also note that the debate, in effect, is even more wide-ranging than we have yet seen. The philosopher Paul Ricoeur (as well as others, including for example Peter Homans) shows how hermeneutics is affected by considerations which emerge not only from Marx but also from Sigmund Freud.[132] One of the most startling features of Ricoeur's discussion from the point of view of the present study is that it serves in effect to demonstrate that conclusions about the importance of preunderstanding can be arrived at from *two radically opposing philosophical traditions*. We have seen that in the tradition of Schleiermacher hermeneutical principles are formulated from the point of view of an emphasis on human consciousness. Freud (together with Nietzsche and Marx) approaches the problem of meaning on the basis of a *rejection* of the category of human consciousness as the key starting point. Because of the complexity of the human mind, Freud argues that meaning is not always synonymous with *consciousness of* meaning. Ricoeur comments, "these

---

132. Ricoeur, *The Conflict of Interpretations: Essays in Hermeneutics*, Studies in Phenomenology and Existential Philosophy, ed. Paul D. Ihde (Evanston: Northwestern University Press, 1974), pp. 99-208, especially pp. 142-50. See also Homans, "Psychology and Hermeneutics," *Journal of Religion* 60 (1975): 327-47.

three exegetes of modern man [Freud, Nietzsche and Marx] . . . all attack the same illusion, that illusion which bears the hallowed name of self-consciousness. . . . These three masters of suspicion, however, are not three masters of skepticism. . . . Marx, Nietzsche and Freud triumph over their doubt about consciousness through an exegesis of meanings. For the first time comprehension is hermeneutics."[133]

However, in each individual case, these thinkers approach questions about meanings with preunderstandings which, in their view, unlock and disclose them. Freud believes that the key to meaning comes from the unconscious psyche. Hence he interprets consciousness from the standpoint of this preunderstanding. Nietzsche approaches the matter in terms of man's will to power. Marx interprets life and history with presuppositions about man as a social being. Their view of "meaning" is inseparable from their own preunderstanding. None of these three thinkers could achieve his goal by ignoring or suppressing his own preunderstanding. "Understanding" dawns in the interaction between preunderstanding and meaning.[134]

We cannot claim, then, that the importance of preunderstanding in New Testament hermeneutics depends either on special pleading in theology or on too narrow a philosophical base. The problems posed by this phenomenon cannot be avoided. In the words of the Church of England's Doctrine Communion Report *Christian Believing,* "No one expounds the Bible to himself or to anyone else without bringing to the task his own prior frame of reference, his own pattern of assumptions which derives from sources outside the Bible."[135]

133. Ricoeur, *The Conflict of Interpretations*, pp. 148-49.
134. Ricoeur, *The Conflict of Interpretations*, p. 150.
135. "The Christian and the Bible," in *Christian Believing: The Nature of the Christian Faith and Its Expression in Holy Scripture and Creed* (London: S.P.C.K., 1976), p. 30.

PART III

CURRENT ASSESSMENTS

The three essays in this section offer surveys of the contemporary hermeneutical scene. As such they provide an overview of some of the major figures and movements that are making an impact on the way hermeneutics is understood and biblical interpretation being done in the present day.

Karlfried Froehlich in "Biblical Hermeneutics on the Move" discusses the problems of contemporary biblical hermeneutics and the problem of how to identify them. He moves on to describe the contexts of biblical interpreters and the need to understand the settings in which exegetical work is done. Froehlich concludes with an illustration of a biblical scholar, Peter Stuhlmacher, who by his ecumenical orientation builds bridges between ecclesiastical traditions but who also combines his professional, academic writings on biblical interpretation with a concern for the needs of the Christian church.

The essay by Thomas W. Gillespie focuses on the fundamental hermeneutical question of how we can understand and express the meaning of the historic literature of Scripture in and for every new and changing historical situation. To come to grips with this, Gillespie examines key hermeneutical terms and how they are being defined by a variety of writers on hermeneutics. The terms include *interpretation, meaning, language,* and *understanding.*

Patrick R. Keifert's essay "Mind Reader and Maestro Models for Understanding Biblical Interpreters" displays two paradigms for biblical interpretation that are prominent today: historical and linguistic. Within each of these, there are various ways of construing an interpreter's self-understanding and the way in which a text can be conceived. The models on which Keifert concentrates are the interpreter as mind reader, maestro, player-coach, deliberator, and storyteller.

With these surveys we see how theories of hermeneutics are enacted in the overall systems of some major figures working in the area of hermeneutics today. Again the picture is one of diversity, but it also shows the possibilities of how hermeneutical understandings can be conceived and developed.

BIBLICAL HERMENEUTICS ON THE MOVE

KARLFRIED FROEHLICH

As we move fully into the eighties, something seems to be happening at the fronts of biblical hermeneutics. It is still too early to assess the new mood after the devastating seventies, but things seem to be moving again, fresh questions appear, new windows are being opened.

1

This optimistic outlook must surely be good news for weary Christians, especially pastors, who feel frustrated and confused by what they have heard from the lecterns of academic theologians in recent years. On the one hand there was plenty of crisis talk. Brevard Childs provided the start in 1970 with his *Biblical Theology in Crisis*. Hans Frei's *Eclipse of Biblical Narrative* followed suit only to make room soon thereafter for the declaration of historical criticism's "bankruptcy" (Walter Wink) and of "The End of the Historical-Critical Method" (Gerhard Maier). On the other hand, everyone noticed a considerable hardening of lines in the older hermeneutical debates. The conservative side went through a resurgence of its more militant positions. After the purge of biblical dissidents in the major seminary of the Lutheran Church – Missouri Synod, the "Battle for the Bible" (Harold Lindsell) was on in the Southern Baptist Convention threatening less radical elements at seminaries like Fuller. The International Council on Biblical Inerrancy is gathering strength since its Chicago Statement of October 1978 and tries to impress its message on the wider public. At the same time, the critical study of the Bible under the auspices of professional societies, the Council on the Study of Religion, and the university departments of religion has been flourishing, reaching out in more and more directions and applying freely the insights of sociology, anthropology, psychology, modern linguistics, and other branches of knowledge with their appropriate methodologies to the biblical texts. Jewish, Christian, and nonreligious scholars collaborate in these efforts as a matter of rou-

Reprinted from *Word & World* 1 (1981): 140-52.

tine and claim attention for a plethora of new theories and possibilities in interpretation. The gulf between the two hermeneutical worlds is widening at a breathtaking pace, leaving few bridges between them.

Many Christians and their pastors are caught in between. Left with the task of applying the biblical message to their daily lives because their churches are committed to the Bible as the norm for teaching, preaching, and living, they often cannot in good conscience endorse the rigid inerrancy propositions of the one side, nor do they find much help for their task from the esoteric work of the other. It is not surprising that many pastors have turned to a new professional emphasis in their ministry, stressing care and counseling more than teaching and giving up more or less on expository preaching. One pastor put it in these terms: "My walls are lined with critical commentaries. I have bought the *Interpreter's Bible* and Kittel's *Theological Dictionary*. I am browsing through the pious popular Scripture series which are full of subjective, irrelevant side remarks, but I just do not find what I'm looking for in order to be able to preach that text to my congregation." Neither do congregations get what they need and are looking for. As a woman said to me recently, "I'm getting tired of those sermons which just repeat in cute language what I can read every day in the paper. Is there nothing the Bible has to say other than this? When the pastor visited me in the hospital he tried valiantly to make me feel better. He even prayed with me a little. But there was no word of comfort from the Bible, no psalm, nothing." A failure of discernment and courage? Maybe. But the "strange silence of the Bible in the church" (James D. Smart) has deeper roots. The hermeneutical confusion of the last decade or so points to a deep insecurity vis-à-vis the normative Bible in church and schools.

The problem of biblical hermeneutics is given with the Bible itself, with its nature as a canonical collection of authoritative writings, and with its linguistic form. Concerning the first point we seem to be somewhat more pragmatic than a previous generation, perhaps as a result of closer ecumenical contacts with the Catholic side. The dialectic of Scripture and church and church tradition no longer bothers Protestants greatly. The resonance which Brevard Childs's proposal has found, to give primary authority for the understanding of biblical texts to their final canonical form, may illustrate the trend.[1] Yet it remains a problem why only the final form of a text should be theologically normative. Neither "canon analysis" nor "canon criticism" (James Sanders) are without serious problems in

---

1. See Childs, *Biblical Theology in Crisis* (Philadelphia: Westminster Press, 1970), especially pp. 99-122.

the present situation. We also speak with relative ease of "God's Word" in relation to Scripture. The recent volume of *Studies in Lutheran Hermeneutics*, prepared under the auspices of the Division of Theological Studies of the Lutheran Council in the U.S.A., documents this fact for Lutheran theologians of all shades.[2] Only the Missouri Synod contributors claim the simple identification of Bible and Word of God as the proper interpretation of the confessional stance,[3] but the distinctions made since Karl Barth between Word of God as event (Christ), witness (Scripture), and proclamation (preaching) have helped other Lutherans, too, to recover the general use of the theological term in reference to Scripture.

The problem of biblical language, however, goes deeper. God did not use a language of his own or the "language of angels" (1 Cor. 13:1) but made human language of particular times and places the vehicle of biblical revelation. Ralph Bohlmann of the Lutheran Church — Missouri Synod, in the volume mentioned above, concludes from this divine authorship that "the Scriptures are qualitatively different from every other form of human expression in every age."[4] One could draw the opposite conclusion: God has the same problem with human language we all have. This is the price of incarnation. Human language is contingent, open, ambiguous, and therefore in need of interpretation. Many factors have to be considered in such an interpretation. Modern linguistic studies give us an idea of their extent. It is not enough to ask for the intention of the original author. Language always involves a speaker and a listener. The process of reception, language as it is *heard*, must be part of the investigation. Modern semantics warns against the determination of the meaning of a word field apart from the conversational and syntactic context. Human language does not communicate unambiguously or in the abstract. It does so in a subtle interaction of contingent factors which are complicated even further in the case of written texts. The entire web of human relationships and their key role in the perception of reality plays into the interpretation of language. There is, nevertheless, reluctance today to attribute to hermeneutics the role of a universal science of understanding all reality simply because of the linguisticality of human perception. Humans themselves have probably not been the same genus throughout the history of the race. Much of what language does has to be seen

2. *Studies in Lutheran Hermeneutics*, ed. J. Reumann (Philadelphia: Fortress Press, 1979). The introductory essay by Reumann not only gives a fascinating account of the discussions within the Division but relates it in a most helpful way to the general situation in biblical scholarship.

3. See S. H. Nafzger's review of the essays in *Studies in Lutheran Hermeneutics*, pp. 119-23.

4. Bohlmann, in *Studies in Lutheran Hermeneutics*, p. 192.

functionally in terms of the act of communication, and precisely in this context it is not identical with reality. We are today more aware of the fact of nonverbal communication and of a world of reality not reached by language.

Biblical hermeneutics, however, is not only a question of human language used by God. In any written text the hermeneutical issue of language and reality takes the concrete form of the relation between language and history. Language points to something. Biblical language, the language of a collection of writings from a distant period of history, points to a history. Its relation to a specific history and to historical reality in general has emerged as one of the major problems of the recent debates. Based on their understanding of inspiration and divine authorship, fundamentalist and conservative interpreters, for instance, have claimed a close relationship. Biblical interpretation is needed, but the need arises more from the use of language than from problems with the reality of the history it points to. The Bible is a book *sui generis* precisely in terms of its unique historical reliability. This is the central point of its widely affirmed inerrancy. Most exegetes, on the other hand, see the distance more clearly. They draw the conclusion from the human language of the Bible that its relation to historical reality is the same as it is in other written sources. This does not mean that the biblical word is not true. Rather, the historical truth in and behind the text, the history to which the text points, is part of the goal of interpretation, not its presupposition, and this goal must be reached by the same means that are applied to all other literature. A third position prominent in the discussion reinterprets the terms of the debate by taking its clue from modern literary criticism. Here the language angle of the text is the primary concern. All texts have a history of their own as soon as they leave the hand of the author and enter the public domain. They become a paradigm for interpretations of reality of which the author may never have dreamed. The historical reality to which the word of the Bible must be related is not only tied to the then and there of ancient history. It is the history—or, to use the more current term, the story—of the hearer today and in all ages. My story participates in the general structure of reality communicated by the linguistic metaphor. The recent theology of the story and the practice of structuralism, while finding a considerable following among exegetes, have also been suspected of being sophisticated tools of a conservative mentality.

In America the most serious development in the turmoil of biblical hermeneutics during the 1970s was the apparent decline of what Childs termed the "Biblical Theology Movement."[5] Highly influ-

---

5. Childs, *Biblical Theology in Crisis*, pp. 13-87.

ential during the 1950s and early 1960s through such writers as
G. E. Wright, B. W. Anderson, Paul Minear, and Floyd V. Filson,
it seemed to provide a middle ground between critical and uncritical
extremes by focusing with equal determination on historical research and theological interpretation of the Bible in and for the
church. The historical investigation of developing traditions in the
biblical community of faith itself seemed to lead directly to extrap-
olations such as a theology of the history of tradition (von Rad) or
the theological concept of *Heilsgeschichte* (Oscar Cullmann). Biblical
history understood as God's mighty acts (G. E. Wright) could be
seen as a vigorous stimulus to Christian witness in society by the
contemporary church without the fear of losing touch with modern
historical consciousness. If one follows Childs's analysis, the movement turned most fervently against the old ethics of theological liberalism and its basis in a misused historical criticism, finding itself
in league with neo-orthodoxy at this point. But it reserved equally
sharp polemics for the fundamentalist position in biblical studies,
and thus made itself a strong advocate of the use of the historical-
critical method in the churches. When the method itself came under
fire, the movement which had suffered heavy blows already in the
1960s was doomed. This may be a somewhat simplistic picture.
Whether the movement really is dead can rightly be doubted. Childs
himself wants to build a "new biblical theology" on a different foundation. The deeper issue in the dissolution of the movement's strength
was not, at any rate, that of method but a changing view of history.
Not only language is ambiguous. History is, too—even a carefully
constructed history of tradition. It always allows for more than one
theological extrapolation in different communities of faith, and the
resulting pluralism has not yet found a common focus. Uneasiness
with the historical-critical method is certainly not enough to provide
common ground and focus for a new movement. Yet it is this methodological issue that seems to keep the discussion in suspense at the
moment.

It is interesting to observe how the predominant concern over
the historical-critical method in recent years has led to talk about
a "precritical," a "critical," and a "postcritical" approach to biblical
interpretation. Such verbal constructions of historical developments
should always be viewed with suspicion. As in most similar schemes,
they express a highly partisan vision, which in this case is no less
biased than the alternative picture of original fidelity, defection, and
return. The distinction of a precritical and a critical era echoes
Ernst Troeltsch's famous analysis which saw the primary characteristic of the modern age in the step from an unscientific to a
scientific worldview. The addition of a postcritical era reveals that
the sequence reflects the program of a generation which, having

lived within the camp of historical criticism long enough, now wants to move out. But "postcritical" itself bestows only an ambiguous identity. Many conservative scholars today seize upon the term in the hope that a jump on the bandwagon of this inner-critical debate will circumvent the need for a real confrontation with the critical method. Obviously the term is usable by both reactionary and avantgarde forces when the repudiation of the dominant parent generation is at stake. In terms of historical periodization, Troeltsch's dichotomy may still be helpful for our understanding of the "modern" age since the Enlightenment of the eighteenth century, although his scheme is really more a historical judgment about the crucial importance of the Enlightenment itself than it is an accurate analysis of two epochs. To add the idea of a "postcritical" age can only compound the historiographical problem. It demonstrates even more clearly the unhistorical character of the scheme and its polemical thrust in the larger battle of our generation to find a new historical identity of its own.

2

These deliberations press home the importance of considering the setting in which exegetical work is done today if we want to understand the promise and the limitations of the hermeneutical debate. Scholars (including this one!) who advance their theories (including theories about the periodization of the history of their field!) are part of a specific sociological setting, a community of scholars in seminaries and universities participating in the general scholarly ethos of their time and yet tied to the life of the church in however faint or indirect a manner individual circumstances suggest. All these factors exert their influence on the direction of their thinking and their agenda. Much has been theorized about the history of biblical scholarship in the abstract, but little attention has been paid to the sociology of professional exegesis.[6] In order to gain a fresh perspective it may be wise to focus not on scholarly hermeneutics as such but on the scholars who formulate its theories, not on interpretation but on the interpreters to whose professional work the exegetical consumer looks for guidance.

Who is the professional biblical interpreter today? Posing the question this way, church people probably think of the biblical professors in our educational institutions, the professionals whose job it is to teach exegetical method to seminarians, to provide expert commentary on Scripture in the classroom and in their writing, and

6. An exception is Patrick Henry's *New Directions in New Testament Studies* (Philadelphia: Westminster Press, 1979).

to contribute to the application of biblical teaching in the discussion of the issues their churches are facing as responsible theologians of the church. What is often forgotten is the fact that they all are also members of the academic establishment of our culture, subjected to the requirements of academic professionalism, susceptible to peer pressure and to the demands of the guild ethos. Their teaching in and for the church owes much to this life setting and cannot be divorced from its dynamics.

Such a guild of professional biblical interpreters in the church is, however, a fairly recent development dating back in its beginnings to the rise of the high medieval universities. In the ancient church the bishops were regarded as the professional interpreters of Scripture. Preaching and the exposition of the Bible was *their* business. Augustine was brought to Hippo Rhegius to fill in as a preacher for the aging bishop who did not feel up to the task. In the Middle Ages, while the exposition of Scripture by the clergy had to be authorized and delegated by the local bishop and excluded the unlearned laity, the highest decisional authority on matters of biblical interpretation was reserved for the *magisterium* of the pope. One can observe how in the late Middle Ages the theological masters of the rising universities started to assert their professional role as the church's exegetes. Without their expert advice popes would not pronounce on matters of faith, and the masters' self-image as sharers in the apostolic *magisterium* of the church is reflected in the sources.[7] Martin Luther the Reformer must be seen in this context. His professional status throughout his life was that of a doctor of Holy Scripture as far as he was concerned, and he used the obligations of this office as a warrant for his reforming activity. In opposition to the papacy, which still claimed the sole right to binding interpretation, he even broadened the base of the shared authority in biblical interpretation far beyond the realm of the academy. In the beginning of his Reformation he regarded all duly called ministers of the gospel as competent interpreters of Scriptures and could locate the authority to judge doctine by the standards of the Bible in the Christian congregation itself. The sobering experience with the actual state of biblical illiteracy during the Saxon visitations and with the independent scriptural exegesis of more radical reformers led, however, back behind this advance. Later developments in the Lutheran territories favored again the academic expert as the authoritative interpreter of Scripture. In fact, during the time of Lutheran Orthodoxy, the theological faculties functioned practically as the *magisterium* of the Lutheran churches.[8] It was in the context of the academy with its biblical experts that the modern historical-critical method emerged. In its application to biblical studies it reflected the double loyalty of the theological professors, both to the ideals of the university of the eighteenth century, committed to the progress of human knowledge and to the cause of the church. In the same limited academic context the picture of a precritical, a critical, and a postcritical epoch of biblical hermeneutics has its *Sitz im Leben*. Its model of a development in three steps has no claim to historical validity but is a value judgment. It explains the present dynamics of an academic field, however, in which the church and all its members have a vital stake.

Our survey has already shown that the history of biblical hermeneutics involved more fundamental shifts than that of the eighteenth century, if we focus on the role of the professional interpreter rather than the method of interpretation. But even if we would consider the latter, one might wonder whether such phenomena as Origen's systematic hermeneutics, the shift from the patristic chain commentary to the scholastic commentary of the twelfth century, the nominalist erosion of trust in an unambiguous biblical language, or the shift to the dominance of the literal sense, did not constitute equally decisive turning points as that marked by the impact of the Enlightenment.

When we turn to an examination of the label "precritical," the problem of the three steps is even more obvious. The label turns out to be simply wrong when we try to verify it outside the limited context which we have sketched. The early history of the biblical canon is full of examples of critical, even historical-critical work. Bishops had to make decisions about the authorship of specific books such as Hebrews, Revelation, and the Catholic Epistles. Church Fathers debated questions of the best text, reliable translations, the historical referent of Old Testament prophecy, and the historicity of New Testament stories. Medieval popes had to render a critical judgment on the biblical evidence concerning Christ's actual poverty. The traditional fourfold sense of Scripture was a sophisticated method of critical biblical interpretation dealing precisely with the relationship between text and history.[9] The simple identification of the two was for medieval exegetes only the first, the surface level, no more. For centuries the designation "letter," literal sense, remained interchangeable with "historia," historical sense. Origen of

8. See W. A. Quanbeck, "The Magisterium in the Lutheran Church," in *Teaching Authority and Infallibility in the Church*, ed. P. C. Empie, T. A. Murphy, and J. A. Burgess (Minneapolis: Augsburg Publishing, 1978), pp. 151-52.

9. For a spirited defense of medieval exegesis, see D. C. Steinmetz, "The Superiority of Pre-Critical Exegesis," *Theology Today* 27 (1980): 27-38; see pp. 65-77 herein.

Alexandria already taught that such a literal, historical sense, while not absent in the Bible, cannot be expected to be the main object of exegesis. There is much more in the Bible than a compend of guaranteed facts. As an inspired book, Scripture must have a spiritual sense everywhere but not necessarily a literal sense also. This assumption called for a very critical attitude toward the surface of a text. There was always the possibility of further levels of meaning behind the words. Building upon Augustine, the medieval tradition standardized the number of the further senses to include three: allegory, tropology (moral sense), and anagogy (eschatological-mystical sense). A widely circulated rhyme in the later Middle Ages which names the four senses reveals the principle under which the "higher senses" were chosen: "The letter teaches facts; allegory what one should believe; tropology what one should do; anagogy where one should aspire." The three spiritual senses represent the three theological virtues — faith, love, and hope. These virtues are the true goal of biblical exposition. Biblical texts are rarely to be taken at face value. There is always something behind them, beyond them which has to be spelled out.

When Luther collapsed the fourfold scheme into a single "literal" sense, he lost an important instrument of biblical criticism. His single sense now had to carry the burden of the *total* meaning of the text.[10] Luther himself eased the problem by concentrating on an internal criticism of the biblical text under the theological axiom: "Scripture is everywhere about Christ." It led him to critical decisions about rank both within the canon and on the fringes of the canon. It also led to his use of the new philological criticism which the humanists had developed for literary texts in general. It was only in the period of Protestant Orthodoxy that the reductionist potential of his insistence on the one literal sense was fully implemented. Verbal inspiration, contrary to Origen's understanding of it, came to mean that the literal level of the biblical text in its identity with history was its only true meaning.

These remarks to not mean to suggest that nothing new happened with the Enlightenment. The unity of text and history stressed so much by Protestant Orthodoxy started to disintegrate under the obvious overload the single literal sense now had to carry. Without denying the ultimate role of the divine author and the rights of dogmatic theology, academic exegetes shifted the hermeneutical focus to the human authors of Scripture in order to speak about literal sense and history in terms verifiable by the rational sciences of their time. For them this was not a proud change from unscientific to

10. For more on this, see my essay "Problems in Lutheran Hermeneutics," in *Studies in Lutheran Hermeneutics*, pp. 127-41.

scientific method or from precritical to critical attitudes. Rather, it was the humbling experience of stepping down from the height of the proud dogmatician who could confidently talk about the "hidden things of God" to the lowly realms of contingent human language and history. In the horizon which interests us here, however, something else is more important: the new concentration on the human author was a clear indication that the academic interpreter of the Bible was now tipping the scale of a double loyalty in favor of academic commitment. Henceforth he would see himself primarily responsible for his colleagues in the developing secular sciences of history and philology, not to his peers and authorities in the church.

The new type of professional interpreter has dominated the nineteenth and twentieth centuries: professional historians who also, secondarily, recognize and often practice their loyalty and responsibility to and in the church. It should be remembered that the latter aspect was rarely missing. Schleiermacher, Harnack, Bultmann, and many others were devoted churchmen whose commitment to their churches must not be doubted. But how can this commitment be carried out effectively if the primary interest of the exegete remains tied to the world of professional scholarship which has its own agenda and its own social dynamics? The question still stands and has to be answered constantly in hundreds of lives to whom pastors and church people look with expectancy but often also with suspicion. To focus attention on the chances for a viable balance between the two loyalties of the professional interpreter seems to me more fruitful today than to debate precritical, critical, and postcritical methods. Is the alternative to the dominant type a new type of church theologian who dabbles in modern scholarship on the side? Karl Barth looked like this to the guild of scholars in the early 1920s. While inadequate, the impression was not totally wrong in terms of Barth's priorities. His relegation of historical criticism to the level of a mere tool for church dogmatics, where he used it himself, probably prevented for some time a penetrating analysis of its ideological character. Today more and more churches seek to exercise stricter control over the teaching of their professional exegetes in the seminaries, degrading the loyalty to the guild of scholars within which these people function to an entirely secondary position. The risks of such pressure are obvious.[11] As long as the professional exegete is located in the setting of modern academe, the churches should expect and respect his or her strong sense of loyalty to the academic context and its common weal. The churches should also expect,

11. Cf. the report of an investigating committee on the question of academic freedom at Concordia Seminary, St. Louis, "Academic Freedom and Tenure: Concordia Seminary (Missouri)," *AAUP Bulletin* 61 (1975): 49-59.

however, that their exegetes recognize the limiting nature of their academic context and relate themselves and their work freely, openly, and loyally to their churches' well-being.

3

The good news for pastors and Christians in the churches is that new models of such a balance of the two loyalties seem to be emerging today. The balance is not just a private matter for the individual exegete but a matter of the public record of his or her work. As an illustration, let me briefly analyze the work of a younger continental scholar who is already influential in Germany through his teaching and writing and whose contribution needs to be better known abroad. Peter Stuhlmacher, former assistant to Ernst Käsemann, is now the successor of his teacher in the second New Testament chair at the University of Tübingen.

Edgar Krentz in his standard introduction to the historical-critical method[12] still classified Stuhlmacher among the critics of the method. One could say, indeed, that in comparison with his German colleagues such as Ferdinand Hahn, Martin Hengel, or Ulrich Wilckens, he is the one who has formulated the clearest and most penetrating scholarly critique of the method's results and presuppositions to date.[13] What he stresses, however, is not so much its failure but its limits, which should, he feels, be easily visible to the self-critical eye. In a masterful survey, Stuhlmacher leads his reader through the problems with some main results of the method's standard branches.[14] Biblical philology still suffers from concentrating

12. Krentz, *The Historical-Critical Method* (Philadelphia: Fortress Press, 1975), pp. 84-85.

13. Only one of Stuhlmacher's pertinent essays is available in English at present: *Historical Criticism and Theological Interpretation: Toward a Hermeneutics of Consent*, translated and with an introduction by R. A. Harrisville (Philadelphia: Fortress Press, 1977). It contains a detailed answer to Gerhard Maier's *The End of the Historical-Critical Method* (St. Louis: Concordia Publishing House, 1977). Others include "Neues Testament und Hermeneutik: Versuch einer Bestandsaufnahme," *Zeitschrift für Theologie und Kirche* 68 (1971): 121-61; "Thesen zur Methodologie gegenwärtiger Exegese," *Zeitschrift für die neutestamentliche Wissenschaft* 63 (1972): 18-26; "Zur Methoden- und Sachproblematik einer interkonfessionellen Auslegung des Neuen Testaments," in *Vorarbeiten zum Evangelisch-Katholischen Kommentar zum Neuen Testament*, Heft 4 (Zürich/Neukirchen: Benziger Verlag und Neukirchener Verlag, 1972), pp. 11-55; "Zum thema: Biblische Theologie des Neuen Testaments," in *Biblische Theologie Heute: Einführüng – Beispiele – Kontroversen*, by W. Schrage et al., Biblisch-Theologische Studien nr. 1 (Neukirchen: Neukirchener Verlag, 1977), pp. 25-60; and especially *Vom Verstehen des Neuen Testaments: Eine Hermeneutik*, Das Neue Testament Deutsch, Ergänzungreihe nr. 6 (Göttingen: Vandehoeck & Ruprecht, 1979). See also the titles listed in note 23 herein.

14. Stuhlmacher, "Zur Methoden- und Sachproblematik einer interkonfessionellen Auslegung des Neuen Testaments," pp. 23-38.

on abstract word history and selective attention to hellenistic lexicography in its standard tools such as the Kittel *Dictionary* or the
Bauer-Arndt-Gingrich-Danker *Lexicon*. Textual criticism is still divided over its primary goal: textual history or critique of variant
readings in order to recover the *Urtext*. Literary criticism all too
often overlooks the need to verify its source hypotheses against a
plausible total picture of the early Christian traditioning process.
Form criticism needs to be aware of the tenuous basis for some of
its major axioms: the assumption of an anonymous corporate author, the attribution of the same literary criteria to both written and
oral tradition, and the postulated correlation of such genres to a
specific *Sitz im Leben*. Redaction criticism lacks clear criteria to judge
the success of its complex working hypotheses. Religio-historical
research needs to revise its theories about hellenization and pre-
Christian gnosticism in light of the complexity of contemporary Judaism which recent scholarship has brought to light. All of this is
obviously a critique from within. It reflects the critic's sensitivity
and loyalty to his academic discipline and its progress.

The limits, not the failure, of the historical-critical method are
also the focus of Stuhlmacher's critique of the method's presuppositions. Historical criticism is not just a tool but an ideology of
considerable dimensions. Whether it must be seen as the direct historical consequence of Reformation theology (Ebeling) or as the
most appropriate modern means to recover the radical confrontation
character of the original gospel (Käsemann) can remain open. But
it still carries with it the overtones of its emancipatory origins and
the resulting freight of its limited scope. Interpreting a biblical text,
the historical-critical exegete is content to ask only questions that
look backward from the present life of the Bible, deliberately creating a distance rather than bridging a gap, isolating a passage
rather than allowing it to speak as part of a unified whole. Much
information about the text can be gathered in this way, but the
intention of the text itself is being slighted. The method's "right lies
in its power to inform, its limit in its restricted perspective."[15] For
Stuhlmacher, historical criticism is not wrong but "in need of further
development." He indicates the direction of this development by
proposing to supplement Troeltsch's three classical principles of criticism (or methodical doubt), analogy, and correlation with a fourth:
the principle of "hearing" (*Vernehmen*). The German term has affinity
to Adolf Schlatter's notion of "perception" (*Wahrnehmen*), as Stuhl-

---

15. Stuhlmacher, "Zur Methoden- und Sachproblematik einer interkonfessionellen Auslegung des Neuen Testaments," p. 47.

macher himself admits.[16] It retains a certain vagueness and open-endedness which renders it somewhat incongruous to Troeltsch's triad. Troeltsch's terms described methodical principles. Stuhl-macher's term focuses on the commitment of the interpreter. As a correlative factor to Troeltsch's methodical doubt, "hearing" means the interpreter's readiness to listen to the text sympathetically in all its claims and dimensions, including the full range of its exegetical history. What Stuhlmacher calls for is the exegete's loyalty to the context of the church's life. To take such a commitment directly into the definition of historical-critical methodology is a bold step. It illumines Stuhlmacher's basic quarrel with the presuppositions of the method as practiced, namely that it is not historical-critical enough with itself and its ideological underpinnings.

Stuhlmacher's controversy with Gerhard Maier proves that he would defend the historical-critical method rather than abandon it when it is attacked in the name of loyalty to an orthodox theory of inspiration. Against Maier he stresses the impossibility of a return to a *hermeneutica sacra,* a hermeneutics of the born-again just for the Bible. Such a step would be a retreat from the church's mission in the world. The exegete cannot eschew the obligation felt in the church ever since its early days to give account of its exegesis before the truth-consciousness of the age. One cannot simply withdraw when it gets critical.

There are some important points, however, where Stuhlmacher's professional loyalty to the context of his church, beyond the realm of the academic setting and his criticism of the method, opens up new perspectives on old issues. First of all, the question of inspiration. Historical criticism had to discount inspiration as a factor in biblical exegesis. Stuhlmacher not only admits the presence of strong inspirational claims in the texts themselves but recognizes inspiration as the presupposition under which all biblical interpretation took place in the church throughout most of its history. Drawing upon the Reformation principle of the "inner testimony of the Holy Spirit," he calls for biblical hermeneutics in the horizon of the Third Article. There are problems with the concrete shape of this emphasis. Maier's criticism, however, that Stuhlmacher does not want to fill his endorsement of inspiration with any concrete content, is unjustified. For Stuhlmacher, it is not the overpowering but the empowering of the elected human witnesses.

16. He was making the connection as early as 1971 in his essay "Neues Testament und Hermeneutik," p. 149. Stuhlmacher's interest in Schlatter, who had been one of Käsemann's teachers, is amply documented. See the section on Schlatter in Stuhl-macher's *Hermeneutik,* pp. 156-62, and his survey of Schlatter's work, "Adolf Schlatter als Bibelausleger," in *Tübinger Theologie im 20. Jahrhundert,* Beihefte zur Zeitschrift für Theologie und Kirche, nr. 4 (Tübingen: J. C. B. Mohr, 1978).

This decision seems to provide new breathing space for a biblical theology that considers Old Testament and New together. Historical criticism had to separate them more and more in order to describe their individual peculiarity. Stuhlmacher shows himself impressed by the work of his Old Testament colleague Hartmut Gese, who has argued for the unity of the Testaments from the nature of early Christian theology.[17] There would be no Old Testament without the New. The dynamic tradition process of Israel's literature crossed the threshold of its Semitic particularity already in the Greek Septuagint and in the universalist tendencies of apocalyptic literature, a movement which the Christian tradition consummated. Stuhlmacher also warns against taking the polemically reduced Masoretic canon as normative for Christian interpretation, rather than considering the full range of Jewish books regarded as normative by Jesus and the early Christians. Precisely the central Christian notions such as justification and resurrection would find their proper connection with Judaism in this broader "canon."

Emphasis on the unity of the Testaments calls for a consideration of a unified vantage point from which to order the manifold emphases of the biblical witnesses. Against Maier's global inspirationalism Stuhlmacher holds firmly to a concept of a discernible canon within the canon. The Reformer's *sola scriptura* did not mean *tota scriptura*, the whole Scripture in undifferentiated unity. It implied, as we have mentioned, a theological critique. With great caution Stuhlmacher has now described this central canon as the biblical message of "reconciliation."[18] Maier and his friends have repeatedly urged that any such distinctions of rind and core are unnecessary and illegitimate,[19] but Stuhlmacher has not been moved, understanding his position as the legitimate quest for the center of Scripture in direct dependence on the theological heritage of the Reformation.

To me as a church historian, the most significant opening is Stuhlmacher's appeal to take the history of interpretation seriously in the exegesis of a text. "Hearing" the text with the interpreter's loyalty to the ongoing life of the church involves openness to its claims which are mediated through the history of its understanding. In antithesis to one of the basic dogmas of biblical criticism, Stuhlmacher holds that the exegetical tradition does not necessarily hinder understanding but may give access to its full potential. I have argued this point myself on the basis of the text's total historicity. In

---

17. See several essays in Gese's *Vom Sinai zum Zion: Alttestamentiliche Beiträge zur biblischen Theologie* (Munich: Christian Kaiser Verlag, 1974) and *Zur biblischen Theologie: Alttestamentliche Vorträge* (Munich: Christian Kaiser Verlag, 1977).

18. Stuhlmacher, *Hermeneutik*, p. 243.

19. See note 23 herein.

order to understand a text, its posthistory is as important as its prehistory and *Sitz im Leben*.[20] Stuhlmacher adds the hermeneutical argument. Drawing on a philosophical tradition that extends from Dilthey to H. G. Gadamer, he states that "every serious historical interpretation must fulfill the requirement of having consciously reflected on the impact of the text in history."[21] Biblical texts as all texts point beyond themselves to the phenomenon of their reception, which may involve modification, even distortion. The history of interpretation thus becomes part of the "horizons" which have to be "fused" in the exegetical endeavor (Gadamer). It seems that Stuhlmacher's insistence on the role of the exegetical tradition will in the long run be seen not only as a contribution to biblical studies but to the much needed new integration of theological scholarship in general.

In his recent *Hermeneutik,* Stuhlmacher repeats that his methodological considerations do not just follow the external logic of the history of scholarship in the field but are demanded by the nature of the texts themselves. This point is underscored when he now calls his own hermeneutical paradigm a "hermeneutics of agreement (*Einverständnis*) with the texts." The focus on the commitment of the interpreter, which we recognized as central, is a necessary part of any true encounter with the biblical material. "Agreement" presupposes "hearing" and thus the willingness to commit oneself to what is being said and meant. Both the text and the history to which it points must remain ambiguous in the horizon of historical criticism as a method. But the "fusion of horizons" takes place within the interpreter, who is thus enabled to lead exegesis beyond the confines of guild loyalty into the realm of common responsibilities of all Christians in the church. In his *Hermeneutik* Stuhlmacher has fully and honestly laid open his hermeneutical presuppositions and emphases as they are developed so far. His students, future pastors for the most part, not only are taught exegetical methodology but are given a rationale for the process in which they are invited to participate. This in itself is an exemplary step.

But the first practical test of this methodology of balanced loyalties is already under way. In 1975 Stuhlmacher published a commentary on the epistle to Philemon as the first installment of the *Evangelisch-Katholischer Kommentar zum Neuen Testament* (EKK), a series which promises to become one of the most significant commen-

---

20. See my inaugural lecture, "Church History and the Bible," *Princeton Seminary Bulletin* 1 (1978): 213-24, especially p. 219.
21. Stuhlmacher, *Hermeneutik*, p. 221.

tary enterprises of the 1980s.[22] The impact of the hermeneutical stance which Stuhlmacher represents can be felt in the meantime in all subsequent volumes published to date. As should be expected, the most striking innovation is the inclusion of material from the history of interpretation in all of them. One recalls that an earlier example of such an approach in the United States, Brevard Childs's commentary on Exodus, did not yet fit in any series and had to be published as a monograph. The new series with its ecumenical orientation should provide an extremely effective platform for a broad influence of the new hermeneutical intentions on Protestant and Catholic churches in Germany. The volumes are still written singly, either by a Protestant or a Catholic author, but a common spirit and a common loyalty both to the exegetical profession in its academic context and to the life of the church are everywhere present.

In the meantime Stuhlmacher has also become an important voice in and for the church outside the academic establishment. The discussion with Gerhard Maier and other evangelicals has continued, especially in the evangelical journal *Theologische Beiträge,* where even the minutes of a conversation of a student group with both Maier and Stuhlmacher were published recently.[23] Stuhlmacher has called himself one "who walks the border between kerygmatic theology, pietism, and biblically-oriented Lutheranism."[24] Such border walks may indeed be a paradigm of the method needed to find the proper balance of loyalties in the case of the professional exegete today. Crossing borders is already in this ecumenical age a constant necessity and a joyful reality for more people than anyone would have predicted some decades ago, despite the hardening of confessional lines and the polarization that characterizes official relations in many cases. It remains a proper activity for Christians including the church's exegetes.

Biblical hermeneutics is on the move. There are signs today that

22. The *Kommentar* is jointly published by the Benziger Verlag (Catholic) and the Neukirchener Verlag (Protestant) under the joint editorship of Josef Blank, Rudolf Schnackenburg, Eduard Schweizer, and Ulrich Wilckens. The following volumes are available: J. Gnilka on Mark (2 vols., 1979), Wilckens on Romans (2 vols, 1978-80), Schweizer on Colossians (1976), W. Thrilling on 2 Thessalonians (1980), Stuhlmacher on Philemon (1975), and N. Brox on 1 Peter (1979).

23. The contributions include H. Lindner, "Widerspruch oder Vermittlung? Zum Gespräch mit G. Maier und P. Stuhlmacher über eine biblische Hermeneutik," 7 (1976): 185-97; Stuhlmacher, "Biblische Theologie und kritische Exegese: Zum Aufsatz von H. Lindner . . . ," 8 (1977): 88-90; Maier, "Einer biblischen Hermeneutik entgegen? Zum Gespräch mit P. Stuhlmacher und H. Lindner," 8 (1977): 148-60; Stuhlmacher, "Hauptprobleme und Chancen kirchlicher Schriftauslegung," 9 (1978): 53-69; and "Zum Thema: Biblische Hermeneutik—Tübinger Studenten im Gespräch mit G. Maier und P. Stuhlmacher," 9 (1978): 222-234.

24. Stuhlmacher, *Schriftauslegung auf dem Wege zur biblische Theologie* (Göttingen: Vandenhoeck & Ruprecht, 1975), p. 61.

at least part of the move could have a double advantage. It might benefit the need for orientation in a profession that finds itself in turmoil, and it might benefit a church that is in need of biblical orientation by that same profession for all its members — teachers, pastors, and congregations alike.

BIBLICAL AUTHORITY *AND* INTERPRETATION: THE CURRENT DEBATE ON HERMENEUTICS

THOMAS W. GILLESPIE

The phrase "biblical authority and interpretation" poses a semantic question of considerable importance. How are *biblical authority* and *interpretation* related? More specifically, what is the semantic value of the copula *and* in the syntax of the phrase? Grammatically, the structure suggests that these two topics are coordinate. The "authority" qualified as "biblical," however, belongs to God in the Reformed tradition, while "interpretation" is a human endeavor. The relationship that is grammatically coordinate is thus semantically subordinate—that is, "interpretation" serves "biblical authority." This service is a necessary one, moreover, for apart from interpretation biblical authority cannot be actualized. If authority may be defined as the legitimate exercise of effective power,[1] then the authority of the Bible is exercised effectively only through biblical interpretation. The interpreter may be a layman reading the Bible "devotionally," or a pastor preparing her sermon, or a highly trained scholar doing technical exegesis. In each and every case this maxim is true: without interpretation the authority of the Scriptures may be formal but not actual. This is not to argue that doctrines of Scripture are without value, but it is to contend that no matter what our view of biblical authority may be, we are compelled to interpret the Bible if we expect to encounter its authority.

For this reason we all have a vested interest in the current debate on hermeneutics — the theory and practice of interpretation. Although occasioned historically by biblical studies, the issue addressed by this discipline is not limited to the Bible. Put simply, the question is this: How is it possible to understand and to express the meaning of historic literature in and for ever new and changing historical situations? The answers proposed depend upon how one conceives of the nature, scope, and function of *interpretation, meaning,*

---

1. So says John Howard Schütz, *Paul and the Anatomy of Apostolic Authority,* Society for New Testament Studies Monograph Series, no. 26 (Cambridge: Cambridge University Press, 1975), pp. 1-21.

language, and *understanding.* What follows is offered as an orientation to the present state of the debate in relation to these issues.

1. INTERPRETATION

In confessing the final authority of holy Scripture in all matters of faith and practice, the Protestant Reformers of the sixteenth century were compelled to face squarely the issue of biblical interpretation. They recognized that the Bible must be interpreted authentically if its authority is to be actualized effectively. Their first step was to reject categorically the allegorical method of biblical interpretation as practiced in medieval Catholicism. Whereas allegory assumed several levels of meaning in every text, the Reformers advocated the view that the Scriptures bear one "plain" meaning, which is the grammatical sense of the text. As an aid to Protestant pastors, whose task was to interpret Scripture to their congregations, handbooks on this grammatical method of exegesis were prepared that dealt with matters of grammar, philology, syntax, and style. In the seventeenth century the Latin term *hermeneutica,* coined from the Greek noun *hermēneia* ("interpretation"), appeared with frequency in the titles of these handbooks and established itself as the technical term for the *theory* undergirding exegesis as the *practice* of interpretation. Later this Latin term was anglicized and entered the English language as "hermeneutics." Today the issues of the nature, scope, and function of literary interpretation are debated with reference to this rubric.[2]

Initially, the scope of Reformed exegesis included both the *verus sensus* ("true sense") of Scripture and its *verus usus* ("true use"). Interpretation moved quite naturally from *explicatio* via *meditatio* to *applicatio.*[3] Any difference sensed by the exegete between an original and a present meaning of a text was transcended intuitively if not theoretically. The study of philology, however, led to an insight that made this naive procedure ever more difficult. For the classical philologians recognized that the meaning of words depends upon their usage, and that usage is a variable dependent upon cultural factors operative at a given time and place in history. What is true of terms, of course, is equally true of discourse. Slowly but surely the *grammatical* meaning of ancient texts was recognized as its *historical* meaning. With this came the gradual realization that the biblical texts

2. See James M. Robinson, "Hermeneutics since Barth," in *New Frontiers in Theology, II: The New Hermeneutic,* ed. J. M. Robinson and J. B. Cobb, Jr. (New York: Harper & Row, 1964), pp. 7-19.

3. See Karl Barth, *Church Dogmatics,* 5 vols., ed. Geoffrey W. Bromiley and Thomas F. Torrance, trans. Geoffrey W. Bromiley et al. (Edinburgh: T. & T. Clark, 1955-57), 1/2: 714, 722ff.

were primarily a witness to their own time.[4] The task of exegesis was accordingly limited to establishing what the texts *meant* in the time and place of their origin, and hermeneutics as the theory of exegesis was identified with the methodology of classical philology. The irony is that at the very moment the past was becoming ever more distant culturally and intellectually, the question of how the literature of antiquity might be allowed to speak its message in the present was divorced from the theory and the practice of interpretation. The more the exegete became a historian, the more the question of the contemporary meaning of biblical texts was left to the devices of pastors and theologians charged with the "edification" of the church. The legacy of this divorce between historical exegesis and contemporary theology remains. But because of its failure to address this issue of the contemporary meaning of ancient literature, traditional hermeneutics is vulnerable to the criticism and challenge of a vision of interpretation that is more comprehensive.

The scope of this vision is stated by its advocates in terms of the etymology and ancient usage of the Greek verb *hermeneūein* ("to interpret") and its derivative noun *hermēneia*. Beginning with the root concept of this word group, "bringing the unclear to clarity," ancient usage is employed to score three points in regard to the overall task of literary interpretation.[5]

The first is that the use of *language* is itself an act of interpretation. Though not conclusive, the evidence concerning the original meaning of *hermeneūein* points in the direction of "speak" or "say." In speaking, the unclarity of thinking comes into clarity. *Hermēneia* in its primitive sense thus connotes "linguistic formulation" or "verbal expression." To speak (or to write) at all is to interpret one's meaning to another.

The second point follows from the first. Not all use of language is clear in its interpretation of meaning. Discourse is not usually univocal. In order to achieve clarity it requires interpretation in the form of *explanation* or *commentary*. The sense of *hermēneia* here is synonymous with its Greek parallel, *exegēsis*, indicating that the familiar distinction between hermeneutics as the theory and exegesis as the practice of interpretation is a modern one that disappears altogether in this vision of the scope of hermeneutics.

The third point suggests the material task of all literary interpretation. As used in antiquity, *hermēneia* also denotes *translation*. We perpetuate this usage by our designation of a translator as an in-

---

4. See Werner Georg Kümmel, *The New Testament: The History of the Investigation of Its Problems*, trans. S. M. Gilmour and H. C. Kee (Nashville: Abingdon Press, 1972), pp. 62ff.

5. Robinson, "Hermeneutics since Barth," pp. 1-6.

terpreter. In translation the meaning that is originally interpreted in one language is reinterpreted in another. What is unclear to auditors or readers in a language unknown to them is made clear by restating it in a known tongue. The apostle Paul's admonition that anyone who speaks in an ecstatic "tongue" unknown to the congregation "should pray for the power to interpret [*hermēneuein*]" (1 Cor. 14:13) is an instance of such translation. Translation thus involves saying the same thing in a different language. But this frequently requires that the meaning be stated differently. For the goal of translation is the equivalence of meaning. It is achieved not by a "wooden" correspondence between the surface structures of two languages but by a dynamic correspondence between the linguistic conventions of two cultures. Meaning is thereby actually transferred conceptually from one culturally determined language world to another. Yet there is more. If the meaning of discourse is constituted by its rational sense *and* its existential significance (as we shall see), then the task of translation is to make that meaning both intelligible and relevant. The subject matter of the original language, if serious, is presumed to have an importance as well as a rationality. Translation of the significance brings the subject matter to bear upon the human condition in general and upon the situation at hand in particular when successful. As the cultural parallels of linguistic convention make possible the translation of the sense of one language act into another, so the analogies of human existence provide the ground for translating significance from one historic situation to another.

To the extent that hermeneutics is informed by the scope of *hermēneia* in its ancient usage, it views "interpretation" in terms of the interrelated functions of bringing the unclarity of thought into clarity through "speech," the unclarity of speech into clarity through "explanation" or "commentary," and the unclarity of meaning (constituted by sense and significance) into clarity through "translation." Whereas traditional hermeneutics limited itself to the second of these three functions, the new hermeneutics seeks to restore the full task of the unified field.

As a minister who regularly engages in preaching, I resonate to this vision of biblical interpretation. For it accurately describes the responsibility which I seek to discharge. Reformed preaching is traditionally a hermeneutical event. Its task is to give contemporary expression to the witness of a historic canonical passage, the assumption being that there is a material relation between the oral discourse of the sermon and the written discourse of its text. The relation between the two poles is established by interpretation, a process that involves a movement of meaning through translation from the language of the text to that of the congregation, from literature to speech, from a past to a present historical setting, and from an ancient to a modern cultural context—and this in the expectation of an eventful hearing of God's Word today. If establishing what a text *meant* in its historical setting is the primary task of the exegete, it is merely the preliminary task of the preacher. The Scriptures are fully interpreted only when what a text meant is translated into what it *means*.

2. MEANING

Implicit in the debate about the scope of interpretation is the question of "meaning." For meaning is the subject matter of interpretation in all of its functions. Traditional hermeneutics focuses upon *textual meaning*, the meaning expressed in ancient literature, which it qualifies as *historical meaning*, the meaning expressed in the text at the time and place of its origin. This is further qualified as *authorial meaning*, the meaning intended by the author or editor of the text, as the case may be. It is possible, therefore, to speak of *the* meaning of the text and to make its clarification the goal of interpretation.

This goal is surrendered, however, by some advocates of the new hermeneutics. For reasons which will be discussed when the issue of *understanding* is addressed, they believe that it is impossible to achieve an interpretation which makes the meaning of the text audible to the modern reader in the same way as it was to the audience for whom it was intended. Further, they argue, when discourse is committed to writing and enters into the stream of literary tradition, it is severed from the intention of its author and attains a "semantic autonomy" which requires its meaning to change with every different situation in which it is read. The focus here is upon the *present* or *contemporary* meaning of the text, which inevitably becomes its meaning to the interpreter. Much confusion is generated in the debate between these so-called "objectivist" and "subjectivist" positions by the lack of a common concept of the nature and scope of "meaning." In order to clarify the confusion, certain distinctions are necessary.

One is the distinction previously mentioned between the *sense* and the *significance* of a text. Initiated by Heidegger in his philosophical work, this distinction is predicated upon his understanding of the nature of language and its relation to both thought and being.[6] In the order of knowing, Heidegger gives the priority to being over

6. The implications of Heidegger's philosophy for hermeneutics are admirably explicated by Anthony C. Thiselton in *The Two Horizons: New Testament Hermeneutics and Philosophical Description* (Grand Rapids: Eerdmans, 1980), pp. 143-204. See also Richard E. Palmer, *Hermeneutics: Interpretation Theory in Schleiermacher, Dilthey, Heidegger, and Gadamer*, Studies in Phenomenology and Existential Philosophy (Evanston: Northwestern University Press, 1969), pp. 124-61.

thinking. Thought is dependent upon the reality of being that calls it forth. It is the human response to the silent toll of being that is heard in the beings that we encounter in our experience. This experience is meaningful when two conditions are met. One is the *intelligibility* of the being of beings which present themselves to view as what they are. This is Heidegger's way of insisting that meaning is not an "add-on," something that thinking attaches to being as an "extra." Meaning as intelligibility is anchored in and expressed by being itself as it unveils itself to thinking through beings. The *significance* which the being of beings has for our universe of concern is the second condition of meaning. Intelligibility alone does not constitute meaning. For something to have meaning it must be related to the concerns of human-being. If thought is dependent upon being, however, it is conditioned by language — the particular language tradition in which it occurs. Because thinking occurs only in and through language, meaning is a linguistic matter. Through the conventions of language, what is intelligible and of concern to a speaker or an author is expressed as the sense and significance of discourse. To speak of the meaning of a text, therefore, is to speak of its sense *and* its significance.

By including within the scope of "meaning" that which is of concern to us, Heidegger's thought rings true to ordinary human experience and common parlance. Like the story of the little boy who was being examined by his minister for confirmation in the Church of Scotland: "Do you understand the Catechism?" the pastor asked. "Aye," the youngster replied, "I understand every word of it, and it dinna mean a thing." Similarly, when people in the pew complain that the Bible has "no meaning" for them, they are not saying that it makes no sense. They are usually saying that the sense of the text has no significance for them. It seems clear, therefore, that an adequate definition of "meaning" must include both sense and significance as constitutive elements.

Before leaving Heidegger, however, it is important to note a hermeneutical inference which he draws from this distinction. The definition of meaning which controls composition also controls interpretation. A text that has meaning *for* an interpreter must be intelligible and significant *to* the interpreter. But it is presumptuous, Heidegger argues, to think of the concerns of the interpreter and the author as being identical. To the extent that they differ, the meaning of the text will also differ, not only from the author to the interpreter but from one interpreter to another. Heidegger thus leads the chorus of the advocates of the "semantic autonomy" of the text. While that is so with regard to the text's significance, is it true of its sense? Is that also a variable or is it a constant?

One who contends strenuously for the stability of textual meaning is E. D. Hirsch, Jr. In fact, it is his conviction that the definition of meaning in terms of the sense and significance of a text is both logically fallacious and hermeneutically pernicious. His intention, therefore, is to defend "the sensible belief that a text means what its author meant." Hirsch carries out his critique of what he calls the "banishment of the author" by defining textual meaning in terms of what I have referred to as its sense. That a text had a significance to its author and its intended audience and that it continues to have mutable significance to its interpreters is not denied. What is challenged is the notion that textual meaning includes both sense and significance. The crux of the matter, according to Hirsch, is that the meaning (sense) of a text is determined by authorial intention and remains constant. Every text represents someone's meaning, for meaning is an affair of human consciousness and not merely of words. Hirsch explains,

> almost any word sequence can, under the conventions of language, legitimately represent more than one complex of meaning. A word sequence means nothing in particular until somebody either means something by it or understands something from it. There is no magic land of meanings outside human consciousness. Whenever meaning is connected to words, a person is making the connection, and the particular meanings he lends to them are never the only legitimate ones under the norms and conventions of his language.[7]

Since the only possible choice is between the author of the text and its interpreter, its meaning must be ascribed to the author if the text is to have any determinate and thus determinable meaning.

The theory of the "semantic autonomy" of the text actually is predicated upon its significance rather than its sense. What changes is not the sense but its significance. Since it is misleading to say that textual meaning changes, Hirsch is intent upon eliminating the terminological confusion by limiting the concept of meaning to that of sense.

> *Meaning* is that which is represented by a text; it is what the author meant by his use of a particular sign sequence; it is what the signs represent. *Significance,* on the other hand, names a relationship between that meaning and a person, or a conception, or a situation, or indeed anything imaginable. . . . Significance always implies a relationship, and one constant, unchanging pole of that relationship is what the text means. Failure to consider this simple and essential distinction has been the source of enormous confusion in hermeneutic theory.[8]

7. Hirsch, *Validity in Interpretation* (New Haven: Yale University Press, 1967), p. 4.
8. Hirsch, *Validity in Interpretation,* p. 8.

Corresponding to this distinction between meaning and significance is another between interpretation and criticism. Hirsch argues that meaning (sense) is the province of interpretation and significance is the domain of criticism. Hermeneutics, accordingly, is understood in the traditional sense of the theory of exegesis. Hirsch's book is in fact a modern statement of the procedures necessary for establishing with some degree of probability *the* meaning of a text, which is the author's meaning, which is the historical meaning.

The insight that theories of changing textual meaning have reference primarily to the mutability of significance rather than sense is helpful. What is missing, however, is a recognition of the fact that textual meaning frequently, if not always, bears both an intentional sense and an intentional significance that depend upon the author. In writing his letter to the Galatians, for example, the apostle Paul certainly intended it not only to have an intelligible sense but to bear a particular significance for the situation of the Galatian churches. It is in fact difficult to imagine how that text could be understood in terms of Paul's intention without reference to both its sense and significance. To limit textual meaning to sense is to foreclose in advance on the fullness of the letter's meaning. Put simply, meaning may be more adequately conceptualized when it includes the interacting poles of sense and significance. Hirsch is convincing only in his insistence that the constant pole in this relationship is the intentional sense expressed by the author. If that pole is the basis for speaking of "validity in interpretation," the other is not irrelevant for establishing criteria for discerning legitimacy in application. For the historical significance intended by an author and understood by the original audience provides a model for developing applicable historical analogies in the process of discerning contemporary significance. Thus the intended significance of the letter to the Galatians was its refutation of the claims of religious legalism against the priority and sufficiency of grace. Although the forms of religious legalism were quite different in first century Galatia and sixteenth-century Europe, the significance which Luther perceived in Paul's letter for his own situation was based upon legitimate historical analogy. The extent to which Luther comprehended the historical sense of this canonical epistle is debatable, but it is beyond question that his interpretation of Galatians would have been deficient had he not translated its historical significance in terms that spoke with power to his own historical situation.

A second important distinction that requires recognition in the discussion of the meaning of "meaning" is that between the *sense* and *reference* of discourse. Actually, this is a refinement of the meaning of "sense" in human speech and writing. Not all speech is referential

in character, of course, but most of it is.[9] And this use of language
has special importance for the Bible in its role as a witness. What
is at stake in the distinction between "sense" and "reference" in the
meaning of discourse was established by the German logicians Edmund Husserl and Gottlob Frege. According to Husserl, a meaning
experience has two components: (1) the "intentional act" (the act
of awareness by which I perceive an object) and (2) the "intentional
object" (the object of awareness as perceived by me).[10] By "intention" Husserl means "awareness" as constituted by act plus object.
Such awareness has both nonverbal and verbal aspects. The former
is constituted by the "experience" as such, while the latter is composed of cognitive, emotive, phonetic, and (in the case of writing)
visual elements which establish and express the "content" of the
experience. For Husserl verbal meaning is a special kind of intentional object. Once expressed it is independent of the generating
psychic experience and objective in its self-identity. Verbal meaning
is thus unchanging and sharable. It is the sharable content of a
speaker's or a writer's experience of an intentional object. As such
the concept of verbal meaning (content) must include both "sense"
(*what* is said or written) and "reference" (what it is said or written
about). Frege demonstrated the necessity of this distinction within
discourse in his famous essay "Sinn und Bedeutung" ("On Sense
and Reference").[11]

Paul Ricoeur develops this distinction fruitfully in his *Interpretation
Theory*.[12] He points to the basic miracle of human communication
whereby we overcome the solitude of our individuality. What is
communicated between us is not our experience as lived but the
meaning (content) of our experience. In other words, experience
remains private while meaning goes public.

The medium of this miracle is the dialectical relationship of event
and meaning in speech as discourse. Ricoeur observes that the primary unit of speech is not the word but the sentence, which has as
its chief function the relating of identification and predication.
Someone says something (predication) to someone else about something (identification). The sentence is thus a "subjective" act in
which signs are integrated to produce an "objective" meaning. All

9. G. B. Caird offers a succinct treatment of the five uses of language, which he
distributes between *referential* and *commissive* uses, in *The Language and Imagery of the
Bible* (Philadelphia: Westminster Press, 1980), pp. 7-36.
10. See Husserl, *Ideas: General Introduction to Pure Phenomenology*, trans. W. R. B.
Gibbon (New York: Collier Books, 1962).
11. An English translation of "On Sense and Reference" is available in *Translations
from the Philosophical Writings of Gottlob Frege*, ed. P. Geach and M. Black (Oxford:
Blackwell, 1952), pp. 56-78.
12. Ricoeur, *Interpretation Theory: Discourse and the Surplus of Meaning* (Fort Worth:
Texas Christian University Press, 1976), pp. 1-24.

oral discourse occurs in the concrete polarity between speech as event and as meaning. In describing this polarity, Ricoeur speaks of a *noetic* act and its *noematic* content, of the "utterer's meaning" and the "utterance meaning." Because of the self-reference of discourse to itself as event, the "objective" pole always points back to the "subjective." Yet the "objective" has an identity of its own once it is actualized, which is its propositional content, the "said as such." For the speech event passes away while its meaning abides in understanding and memory, and can thus be repeated.

The "objective" side of the dialectic, however, has an inner dialectic of its own between the "what" of discourse (its sense) and the "about what" (its reference). Ricoeur argues that speech is ordinarily directed beyond itself. The sense is immanent to the discourse and objective in the sense of ideal. The reference expresses the movement in which language transcends itself and makes contact with the world. Put otherwise, the sense correlates the identification function with the predication function in the sentence and generates thereby the reference which relates speech to the world of objective reality. The structure of the sentence (its sense) is used by the speaker to indicate something beyond the sentence (its reference). Both, according to Ricoeur, are dependent upon the intention of the speaker and constitute together the meaning of the speech-act.

When he comes to the subject of meaning expressed in written discourse, Ricoeur seeks to find a way between "the intentional fallacy" (in which the intended meaning of the author becomes the norm of valid interpretation) and "the fallacy of the absolute text" (in which textual meaning is treated as authorless). The former overlooks the semantic autonomy of the text, he explains, while the latter forgets that a text remains a discourse told by someone to someone else about something. The necessity of this quest is occasioned by the very nature of writing.

The theory of semantic autonomy is required, Ricoeur argues, by the fact that writing explodes the dialogical situation which characterizes oral speech. Oral discourse is predicated upon a face-to-face relationship between speaker and hearer which allows for questions and answers about the speaker's intended meaning. With the inscription of meaning, however, the possibility of a real dialogue between text and interpreter is severely limited. Ambiguity in the text creates the possibility of multiple meanings. Thus it may be construed differently by interpreters without having the power to correct misunderstanding. Nevertheless, the range of possible meaning is not limitless. The autonomy of the text, Ricoeur acknowledges, is not absolute. It remains, even at a greater distance than is common to oral discourse, in a dialectical relationship with the intention of the author. Thus Ricoeur cites with approval the view of Hirsch that interpretation can achieve probable validation with regard to the sense of a text if not absolute verification.[13] With this concession, however, Ricoeur seems to give back what he has taken away by his advocacy of semantic autonomy. The latter turns out to mean little more than a recognition of semantic ambiguity that is characteristic of all discourse, and, in the case of literature, impossible to clarify by direct appeal to the author. Here the semantic autonomy of a text is based upon the absence of its author rather than upon a banishment of its author from consideration.

If writing limits the dialogical character of speech, it also transcends the situational nature of oral discourse. When meaning is committed to writing, it escapes the immediate and original horizons of the author. This impacts the reference of meaning decisively. For the ordinary ground of reference in our conversations is the common situation of speaker and hearer. We refer to realities which are ostensive, and even when reference is made to inostensive realities they can be identified more clearly by the speaker where there is confusion over what he or she is talking "about." Authors of literature and their readers, other than those originally intended, do not, however, share a common situation. The reference pole of meaning is for this reason more difficult to establish than the sense pole. Fortunately, human beings who do not share a common situation do share a common world. To the extent, therefore, that textual meaning refers a reader to realities which transcend situations and which constitute the world of human experience, it opens up for the reader the possibility of experiencing those realities personally and thus appropriating at a level of fundamental depth the meaning of the text as reference. When that occurs, of course, "reference" has achieved "significance." For Ricoeur the referential aspect of textual meaning is of central importance for interpretation theory, and it will be discussed further when the counterpart of "meaning" is taken up, namely, "understanding."

For biblical interpretation, the following results of this exposition of the meaning of "meaning" may be offered in summary fashion. The Bible is written discourse. It participates fully in the nature of such discourse. The meaning of a biblical text is, therefore, constituted by its sense, its reference, and its significance. Consequently, textual meaning is nuanced according to the particular constitutive element of meaning that is under consideration. The sense of a text is determined by the linguistic conventions of biblical Hebrew and Greek. Meaning at this point bears the sense intended by the author or editor and is a constant. Where the sense of a text is theologically referential, as the Bible is in its witness to God, to Jesus Christ, to

---

13. Ricoeur, *Interpretation Theory*, p. 78.

the Holy Spirit, or to the themes of the gospel, it directs the reader beyond the text itself to the realities attested. The assumption is that such realities are potentially significant to the interpreter.

3. LANGUAGE

However the scope of meaning is defined, the relationship of meaning to language is intrinsic and indisputable. Meaning is expressed *in* language and understood *through* language. Language figures prominently, therefore, in hermeneutical theory of both the traditional and contemporary types.

Traditional hermeneutics has been strengthened in its aim of establishing the historical meaning of ancient texts by recent developments in the related fields of linguistics and semantics. Ferdinand de Saussure, the founder of modern linguistics, distinguished in French between language as *langue* (system) and language as *parole* (speech). *Langue*, the linguistic code with its specific structure, is collective, anonymous, systematic, and compulsory. *Parole*, the actualization of the linguistic code, is individual, intentional, arbitrary, and contingent. The former is a system, the latter an event. Linguistics is the science of language systems. Semantics is the science of the sense conveyed by language events.

Regarding linguistics, Saussure laid down three axioms which continue to influence the field. First, language functions on the basis of human convention. Second, a distinction must be made and observed between synchronic and diachronic linguistics. Third, language is by nature a structured system.

The last principle conveys the insight that language is a system of interdependent terms in which the value of each term depends upon the presence of the others. All words used to give expression to meaning, in other words, limit each other in a reciprocal manner. From this is derived the concept of literary context. For Saussure, context is established by the interaction of syntagmatic and paradigmatic relations within the system. The former are the relations between words in the same sentence, paragraph, or work, while the latter are the relations of words used to others in the code which might have been used as substitutes. These contextual relations constitute "the particularity of meaning" conveyed by a given text. Together they form "the semantic field" of discourse.

Because language systems are dependent upon the conventions of language use, they are subject to change. This mutability of *langue* necessitates the distinction between synchronic and diachronic linguistics. Diachronic linguistics is concerned with the history of developments in language, with how usage changes the language system at given historical points and thus changes the meaning of discourse.

Synchronic linguistics is focused upon the use of language at one particular point in time. Diachronic description thus depends upon synchronic description, but not the reverse. *Parole* (speech), in other words, is always synchronic. And semantics, as the science of the sense expressed in speech, is related to synchronic linguistics and is oriented to history for this reason. Semantics takes seriously the diachronic distance between the text and its interpreter, and recognizes the necessity of discerning its linguistic sense within the horizon of its synchronic possibilities. By limiting itself to the original language world of the text, semantics is virtually synonymous with traditional hermeneutics. The same limitation distinguishes semantics from the new hermeneutics which seeks to bridge the diachronic distance and the situational difference between the text and its interpreter.

The axiom that language functions on the basis of human convention has a direct bearing upon the issue of the relation between language and thought. Answers to this question tend to fall into two traditions. Saussure and the majority of modern linguists contend, on the one hand, that there is no inherent dependency of human thought upon conventional and accidental differences of morphology and grammar. The same applies to lexicography. The fact that a language system has no word for a particular concept is no indication that the concept cannot be expressed within that system. It is on this premise that James Barr challenges Thorleif Bowman's exposition of the venerable distinction posited by biblical scholarship between Greek and Hebrew thought on the basis of their respective surface grammars.[14] Ernst Cassirer, Martin Heidegger, Hans-Georg Gadamer, and Ludwig Wittgenstein argue, on the other hand, that language decisively influences human thought and world-views. Because it comes to expression in language, thought is shaped by the unique language tradition in which it occurs. This is particularly true of human "preunderstanding," a concept that plays an important role in the interpretation process. The two positions are not, as Anthony Thiselton recognizes, mutually exclusive.[15] Citing the conclusion of B. L. Whorf that language is both conventional and influential upon thought and culture, Thiselton argues that the issue of whether language actually *shapes* our cultural views or merely *serves* them on the basis of agreements established previously by convention is moot; it can be answered both ways. He thus concurs with Saussure and Barr in their conviction that the structures of language are mere linguistic accidents which do not determine

---

14. See Barr, *The Semantics of Biblical Language* (London: Oxford University Press, 1961), pp. 46-79.

15. See Thiselton, *The Two Horizons*, pp. 133-39.

thought, worldview, or preunderstanding. Languages differ, but not absolutely. The differences between them are differences of language *uses* or "language games" (Wittgenstein). This is what makes all languages intertranslatable. But Thiselton goes on to point out that though these uses are established merely by convention, they do in fact exert influence upon the way human beings see things conventionally. Conventionality hands on an inherited language tradition which makes certain questions either easier or more difficult to ask. Thus it is language use, rather than the accidents of surface grammar and lexicography, which conditions thought. Gadamer summarizes the point: "If every language represents a view of the world, it is this primarily not as a particular type of language (in the way that philologists see it), but because of what is said or handed down in this language."[16]

Undergirding the conventionality of language is the reality of a shared world. This, according to the early Heidegger, is the primordial assumption which makes communication possible in discourse. The sharing of meaning between human beings is not predicated ultimately upon abstract considerations of logic but upon the common world of understanding which has developed among them. "In discourse Being-with becomes 'explicitly' *shared;* that is to say, it *is* already, but it is unshared as something that has not been taken hold of and appropriated."[17] Gadamer also emphasizes that a common world is always the presupposition of speech. For this reason the use of language cannot be altered arbitrarily. Because they live, language traditions do change and grow. They influence human horizons and yet they are not prisons. For through the use of the language tradition fresh experiences and perceptions develop new concepts that come to expression in new language uses. In this way language use is changed conventionally but not arbitrarily.

This discussion of the conventionality of language has a direct bearing upon biblical interpretation. It compels us to recognize that the surface grammar and syntax of biblical Greek and Hebrew are "linguistic accidents" which do not determine the way reality is experienced and expressed. Biblical texts are, however, influenced and shaped by the conventional uses of language common to their time and place. The assertion, often made, that the language of the Bible is "culturally conditioned" is thus a truism. At the same time, the conventionality of language warns us not to press the cultural differences between biblical times and our own too hard. For they are not absolute differences. The language uses of Scripture have parallels in the conventions of other languages, including our own,

16. Gadamer, *Truth and Method* (New York: Seabury Press, 1975), pp. 399-400.
17. Heidegger, *Being and Time* (Oxford: Blackwell, 1962), p. 205.

and it is this linguistic fact which makes them both understandable and translatable.

Corresponding to the question of the relationship between language and thought is that of the relationship between language and reality. What is the connection between the sense of human discourse and its reference? T. F. Torrance is probably right in his opinion that the relation of statements to reality cannot be expressed in statements.[18] Yet the question is a crucial one in that it bears upon the way we conceive of truth. For example, if truth is limited to the sense of discourse, it loses touch with the reality of its reference. Both Protestant Orthodoxy and the Rationalism of the Enlightenment fell into this trap. Each in its own way identified truth in language with its propositional or logical content. Hermeneutics in the post-Reformation period thus focused upon the grammatical content of biblical texts to the exclusion of their reference. Recognizing that speech seeks to convey more than rational content, Schleiermacher and Dilthey oriented the truth of discourse respectively to the "psychic experience" and the "lived experience" of the speaker or author. Here the primary reference of language was identified with what Husserl would later call the "intentional act" of the subject. Rudolf Bultmann, following the early Heidegger's analysis of human-being, similarly viewed discourse as the externalization or the objectification of the existential self-understanding of the speaker or author. His hermeneutical program of "demythologizing" biblical texts aimed at interpreting the objectifying mythological language of the Scriptures by means of the categories of human existence provided by Heidegger. Truth here is a matter of "authentic existence," which Bultmann equated with faith.

Both this rationalizing and subjectivizing of the truth of language results in a reduction of the fullness of discourse. If in discourse someone says something about something to someone else, the hermeneutics of Protestant orthodoxy reduced the truth of language to the "something" said (or written), and the line of hermeneutics from Schleiermacher to Bultmann reduced the truth to the "someone" who speaks (or writes). What is missing is the reference of discourse to realities which transcend both speech and its speaker. This omission precludes speech from having its say "about" such realities.

In the hermeneutical reflections of Hans-Georg Gadamer, the use of language is oriented neither to the rationality of the text nor to the subjectivity of the author expressed in the text but to textual

18. See Torrance, *Space, Time and Resurrection* (Grand Rapids: Eerdmans, 1976), pp. 10-11.

content understood as its subject matter.[19] James M. Robinson calls this "an ontological turn" in the discussion.[20] In a clever play upon German words, Gadamer focuses attention upon the dialectical relationship between the *Sprache* (speech) and the *Sache* (subject matter) of literature. By this he wishes to emphasize that in every serious text someone says something to someone *about something*. The reference of speech is its subject matter. And the subject matter provides the bond between a text and its interpreter. For in the act of interpretation, Gadamer argues, the subject matter "emerges" (*herauskommt*) in the interaction between the text and the interpreter. This "coming-into-language of the subject matter itself" is the material issue of hermeneutics.

Paul Ricoeur follows Gadamer's lead in this concern to do justice to the referential function of discourse. As previously noted, textual meaning for Ricoeur is constituted by the sense and the reference of the text. As constituted, the text not only opens up the world of reality to which it bears witness but actually projects such a possible world. The meaning of a text is therefore neither lurking somewhere *behind* the text in the subjectivity of the author nor *in* the grammatical structure of the text. It is manifest *in front of* the text. In a word, discourse enables reality to manifest itself to the interpreter.[21]

It is crucial to note that for both Gadamer and Ricoeur the subject matter or reference of discourse is not merely *conveyed* by but *manifested* through the language of the text. To get at this "manifestation" function of language, Gadamer traces "the emergence of the concept of language in the history of Western thought."[22] Beginning with Plato's analysis of the nature of language in the *Cratylus*, Gadamer notes that an epoch-determining decision was made here which continues to influence the philosophy of language. Plato chose to view words as *signs* rather than as *images*. It is the nature of signs that they have their being solely in their function, in the fact that they point to something else. A sign thus acquires its meaning as a sign only in relation to the thing signified. It is not something that establishes a content of its own. The image, by contrast, does not gain its function of pointing or representing from the thing signified but from its own content. An image is not a mere sign, for in it the *Sache* imaged is itself represented, caught, and made present. By its resemblance character, it makes present in itself what is not otherwise present. Yet this understanding of the nature and function of the word is thoroughly discredited by Plato. In place of the image

19. In addition to Gadamer's *Truth and Method*, see Palmer's *Hermeneutics*, pp. 194-222, and Thiselton's *Two Horizons*, pp. 293-318.
20. Robinson, "Hermeneutics since Barth," pp. 69ff.
21. See Ricoeur, *Interpretation Theory*, p. 92.
22. See Gadamer, *Truth and Method*, pp. 366-97.

(*eikon*), he sets the sign (*semeion*). This, for Gadamer, represents a tragic loss.

Plato considered thought to be silent. Thinking is essentially speechless. It is not dependent upon language. He thus separated thought from language in this radical way and viewed words as mere signs at the disposal of thought. Words refer to something, to the idea or to the *Sache* intended, and thus bring the *Sache* into view. Yet here the words adopt a wholly secondary relation to the *Sache*. They are mere tools of human communication. Gadamer concludes that this pragmatic or technological view of language has led to the forgetfulness of language in the Western cultural tradition.

His own position is that language is something other than a mere sign system. It has a resemblance to an image. The word has "a mysterious connection with what it represents, a quality of belonging to being." This is meant in a fundamental way. Language is not wholly detached from the intended *Sache*. It is not merely an instrument of subjectivity. Rather, it has an ideality which lies in the word itself, which is its meaning (or, as Ricoeur would say, its "sense"). It is meaningful already. Gadamer concedes that language arises out of experience, but argues that experience itself is linguistic. It is of the nature of experience that it seeks and finds words that express it. We seek for the right word, the word that belongs to the *Sache*, so that in it the *Sache* itself comes into language. This is not a matter of simply copying. The word participates in the *Sache* and the *Sache* in the word, and it is this mutual participation of language and being which makes language something more than a mere system of signs.

How reality which transcends language can manifest itself through language that attests to it is suggested to Gadamer by Aquinas. The word, according to Thomas, is like a *mirror* in which its *Sache* is seen. What is curious about this mirror, however, is that it nowhere extends beyond the image of its object. Nothing is mirrored in it but this one thing, so that it reproduces only its own image. What is remarkable about this image is that the word is understood here entirely as the perfect reflection of the *Sache* — that is, as the expression of the *Sache* — and has left behind the thought to which it owes its existence. The word thus does more than express the mind. It reflects the intended subject matter. The starting point for the formation of the word is the intelligible *Sache* that fills the mind. But the thought seeking expression through speech *refers* to the subject matter of discourse rather than to the mind which produces it. Thus the word that is the expression of the mind is concerned with the image of the being which it attests. Through the image created by discourse is reflected the reality attested. It is for this reason that Gadamer asserts that in discourse the *Sache*, the subject matter, "emerges." The function of language as *parole* (speech) is not merely to "point" to realities which transcend language, but to "show" such realities. In brief, "saying" is a way of "showing."

Gadamer's dialectic between *Sprache* and *Sache*, in which the subject matter of a text is manifested through its language, has its parallel in Ricoeur's dialectic between *sense* and *reference* in discourse. Both philosophers provide biblical interpreters with a formal analysis of how the scriptural texts function theologically as a witness to the God who reveals himself to us in his Word. It is by means of the power of the sense of a text to refer us to God that God continues to manifest himself through the text. Calvin's doctrine of the correlation between the Word and the Spirit in the interpretation of Scripture assumes the same dialectical functioning of language. As is well known, Calvin taught that in spite of the many rational arguments which may be adduced in support of the belief that the Scriptures are the Word of God, the assurance of their truthfulness comes only through "the internal testimony of the Spirit" (*Inst.*, 1.7.4). His point is not that the Spirit whispers assurances into the ear of the reader that what the text says is true. It is rather that the witness of the text to God is confirmed to the reader by the Spirit of God who manifests himself through this testimony. The following explanation provided in the *Institutes* scores the point clearly:

> Therefore, being illuminated by [the Spirit], we now believe the divine original of the Scripture, not from our own judgment or that of others, but we esteem the certainty, that we have received it from God's own mouth by the ministry of men, to be superior to that of any human judgment, and *equal to that of an intuitive perception of God himself in it.* (*Inst.*, 1.7.5; italics mine)

This is the key to Calvin's own hermeneutical procedure. With regard to the exegesis of the epistle to the Romans, Barth once noted

> how energetically Calvin, having first established what stands in the text, sets himself to re-think the whole material and to wrestle with it, till the walls which separate the sixteenth century from the first become transparent! Paul speaks and the man of the sixteenth century hears. The conversation between the original record and the reader moves round the *subject-matter* [*Sache*], until a distinction between yesterday and to-day becomes impossible.[23]

The *Sache* to which Barth refers here is, in his own words, none other than "the spirit of the Bible, which is the Eternal Spirit." It is the Spirit of the God who continues to reveal himself in and through his Word that constitutes the theological subject matter of

23. Barth, *The Epistle to the Romans*, trans. Edwyn C. Hoskyns (London: Oxford University Press, 1950), p. 7; italics mine.

the Scriptures and that transcends the centuries and cultures which separate the world of antiquity from the modern world, and thus provides the abiding theological reference of biblical discourse. It was the achievement of Calvin, according to Lucien J. Richard, that he broke through the medieval notion of the Bible as a source of information *about* God to a position in which the Scriptures afford the reader a knowledge *of* God.[24] The basis of this position is his correlation of the Word and the Spirit, the testimony of the Bible to God with "the internal testimony of the Spirit" which is manifested to the reader through the Scriptures. It is thus through the interpretation of the Scriptures that their authority, which belongs to God, is experienced. How this occurs "through understanding" is the final issue of the present debate on hermeneutics.

4. UNDERSTANDING

The meaning expressed in language is through language understood. If the expression of meaning is the task of the speaker or author, the understanding of this expressed meaning is the task of the hearer or reader. Meaning and understanding are thus correlatives joined by discourse. The nature and scope of the latter, accordingly, is determined by that of the former.

Modern hermeneutics was founded by Friedrich Schleiermacher, who made "understanding" the focal problem of the discipline.[25] That meaning is understood through language is a fact of human experience. Yet communication is a mystery that calls for reflection. Schleiermacher approached the matter from the side of the interpreter, identifying understanding as the specific hermeneutical issue. How does understanding occur? On what basis can it be achieved? In response to such questions, Schleiermacher defined hermeneutics as "the science and art of understanding." In that it clarifies theoretically how understanding actually occurs, hermeneutics is a science. With respect to its practice, it is an art.

Literary meaning for Schleiermacher is formed by the interaction of two structural moments, the grammatical composition of the text and the idea of the author expressed in it. Conversely, understanding occurs when the interpreter reexperiences the mental processes of the author through the grammatical formation of the text. Understanding, in other words, is essentially an act of *re*-cognition. As meaning moves from thought to language via composition, understanding moves from language to thought via interpretation. The

24. See Richard, *The Spirituality of John Calvin* (Atlanta: John Knox Press, 1974), pp. 1-11.
25. See Palmer, *Hermeneutics*, pp. 84-97.

same two interacting moments are involved in both meaning and understanding, only in the reverse order.

In his early reflections upon hermeneutics, Schleiermacher assumed a strict correlation between language and thought. The grammatical and psychological moments of understanding were so closely related that interpretation was oriented to language. The subjectivity of the author was discernable *in* the objectivity of the text. E. D. Hirsch, Jr., follows Schleiermacher closely at this point. His restriction of textual meaning to what Ricoeur calls the "sense" of the text in distinction from what Hirsch himself terms its "significance" has been noted. Quite naturally, this limitation has an impact upon his definition of "understanding." In understanding, he writes, "one submits to another — literally, one stands under him."[26] That is to say, the interpreter submits to the thought of the author as it is expressed in the grammatical sense of the text. In this Hirsch is faithful to the early reflections of Schleiermacher.

Later, however, Schleiermacher shifted the emphasis from grammatical to psychological interpretation in the belief that language does not fully express the thinking of an author. The task of hermeneutics was now focused upon discerning the meaning of an author *through* the text. What understanding requires is not only knowledge of the author's vocabulary, grammar, and style, but a divinatory intuition through empathy with and imagination of the author's experience. This divinatory method he defined as "that in which one transforms oneself into the other person in order to grasp his individuality directly." It is made possible, according to Schleiermacher, by the shared "relationship to life" of the author and the interpreter. This concept provided him with the metaphysical universal necessary for communication to occur across the distance which separates cultures and historical eras. Understanding now involved more than *re*-thinking what an author thought. It required *re*-experiencing that which in the life of the author generated the thought.

The biographer of Schleiermacher Wilhelm Dilthey saw in hermeneutics the possibility of a foundation for the humanities that would make them truly *Geisteswissenschaften* (literally, "sciences of the spirit").[27] His quest was for a "humanistic methodology" that would provide objective validity to the yield of all disciplines which have as their task the interpretation of the expressions of the inner life of humans. The difference between the natural and human sciences, according to Dilthey, is one of goals. The natural sciences seek to *explain* nature in terms of causality; the human sciences seek

26. Hirsch, *Validity in Interpretation,* p. 143.
27. See Palmer, *Hermeneutics,* pp. 98-113.

to *understand* the inner life of fellow human beings in terms of shared meaning. Meaning for Dilthey is human experience known from within. Because human life is "historical," the expressions of human meaning are also historical and therefore relative. Understanding occurs through a mysterious process of mental transfer. Following Schleiermacher, Dilthey saw this transposition as a reconstruction and a reexperiencing of another person's inner world of lived experience. Experiences of life, however, are preconceptual acts of human consciousness before they are rational concepts. When expressed they have conceptual content, but this content is itself a witness to the preconceptual experience which grounds it. The formula for hermeneutics is thus: experience, expression, understanding. Understanding occurs when the interpreter, through an expression of lived experience, reexperiences the experience which generated the expression. Dilthey described this process as one in which the mind of the interpreter grasps the mind (*Geist*) of an author. This involves more than a purely cognitive act, for it is an act of comprehension which transcends conceptualization. As for Schleiermacher, so also for Dilthey, understanding occurs by the transposition of the interpreter into the author through an act of imagination at the level of lived experience.

Picking up on Dilthey's recognition of the radical historicality of human life, Martin Heidegger subjected human-being (*Dasein*) to a radical analysis in his magnum opus, *Being and Time*. Here understanding is identified as one of the "existentials" that constitute human-being. That is to say, understanding is an *a priori*, a given prior to cognition, a primordial awareness of the possibilities of human-being. At the cognitive level, as already noted, understanding requires both intelligibility and significance. These purely cognitive functions of understanding are generated, however, from existential awareness of human possibilities, and this awareness in turn is based upon the ability of human-being to exist in various ways. From this primordial level of awareness, understanding moves through cognition to expression in the use of language. What comes to expression in discourse is the projection of an understanding of a possibility of human-being. To understand this projection through interpretation involves more than merely comprehending the information provided in the text about what is understood by its author. Understanding is achieved when the interpreter appropriates personally the possible way of being human projected by the text.

Heidegger's analysis of understanding entered the domain of biblical studies primarily through the hermeneutical program of Rudolf Bultmann. What is of importance to Bultmann is not the objectifying language of the New Testament but the existential possibilities of human-being projected through it. Faith, for Bultmann, represents one such possibility. The literature of the New Testament is written out of faith. It attests to the kerygma that calls for faith. Although couched in the objectifying mode of language which Bultmann calls "myth," the New Testament message is to be interpreted in terms of the primordial possibilities of human-being which it expresses in this manner. What Bultmann intends by his program of "demythologizing" is thus not the removal of myth but rather its "existential interpretation." Understanding occurs when the existential possibilities of the language of faith are appropriated by faith and result in a new "self-understanding" (*Selbstverständnis*) or "understanding of existence" (*Existenzverständnis*). It is appropriate, therefore, that the collected essays of Bultmann should be published under the title of *Glauben und Verstehen* ("Faith and Understanding").

It is true that both Heidegger and Bultmann distance themselves from the Romantic hermeneutics of Schleiermacher and Dilthey, so-called because of its psychological focus in the interpretation process. Yet it is equally true that they share with Romantic hermeneutics a common orientation of interpretation to the self of the author. Both approaches make the same two assumptions. One is that written discourse is a form of self-expression. The other is that the ultimate reference of such discourse is something in the life of the author. When conceived of psychologically, this reference is the "experience" of the author which generated the expression and which is understood when it is reexperienced by the interpreter. When it is conceived of existentially, the reference of discourse is the "self-understanding" of the author which projects a possibility of human-being and is understood when this possibility is personally appropriated by the interpreter. What drops out of serious consideration is the *intended* reference of discourse, the *Sache* which may and often does transcend both language and the user of language. Thus the impression given by Bultmann is that no matter what the biblical texts speak "about," their ultimate subject matter is human existence. Not many would deny that the biblical texts emerge out of human existence, but when their interpretation is oriented exclusively to human existence it tends to reduce the theological and christological references of the Scriptures to anthropology. This tendency is the fundamental objection raised against Bultmann by his critics, particularly Karl Barth.[28]

Precisely at this point, Gadamer seeks to move the discussion beyond the achievements of his former teachers Heidegger and Bultmann by orienting hermeneutics to language and its subject matter rather than to the existential understanding of the author objectified

28. See Barth, *Rudolf Bultmann: Ein Versuch ihn zu Verstehen,* Theologischen Studien nr. 34 (Zürich: Evangelischer Verlag, 1952).

in the text. Whatever the particular subject matter of a text, he argues, it belongs to historical reality. Gadamer, following Husserl, recognizes that our human experiences of such reality occur within the intentional horizon of consciousness, a fact which eliminates the possibility of pure objectivity in the realm of knowledge and relativizes all human understanding. Yet historical realities cannot be reduced to human experience. Not only are they ontologically prior to experience, but they determine the manner in which they are interpreted by experience through the "world" of the individual established by their social and cultural forms (including language). One way of putting it is that we belong to history before history belongs to us. Meaning therefore transcends the horizon of experience of the individual. It is constituted by our heritage, the tradition in which we live. Communication occurs, accordingly, within the tradition and by means of the transmission of the tradition. The problem of hermeneutics for Gadamer is this act of transmission in which past and present are constantly being mediated.

This process of "effective history," as Gadamer calls it, is made possible by "the fusion of horizons" represented by author and interpreter. Gadamer's point is that neither can escape the horizons established by their respective "worlds." The greater the historical and cultural distance which separates them, the greater the difficulty in effecting this fusion. Gadamer rejects the Romanticist notion that the distance can be bridged by the transposition of the interpreter into the psychological life of the author for the sake of establishing "contemporaneity." He also rejects the assumption of traditional hermeneutics that it is possible to interpret ancient texts "objectively," agreeing with Bultmann that interpretation without presuppositions is an impossible ideal. For our "prejudices" (understood by Gadamer as "pre-judgments") are the constitutive factors of our historical being. What Gadamer seeks to achieve is a productive rather than a distortive use of "pre-judgments" in the process of interpretation. This is made possible by conceiving understanding not in terms of re-cognition but in terms of translation of meaning. The objective of understanding is the establishment of material agreement on the subject matter. The interpreter comes to this goal when the subject matter emerges out of the dialogue with the text and becomes meaningful within the horizon of the interpreter. While Gadamer concedes that it is rash to say that an interpreter understands the subject matter of a text better than its author, he insists that the interpreter always understands it differently. In connection with this statement, it is helpful to note that he is speaking of the *reference* of the text and not its *sense*.

The concepts of "horizon," "world," and "prejudice" in the thought of Gadamer point up the reality and importance of what is called in the new hermeneutics "preunderstanding." Actually, this represents the logical conclusion of the venerable doctrine of "the hermeneutical circle" in traditional hermeneutics. This principle was first established by the classical philologists with reference to the grammatical meaning of the sentence. The meaning of a sentence, it was recognized, depends not upon the semantic value of individual terms as they appear in a lexicon but upon their semantic value as determined by their mutual relationship within the sentence. This relationship is between the "parts" (terms) and the "whole" (sentence). Interpreters may begin with the parts but they construe the meaning in terms of the whole. Conversely, they may intuit the meaning of the whole and seek confirmation by an examination of the parts. Either way, understanding occurs by a circular process in which meaning emerges out of the interaction between the parts and the whole. Schleiermacher applied this principle to understanding itself. He perceived that we understand something by comparing it with something we have already understood. At the level of subject matter as well as grammar, therefore, understanding emerges out of a circular interaction between the part (what is being understood) and the whole (what is already understood). In Heidegger this theme is developed under the concept of "fore-having" which grounds all understanding. Gadamer discusses the matter beneath a quotation from Luther to the effect that "he who does not understand the subject-matter under discussion cannot elicit the meaning of the words."[29] This foundational "preunderstanding" may, but need not, be rigid. If the interpreter knows everything better than the author, the text will be muted in its ability to have its say. The "closed mind" of the interpreter precludes new insights into the subject matter of the text. If the interpreter remains "open minded," the text may provide new understanding. Thus in place of the plea for exegesis without presuppositions made by traditional hermeneutics, the new hermeneutics calls for an openness to what the text has to say on the subject matter with a view to greater understanding.

Ricoeur's discussion of the nature of "understanding" and how it is achieved is of special interest in that he combines theoretically the legitimate concerns of Hirsch and Gadamer as expressed above. His agreement with Hirsch regarding the real possibility of validity in interpretation with regard to textual sense has been noted. For Ricoeur, however, the role of the intention of the author is less important than for Hirsch. Not that a text bears no intentional meaning. Ricoeur's point is that since the author is unavailable to the interpreter for questioning about ambiguous meaning in the text, the interpreter has access to the author's intention only in its expres-

---

29. Gadamer, *Truth and Method*, p. 151.

sion in the text. Lacking a court of appeal beyond the text, the interpreter must assume that the "utterer's meaning" is present in the "utterance meaning." It is the latter, therefore, that must be understood. Understanding, according to Ricoeur, begins with the sense of the text and follows it out to what it points to, its reference. The formula offered for the process of construing textual sense is: understanding — explanation — comprehension. A circular process is involved here which begins with understanding as a naive, intuitive grasp of the content (a guess), validates the guess by explanation (arguments from grammar, syntax, style, genre, context, etc.), and issues in comprehension as a more sophisticated form of understanding. By introducing the concept of "explanation" into the interpretation process, Ricoeur moves away from Dilthey's claim that nature is explained and the mind is understood. His reason is the simple observation that one explains something to people in order that they may understand. And what they understand they may then explain to others. If the initial guess at understanding is synthetic, explanation is analytic. It explores the full range of possible meanings in the text, including possible primary and secondary meanings. But this range is not unlimited. By means of the arguments from explanation, a particular meaning may be established with some probability as *the* meaning of the text. This is the basis of validation in the circular interpretation process. For Ricoeur, however, this validation applies equally to the sense and to the reference of textual meaning, its ideal sense and its subject matter. Meaning is not only the ideal object intended by the author, but the actual reality aimed at by the ideal object as well. To understand a text is to be led by its dialectical movement from sense to reference, from what it says to what it talks about.

The possibility of understanding the sense of a text is for Ricoeur grounded in "the universality of sense." The "ideality" of textual sense, its *noematic* content, is the logical dimension of its proposition. Following Husserl, Ricoeur describes this logical content of all intentional acts as a *noematic* object that is neither a physical nor a psychic reality. As such it enjoys a rationality that is intelligible across historical and cultural distance. Consequently, meaning and understanding are both less historically and more logically determined than Dilthey and the historicist tradition allowed. Ricoeur openly challenges the epistemological presupposition that the content of literary works receives its intelligibility from its connection to the social and cultural conditions of the community that produced it or to which it was originally destined. Literature, because of the nature of writing, slips the chain of its original historical situation and becomes a kind of atemporal object. The access to writing thus implies the overcoming of the historical process by the transfer of discourse to a sphere of ideality which allows an indefinite widening of the sphere of communication.

This applies also to the reference of the text, at least to the extent that the reference is a subject matter which itself transcends a human situation and involves a human world. With regard to the referential function of texts, Ricoeur argues that two attitudes are possible. On the one hand, the interpreter may remain in a state of suspense as regards any kind of referred to reality. On the other hand, the interpreter may actualize the potential of the subject matter by imaginatively relating it to a new situation. Because the text opens up a possible world to the interpreter, the "world of the text" or the "text world," the interpreter may enter that world and appropriate personally the possibility of human-being which it projects. When that occurs, the meaning of the text is actualized in understanding.

Ricoeur asks what is to be understood and consequently appropriated in the text. His answer is not the intention of the author, which is supposed to be hidden behind the text; not the historical situation common to the author and the original readers; not even their understanding of themselves as historical and cultural beings. What has to be understood by appropriation is the meaning of the text itself, conceived in a dynamic way as the direction of thought opened up by the text. In other words, what has to be appropriated for understanding to be completed is nothing other than the power of disclosing a world that is the reference of the text. This concept of "understanding," Ricoeur acknowledges, is close to what Gadamer calls "a fusion of horizons" in which the world horizon of the reader is fused with the world horizon of the writer as both focus upon the subject matter. The mediating link between the two in this process of horizon fusing is the ideality of textual sense. For it is the *noematic* content of the text, its sense in dialectical relation to its reference, which spans the cultural and historical distance between the author and the interpreter. Indeed, when Ricoeur speaks of literary "distanciation," he means the distancing of the text from its author and original situation. The gulf between the interpreter and the author need not be bridged by the interpreter making an impossible leap into the past or into the lived experience of the author. It has been bridged by the text itself. A text is indeed historical in its origin, but it is also present in its power to communicate its sense and to open a world to its reader by its reference. In this conviction, Ricoeur is bold to claim that the letters of Paul are no less addressed to him than to the Romans, Galatians, Corinthians, and Ephesians. For the meaning of a text can be understood by anyone who reads. And to appropriate that meaning is to understand.

Clearly Ricoeur overstates the case when he contends that literature is atemporal by virtue of its being literature, and that textual interpretation is for this reason oriented more to logic than to history. The recognition of modern linguistics that language use is both synchronic and diachronic requires the "said as such" of discourse to be interpreted in the light of its particular synchronic period of origin. The necessity of a historical understanding of the sense of textual meaning is thus linguistically grounded. At the same time, the claims of radical historicism are patently false. If literature were totally determined by the historical and cultural situation of origin, if there were no common world binding the situations and transcending them, then neither historical understanding nor cross-cultural communication would be possible. That both are in fact possible indicates that the truth of historical relativism is only relatively true. There is something like Ricoeur's "universality of sense" which makes possible both understanding and translation of textual meaning.

Quite evidently, Ricoeur conceives of "understanding" at a variety of levels which correspond to his conception of meaning. The intuitive "guess" which initiates textual understanding and must be confirmed or corrected by explanation in order to attain comprehension is limited to the *noematic* content of the text, the "what" of the textual sense, the "said as such." At this level, Ricoeur concurs with Hirsch that the sense of the text bears a determinate and thus a determinable meaning. It remains constant in the interpretation process. But this constant factor directs the interpreter to its reference, the "about what" of the text. This also is determined by authorial intention and remains the same in interpretation. At the point of reference, however, the interpretation process encourages diversity rather than uniformity of understanding. Because interpreters bring to the text their own preunderstandings of its subject matter, and because understanding of the subject matter moves in a circle from this preunderstanding to understanding the text on its subject matter to greater understanding, there is bound to be a difference in the way textual meaning (sense plus reference) is comprehended. With appropriation, the variation factor in understanding increases, and in application it is maximized.

By analogy, the relationship of understanding to meaning is like that of a harbor buoy to its anchor. Textual meaning is the anchor which tethers the buoy of understanding to the sense, the reference, and the significance intended by the author. The chain that connects them is the interpretation process. At the level of comprehending the sense of the text the chain holds firm. At the level of appropriating the reference it begins to move with the currents introduced by the interpreter's preunderstanding of the subject matter. And at the level of applying the significance of the text it floats with the changing conditions of the seas of history. Yet even here it does not run free. For the significance of the test is still anchored to the author's intention and moves only within the range permitted by appropriate historical analogies.

Does the meaning of a text then change? No. What changes is our understanding of that unchanging meaning. The fullness of textual meaning and textual understanding make change inevitable. For understanding fully is a process that moves from comprehension of the sense of the text to appropriation of the reference to application of its significance. And the further the process moves from the sense of the text, the greater the difference will be between the interpreter's understanding and the author's meaning with regard to the subject matter.

5. CONCLUSION

One clear result of this cursory presentation of the issues involved in the current debate on the nature, scope, and function of interpretation should be the recognition of their intrinsic interdependence. *Hermeneutics* is the theory and practice of *interpretation*, which is the process whereby one achieves *understanding* of textual *meaning* as expressed in written *language*. The semantic value of each term in this description is mutually determined by its interaction with the others. While language provides the unifying concept (the point at which the others meet), meaning establishes the foundation concept upon which the others build. The correlative relation between meaning and understanding is evident, the nature and scope of the former bearing determinative influence upon the nature and scope of the latter. In domino fashion, understanding then specifies the goal of interpretation, which in turn creates the vision of hermeneutics.

MIND READER AND MAESTRO: MODELS FOR UNDERSTANDING BIBLICAL INTERPRETERS

PATRICK R. KEIFERT

The task and results of biblical interpretation will vary greatly, depending upon the interpreter's own self-understanding and, at the same time, the interpreter's estimate of the character of the text to be interpreted. When we say "the Bible is Christian Scripture," we claim at least that "it ought so to be used in the common life of the church as to nurture and preserve her self-identity."[1] It follows, then, that if the interpreter understands the text as Scripture,[2] then the interpreter's self-understanding of the interpretive task is grounded in the common life of the church, in the church's nurture and preservation of its self-identity.

Certain models of the interpreter's self-understanding within the interpretive task might be found more in keeping than others with the common life of the church, its nurture and preservation. I will

---

1. David H. Kelsey, *The Uses of Scripture in Recent Theology* (Philadelphia: Fortress Press, 1975), p. 150. The interpretation of any text involves the text in relationship to itself, other texts, the author, and its readers. The arrangement of these four factors in relationship with one another creates the spectrum of possible theories of interpretation. This essay explores only two of those possible arrangements: the one primarily normed by authorial intention and the other focusing on the contemporary readers or audience. In neither case are the factors in the interpretation of the text ignored. It is a matter of degrees and emphases.

It is clearly possible to interpret the texts of the Bible without understanding them as Christian Scripture. They may be studied as literature or as a historical source by methods of inquiry unrelated to their status as Scripture. Here I follow Kelsey's discussion of Scripture *(The Uses of Scripture in Recent Theology,* pp. 89-112).

2. This essay is an exercise in systematic theology, not fundamental theology. My concern here is to examine possible models for the self-understanding of the churchly interpreter of the Bible. Therefore, no argument will be made regarding the possibility of the truth of Scripture to any audience outside the church. Rather, I will be concerned to examine how Scripture functions for the Christian community. I do not intend this bracketing to imply that such an argument concerning the truth of Scripture cannot or should not be made. Indeed, I am convinced that such an argument is both possible and necessary; it simply lies outside the central concerns of this essay. Likewise, I do not deny the doctrine of inspiration, but it too is outside the direct concerns of this essay.

Reprinted from *Word & World* 1(1980): 153-68.

explore several models of the interpreter's self-understanding of the interpretive task, pair them with the corresponding understanding of the text, and evaluate their usefulness for interpreting the Bible as Christian Scripture.[3] Models that consciously begin with contemporary readers and audiences, I will argue, have significant advantages over those that primarily ground meaning in the consciousness of the author. Or, to put it another way, those models that seek first to bridge the gap between the life and practice of the contemporary audience and interpretive theory are relatively more adequate compared to those that primarily seek to bridge the historical gap between what the text meant and what it means today.

HISTORICAL AND LINGUISTIC PARADIGMS

Two basic paradigms for the biblical interpreter and text hold the field today: historical and linguistic.[4] The interpreter might understand his or her role primarily as that of historian and think of the biblical text to some degree as a historical document.[5] Such an

3. By the term *model* I am referring to the use of "an image employed reflectively and critically to deepen one's theoretical understanding of a reality" (see Avery Dulles, *Models of the Church* [Garden City, N.Y.: Doubleday, 1978], pp. 19-37). Some models are readily imagined (e.g., my Maestro and Player-Coach models), while others are more abstract (e.g., those of the Deliberator and the church as Sacrament of Dialogue). The term *model* has for some time been in use in the physical and social sciences. I. T. Ramsey, among others, has shown its fruitfulness for theology (see Ramsey, *Religious Language* [New York: Macmillan, 1963] and *Models and Mystery* [New York: Oxford University Press, 1964]; see also Max Black, *Models and Metaphors* [Ithaca, N.Y.: Cornell University Press, 1962]). In their use in theology, however, models renew the attempt to relate language and the ultimate mystery of reality. In this attempt, says Dulles, one must recognize that "religious experience has a depth that has no correlation in our experience of the physical universe" (Dulles, *Models of the Church*, p. 30).

I will be using models to explain and synthesize what I believe is generally held by churchly interpreters of the Bible and also to explore possible new insights into the interpretive enterprise. The Mind Reader model will be of the former type, and the other models of the latter. The exploratory and heuristic models in no way suggest that I have rejected what Dulles calls the "abiding objective norm in the past, that is, in the revelation that was given once and for all in Jesus Christ" (*Models of the Church*, p. 32). I am using these heuristic models to order our abiding experience of that revelation.

4. This truism was reflected in the arrangement of the various program categories of the 1980 Centennial Meeting of the Society for Biblical Literature. The call for papers was divided between approaches to the Bible through historical paradigms on the one hand and linguistic paradigms on the other.

In this essay I will use the term *paradigm* to mean a model of interpretation that has received general acceptance and encompasses various models and types within it. Thus, the historical paradigm can include more than one type of interpretive method—for example, source, form, redaction, and sociological criticism. The linguistic paradigm includes both traditional literary types of interpretation and structuralist and deconstructionist criticism.

5. By speaking of the Bible as a historical document, I in no way wish to ignore the many other literary forms besides historical narrative in the text.

interpreter would use the text to authorize claims either in reference
to the events behind the text or to the "mind" of the community of
the faithful who are witnesses to those events. In either instance the
interpreter's task is essentially historical. The appropriate primary
claims resulting from such an interpretation will tend to be historical as well.

Another interpreter might also understand the task from the side
of the contemporary reader or audience and thereby downplay the
historian's task, though not necessarily exclude it. In this self-understanding the text is essentially understood as literary text, which is
not to say that it is exclusively fictional.[6] As in the earlier understanding of the text as history and the interpreter as historian, there
are within this self-understanding two broadly construed choices.
Either the text's authority lies primarily in its effect within the contemporary audience, or it has its authoritative status within its own
structure.

There are, then, at least four possible basic types for the interpreter's self-understanding and, broadly construed, four possible
theories of the text. They need not be mutually exclusive; they can
be integrated in various ways. Such an integration, however, first
requires some clarity on their essential characteristics and functions.
Before I attempt such an integration, I shall briefly describe these
four types from the side of models for the interpreter's self-understanding of the interpretive task. The first two, historical types, and
the fourth, a linguistic type, will be given short and, by implication,
secondary consideration; the third (also linguistic) will be given a
more extensive and developed consideration.

Historical Paradigm: Two Types[7]

The interpreter can understand the interpretive task as an attempt
to discern what actually took place in the history to which the text
refers. For example, when Vincent Taylor interpreted Mark, he was

6. I choose to avoid a fast terminological distinction between fiction and history.
To a great extent I am in sympathy with Barbara Herrnstein Smith, who rejects the
overt distinctions between categories of poetry and history in recognition of "covert"
categories — that is, "categories implicitly acknowledged and respected in the culture,
and learned by its members, but cutting through and across the distinction presumably reflected in traditional terms such as poetry, prose, literature, fiction, and non-
fiction" (see Smith's *On the Margins of Discourse: The Relation of Literature to Language*
[Chicago: University of Chicago Press, 1978], pp. 45ff.). As I will point out shortly,
I wish to distinguish between historical and literary criticism but not propose the
great divide imagined by interpreters who hold one paradigm over the other.

7. By the term *type* I am referring to particular developments of either the linguistic or the historical paradigm that might be methodological types and yet remain
within the same general paradigm. For instance, both source criticism and redaction-
criticism fall within the historical paradigm, although each orders the historical
enterprise quite differently.

concerned to underline its value or use as history.[8] Taylor was by no means uninterested in the gospel's literary style and formal characteristics; he was, however, concerned to subordinate such observations in service of his goal to establish the outline of Jesus' ministry.[9] The motives of the author (whom Taylor identified as John Mark, a follower of Peter) were taken into account and carefully subtracted from the text in order to discern the events behind the text. Apologetic aims, liturgical interests, and doctrinal motives were taken into account in order to ascertain what Jesus actually said and did.[10] In spite of textual redaction, Taylor could, in his role as historian, confidently speak of the "objectivity of the gospel."[11] For Taylor, Mark could authorize claims regarding the life and ministry of Jesus that could in turn be normative for the life and ministry of the contemporary church, though the delineation of such norms was beyond the scope of Taylor's endeavor.

A second, and perhaps more subtle, type of the first paradigm (the interpreter of Scripture as historian) focuses on a particular historical event: the mind or consciousness of the author and the original audience. In this second type of the interpreter as historian, the goal of the interpretive task focuses on repeating the intention of the author in relationship to the original audience. For example, Willi Marxsen, in his interpretation of Mark, consciously speaks of the interpreters task as "repeating (nachsprechen) what the author had meant to say to the original audience."[12] Marxsen can clearly distinguish between what he calls "exegesis" and "history," insofar as history would be viewed as an attempt to go behind the text to establish what really happened in the life of Jesus. For Marxsen the exegesis of Mark excludes "from the outset . . . what really happened" as the subject matter for its investigation.[13] In this way he makes clear his polemic against the form-critical school which had sought to isolate the earliest reliable synoptic material as the basis for a reconstruction of the historical Jesus.

Interpreter as Mind Reader

To a great extent this second type of the historical paradigm for understanding the interpreter and the character of the text dominates the use of the biblical text in major portions of the church

8. See Taylor, *The Gospel according to St. Mark*, 2d ed. (London: Macmillan, 1966), pp. 130-49.

9. See Taylor, *New Testament Essays* (London: Epworth, 1970), pp. 95-118.

10. See Taylor, *The Gospel according to St. Mark*, pp. 131-35.

11. Taylor, *The Gospel according to St. Mark*, p. 135.

12. Marxsen, *The Beginnings of Christology: A Study in Its Problems* (Philadelphia: Fortress Press, 1969), p. 3. See also his *Mark the Evangelist: Studies on the Redaction History of the Gospel* (Nashville: Abingdon Press, 1969) and *New Testament Introduction: An Approach to Its Problems* (Philadelphia: Fortress Press, 1968), pp. 134-45.

13. See Marxsen, *The Beginnings of Christology*, pp. 3ff.

today.[14] We clearly distinguish between what the text meant and what it means.[15] The norm, of course, is what it meant. We say to ourselves, "How would the original author have meant this expression?" Or, "What did the original author and audience have in their minds when they wrote and heard this text?" The interpreter, then, must "psych-out" the original author and audience. The authority of the text depends upon the possible analogies between the minds then and now. Interpretations within this type receive titles like *The Mind of Mark*[16] and *Community of the New Age;*[17] the former emphasizes the authorial side of this interpretive type and the latter the audience side. This search into the consciousness of the original author or community might well be called the Mind Reader model.

The churchly interpreter who would use the Mind Reader model should note possible pitfalls. Quite often this model ignores the

14. Norman Perrin has suggested that "we need to be able to understand the language in which a text is written, the nature of the text itself as a historical and literary artifact, the circumstances in which and for which it was written. We need, further, to understand as far as we can the intent of the author in writing the text and the meaning understood by those for whom the text was written" (*Jesus and the Language of the Kingdom: Symbol and Metaphor in New Testament Interpretation* [Philadelphia: Fortress Press, 1976], p. 4).

15. Raymond Brown states this general principle when he writes that "to determine the sense of a written work is largely to determine what its author meant when he wrote it" and that "the principal task of interpretation centers around the author's intended meaning" (*The Jerome Biblical Commentary,* ed. R. E. Brown, J. A. Fitzmyer, and R. E. Murphy [Englewood Cliffs, N.J.: Prentice-Hall, 1968], 2: 606, art. 5). In his last major publication before his death in November 1976, Norman Perrin wrote, "Biblical scholars tend to be primarily historical scholars, so much so that 'Biblical criticism' almost always means 'historical criticism of biblical texts' " (*Jesus and the Language of the Kingdom,* p. 5). Nor is fascination with and acceptance of this historical approach restricted to the professional experts. Indeed, as Edward Krentz (writing in 1975) points out, the historical-critical method of biblical exegesis is generally accepted as a valid and in fact *necessary* approach to the biblical writings, not only in scholarly circles but also at the level of the official pronouncements of various Christian churches (see Krentz, *The Historical-Critical Method* [London: S.P.C.K., 1975], pp. 2-3).

16. Quentin Quesnell, *The Mind of Mark: Interpretation and Method through the Exegesis of Mark 6:52* (Rome: Pontifical Biblical Institute, 1969). The search for the author's intention springs from the Romantic hermeneutical tradition of Schleiermacher and Dilthey and its insistence that genuine understanding of a text involves and aims at what Paul Ricoeur refers to as "a 'congenial' coincidence with the 'genius' of the author" (*Interpretation Theory: Discourse and the Surplus of Meaning* [Fort Worth: Texas Christian University Press, 1976], p. 92). Thus, for example, Benjamin Jowett, an important nineteenth-century English New Testament scholar and contributor to the programmatic *Essays and Reviews* published in 1860, is quoted as having declared that "the true use of interpretation is to get rid of interpretation and leave us alone in company with the author" (see E. C. Blackman, *Biblical Interpretation: The Old Difficulties and the New Opportunity* [London: Independent Press, 1957], p. 206).

17. Howard Clark Kee, *Community of the New Age: Studies in Mark's Gospel* (Philadelphia: Westminster Press, 1977). In discussing the contribution of E. D. Hirsch, Jr., to the hermeneutical discussion, Kee makes a special point of praising Hirsch's treatment of the concept of the author (see Hirsch, "In Defense of the Author," in *Validity in Interpretation* [New Haven: Yale University Press, 1967], pp. 1-23).

various senses in which the word "author" can be used. The expression "author" can refer to several different personae. First, it can refer to a biographical flesh and blood person. For example, Paul of Tarsus would count as the biographical author. Within this biographical "author" would be the peculiar personal idiosyncracies that might be hinted at in Galatians and in 1 and 2 Corinthians[18] but are unavailable to anyone but his closest intimates. Second, there is the career author. In the case of Paul one can discern a career author by tracing the supposed development of Paul, the career author, from 1 Thessalonians through Romans.[19] Third, there is the public figure which in the case of Paul can best be characterized by his portrayal in Acts and, subsequently, in the church's development of his public character to this day.[20] Finally, there is the implied author, the persona that the reader creates in his/her mind and projects into the text in order to follow the narrative.

Without further detail, I hope that the outline of a spectrum of possible meanings and theories of author can be discerned from these four possible meanings for the term *author*.[21] Each might be the appropriate meaning of *author* in the expression "author's intention," depending upon the situation in which the expression is used and the text with which it is used as an interpretive device. For example, in the case of Mark, the "author's intention" has a very limited use. We do not have enough data to say much about the biographical or career "author" and not much more to say about the public author. We are left more often than not with the implied author of Mark, that *persona* the interpreter creates to bring a consistent meaning to the entire text.[22]

And yet it is insufficient, though necessary, to chasten this model with these various references for the word *author*. Quite often the Mind Reader model ignores the great complications in deciphering another human consciousness.[23] Fishing expeditions in the territory of another person's consciousness, even one who is present with you in conversation, are tricky at best. How much more difficult must

18. See Robert Jewett, *A Chronology of Paul's Life* (Philadelphia: Fortress Press, 1979), pp. 29-30.

19. See Jewett, *A Chronology of Paul's Life*, pp. 1-24, 63-92.

20. See Jewett, *A Chronology of Paul's Life*, pp. 1-24, 63-92.

21. See Wayne C. Booth, *Critical Understanding: The Power and Limits of Pluralism* (Chicago: University of Chicago Press, 1979), p. 268.

22. See Wolfgang Iser, *The Act of Reading: A Theory of Aesthetic Response* (Baltimore: The Johns Hopkins University Press, 1978), p. 18.

23. No more sophisticated and thoughtful "defense of the author" exists than that of Hirsch in his books *Validity in Interpretation* and *The Aims of Interpretation* (Chicago: University of Chicago Press, 1976). He attempts to avoid both of the pitfalls to which I refer in this essay, although in the end I believe he succumbs to both. For an excellent analysis of Hirsch's failure on this score, see David Couzens Hoy, *The Critical Circle: Literature and History in Contemporary Hermeneutics* (Berkeley and Los Angeles: University of California Press, 1978), pp. 11-35.

it be to attempt the same feat with a person dead two thousand years! With a contemporary person we have at the minimum the numerous nonverbal signals of body language and prelinguistic background that we share. In some cases this may follow a relatively long period of familiarity with this person. The experienced interpreter of human nature would be reticent to claim to understand, without considerable reservations, the mind of any person who might out of the blue speak to him or her. Though the Bible may not speak out of the blue, it is for us devoid of many contextual preunderstandings that a conversation implies. In the case of Mark, for example, where we have primarily the implied author, little or none of the complex contextual material is present that would make reading Mark roughly analogous to a conversation or even a letter from a contemporary.

I hope that even with these short observations, the impasses that confront the Mind Reader model are evident. This is not to say it does not have a place among appropriate means of interpreting the biblical text. I hope to leave with you, however, the significant reservations and limitations involved in such a model. It should be clear that such a model would be insufficient for the churchly interpreter, and certainly an extremely limited manner in which to have the Bible be Scripture for the church. If the Bible is to be used "in the common life of the church as to nurture and preserve her self-identity," then other models would have to supplement and perhaps encompass it.

The Linguistic Paradigm: Two Types

Other models are available as a result of contemporary hermeneutical discussions. The hermeneutical principle of authorial intention, which provides the major hermeneutical grounding for the historical-critical method in biblical exegesis, has been brought into question by opposing theories.[24] L. Griffin, for example, writes of a "new tendency" which questions "the adequacy of the author's intention as an explanation of his product" and claims "that the author's intention is only a partial explanation, and that in fact any real explanation must be had through insistence on the work itself which in fact may exceed the author's intention or indeed may fall short

24. While it is clear that historical-critical biblical exegesis makes use of a wide variety of methods and approaches, I shall in this essay use the terms *historical-critical method* and *historical-critical exegesis* to refer globally to these various methods insofar as they are governed by the principle of authorial intention and are thus (ultimately) directed toward discovering the author's intention or intended meaning as understood by the original readers or addressees in the historical situation in which the writing arose.

of it."[25] In Anglo-American literary-critical circles,[26] the principle of authorial intention has for some time been the subject of lively debate, and indeed this principle has been dubbed by Wimsatt and Beardsley the "Intentional Fallacy."[27] As Amos Wilder puts it, "in literary criticism attention has now for some time been directed to the given work as a self-sufficient aesthetic whole which should be allowed to make its own impact apart from extraneous consider-ations having to do with the author and his circumstances or intentions."[28]

As I stated above, there are two broadly construed choices within the linguistic paradigm. The one would focus on the "world" created by the text in its effect on the contemporary reader. Likewise, this choice would take note of the complex relationship the reader es-tablishes with the text. Of this choice I will later have much to say. The second alternative within the linguistic paradigm is the struc-turalist approach to texts,[29] which is in many ways the antithesis of the historical paradigm. If the historical approach provides the tools for uncovering and analyzing the author's intended meaning, structuralism aims at uncovering and analyzing the deep structures of the text itself, which are quite independent of what the author may or may not have intended.[30] For the structuralist approach, to use Paul Ricoeur's words, a text is "an absolute object for and in itself."[31] Therefore, the text's meaning is a function of the interre-

25. See Griffin, "Hermeneutics," *Irish Theological Quarterly* 37 (1970): 237-38. Of this "new tendency," Griffin writes that it "does have the good effect of taking biblical hermeneutics out of its isolation and inserting it into the larger field of general interpretation" (p. 242).

26. I refer here not to what is commonly known as "literary criticism" among biblical scholars but to what R. W. Funk calls "literary literary criticism" (see Funk's foreword to *Semeia* 8 [1977]: vii). Through this essay, the term *literary criticism* will be used in this sense.

27. See G. Hermeren, "Intention and Interpretation in Literary Criticism," *New Literary History* 7 (1975-76): 57-82, especially p. 57. See also W. K. Wimsatt, *The Verbal Icon: Studies in the Meaning of Poetry* (Lexington: University of Kentucky Press, 1967), especially "The Intentional Fallacy," an essay written in collaboration with M. C. Beardsley (pp. 3-18).

28. Wilder, *Early Christian Rhetoric: The Language of the Gospel* (Cambridge: Har-vard University Press, 1972), p. xxv.

29. For a good introduction to the structuralist approach to texts, see R. Scholes, *Structuralism in Literature: An Introduction* (New Haven: Yale University Press, 1974). See also R. Barthes, "Introduction à l'analyse structurale des récits," *Communications* 8 (1966): 1-27.

30. See Robert Everard C. Johnston, "Text and Text-Interpretation in the Thought of Paul Ricoeur" (licentiate diss., Katholieke Universiteit te Leuven, 1977), p. 2. Mr. Johnson's dissertation and an as-yet-unpublished book-length manuscript of his on Paul Ricoeur's hermeneutical theory have been of considerable help in sorting out some of the argument of this essay.

31. Ricoeur, "Du conflit à la convergence des méthodes en exégèse biblique," *Exégèse et herméneutique*, by R. Barthes et al. (Paris: Ed du Seuil, 1971), p. 38.

lations among its elements. Authorial intention is thus considered irrelevant so far as the meaning of the text is concerned. Though considerable and fruitful discussion has been dedicated to the use of structural analysis of the biblical text, models dependent on this type of interpretation will not be my major concern in this essay. I have, instead, chosen to focus on that choice within this paradigm which concerns itself with the relationship between the contemporary audience and the world that the text creates.

Recently much discussion of the Bible as Scripture and as authoritative has focused on models of interpretation that are roughly within this broad type. I will call it the contemporary audience type. Instead of understanding the biblical interpreter's task as negotiating the gap between what was once said and what might appropriately be said today, what the text meant and means, much recent thought has turned to negotiating the gap between hermeneutical theory and pastoral praxis. To one degree or another they have taken seriously Johannes-Baptist Metz's observation that "the fundamental hermeneutical problem of theology is not the problem of how systematic theology stands in relation to historical theology, how dogma stands in relation to history, but what is the relation between theory and practice."[32]

David Kelsey, though in many important ways quite unlike Professor Metz in theological outlook, suggests that Scripture's authority is conferred upon it and is in a reciprocal relationship with the audience, or community, that understands it as authoritative.[33] Kelsey, I believe, rightly observes that the church's influence on the interpreter's view of Scripture is crucial. Professional interpreters might make suggestions as to how the text should be understood, but such suggestions grow out of and respond to the common life of the church both in its liturgical and moral forms.[34] It is then quite sensible to argue, as I have suggested above, that *the fundamental form of the Christian interpretation of Scripture is the life, activity, and organization of the Christian community.*

Interpreter as Maestro[35]

Such interpretation can, I believe, be understood best under the category of performance of the biblical text. By analogy this might

32. Metz, "Relationship of Church and World in the Light of Political Theology," in *Renewal of Religious Structures*, vol. 2 of *Theology of Renewal*, ed. L. K. Shook (New York: Herder & Herder, 1968), p. 260.

33. See Kelsey, *The Uses of Scripture in Recent Theology*, p. 150.

34. See Kelsey, *The Uses of Scripture in Recent Theology*, pp. 208ff.

35. I use the term *maestro* in the sense of the master of any art. In this case, the conductor of a chamber orchestra has clarified the model. The model first occurred to me when I heard a lecture by N. L. A. Nash that to my knowledge has not been published.

mean comparing the interpretation of the biblical text to a chamber orchestra playing a Mozart symphony. We have a group of people interpreting a text. It is possible that they are playing the piece incorrectly, or at best, poorly. The score may include misprints, or the orchestra may simply misunderstand the signs on the score, or the players may lack the basic technical skills to perform the score. Even if the orchestra is quite capable technically of performing the score, critics might conclude that it is unfaithful to the score, that the performance lacks a certain truthfulness. Though all of these faults might be present, the text could be to some degree faithfully enacted.

A model of the interpreter of the biblical text based on this analogy would not exclude the important work of the historical critic. A determination of whether the score had been corrupted would require careful textual criticism. A determination of the range of possibilities for the particular form of symphony, its *Sitz im Leben,* and the editorial developments of the form in the hand of the master would certainly require the work of the form and redaction critic. But these would not be the focus; nor would the problems raised by them be the primary concern of the performance. Any model based on this analogy between the performance of a symphony and the performance of the biblical text would focus on the performance itself as the crucial context and norm for the interpretation. This shift of focus, though not rejecting the historical-critical method, places the conclusions and significance of those conclusions in a completely different order of value. The interpreter, let us say on a Sunday morning, changes from Mind Reader to Maestro.

I have recently had the opportunity to observe the work of the St. Paul Chamber Orchestra under the direction of Pinchas Zukerman. Mr. Zukerman's delightful manner, his expressive care for the truth of the performance and the fidelity of the music, have helped crystalize my thoughts on this model. The director of a chamber orchestra is perhaps not quite as crucial as the director of a symphony orchestra. Nonetheless, the director's task is primarily to allow the individual members as an ensemble to create the music. As the principal interpreter of the text, the director leads the ongoing discussion called interpretation. Each member of the chamber orchestra must and does have an interpretation of the piece. In the case of the St. Paul Chamber Orchestra many of the members offer considerable skills and detailed information about the history and form of the text. The director must identify the interpretation most appropriate, not only for the original performers, but most especially for the contemporary performers.

Interpreter as Player-Coach [36]

Perhaps the Maestro model is too elitist. At any rate, it could lead to too great an emphasis on the virtuoso character of the interpreter. It is, however, true that much of the necessary and crucial work of interpretation is done alone and then brought to the community for discussion and enactment. In this case, the Player-Coach model might help clarify the role of the interpreter in the interpretation of Scripture within the community.

In this model the text is the playbook, often referred to as the Bible of the Game. Any player caught not only in ignorance of but also unable to execute the playbook—to digest it inwardly—in the moment of action will suffer rather grave consequences. The character of the interpretation of the text as a cooperative team play suggests the communal character of the Bible as Scripture.

Once again to lessen the possibility of an authoritarian model of the interpreter, each coach, too, must venture onto the field of play. In the heat of the skirmish, each interpreter must bring about a mutual interpretation that is finally judged by its success on the playing field. This model recognizes the vulnerability of the interpreter who has not developed the community of trust and high morale necessary for the test of the community in the game. Anyone who fails to include the community in his or her interpretation risks getting sacked.

Two other possible objections might arise out of the Player-Coach model of interpreter. First, one might object to the analogy between interpreting Scripture and a game. "Interpreting Scripture is serious business, not a game," one might object. This is true. On the other hand, one need only observe the professional athlete before the beginning of the game or in the heat of a crucial play. Think of the hours of individual and team practice and study, long and tedious repetitions of exercises, the struggle for excellence in mind, body, and spirit. If the average professional interpreter of Scripture within the community of the church engaged in such "play" one might not make such an objection.

A second objection might be to the violent images employed in some instances of this model: the player-coach may play on a hockey team. Surely no model can be effectively analogous at all points or

36. In using the model of Player-Coach I am drawing an analogy with games and the interpretive enterprise. In doing so I recognize that I am opening the door to possible misunderstandings of my intentions; I want to stress that this choice is not capricious and that it does not imply any skepticism on my part. There has been considerable discussion of game theory and interpretation theory; see Wayne C. Booth, *Critical Understanding*, pp. 29-30.

sufficient for all moments in this argument. However, the possibilities of violence, especially the possibilities for oppression both within and without the community of interpreters, must not be forgotten. In fact, the churchly interpreter might well be quite suspicious of any model of interpreter that ignores the possibility of such systemic distortion within and without the community.[37]

Interpreter as Deliberator

In noting the possibility of violence and oppression within the community of interpretation, Johannes-Baptist Metz's concern for theory and praxis comes home again. Though my focus is on the imaginative character of interpretation of the Bible as Scripture, this "does not make it any less political activity";[38] it truly is a political act. The imaginative and the political character of interpretation are equally significant and necessary.[39] This political character of interpretation might be developed under the model of the interpreter as Deliberator.

In the face of violence and oppression, the community needs to deliberate; at its best, it acts out its shared hope as a result of a deliberative and persuasive discourse. When the professional interpreter of the Bible engages in the enactment or performance of the text within the community, she or he leads such deliberation. The sermon, for example, need not, in its concern for the truth, be an edict or prescription of the dos and don'ts of the community. It can be a winsome deliberation upon the truth that the community shares, without lessening the proclamatory or prophetic character of the interpretation. For the Christian deliberator cannot escape pronouncing the mercy and judgment of God or escape its way in her life.[40] Such pronouncing includes all the members in the community in a same-saying *(homilia)*, not in angry fiats and coercive sophis-

---

37. There have been important discussions concerning the integration of hermeneutical theory and practice with regard to political philosophy. The implications of these discussions are too extensive to discuss in any detail here. On the specific topic of systematic distortion within the community of discourse, see Jürgen Habermas, *Legitimation Crisis* (Boston: Beacon Press, 1975) and *Theory and Practice* (Boston: Beacon Press, 1971).

38. Stanley Hauerwas, "The Moral Authority of Scripture: The Politics and Ethics of Remembering," *Interpretation* 34 (1980): 364.

39. See Langdon Gilkey, *Reaping the Whirlwind: A Christian Interpretation of History* (New York: Seabury Press, 1976). See especially his discussion of the intimate relationship between the imaginative character of interpretation and political activity and meaning (pp. 57ff.).

40. The models underline the old saw that the preacher cannot escape the message preached. The interpreter is never external from the interpretation — perhaps alienated from it, but not outside it.

tries.[41] Either the power of the promise that calls us together and
the hope it engenders is sufficient for creating servants of the world,
or the community will ultimately fail.

Under the model of Deliberator the interpreter would not be set
afield to force members of the community to the truth.[42] Deliberation dependent upon the proclamation of the promise that has
brought the community of the faithful into existence draws the community into enacting the text in daily life. Deliberators do not need
canned solutions or any authority other than their shared trust in
the promise that enables the community. Deliberators persuade;
Christian deliberators give good reasons for the hope we share.[43]

Interpreter as Storyteller

These good reasons that deliberation discovers can take the shape
of a story. Some would argue that the character of the biblical text
is far closer to story than it is to history.[44] Others would, along with
Hans Frei, characterize Scripture as having a "history-like" quality,
but they would also say that the real meaning of the text does not
reside in how accurately or inaccurately it reports historical events.[45]
Such an understanding of the text of Scripture might mandate the
model of the interpreter as storyteller.

41. As a student pastor, I served as assistant to a pastor who would translate his
text each Monday morning and spend the rest of the week working the text over with
members of the parish. No hospital visit or administrative meeting went by without
some shared reflection on the text. Those who had been in contact with him during
the week would probably recognize much of Sunday's sermon as a part of their own
interpretation of that text during that week.

42. For a further development of this theme, see Hans Küng's short meditation
The Church: Maintained in Truth (New York: Seabury Press, 1980) and the discussion
of infallibility versus indefectibility in *Lutherans and Catholics in Dialogue VI*, ed. Paul C.
Empie, T. Austin Murphy, and Joseph A. Burgess (Minneapolis: Augsburg Press,
1978).

I find the introduction to *Preaching the Story,* by Edmund A. Steimle, Morris J.
Niedenthal, and Charles L. Rice (Philadelphia: Fortress Press, 1980), most instruc-
tive, especially in its call for a "holistic view of preaching," which includes four
factors: "the preacher, the listener, the churchly context including the institutional
organization, and the message. Any really comprehensive view of preaching must do
justice to all four factors, without focusing unduly on any one of them" (pp. 1-2).

43. For a general introduction to how stories might be a form of persuasion in
our contemporary situation, see Wayne C. Booth, *Modern Dogma and the Rhetoric of
Assent* (Chicago: University of Chicago Press, 1974), especially pp. 180ff. For a marvelous development of this rhetoric of persuasion in a Christian theologian, see Robert W. Jenson, *Story and Promise: A Brief Theology of the Gospel about Jesus* (Philadelphia:
Fortress Press, 1973).

44. See, for example, James Barr, *The Bible in the Modern World* (New York: Harper
& Row, 1973), pp. 147-48; see also Barr's "Story and History in Biblical Theology,"
Journal of Religion 46 (1976): 1-17.

45. See Hans Frei, *The Eclipse of Biblical Narrative* (New Haven: Yale University
Press, 1974).

Stanley Hauerwas, in a most insightful essay, integrates his concern for the political and ethical use of Scripture in the Christian community with the role of narrative and imaginative *discrimen*[46] in the interpretation of the Bible as Scripture.[47] He speaks of the moral authority of Scripture under the heading of the "Morality of Remembering: the Scripture as Narrative."[48] The "narrative of Scripture not only 'renders a character'[49] but renders a community capable of ordering its existence appropriate to such stories."[50] Thus, Scripture need not be ordered by a dogmatic canon within a canon, but one can understand the whole of Scripture as "one long 'loosely structured non-fiction novel' that has sub-plots that at some points appear minor but later turn out to be central."[51] The character of the community that it creates and requires "must be able to make the narratives of Scripture central for its life."[52] It is a community that "knows it has a history and tradition which separates it from the world."[53]

I would not want to reduce this model to this ethical dimension, nor would I want to exclude it. It should, however, be encompassed within a broader theology of narrative. Gabriel Fackre has made just such an attempt to explore the Christian story. He sets out to do a Christian systematic theology based on and reflected in a "narrative interpretation of basic Christian doctrine."[54] He understands as his "ultimate source of the Christian Story . . . the Scriptures of the Old and New Testament." The authority of the Bible rests in "its testimony to the decisive events in the faith narrative."[55] The story is subject to the norm of the Bible; "it must be 1) rooted in the biblical source and accountable to its Storyline norm, 2) continuous with the traditions of the Church, past and present, 3) intelligible to those to whom it is addressed, connected to the realities of their time and place, and illuminative of their lived experience."[56]

46. On the use of this term, see Kelsey, *The Uses of Scripture in Recent Theology*, p. 160. Kelsey in turn has borrowed the concept from Robert C. Johnson, *Authority in Protestant Theology* (Philadelphia: Westminster Press, 1959), p. 15.

47. See Hauerwas, "The Moral Authority of Scripture," p. 364.

48. Hauerwas, "The Moral Authority of Scripture," p. 365.

49. Kelsey interprets Barth in this manner; see *The Uses of Scripture in Recent Theology*, p. 39.

50. Hauerwas, "The Moral Authority of Scripture," p. 366.

51. Hauerwas, "The Moral Authority of Scripture," p. 366.

52. Hauerwas, "The Moral Authority of Scripture," p. 367.

53. Hauerwas, "The Moral Authority of Scripture," p. 367; one need not take a sectarian position to affirm this notion.

54. Fackre, *The Christian Story: A Narrative Interpretation of Basic Christian Doctrine* (Grand Rapids, Eerdmans, 1978).

55. Fackre, *The Christian Story*, p. 22.

56. Fackre, *The Christian Story*, p. 39.

Fackre seeks the "core"[57] of the Christian faith under the imaginative *discrimen* of several "acts in the Christian drama . . . chapters in the Story" — "Creation, Fall, Covenant, Christ, Church, Salvation, Consummation, with their Prologue and Epilogue, God."[58] This development of the Storyteller model still has several steps to go before completely bridging the gap between story and audience, but it points in the right direction.[59] It is sufficiently exciting to see the shape of a new relationship between biblical interpretation and systematic theology in this development of this model.

QUESTIONS AND OBJECTIONS

Several questions and objections can and should be raised to the theory of interpretation that supports these latter models. Every performance or enactment of a musical score or a dramatic or literary text is a new event in the history of the meaning of the text. Texts, as Paul Ricoeur notes, have itineraries.[60] Or, as Hans-Georg Gadamer puts it, "the discovery of the true meaning of a text or a work of art is never finished; it is in fact an infinite process."[61] In the case of great classical texts or scores this is quite clear. But is this apparent relativism not contrary to the finality of God's work in Jesus the Christ? Do these models imply a diminution of Christian claims to truth? Is it entirely true of the texts of Scripture to suggest that they are merely "history-like," or "fictional" narratives? Have we given up on the historical claims of the Christian texts?

We do ourselves a disservice if we appropriate these models based upon a linguistic paradigm of text and interpreter without addressing these important theological and historical truth questions. Though I cannot give any complete argument here, some suggestions follow. It is possible to perform Mozart not only badly but incorrectly. The incomplete character of the interpretive enterprise does not legitimate all interpretation. To say that historical perception and enactment of truth is always partial, always provisional, does not lead to the conclusion that we are simply incapable of

57. Fackre, *The Christian Story*, p. 14. Fackre follows the suggestion of Martin E. Marty in *The Fire We Can Light: The Rise of Religion in a Suddenly Different World* (Garden City, N.Y.: Doubleday, 1973), p. 219, where he suggests that we core and care.

58. Fackre, *The Christian Story*, p. 15.

59. The same might be said of Hans Frei's development of his theoretical work *The Identity of Jesus Christ: The Hermeneutical Bases of Dogmatic Theology* (Philadelphia: Fortress Press, 1975).

60. So he said in a paper entitled "The Bible and Imagination" presented at the William Rainey Harper Conference on Biblical Studies held 3-5 October 1979 at the Divinity School of the University of Chicago.

61. Gadamer, *Truth and Method* (New York: Seabury Press, 1975), p. 265.

acting and speaking truly. Certain ways of enacting, performing, enlivening the Christian texts are false. Though the cases are seldom clear-cut and often require centuries of mutual conversation, truth claims regarding interpretation of the Christian Scriptures remain appropriate.[62]

Such conversation cannot be judged by some supposed external principle that will provide a final test.[63] Only in a community which I would like to characterize as "a sacrament of dialogue"[64] can this conversation take place. In such a sacramental community the truth of the Christian texts becomes present in the community's mutual trust and hope. This is a trust and hope called into existence by the word of promise and manifested in the sacramental presence of Christ in his church.[65]

This model of the church eschews the constraint of conversation concerning the truth of the Christian texts as to what has previously been established as what they "originally meant." Without denying the place of the text, form, and redaction critics, it is still necessary to seek appropriation in the present situation. On the other hand,

62. Several important distinctions can and should be made regarding the character of the truth claims of the Bible. First, the character of the biblical text is in most cases practical conversation in which arguments or claims to truth are basically superfluous. However, in those places within the Bible where certain arguments or thematic discourse predominates, truth claims do appear. Second, the character of much preaching may not require such explicit arguments or truth claims, but eventually the professional interpreter of the Bible as Scripture will need to make argument for its explicit truth claims. For a further discussion of the relationship between truth claims and practical and thematic discourse, see Jürgen Habermas, "Wahrheitstheorien," in *Wirklichkeit und Reflexion,* Festschrift für Walter Schulz (Pfullingen: Neske, 1973), pp. 211-65.

63. This is, of course, at odds with the correspondence theory of truth quite often presumed in discussions of the truth claims of theology. This does not reject the possibility of critical appraisal of interpretations, as if to say "Any interpretation will do as long as you feel strongly enough about it." It is dependent on whether or not a claim can be justified—that is, maintained (cf. Habermas, "Wahrheitstheorien," pp. 211-12). What I am trying to underscore in this essay is that such arguments of justification cannot ignore the question of worth or value in maintaining truth claims. The participation of the interpreter with the text can have a moment of critical explanation but must return to a moment of second naivete (see Ricoeur, *Interpretation Theory,* pp. 71-88; see also *The Philosophy of Paul Ricoeur: An Anthology of His Work,* ed. Charles E. Regan and David Stewart [Boston: Beacon Press, 1978], pp. 149-66).

64. This develops the discussion by Edward Schillebeeckx in *Christ the Sacrament* (New York: Sheed & Ward, 1963). God initiates the dialogue and continues to authorize it by means of the promise proleptically available in the life, death, and resurrection of Jesus Christ and continually present by the promise of the Spirit.

65. In his *Models of the Church,* Avery Dulles develops five models for the church: Institution, Mystical Communion, Sacrament, Herald, and Servant. I envision an ecclesiology congruent with my models for understanding the biblical interpreter as a community which encompasses the church as institution, mystical communion, and servant with the church as sacrament and herald.

we cannot forsake understanding what the author meant. Here, however, I prefer Gadamer's description of this search for authorial intention as an attempt "to recapture the perspective within which he . . . formed his views" and endorse Collingwood's dictum that "we can understand a text only when we have understood the question to which it is an answer."

Nothing within this understanding of truth in relationship to the sacrament of dialogue, which takes place in the church, is incompatible with the finality of the work of Christ. Indeed, it recognizes and takes account of the radical eschatological character of the message and work of Christ, the principally promissory character of it.

I am not prepared to suggest that the linguistic paradigm can be sufficient for the interpretation of Scripture or that my concern for relating theory and practice so intimately can leave behind the historical questions that might be raised. To take the interpretation of Mark as an example, it is one thing to question Vincent Taylor's hierarchy of values when he interprets Mark; it is another to claim that he is quite mistaken in detecting and examining historical referential claims in the text. Mark does not simply give symbolic expression to certain pervasive features of the human drama; his Gospel also expresses his confidence in the person Jesus and the promise which he embodied. Certain historical claims are made that remain subject to historical examination and are characteristic of the Christian teaching.

I hesitate to make some great divide between literary criticism and historical interpretation. All too often such differences are exaggerated. Some perceive the literary critics' judgments to be "merely subjective" in character, lacking any significance as knowledge.[66] On the other hand, many nonhistorians suggest that historical methodology is hopelessly positivistic, a claim I cannot support.[67] There is, nonetheless, a difference between literary criticism and historical criticism.

Here I must appeal both to the complexity and perhaps essential mystery of the reality to which the Christian texts point and the

66. Gadamer criticizes Kant, insisting that "art is knowledge and the experience of the work of art is a sharing in this knowledge" (*Truth and Method*, p. 8).

67. Significant responses have been made to the positivist critical philosophers of history such as Popper and Hempel. Positions which are in some way supportive of my general proposal are presented by the critical philosophers of history who understand history primarily in terms of the genre of narrative (e.g., Gallie, Danto, and Morton White). Earlier forms of this viewpoint can be found in Dray's continuous series model of explanation, in W. H. Walsh's account of history as "significant narrative," and in certain aspects of the theories of Croce and Collingwood. A moderating position between the realists and the reconstructionists that hold considerable persuasive power is Maurice Mandelbaum's *Anatomy of History* (Baltimore: The Johns Hopkins University Press, 1977).

importance of the ongoing conversation of the community, the sacrament of dialogue which is grounded in the gospel and the promise of the Spirit.

Advantages

In the meantime, certain advantages accrue from these linguistic models that, by way of summary, commend them to the professional interpreter of the Bible as Scripture within the Christian community.

First, though they downplay the historical gap, they are strong in their ability to address the relationship between the Christian message and Christian living today. Their dependence upon a close tie between theory and practice avoids the bracketing of preaching, pastoral care and counseling, and political issues away from direct implication in the interpretive process. They counteract the opinion of one of my exegetical teachers who said at the conclusion of a strenuous textual, source, form, and redactional analysis of a text, "the rest is homiletics," as if to say the rest is either easy or, worse, less significant.

Second, these models restore the devotional and liturgical uses of Scripture to a fuller place in the interpretive process both in the understanding of the text and the self-understanding of the interpreter. In this way, they take more seriously the place of preunderstanding and elevate its often secondary and solely negative role to a positive source for the interpretation of the text.

Third, these models imply a reevaluation, but not a rejection, of classical nineteenth-century hermeneutics of suspicion (e.g., historical consciousness).[68] These models point beyond what some have described as "critical description and capricious faith" of much biblical interpretation.[69] Rather than disparaging the accomplishments of historical critics, my intention has been to bring as much disci-

---

68. In principle I would argue that all of the classical hermeneutics of suspicion should be encompassed within this argument if it were to be developed. The work of Freud, Marx, Nietzsche, and Feuerbach need not be neglected or ignored but can be incorporated into and encompassed by the experience of good will and trust engendered by the promise of Christ, to which the Christian texts are a witness and which the community experiences.

69. See Martin J. Buss, "Understanding Communication," *Encounter with the Text: Form and History in the Hebrew Bible*, ed. Martin J. Buss, Semeia Supplement 8 (Philadelphia: Fortress Press, 1979), p. 33. Buss argues that much "biblical scholarship . . . oscillates between critical description and capricious faith, calling the one 'historical' and the other 'theological.' " I can only agree with this analysis of much of the churchly interpretation done with the best of intentions to reproduce the author's intention consistent with the historical context. Unfortunately, much of the interpretation of Scripture that follows the literary paradigm — especially some of the interpretation done under the category of "story" — engages in both capricious faith and irresponsible description. Slapping a story onto a pericope is not at all what my models imply or mandate.

pline to the side of appropriation and enactment of the texts as has
been the case in the historical analysis of the texts. The work of the
historian need not be neglected but can be incorporated critically
and encompassed by a more complete understanding of the interpretive enterprise.

Fourth, the focus on performance and enactment leads the Christian community to action. The model of the church as servant to
the world can find a much more conducive environment within these
models of the interpreter's self-understanding of the interpretive task
than in the Mind Reader model. Moreover, they can perhaps be a
step on the road to the oft spoken but seldom manifested theology
of the laity both within and without the doors of the local
congregation.

PART IV

CONTEMPORARY APPROACHES

In addition to the hermeneutical perspectives already encountered, there are numerous other approaches that may be characterized by their particular emphases. This section presents a sampling of these specialized approaches.

What might be termed a "theological approach" to hermeneutics is exemplified by the work of the Swiss theologian Karl Barth (1886-1968). Barth always sought to do "theological exegesis," and the hermeneutical approach evident in his major work the *Church Dogmatics* is examined here by Thomas Provence.

Peter W. Macky surveys literary approaches to New Testament interpretation that stress imaginative elements rather than only historical or rational dimensions.

One of the most sophisticated contemporary hermeneutical approaches is structuralism, a linguistic movement that turns attention away from questions relating to a document (e.g., its historical composition) to the linguistic structures of texts — how they are "read" and what signification they have. Richard Jacobson's essay, "Structuralism and the Bible" describes the main features of this method.

In René Padilla's essay "The Interpreted Word: Reflections on Contextual Hermeneutics," traditional hermeneutics and the historical-critical method are contrasted with a contextual approach that takes the "hermeneutical circle" seriously and seeks the contextualization of the Christian gospel as a means for presenting Scripture to the world's varied cultures and peoples.

Cultural anthropologist Charles H. Kraft presents a discussion of theological hermeneutics that is informed by the insights of cultural anthropology. In his "Supracultural Meanings via Cultural Forms," Kraft advocates a dynamic understanding of the hermeneutical process that may be termed "ethnolinguistic" or "ethnohermeneutics."

An increasingly prominent theological movement is liberation theology. This theological position approaches Scripture with the concerns of the poor for liberation and justice foremost in mind. It stresses the truth that comes through "praxis" and recognizes that biblical interpretation, particularly in wealthy Western nations, falls prey to ideological captivities. This is expounded in José Miguez Bonino's essay "Hermeneutics, Truth, and Praxis."

The concerns of feminist theologians are represented here by Elisabeth Schüssler Fiorenza, whose contribution is entitled "Toward a Feminist Biblical Hermeneutics: Biblical Interpretation and Liberation Theology." She suggests liberation theology extend its ideological suspicion to Scripture itself. She advocates a recognition of the sexism of Scripture and Christian theology while seeking a feminist interpretive paradigm of "emancipatory praxis."

Each of these approaches is making significant contributions to hermeneutical understandings on the contemporary scene. None will be able to dominate. Each will offer a perspective to which some will be drawn. But through them all is the serious attempt to grapple with the problematic issues that arise when one seeks to interpret Scripture.

THE SOVEREIGN SUBJECT MATTER: HERMENEUTICS IN THE *CHURCH DOGMATICS*

THOMAS E. PROVENCE

One year after the publication of *Fides Quaerens Intellectum*, Karl Barth produced the first half-volume of what was to become his life work, the massive *Church Dogmatics*. The first volume of the *Church Dogmatics* (which included two half-volumes) amounted to an extensive revision and expansion of his now abandoned *Christliche Dogmatik* and reflected the significant way in which the study of Anselm had changed his thinking about the interpretation of Scripture. To be sure, Barth continued to insist that the goal of interpretation was to meet and understand the subject matter of the text, but now he came to believe that it was possible to meet this subject matter only if the subject made itself known to the interpreter.

The first volume of the *Church Dogmatics* deals with the doctrine of the Word of God. In it Barth considers the doctrine of Scripture and, in the second half-volume, offers his understanding of the nature of hermeneutics. It will become apparent that Barth's doctrine of Scripture can be understood only in the light of his hermeneutical position. His understanding of Scripture as the witness to revelation, necessary for understanding this revelation, yet not itself the revelation, flows directly from his conception of language and its interpretation. In turn, his understanding of language in general and religious language in particular proceeds from his study of Anselm's methodology. To fail to understand these connections is to fail to understand one of the most important elements of Barth's thought.

Barth insists, in the *Church Dogmatics*, that biblical hermeneutics is really no different from general hermeneutics. "There is no such thing as a special biblical hermeneutics."[1] All hermeneutical meth-

---

1. Barth, *Church Dogmatics*, 5 vols., ed. Geoffrey W. Bromiley and Thomas F. Torrance, trans. Geoffrey W. Bromiley et al. (Edinburgh: T. & T. Clark, 1955-57), 1/2: 456. Subsequent references to this text will be made parenthetically in the text, using the abbreviation *CD*.

Reprinted from "The Hermeneutics of Karl Barth" (Ph.D. diss., Fuller Theological Seminary, 1980), pp. 136-76.

odology ought to operate on common ground with common presuppositions. According to Barth, "biblical, theological hermeneutics
is not claiming for itself a mysterious special privilege" (*CD*, 1/2:
727). This is not to say, however, that general hermeneutics and
biblical hermeneutics actually do function in the same manner, only
that they would do so if each were to recognize how any text is to
be interpreted.

There is, says Barth, only one general task of hermeneutics. As
an interpreter of the Bible, "I must try to hear the words of the
prophets and apostles in exactly the same freedom in which I attempt to hear the words of others who speak to me or have written
for me as in the main intelligible words" (*CD*, 1/2: 723). In the
interpretation of Scripture, as in the interpretation of any other text,
it is necessary to employ the tools of "literary-historical investigation." Indeed, says Barth, "at the start of this attempt [of biblical
interpretation] we still find ourselves wholly upon the plane of general hermeneutics" (*CD*, 1/2: 723).

There is, of course, genuine disagreement between the practitioners of general hermeneutics and those who interpret the Bible.
Barth claims, however, that such disagreement does not come about
from the use, in biblical hermeneutics, of special and mysterious
means of interpretation. Instead, the conflict arises from the failure
of general hermeneutics to recognize and appreciate the significant
insight into the general methodology of interpretation which is provided by the practice of biblical hermeneutics. "It is from the word
of man in the Bible that we must learn what has to be learned
concerning the word of man in general. This is not generally recognized. It is more usual blindly to apply to the Bible false ideas
taken from some other source concerning the significance and function of the human word" (*CD*, 1/2: 466). The principles of exposition which Barth discusses are, he believes, valid for all texts. He
asserts, "because they are valid for biblical exposition they are valid
for the exposition of every human word, and can therefore lay claim
to universal recognition" (*CD*, 1/2: 466).

THE NATURE OF LANGUAGE

In Barth's view, a study of biblical hermeneutics can provide important insights into the nature of all human utterances. Based upon
these insights, Barth developed a theory of language and meaning
which, while derived from observations of biblical language, is descriptive of language in general.

According to Barth, the words of an author evoke a picture, or
image, of that which is said or written. "The image which [the

authors] conjure up reflects the image of an object" (*CD*, 1/2: 723).[2] In other words, an author has a particular picture of his world and of the realities that surround him. He then puts this picture into words which reflect the object which he perceives in his world. The reader or hearer of these words then obtains a "picture of [the author's] expression." The task of interpretation is the task of reproducing this picture.

Words, then, direct the thinking of the hearer to the object evoked by the word. This thought is reminiscent of Barth's thinking in his book on Anselm: "We can think of an object by thinking of the word that describes it, that is by obeying the directions which our thinking receives from the sign language of this word and so considering what claims to be the thought of the object concerned."[3]

Words are directional signals to an object which is beyond them; they have no ontological force of their own. Neither do words direct us to an author's inner thoughts and feelings. Instead, they point to an object beyond both author and interpreter. Indeed, says Barth, "the understanding of [a human word] cannot consist merely in discovering on what presuppositions, in what situation, in what linguistic sense and with what intention, in what actual context, and in this sense with what meaning the other has said this or that" (*CD*, 1/2: 464). The point of interpretation is not found in understanding the words of the text as such nor in entering into the thoughts of the author. Instead, understanding properly occurs when the object evoked by the words of the author is reproduced in the mind of the interpreter.

Indeed, for Barth true understanding does not take place until the image of the subject matter of the text is in some real sense reproduced in the mind of the reader. "We can speak meaningfully of hearing a human word only when it is clear to us in its function of referring to that which is described or intended by the word, but when this its function becomes an event before us, when therefore it happens that by means of the human word we ourselves catch sight to some degree of that which is described or intended" (*CD*, 1/2: 464-65).[4] If an interpreter does not "catch sight" of what is

2. Translation mine. The German original reads "Es spiegelt das Bild ihrer Worte das Bild eines Gegenstandes" (*Die Kirchliche Dogmatik*, 5 vols. [Zürich: Evangelischer Verlag, 1939-60], 1/2: 811; subsequent references to this work will be cited using the abbreviation *KD*).

3. Barth, *Anselm: Fides Quaerens Intellectum*, trans. Ian W. Robertson (New York: Meridian Books, 1960), p. 163.

4. Translation mine. The German original reads "Gerade vom Hören eines menschlichen Wortes kann doch sinvollerweise nur da die Rede sein, wo es uns nicht nur in seiner Funktion des Hinweisens auf ein durch das Wort Bezeichnetes oder Gemeintes deutlich wird, sondern wo diese seine Funktion uns gegenüber Ereignis wird, wo es also geschieht, dass wir durch das Mittel des menschlichen Wortes in irgendeinen Mass selber ansichtig werden" (*KD*, 1/2: 514).

described or intended, then the language of the text has been unable
to accomplish its purpose of evoking a subject matter. The words
must so project an image of the object that this image "becomes an
event before us" *(uns gegenüber Ereignis wird)*. Otherwise, the interpreter works in vain.

Thus, to use a simple example, the word *unicorn* has meaning for
us only when we are able to conceive in our mind's eye an animal
which is like a horse but which also has a single horn growing out
of its head. On the other hand, if we say the syllables of the word
unicorn to a child who is not yet familiar with mythological beasts,
there will be no understanding because the child will not know what
image the word is to evoke in his mind. Understanding cannot take
place until he realizes the reality to which *unicorn* points.

Barth's insight led him to formulate what he believed was a principle which would govern all hermeneutics, both biblical and general: "the *universal* hermeneutical rule applies that a text can be read,
understood, and expounded *only with reference* to and in the light of
its object" (*CD*, 1/2: 493; italics mine).[5] The determination of the
meaning of any particular text is dependent upon a previous understanding of the subject matter. A text has meaning and is understood
insofar as the interpreter knows the referent of that text. No text can
be understood without such knowledge, for without it the text can
only be forms without content.

This means, according to Barth, that the object, or subject matter, of a text controls the meaning of that text and, ultimately, our
understanding of it. Thus far, Barth claims, biblical and general
hermeneutics are in accord. But Barth goes on to say that this fact
necessarily implies that "interpretation is not a conversation *inter
pares*, but *inter impares*" (*CD*, 1/2: 720). The subject matter of any
text is, in some sense, sovereign. If we wish to hear what it has to
say to us, we must submit ourselves to it.

THE DISPUTE WITH GENERAL HERMENEUTICS

It is at this point, Barth states, that biblical hermeneutics parts ways
with general hermeneutics. In principle this ought not to be the
case, says Barth, since both are governed by the same hermeneutical
rule, a rule that implies that the interpreter must subordinate himself to the subject matter of the text. In fact, however, the two kinds
of hermeneutics stand at odds. Barth outlines the major point of
disagreement:

5. Translation mine. The German original reads "Gilt die allegemeine hermeneutische Regel, dass ein Text nur im Wissen um seinen Gegenstand und von diesem
her recht gelesen, verstanden und ausgelegt werden kann" (*KD*, 1/2: 546).

It is only within definite limits that general hermeneutics is accustomed to take seriously the idea that what is said in a text, that is, the object which we have to reproduce might bring into play other possibilities than those previously known to the interpreter. . . . It thinks it has a basic knowledge of what is generally possible, of what can have happened, and from this point of view it assesses the statement of the text, and the picture of the object reflected in it as the picture of a real, or unreal, or doubtful happening. It is surely plain that at this point an alien factor is exercising a disturbing influence upon observation. (*CD*, 1/2: 725)

Practitioners of general hermeneutics come to every text with an a priori judgment that certain things are possible and others impossible. Therefore, when they are confronted with a subject matter which they have decided is unreal, the subject matter is unable to have its proper role in bringing about understanding.

Even though the one universal rule of hermeneutics is that the subject matter of the text must be allowed to have its decisive role in bringing about understanding, many interpreters refuse to allow the subject that freedom. Yet, says Barth, "strict observation obviously requires that the force of a picture meeting us in a text shall exercise its due effect in accordance with its intrinsic character" (*CD*, 1/2: 725). Thus, general hermeneutics is often inconsistent with its most basic principle.

To be sure, Barth says, there are those who will advance the argument that biblical hermeneutics simply imposes its own special methodology upon all sorts of interpretation. Barth admits that the principle of the sovereignty of the object of a text is an insight which derives from biblical hermeneutics. But the source of the principle cannot invalidate its truth. "That it derives this hermeneutic principle from the Bible itself, i.e., that the Bible itself, because of the unusual preponderance of what is said in it over the word as such, enforces this principle upon it, does not alter the fact that this principle is necessarily the principle of all hermeneutics" (*CD*,1/2: 468). If general hermeneutics would learn the lesson which is to be gained from the insights of biblical hermeneutics, there would be no conflict between the two, for then interpreters would allow the subject matter of every text to have its decisive role in determining the meaning of the text.

THE PECULIAR CHARACTER OF THE BIBLICAL OBJECT

Insight into the fact that every text must be interpreted in the light of its subject matter comes about "because of the unusual preponderance of what is said in [the Bible] over the word as such" (*CD*,

1/2: 468).[6] That is, the object of the biblical text so overwhelms the words of the text that it becomes obvious that a text must be interpreted by means of its object.

What, then, is the object of the Bible which has this "unusual preponderance" over the words of the text of Scripture? "The object of the biblical texts is quite simply the name Jesus Christ, and these texts can be understood only when understood as determined by this object" (CD, 1/2: 727). Jesus, the living Word of God, is the subject matter of the Bible, and if one is to understand the Bible, he must understand it because he has perceived the image of the Word of God about whom it speaks.

Because Jesus Christ, as the subject matter of the Bible, dominates the words of the biblical text much more obviously than does any other textual subject matter, the principle of the universal rule of hermeneutics becomes especially apparent in biblical interpretation. As the eternal God, the subject matter of the Bible claims, in a particularly forceful manner, "the freedom [of any object of any text] to assert and affirm itself over against these presuppositions of ours, and in certain cases to compel us to adopt new presuppositions, as in fact it can do" (CD, 1/2: 726).

The central difference between biblical interpretation and the interpretation of any other text lies in the "majesty" of the subject matter of the Bible. Indeed, Barth argues, the reality of the objects of all other texts depend, in an ultimate sense, upon the reality of the majesty of the biblical object. This is "a majesty without which [every other human word] would be meaningless if [the human word in the Bible] were only an exception and not the law and the promise and the sign of redemption which has been set up in the sphere of all other human words, and of all that is said by them" (CD, 1/2: 472). The "majesty" of the biblical subject matter has an ultimate significance because the object of the biblical text confers meaning not only upon the Bible, but upon every text since he is the Creator of the object of every object of every text.

Barth's thought here is reminiscent of that of his work on Anselm where he points out that the issue of the existence of God is not merely the issue of the existence of an object, but of "the *existere* of Truth itself which is the condition, the basis and indeed the fashioner of all other existence, the simple origin of all objectivity, of all true

6. Barth uses several words, more or less interchangeably, in reference to the subject matter of a text, including *das Gesagte* ("that which is said"), *das Bezeichnete* ("that which is described"), *das Gegenstand* ("the object," or, more properly, "that which stands over against"), and *die Sache* ("the subject matter"). Sometimes such words as *theme* or *matter* or *substance* are used to translate the latter two German words, which are the ones he uses most often.

outward being, and therefore also of all true inner being."[7] God is creative Truth; therefore all truth has its validity only because it receives it from the Creator. For this reason, the subject matter of the biblical text has an ultimate significance in the interpretation of every text, because every other subject matter is dependent upon God for its truth.

THE FREEDOM OF THE SUBJECT MATTER

Because the object of the Bible is no less than Jesus Christ, the sovereign Lord, it is conceivable that an interpreter might grasp the meaning of the words of the Bible but not really understand it if he is not acquainted with the biblical subject matter. This corresponds with the idea Barth had learned from Anselm. In the *Proslogion* Anselm had written, "a thing is conceived in one way when it is the word describing it that is conceived, in another way when the thing itself is known."[8] True understanding, Barth claimed, occurs only in the second case since only then is the subject matter, which determines the meaning of the word, understood.

In ordinary human texts Anselm's insight can pose no difficulty, for we are sufficiently acquainted with the objects of our world that when a text speaks of such objects, we understand both word and object. When the text refers to a humanly inconceivable object such as the Word of God, however, the object must make itself known if the text is to be understood. In an ultimate sense, then, the understanding of the biblical material rests not upon the hermeneutical skills of the interpreter but upon the sovereign freedom of the object, God's Word. For this reason, says Barth, "revelation speaks, even in the Bible, if, then and there where God wishes it to do so."[9]

If the biblical exegete recognizes that the subject matter of the Bible determines understanding and if he further understands that the biblical subject matter is free to make himself known to whomever he wills, the exegete will understand two of the basic principles for understanding the Bible. Barth states,

> if the exposition of a human word consists of the relating of this word to what it intends or denotes [*zu der von ihm gemeinten oder bezeichneten Sache*], and if we know the sovereign freedom, the independent glory of this subject-matter [*die Selbstherrlichkeit dieser Sache*] in relation both

7. Barth, *Anselm*, p. 98.

8. Anselm, quoted by Barth in *Anselm*, p. 163. It is worth noting that Barth applies Anselm's insights to a peculiarly post-Kantian problem—how the existence of God can be something more than a projection of human imagination. No doubt Anselm was not directly concerned with this problem in his writings.

9. Barth, *Theologische Fragen und Antworten* (Zürich: Evangelischer Verlag, 1957), p. 181.

to the word which is before us and to ourselves, we will be whole-
somely restrained at the very least in our usual self-assured mastery
of the relationship, as though we already knew its content and our
exposition could give more than hints in its direction. (*CD*, 1/2:
470-71)

These principles have a negative force to them. They warn the interpreter away from a self-assurance that assumes that true understanding is possible through the application of exegetical methods
and hermeneutical principles.

THE LIMITATION OF THE INTERPRETER

Clearly, Barth did not believe that the means of understanding the
Bible were directly available to the interpreter. The character of the
biblical subject matter, the sinfulness of the interpreter, and the limitations of the methodology all preclude such a possibility. Thus, an
expositor of the Bible may labor diligently over the text for days,
even years, without really understanding it. According to Barth,
"if it is really the case that a reader of the biblical Scriptures is quite
helpless in face of the problem of what these Scriptures say and
intend and denote in respect of divine revelation, that he sees only
an empty spot at the place to which the biblical writers point, then
in a singular way this does set in relief the extraordinary nature of
the content of what these writers say on the one hand, and on the
other the state and status of the reader" (*CD*, 1/2: 469).

On the one hand, the reader of the Bible may not understand its
subject matter because of its "extraordinary nature." Barth is here
thinking of the freedom of God to reveal himself to whom he wills.
Because Jesus Christ is one who stands over against us (a *Gegenstand*)
rather than an inanimate and static object, he is free to make himself
known to one but not to another. Jesus Christ can never be mastered
through exegetical skills but himself determines who shall know him.

Barth may also be thinking of the incomprehensibility of God, a
theme with which he had had to wrestle in his work on Anselm. We
know the objects of most texts through prior experience with them.
When we read about a tree, for example, we understand the text
because we understand the object. When the text has to do with
God, however, we cannot depend upon our previous perception of
him since he is incomprehensible. For Gaunilo, one of Anselm's
objectors, "the word itself could not provide him with a knowledge
of God unless some extension of what the word is meant to denote
were also given to him from another source."[10] But this is an impossibility with God. Knowledge of God must, therefore, come from

10. Barth, *Anselm*, p. 79.

the biblical text itself through "words which even in themselves do not remain 'mere' words but are a divine revelation."[11] To understand the object of the Bible, then, requires a decisive act on the part of the incomprehensible God.

On the other hand, a reader of the Bible may not know the subject matter of the biblical text because of his own "state and status." Man is morally and physically incapable of such knowledge. As sinful creatures, humans have no capacity in themselves to know the Word. It is, says Barth, a measure of God's grace that men can come to know the Word. "God's Word is no longer grace and grace itself is no longer grace, if we ascribe to man a predisposition towards this Word, a possibility of knowledge regarding it that is intrinsically and independently native to him" (CD, 1/1: 194). The effect of sin is so pervasive that man is not only ignorant of God, he has no resource, or faculty, by which to know him.

Indeed, according to Barth, the chasm between God and man is so great that even man's knowledge of God is not a result of a divinely endowed capacity for such knowledge. "The possibility of knowledge of God's Word lies in God's Word and nowhere else" (CD, 1/1: 222). Man can never have a faculty for knowledge apart from the knowledge imposed by the Word itself. For it to be otherwise would be to make man, even if it be regenerate man, the criterion for truth about God's Word. But if this were the case, there could be no certainty of knowledge of the Word since knowledge would be wrapped in a subjective knower instead of the objective reality (CD, 1/1: 210-19). Instead, "the knowability of the Word of God stands or falls . . . with the act of its real knowledge, which is not under our control. . . . In faith man has and knows and affirms only this possibility of knowledge of God's Word, the possibility which lies in the Word of God itself, has come to him in the Word, and is present to him in the Word" (CD, 1/1: 224). Thus, man is utterly dependent upon the sovereignty of the Word for his knowledge of it.

Once again echoes of Barth's work on Anselm resound. In Fides Quaerens Intellectum Barth wished to establish the absolute objectivity of God. God as eternal object "emerges as something completely independent of whether men in actual fact conceive it or can conceive it."[12] God's existence, Barth says, is in no way dependent upon man's self-certainty. Instead, man's knowledge is dependent upon the objective existence of God apart from man's knowing.

In the Church Dogmatics Barth continued to emphasize the priority of the object known over the knowing subject. Knowledge "means

11. Barth, Anselm, p. 82.
12. Barth, Anselm, p. 74.

that the reality of the object concerned, its existence and nature, being true in themselves, now become in some way, and with some degree of clarity and distinctiveness, true for men too" (*CD*, 1/1: 188). But the knowledge of the Word of God is conditioned upon the gracious activity of the Word itself. Men are foolish, therefore, when they insist that they could know God. For God's reality precedes the knowledge of any knower. It is arrogance to believe that knowing can validate existence. Also, man's utter incapacity to know the Word of God apart from the sovereign activity of that Word demonstrates that knowledge is dependent upon the object to be known rather than the knower. "In short the binding nature of what we affirm and deny depends wholly and utterly on our own relevance to the subject matter [*Sache*] as speakers and hearers. But our own relevance to the subject matter depends wholly and utterly, not on us, but on the subject matter itself" (*CD*, 1/1: 198).

Since understanding the biblical text requires an acquaintance with the object about which it speaks, the Word of God, Jesus Christ, and since knowledge of the Word depends solely on the initiative of the Word toward man, it follows that there can be no understanding of the Bible without the prior gracious activity of its subject matter. Understanding is not dependent upon understanding the various words of the text; for it is one thing to understand the word which signifies the object and another to understand the object itself. Again, understanding is not dependent upon our efforts to know the object of the Bible nor our capacity to understand him; for knowledge of the Word of God comes about wholly through his sovereign and gracious activity.

THE LIMITATIONS OF EXEGESIS

Since the words of Scripture are pointers to the picture of the object about which the Bible is written, an interpreter wrongly concerns himself with the words of the Bible as though they were the object which gives meaning. "It would not strictly be loyalty to the Bible, and certainly not thankfulness for the Word of God given and continually given again in it, if we did not let our ears be opened by it, *not to what it says, but to what He, God Himself, has to say to us* as His Word in it and through it" (*CD*, 1/2: 527; italics mine). A hermeneutic which focuses upon the literary-historical character of the Bible without recognizing that this character is a means to the perception of the object of the text is wrong-headed and likely to go astray.

Indeed, Barth claims, such misdirected exegesis can distort the message of the Bible and stifle the subject matter of the Bible. This danger caused Barth to assert that "exegesis . . . entails the constant danger that the Bible will be taken prisoner by the Church, that its own life will be absorbed into the life of the Church, that its free power will be transformed into the authority of the Church, in short that it will lose its character as a norm magisterially confronting the Church" (*CD*, 1/1: 106). If the interpretation of the Bible is a matter of subjecting the text to human methodologies, then there is the consequent possibility that the methodologies will become masters of the text, and therefore authorities in the church.

Barth believed that the liberal hermeneutics of his own day had fallen prey to "the sickness of an insolent and arbitrary reading in" (*CD*, 1/2: 470) in biblical interpretation. It was the tendency of the liberals, following Friedrich Schleiermacher, when they dealt with the Bible, "instead of proceeding from the substance [*Sache*] to the word, to go first to the word, i.e., to the humanity of the speakers as such" (*CD*, 1/2: 470). By proceeding in this manner, these interpreters revealed that they knew neither the subject matter nor the mystery of its sovereign freedom.

By dealing with the words of the text rather than its object, however, the liberal exegetes could deal only with the limitations, or humanity of the biblical authors and their texts. Liberalism could confidently deal with the Bible by means of the historical method, but the result was the discovery of a thoroughly human Jesus who had nothing to do with the free and sovereign subject matter of Scripture.

The "theological historicism" of liberalism had concluded that the primary goal of biblical interpretation was "to penetrate past the biblical texts to the facts which lie behind the texts in order to find revelation in these facts" (*CD*, 1/2: 492). But such a view entirely missed the purpose of interpretation. The text was read "differently from what it is intended to be and can be read" (*CD*, 1/2: 493) because it was not read in the light of its object.

It is no wonder, then, that Barth was so pessimistic about the possibility that exegetical methods could bring about true understanding of the biblical material. Such methods can all too easily lull the interpreter into the subjectivist trap of believing that his method captures the Word of God. But this sort of thinking takes no account of the fact that the Word is himself Master of all methods and will not be bound by any. "One cannot lay down conditions which, if observed, guarantee hearing of the Word. There is no method by which revelation can be made revelation that is actually received, no method of scriptural exegesis which is truly pneumatic, i.e., which articulates the witness to revelation in the Bible and to that degree really introduces the Pneuma" (*CD*, 1/1: 183). Therefore, says Barth, "the only proper thing to do here is to renounce altogether the search for a method of hearing God's Word" (*CD*, 1/1: 184).

THE NECESSITY OF THE TEXT

It should now be apparent that Barth wished to make the sharpest possible distinction between the words of Scripture and their subject matter, which is Jesus Christ. An interpreter might grasp the meaning of each word in the biblical text and yet, because he goes first to the word rather than the substance, or subject matter, still not actually understand it. Exegetical methods are ultimately quite limited. Nevertheless, there is no knowledge of the biblical subject matter apart from the words of the Bible. Even though one can only understand the text by means of an acquaintance with the subject matter, the knowledge of the subject matter itself comes about, when the sovereign Word wills, through the text itself.

Barth's argument here appears to be circular. An interpreter understands the Bible only when he is acquainted with the subject matter of the Bible, Jesus Christ. Yet, he cannot discover this subject matter through human methods of exegesis since it is sovereign and free from the words of the text as such. Nevertheless, it is only through the text that he may gain knowledge of the subject matter. The interpreter must understand the text by means of the text.

The subject matter of the Bible, Barth insists, is to be found in the text of the Bible itself. "The relationship between theme [*Gegenstand*] and text must be accepted as essential and indissoluble" (*CD*, 1/2: 493). To deny this is to seek the object of the text somewhere beyond or outside of the text, an attempt characteristic of the sort of historicism which endeavors to discover facts which lie behind the biblical text. But such a procedure violates the nature of texts, for texts carry their content within their form, their objects within their words. Indeed, the church "can distinguish between seeing Jesus Christ, hearing His prophets and apostles and reading their Scriptures, and yet it cannot separate these things" (*CD*, 1/2: 583).

This is why Barth insisted that the Scriptures are essential for the church, that in fact they are in a limited, but important, sense the Word of God.

> "It holdeth God's Word," is what Luther once said about the Bible. . . .
> It only "holds," encloses, limits and surrounds it: that is the indirectness of the identity of revelation and the Bible. But it and it alone does really "hold" it: it comprehends and encloses it in itself, so that we cannot have the one without the other; that is why we have to speak about an indirect identity. (*CD*, 1/2: 492)

It is the Bible, and the Bible alone, which points to the one object of Scripture, Jesus Christ. Therefore, while the object of the text is not the text itself, and in fact must be distinguished from it, nevertheless one can never know the object of the Bible, and so understand it, without reading the biblical stories.

But how does the interpreter come to know the object of the Bible if this object is both free from the text and in an "essential and indissoluble" relationship with it? Barth deals with the answer to this question in a short paragraph in his book on the method of Saint Anselm.

The problem that faced Anselm in his debate with Gaunilo, the monk who questioned his proof, was that for Gaunilo the word *God* (in Latin *Deus*) "could not provide him with a knowledge of God unless some extension of what the word is meant to denote were also given to him from another source."[13] But since God is incomprehensible, the word which refers to him is unlike any other word. There is not, nor can there be, any source for knowledge of God apart from the words which refer to him.

Here, however, Anselm and Gaunilo differed. For Anselm, the words themselves could become the means of revelation so that God could make himself known through the very words of the Bible. Therefore, the Word of God is free in relationship to the words of the text; he does not have to reveal himself through them and does so in freedom. Yet, when the Word does reveal himself, he chooses to do so in an "essential and indissoluble" relationship with the text, by revealing himself through the words themselves. For Gaunilo, on the other hand, such a conception was an impossibility. "That there could ever be words which even in themselves do not remain 'mere' words but are a divine revelation in the guise of something 'conceived' by a human brain in accordance with human logic and expressed in human Latin — that, in complete contrast to Anselm, was for him a totally foreign concept.[14] For Barth, as for Anselm, the divine Word was both free in relationship to the text and in an "indissoluble" relationship with it whenever the Word desires to reveal himself through it.

THE NEED FOR METHODOLOGY

The "indissoluble" yet "free" relationship between the subject matter of the Bible and its text enables Barth to make two further assertions about biblical interpretation which appear, at first, to be contradictory. On the one hand, our human conceptions are to be

13. Barth, *Anselm*, p. 79.
14. Barth, *Anselm*, p. 82.

subordinated to the scriptural witness: "the necessary and fundamental form of all scriptural exegesis that is responsibly undertaken
and practiced in this sense must consist in all circumstances in the
freely performed act of subordinating all human concepts, ideas,
and convictions to the witness of revelation supplied to us in Scripture" (*CD*, 1/2: 715). On the other hand, only a few pages later
Barth claims that our human systems of interpretation are all we
have to help us read the Bible. The interpreter "will everywhere
betray the fact that . . . he has approached the text from the standpoint of a particular epistemology, logic or ethics, of definite ideas
and ideals concerning the relations of God, the world and man, and
that in reading and expounding the text he cannot simply deny
these" (*CD*, 1/2: 728). Such a statement, Barth says, may appear
shocking at first, but in truth "without such systems of explanation,
without such spectacles, we cannot read the Bible at all" (*CD*, 1/2:
728).

How can Barth affirm these widely divergent and apparently
contradictory assertions? The answer lies in the fact that, in Barth's
view, human systems are to be subordinated to the *subject matter* of
Scripture, but employed in dealing with the *words* which reflect the
subject matter. It is impossible to deal with the words of the Bible
without understanding them through some preexisting presuppositions; yet, when we are encountered by the object of the text, all
such human presuppositions must be surrendered in order that we
might be challenged by the subject matter itself.

There are two reasons why we must submit our hermeneutical
systems to the sovereign object. First of all, "when the Word of God
meets us, we are laden with the images, ideas and certainties which
we ourselves have formed about God, the world and ourselves. In
the fog of this intellectual life of ours the Word of God, which is
clear in itself, always becomes obscure" (*CD*, 1/2: 716). Because of
the obscurity of our world, we tend to dominate the Word of God
and make it over into our own image. Man always tries "to justify
himself from his own resources in face of a God whose image he has
fashioned in his own heart." But this is idolatry and stands under
the judgment of the one true God. Therefore, "to try to hold together
and accept *pari passu* both the testimony of the Bible which has this
content [i.e., Jesus Christ as Lord] and the autonomy of our own
world of thought is an impossible hermeneutic programme" (*CD*,
1/2: 721).

Additionally, Barth says, the Bible itself comes to us "in the form
of the human word of the prophets and apostles." We therefore
encounter obscurity in the very words of the Bible itself. "The divine
Word itself," says Barth, "meets us right in the thick of that fog of
our own intellectual life, as having taken the same form as our own

ideas, thoughts and convictions" (*CD*, 1/2: 716). The very words of the Bible itself could misdirect us if we insist upon judging these human words by our own human methods for we will not allow the sovereign subject matter to have its sovereignty over us.

Nevertheless, says Barth, "there has never been an expositor who has allowed only Scripture alone to speak" (*CD*, 1/2: 728). Instead, each of us, as we read the Bible, imposes upon the subject matter "one or other of the possibilities of meaning already known to us through our philosophy" (*CD*, 1/2: 729). But this is not necessarily evil, for in order to reflect upon anything we must make use of a conceptual framework, or "philosophy," in order to make sense of it.[15]

The system of thought, or philosophy, which we bring to the biblical text can be a means to the end of picturing the object of the text. But it can only be a *means* to such an end. For the system of thought is servant to the subject matter of the text. "The use of a scheme of thought in the service of scriptural exegesis is legitimate and fruitful," says Barth, "when it is determined and controlled by the text and the object [*Gegenstandsbild*] mirrored in the text" (*CD*, 1/2: 734).

Therefore, a particular philosophy used in exegesis "can claim no independent interest in itself" (*CD*, 1/2: 731). Indeed, "there is no essential reason for preferring one of these schemes to another" (*CD*, 1/2: 733). A human system of thought must always be subject to the object of the text lest the system dominate the text and there be no understanding at all. Still, insofar as the Bible is human word, it must be interpreted using human thoughts to evoke that image of the object which constitutes the meaning of the text.

HISTORY AND UNDERSTANDING

For Barth, then, hermeneutical and philosophical systems are useful in providing a framework for understanding the subject matter of the Bible. As the framework is erected, the biblical subject matter brings about understanding in that he freely and sovereignly reveals himself to the interpreter through the words of the text. Yet, this formulation raises another problem. The object of the Bible is Jesus Christ, a man who lived in first-century Palestine, attracted followers, was crucified and raised from the dead. He was, in other words, a historical personage who lived and worked twenty centuries ago,

15. Cf. Ian Barbour's concept of models as "useful fictions." He explains that "a 'useful fiction' is a mental construct used instrumentally for particular purposes but not assumed to be either true or false" (*Myths, Models and Paradigms* [New York: Harper & Row, 1974], p. 38).

separated from us both in space and in time. How then can Barth assert that the biblical text, which is a report of his life and work, is understood by us today because of him who lived long ago? This is, in fact, the question raised by G. E. Lessing when he referred to the "ugly, wide ditch" which separates today from any historical event.[16]

Lessing had written that "accidental truths of history can never be proof of the necessary truths of reason."[17] By this he meant that the category of history and the category of reason are different. The fact that a particular event occurred in time can never be, in itself, a ground for establishing a universal truth. Thus, the fact that Jesus lived, was crucified, and raised again can never provide sufficient reason for us to believe that God has saved us from our sins.

Lessing believed that the answer to the problem consisted in recognizing that "religion is not true because the evangelists and apostles taught it; they taught it because it is true."[18] Thus, Christianity was true not because God acted in history through Jesus Christ but because there was a universal truth within it recognizable at any moment in history. While historical events might not carry the burden of necessary truths of reason, nevertheless, reason, or truth, is apparent in the gospel during every age. There is no real distinction between the first century and our own.

For Barth, however, Lessing's solution was worse than the problem.

> When we are able to eliminate our non-contemporaneity with Christ and the apostles by putting ourselves on the same soil as them or putting them on the same soil as us, so that, sharing the same prophetic Spirit and having the measure of inner truth in our own feeling, we can discuss with them the gross and net value of their words, . . . then the concept of the Word of God is humanised in such a way that it is no wonder that people prefer to use it comparatively rarely and in quotation marks. (*CD*, 1/1: 147)[19]

If the distinctiveness of the history of Jesus is taken away, then the truth of the gospel is always and everywhere true for men, and so a human possibility. If Lessing is correct, then God did not break into history once and for all in the man Jesus. Instead, Jesus becomes an example of what can happen to any man who grasps the inner truth of religion.

---

16. Lessing, "On the Proof of the Spirit and of Power," in *Lessing's Theological Writings*, ed. H. Chadwick (London: A. & C. Black, 1956), p. 55.

17. Lessing, "On the Proof of the Spirit and of Power," p. 53.

18. Lessing, quoted by Barth in *CD*, 1/1: 146.

19. Note that Kierkegaard also dealt extensively with Lessing's problem in his *Concluding Unscientific Postscript*, trans. D. F. Swenson (Princeton: Princeton University Press, 1944), pp. 86-97.

Therefore, says Barth, man cannot eliminate the distinction between the past and the present. When we attempt to unite the two, we inevitably distort the past. "For all our respect for the greatness and vitality of history, it is we the living who have right on our side and who thus finally fix and manipulate the norm and the conditions of this togetherness" (*CD*, 1/1: 147). The past is always interpreted in the light of the present and so is transformed into the image of the present.

If there is to be real contemporaneity so that the subject matter of Scripture revealed then and there can be known to us here and now, then "it can be understood only as an expression of the fact that God's Word is itself God's act" (*CD*, 1/1: 147). This is what Barth calls "contingent contemporaneity" (*CD*, 1/1: 145). If the interpreter of the twentieth century is to know the subject matter of the Scriptures who appeared in history during the first century, there must be a real contemporaneity *(Gleichzeitigkeit)* so that the once-for-all-time of Christ becomes simultaneous with the time of the exegete. At the same time, such simultaneity is always contingent upon the sovereign activity of the Word of God itself. Therefore, this contemporaneity "has nothing directly to do with the problem of historical understanding" (*CD*, 1/1: 147). It is not something accessible to man's methodology but is completely dependent upon God's sovereignty.[20]

In the *Church Dogmatics*, then, we encounter a refinement of Barth's earlier thought expressed in the *Epistle to the Romans*. There Barth had asserted, "the past can speak to the present; for there is between them a simultaneity [*Gleichzeitigkeit*] which heals the past of its dumbness and the present of its deafness. . . . This simultaneity makes possible an intercourse in which time is at once dissolved and fulfilled, for its theme [*Sache*] is the non-historical, the invisible, the incomprehensible."[21] Barth believed, at the time of the Romans commentary, that Lessing's "ugly, wide ditch" could be bridged if the man of today understood the one theme running like a thread through all time.

By the time of the *Church Dogmatics*, however, Barth had some significant alterations in his thinking. The most important change had to do with the nature of the theme which ties the past to the present. In the *Epistle to the Romans* Barth had defined this theme existentially. The theme was the fact that man stands in uncertainty.

20. Note Barth's (unacknowledged) dependence on the concept of contemporaneity developed by Kierkegaard in his *Philosophical Fragments*, rev. ed., trans. David F. Swenson and Howard V. Hong (Princeton: Princeton University Press, 1962), especially pp. 83-84.

21. Barth, *The Epistle to the Romans*, trans. Edwyn C. Hoskyns (Oxford: Oxford University Press, 1933), p. 145.

"We stand at the barrier between death and life, between deep-seated corruption, which is the denial of God, and the righteousness of God, which is the denial of men."[22]

In the preface to the first half-volume of the *Church Dogmatics* Barth stated, "I have excluded to the very best of my ability anything that might appear to find for theology a foundation, support, or justification in philosophical existentialism" (*CD*, 1/1: xii). Therefore, he rejected the definition, in existential terms, of the theme of history put forward in his commentary. In place of the theme of history Barth substituted the subject matter of the Bible, Jesus Christ, the Word of God. That which ties the past with the present is not the uncertainty of man but the sovereign Word of God.

A second major difference in Barth's later thinking is that the Word of God *is* historical in contrast to the "nonhistorical" theme of history in the Romans commentary. The difference here certainly stems from Barth's later recognition that the Bible speaks of a revelation which is once for all rather than a timeless truth accessible to all men. The historicity of the Word need not mean that it is historically accessible to the historical method, in Barth's thinking, but it does mean that God broke into history in the man Jesus Christ.

A final difference in Barth's later thought has to do with the way in which the simultaneity of times is to be perceived by man. In his commentary on Romans Barth is unclear as to how the theme of history is recognized. He does assert that knowledge of this theme comes about "quite apart from the study of documentary sources." Indeed, "the value of history is displayed in that which precedes its critical investigation. . . ." He does say, "to us . . . the union of 'here' and 'there,' which is established only by God and can be awaited only from Him, is likewise impossible."[23] Yet, how God brings about the knowledge of this theme is not in view.

In the *Church Dogmatics*, on the other hand, Barth indicates that the knowledge of the object of the biblical text, and so the simultaneity of our time and his time, comes about purely by the act of God and is expressed by the concepts of election, revelation, calling, separation, and new birth. These concepts focus upon God's action rather than man's understanding. "In the sense of the biblical authors one can only understand the concepts as terms for God's free acts, or else they are not understood at all. They tell us that without elimination of the distinction the time of Christ by God's free act becomes contemporaneous with the time of the prophets and apostles" (*CD*, 1/1: 148). Lessing's ugly ditch, then, is bridged "solely and simply through the power of the biblical Word itself, which now

22. Barth, *The Epistle to the Romans*, p. 147.
23. Barth, *The Epistle to the Romans*, pp. 145, 146, 148.

makes a place for itself in a very different time" (*CD*, 1/1: 149). This is why the simultaneity between now and then is contingent. It is entirely dependent upon the act of the Word of God itself.

Therefore, even though the Bible deals with a theme that is long ago and far away, it may be understood by an interpreter today because the theme, the Word of God, acts by making a place for itself in our time. Such an act is always contingent, however, because the Word acts in sovereign freedom to make its time simultaneous with that of the interpreter. The interpreter can do nothing to place himself into the time of the Word or to bring the Word into his own time. Lessing's ditch may be bridged, but only from the other side.

INSPIRATION AND UNDERSTANDING

The bridge by which the "ugly ditch" between past and present is made passable Barth calls *theopneustia*, inspiration. Inspiration is that process by which the revelation of God in Jesus Christ became understood first of all by the prophets and apostles and then, through them, by modern man. There are, according to Barth, two moments of inspiration: one involving the biblical authors and another involving their present day interpreters.

Through inspiration the prophets and apostles stood in a special relationship with the revelation. This relationship was characterized by "the special attitude of obedience in those who are elected and called to this obviously special service. The special element in this attitude of obedience lay in the particularity, i.e., the immediacy of its relationship to the revelation which is unique by restriction in time, and therefore, in the particular nature of what they had to say and write as eyewitnesses and earwitnesses, the first fruits of the Church" (*CD*, 1/2: 505). In other words, inspiration of the biblical witnesses was brought about by a special relationship to the Word of God characterized by obedience and closeness in time.

The obedience of the witnesses was always rendered freely and therefore "they themselves and of themselves thought and spoke and wrote what they did think and speak and write as genuine *auctores*" (*CD*, 1/2: 505). They controlled their own thinking and writing; God did not wrest their faculties from them to make them his vessels. That their act as a free act "acquired this special function, was placed under the *autoritas primaria*, the lordship of God, was surrounded and controlled and impelled by the Holy Spirit, and became an attitude of obedience in virtue of its direct relationship to divine revelation—that was their *theopneustia*" (*CD*, 1/2: 505). The writing of Scripture was not some mystical process by which the Holy Spirit took over the will of the authors, denying them their freedom. Rather, it was an action taken by men in special relationship to the revelation and confirmed by the Spirit as his work.

Inspiration, therefore, points not to the Bible as the Word of God but to the event in which the biblical authors heard the Word of God. Thus, it is directed toward the present when twentieth-century man hears that same Word through the voices of the biblical witnesses. When we read and hear them we stand "remembering that it was once the case that their voice reproduced the voice of God, and therefore expecting that it will be so again" (CD, 1/2: 506).

There are two facets to the concept of inspiration. One, reflected in the thought of 2 Timothy 3:16 and 2 Peter 2:19-21, refers to the original inspiration of the biblical authors. The second, developed in 2 Corinthians 3:4-18 and in 1 Corinthians 2:6-16, focuses upon the work of the Holy Spirit in the present causing men to understand the Scriptures. The passage in 2 Corinthians 3 points out that the Scriptures are veiled to the Jews. Access to Scripture can come about for them only by a return to the Lord. Christians, however, "know how to read and receive what the Jews read but do not know how to read and receive. But we do so, not by virtue of any capacity of our own as distinct from them, but only of the Lord who is the Spirit—or from the Lord the Spirit (v. 18)" (CD, 1/2: 515).

The second passage, 1 Corinthians 2:6-16, reveals, in Barth's mind, the relationship between the inspiration of the authors of Scripture and the reader's understanding of their words. Paul understands himself as one who has received the divine Spirit and so knows the things given to him by God. He is an inspired apostle. But he knows that there are two other types of men in the world. There is "man in himself and as such" and there is "the man endowed with the Spirit and enlightened and led by the Spirit" (CD, 1/2: 516).

The natural man "does not receive what on the basis of the work of the Spirit is said in this way about the benefits of God." The spiritual man, on the other hand, "sees and understands what that other who is himself taught and led by the Spirit [i.e., the apostles and prophets] says." Therefore, for the reader to understand, three keys must be available. There must be first of all the benefit of revelation; second, "the apostle, who himself is empowered by the Spirit to know and declare that which is hidden"; and finally the hearer, who holds the key as to "whether by the help of the same Spirit . . . he himself will be a spiritual man who will listen to what the apostle has to say to him" (CD, 1/2: 516).

Barth detects early in the history of the church a tendency to deemphasize the present work of the Spirit in inspiration. Quite early on the Church Fathers indicated a desire "to concentrate interest in the inspiration of Scripture upon one particular point in that circle, and to limit it to it; namely, to the work of the Spirit in the emergence of the spoken or written prophetic and apostolic word as such" (*CD*, 1/2: 517). Barth asks if this inclination is "not the attempt to make the miracle of God in the witness of His revelation perspicuous to everybody, conceivable in its inconceivability, natural for all in the emphasizing of its supernatural character, a factor with which we can reckon even though we do ascribe it to the Holy Spirit" (*CD*, 1/2: 517). This tendency is evident throughout the history of the church and is simply another example of how man wishes to make the knowledge of God accessible to himself rather than recognizing it as an aspect of the divine freedom.

PRAYER AND UNDERSTANDING

The understanding of the Bible is a result of the activity of its subject matter, Jesus Christ, through the inspiration of the Holy Spirit. It is purely a matter of the sovereignty of this object that he causes an interpreter to know him as the object of the Scriptures. No methodology, no finely honed historical skills can bring about true understanding. There is, however, one thing that the interpreter, on his part, can do to bring about this understanding. This one activity cannot insure that understanding will, in fact, take place, but it does demonstrate the interpreter's awareness that he is dependent upon God for his understanding. This one thing that can be done is prayer.

Prayer must not be taken to be a strange and mystical method by which we come to an understanding of the Bible. To search for the witness to the divine revelation in the Bible requires both study and prayer. Both are human activities. But the witness to revelation "does not lie—and this is why prayer must have the last word—in our power but only in God's" (*CD*, 1/2: 531). Prayer, then, is an expression of our dependence upon the sovereign object of the text for understanding.

Prayer is, in fact, the most important factor in all our human effort to understand the Bible. "Because it is the decisive activity," says Barth, "prayer must take precedence even of exegesis, and in no circumstances must it be suspended" (*CD*, 1/2: 695). Understanding may come about apart from the work of historico-critical exegesis, but it can never take place apart from our expression of dependence upon God. Barth writes, "we cannot read and understand Holy Scripture without prayer, that is without invoking the grace of God. And it is only on the presupposition of prayer that all human effort in this matter, and penitence for human failure in this effort, will become serious and effective" (*CD*, 1/2: 684). Since prayer is a recognition of the interpreter's dependence upon God, through it God may cause the methods available to us to become effective. Human endeavor may become fruitful if it derives its effectiveness from God.

Prayer, therefore, is the confession that it is impossible to finally understand the Bible in our own power through our hermeneutical skills alone. Only God, as the object of the Scripture and so the determiner of its meaning, can graciously bestow meaning upon the biblical text. Prayer, according to Barth, is the means by which we place our understanding at the mercy of the subject matter of the text.[24]

Thus, in volume 1 of the *Church Dogmatics* Barth defines clearly and explicitly his view that the biblical text, in fact any text, can be understood only insofar as the interpreter understands its subject matter. This was not really a new view for Barth; he had defined his hermeneutical position in a similar fashion in his early writings. What was new in Barth's thinking was that he now believed that there could be no understanding of the Bible apart from the initiative of the divine subject matter, a view which precluded dependence upon hermeneutical methods for bringing about understanding.

Barth's view of hermeneutics sent shock waves throughout the theological world. Some theologians, particularly those from the liberal tradition, reacted strongly against Barth; others, generally younger and as fed up as Barth was with liberalism, saw him as the bright hope for the future of theology. One of these latter scholars, Rudolf Bultmann, found himself at one with Barth in the days of the Romans commentary but later opposed Barth's repudiation of hermeneutical methodology. Much of Barth's understanding of hermeneutics, as well as his influence upon a new era in the history of hermeneutics, may be understood by following the discussion, which was to continue for thirty years, between Karl Barth and Rudolf Bultmann.

---

24. Elsewhere Barth states that "theological work cannot be done on any level or in any respect other than by freely granting the free God room to dispose at will over everything that men may already have known, produced and achieved, and over all the religious, moral, intellectual, spiritual, or divine equipage with which men have traveled" (*Evangelical Theology: An Introduction*, trans. Grover Foley [Garden City, N.Y.: Doubleday-Anchor, 1964], p. 147).

THE COMING REVOLUTION: THE NEW LITERARY APPROACH TO NEW TESTAMENT INTERPRETATION

PETER W. MACKY

A woman and a man stood beneath the soaring stained-glass window, the most inspiring of all the glorious parts of the cathedral. As the woman looked in silence from a distance, the man stepped close, peering at the glass and moving from panel to panel. As they walked away the woman said:

"Did you ever see such a magnificent picture? I felt as if I was in paradise as I stood in front of it."

"Oh, yeah," the man replied. "But, you know, that glass is rather hard to see through. I could barely make out the trees outside."

For too long now we have believed that the Bible is a window through which we are intended to see what lies behind it. We have supposed that the primary purpose of the biblical writers was to report historical events but that unfortunately they did not do an adequate job. Their glass was stained.

But perhaps the colors in the glass are the meaning and not just an obstacle. Perhaps the Bible is a glorious stained-glass window and we have been looking at it with blinded eyes.

That, in brief, is the contention of a growing number of biblical scholars who are looking at the Bible with a new literary approach.

In 1970 I finished a book on biblical interpretation entitled *The Bible in Dialogue with Modern Man*.[1] That book attempted to present the most important debates on biblical interpretation over the 1,940 years since the time of Jesus' ministry. Looking back at the book I see hints of what has become quite obvious now: we were at the end of an era in biblical studies. I wish I had seen it then, but it was only a cloud the size of a man's hand on the horizon. The revolution in progress is this: we are moving from the historical era to the

---

1. Macky, *The Bible in Dialogue with Modern Man* (Waco, Tex.: Word Books, 1970).

Reprinted from *The Theological Educator* 9 (Spring 1979): 32-46.

literary era in biblical studies. "Today the historical-critical paradigm is in process of potentially revolutionary change."[2]

This change is a paradigm shift, to use the language of Thomas Kuhn in *The Structure of Scientific Revolutions*. A paradigm shift is the movement from one particular hypothesis on the subject before us to another. It is a time of turmoil, of great conflict, of name-calling, of threat to the established order. But it appears to be moving steadily.

Biblical scholarship has endured such a paradigm shift once before, a movement from the philosophical to the historical approach to the Bible. Up until the Reformation, theologians approached the Bible from philosophical-theological perspectives seeking the ideas to be found there.

The reformers, however, rejected church theology and philosophical systems as their starting point. They advocated finding the historical meaning of the text by reading the Bible in the light of its own times. The reformers were still looking primarily for ideas to use in their own time, but they started a new way of looking. This new way sprang to full life in the Enlightenment and its development of historical criticism which was adopted by biblical scholars in the nineteenth century.

The crucial change, the paradigm shift, from philosophy to history was this: the goal was no longer to find ideas to use in the present; now the goal was to uncover events in the past. The historical critic's goal was to answer the question of what really happened? Naturally the historian paid attention to ideas, but they were simply part of the pattern of events that had to be woven into a whole by the historian.

Today we cannot doubt that that was a revolution, and indeed a fruitful one. Much of what is now taken for granted by conservative and liberal alike on text, language, form, context, and so on, is the result of two hundred years of historical criticism.

Now too it is clear that with the rise to power of historical criticism the older philosophical-theological approach did not disappear, especially in the various orthodoxies (Catholic, Eastern, Reformed, Lutheran, and others). Likewise, we can anticipate that the historical approach is not going to disappear with the advent of the literary approach. What will happen is that the absolutism of the historical is going to be undermined. In addition it is possible that the absolutism of the philosophical approach in the orthodoxies may begin to be subtly undermined also. But that remains to be seen.

2. N. R. Petersen, *Literary Criticism for New Testament Critics* (Philadelphia: Fortress Press, 1973), pp. 9-10.

In this article the thesis that we are now in a revolutionary stage in biblical studies will be explained, argued for, and its implications for the future suggested. The first section will show the anomalies in historical criticism of the Bible, for it is precisely the recognition of weaknesses that leads to a revolution. The next section will be concerned with seeing the Bible's literary dimension and explaining the new literary approach and why it is offered. The third section will be a more detailed look at one aspect of the literary approach, God's accommodation in metaphor, symbol, and the imagination. Finally, based on the arguments of the preceding sections we shall discuss transculturation.

THE ANOMALIES IN HISTORICAL CRITICISM OF THE BIBLE

From the very beginning of historical criticism in the Enlightenment, conservative theologians have objected that it was not as objective and presuppositionless as it claimed. In particular, British biblical scholars as a whole took a moderate view on this matter, seldom adopting the "functional atheism"[3] that was common among German historical critics of the Bible. The British early recognized that "all historians write on the basis of their personal philosophies, none of which can be proved or disproved."[4] Alan Richardson's *History, Sacred and Profane,* is an excellent presentation of this perspective view of history.

In particular, moderate biblical criticism has long noted what George Ladd states succinctly: "Underlying the ebb and flow of successive schools of criticism is to be found the continuing theological assumption that the nature of God and history is such that a proper critical method can make no room for the immediate acting of God in history."[5] Ladd then goes on to present the typical British view that this assumption is false and that historical criticism can function more accurately without it. Ladd's own "evangelical criticism," his "historical-theological method," shows well how this may be done.[6]

Such evangelical objections are nothing new, but when we hear left-wing scholars raising profound objections, that is new. For example, some of Bultmann's students have propounded the new hermeneutic based on Heidegger's views of the power of poetry. Gerhard

3. See Walter Wink, *The Bible in Human Transformation* (Philadelphia: Fortress Press, 1973), p. 4.
4. Macky, *The Bible in Dialogue with Modern Man,* p. 134.
5. Ladd, *The New Testament and Criticism* (Grand Rapids: Eerdmans, 1967), p. 49.
6. See Ladd, *The New Testament and Criticism,* pp. 13, 16.

Ebeling proclaims, "the primary phenomenon in the realm of understanding is not understanding of language, but understanding through language."[7] His meaning is that the Bible is not a problem we are in charge of solving, which is the historical critic's view. Rather *we* are the problem, and we need to stand under the light of the Bible to let it solve us. This does not deny the necessity for historical study as a preliminary. The major protest is that for too long scholars have stopped when historical results were obtained instead of going beyond them.

Even more revolutionary in his criticism is Walter Wink, who argues in *The Bible in Human Transformation* that historical criticism of the Bible is a false ideology he calls "objectivism." His specific objections are (1) that this approach is not neutral and objective but is a handmaiden of the particular philosophical-theological perspectives of its users; (2) that as a result, historians come up with widely varying "assured results," as can be seen in the contradictory portraits summarized in Bowman's *Which Jesus?*; (3) that the attempt at objectivity produces a heavy-handed rationalism that ignores much of the emotional, irrational, imaginative aspects of human life that are continuously present in the Bible; and (4) that by standing over the Bible like a coroner over a corpse, historical critics are unable to stand under the Bible and hence are unable to understand it.

Scholars of literature, in addition, have suggested that the biblical critic's concern for what lies behind the text (rather than for the text itself) is a waste. Roland Frye notes, for example, that in literature there have been scholars who tried to divide works into sources, but "it has been found that such analyses are at best only marginally productive, and far more often they are counterproductive. They almost always divert attention from the literary work itself by breaking it up into fragments. In my field such efforts are called disintegrating criticism . . . [which] has been almost entirely abandoned as unproductive."[8]

A writer with a unique perspective drew similar conclusions: "C. S. Lewis, speaking both as a literary critic and a writer whose works had been analyzed by critics, records his distrust of critics who presume to explain the process that lies behind a written text, noting that the critics who theorized about the composition of his

7. Ebeling, "Work of God and Hermeneutic," in *New Frontiers in Theology, II: The New Hermeneutic,* ed. James M. Robinson and John B. Cobb, Jr. (New York: Harper & Row, 1964), p. 93.

8. Frye, "A Literary Perspective for the Criticism of the Gospels," in *Jesus and Man's Hope,* ed. D. G. Miller and D. Y. Hadidian (Pittsburgh: Pittsburgh Theological Seminary Publications, 1971), p. 214.

own works had never once been right."[9] The crucial criticism is not that it is improper to look behind a literary text. Rather the accusation is that only highly speculative results are possible so it is a waste of time to try.

The conclusion which this series of objections thus brings us is this: historical criticism cannot do what it claimed it would — namely, provide an adequate interpretation of the Bible. A child stood up and said, "But the King has no clothes on." So the King is sliding off his throne. A new day is dawning with the new literary approach.

SEEING THE BIBLE'S LITERARY DIMENSION

The new literary approach is not to be confused with the Bible-as-literature movement of liberalism at the turn of the century. That movement denied the authority of the Bible as the Word of God, asserting that it was just another example of religious literature.

In addition this new approach is not to be confused with the literary criticism that has been practiced by biblical scholars for several centuries. The questions of author, date, audience, place of origin, sources, and so on are historical questions. They do not touch the literary-aesthetic qualities with which the new literary approach is mainly concerned.

This new approach suggests there is a third dimension to the Bible that has been largely ignored. The philosophical-theological search for useful ideas sees one dimension. The historical search for background provides insight into a second dimension. Now the claim is being made that the depth dimension has been missed, that the literary/aesthetic dimension of much of the Bible must be plumbed.

For too long biblical scholars have been living in a two-dimensional world. Flat. Now the sky and the mountains and the bottom of the sea have come into view. This approach has been developed on the basis of the new criticism or formalistic criticism that sprung up in literary circles in this country in the 1930s and 1940s. This new approach concentrates on the work itself, rather than moving away from the work to something else, whether author, readers, historical background, or ideas. To get to the depths of a work "we must narrow our attention to what the literary work says, and to do that we must first consider how it is said."[10]

In this section we will consider three aspects of this subject: the

9. Leland Ryken, "Literary Criticism of the Bible: Some Fallacies," in *Literary Interpretations of Biblical Narratives,* ed. K. R. R. Gros Louis (Nashville: Abingdon Press, 1974), pp. 36-37.

10. W. L. Guerin et al., *A Handbook of Critical Approaches to Literature* (New York: Harper & Row, 1966), p. 47.

meaning of a new literary approach, the assumptions lying behind it, and the argument for using it to see the depths of the Bible.

What is the new literary approach? This approach does not ignore the insights gained from traditional interpretations. Traditional approaches have been textual-linguistic, historical-biographical, and moral-philosophical, and all have offered considerable insight. But now we must go beyond these and ask what the particular work itself has to contribute because of its own form. Norman Perrin points to the kinds of questions that must be asked of a narrative by mentioning "the inter-relatedness of plot movement, activity of the characters involved, the human encounters and their outcomes."[11]

Leland Ryken gives a more detailed list of questions used in the literary approach: "How is the story structured? What are the unifying narrative principles . . . ? What is important about the ordering of events? . . . What archetypal plot motifs are important in the story? How is the thematic meaning of the story embodied in the narrative form? . . . What are the meanings of the poet's concrete images and metaphors and allusions? What feelings are communicated by his hyperboles, images, exclamations . . . ?"[12]

Clearly this approach is an attempt to pay much closer attention to the text itself than is done in other approaches. Unlike the historical approach, it is not looking for the historical process that led up to this text but is concerned with seeing and hearing the fullness of the text itself. Unlike the philosophical-theological approach, it is not using the text to develop a system of doctrine but is concerned with the text as it is. This does not mean that those other questions are forbidden. It just means that if this text is God's Word to us, our primary and ultimate task is to hear it in all its fullness.

The assumptions undergirding this approach. At the root of this approach is the belief that human language has a variety of functions. Most people believe that conveying information is the purpose of language, and so in reading the Bible they look for information. But to inform, to declare, to assert constitute only one of several functions of language. A second very important function is based on the biblical view that language, the Word, is powerful, that it effects change, that it performs actions (cf. Genesis 1; Jeremiah 1:9-10; Mark 1:25-26; 2:5, 11). This kind of language is called performative. Examples of performative language are the minister marrying a couple, the jury foreman announcing a verdict, and one person making a promise to another. Literary language is this kind of language, for at its best it does something to the reader, making him someone

11. Perrin, *Jesus and the Language of the Kingdom* (Philadelphia: Fortress Press, 1976), p. 148.
12. Ryken, "Literary Criticism of the Bible," p. 24.

different. This difference involves not merely an increase in information but a new experience, a new feeling, perhaps even a new life.[13]

The possibility of this happening in literature is seen in Aristotle's distinction between "rhetoric" and "poetics," background pointed out by William Beardslee in *Literary Criticism of the New Testament*.[14] "Rhetoric" is an ornamental form used to make content more attractive. Biblical scholars have usually treated the biblical narrative-poetic materials this way. But in "poetics" the form is essential to the meaning. Almost he could have said, "the medium is the message." The new literary approach claims that to a significant extent the Bible is "literary" or "poetic," that its meaning is not separable from its form.

This insight has been stressed above all about Jesus' parables, especially by Dan Via. His book *The Parables* offers the basic theory used to see deeply into some of Jesus' parables. In a later article he summarizes the view this way:

> The narrative parables, as fully realized artistic works, present a union of form and content so that meaning depends as much on form as on content. The content is composed of the episodes in the protagonist's fate—his actions or nonactions, his encounters, and his moments of recognition and understanding. The form is not the disposal container for these parts but is rather the arrangement and fusion of them. Form exerts a kind of pressure on the matter, or content, with the result that meaning is diffused throughout the texture of the parable. Meaning, then, is not found in any one isolable part or "point" but in the configuration of action and understanding as a whole.[15]

Most conservative biblical interpreters have imagined God's self-revelation as a treasure hidden inside an earthen vessel which was the biblical form; once you have found the doctrine inside, you have all you need and then you can ignore the stories. The new literary approach suggests, however, that God's self-revelation is the story itself; the story is a flower that is beautiful when whole, but is destroyed when you pull it apart to try to see what is inside it that makes it beautiful.

In a literary work the author intends that something happen to the reader; he does not intend merely to pass on information. In particular, literary works touch our imaginations, providing us with

13. Cf. R. C. Tannehill, *The Sword of His Mouth* (Philadelphia: Fortress Press, 1975), pp. 1, 7.

14. Beardslee, *Literary Criticism of the New Testament* (Philadelphia: Fortress Press, 1970), pp. 3-4.

15. Via, "The Relationship of Form to Content in the Parables: The Wedding Feast," *Interpretation* 25 (1971): 175.

new, vicarious experiences that make us somewhat different people. Experiences cannot be fully contained in ideas, or information. Thus a literary work cannot be fully translated into other words. James Barr expresses this basic insight well:

> In so far as a work is really literary and not merely information . . . it can perhaps be said to be its own meaning. . . . For a work to be literary in character means that it does not have a detachable meaning which might have been stated in some other way; the way in which it was stated in the work is in fact the message or the meaning of this work. Any comment on such works can therefore aim only at elucidating the work and sending the reader back to the work itself.[16]

"Back to the work itself" could well be the motto of the new literary approach. Commentary may be helpful as a means of helping readers understand the text, but neither the theology nor the history behind the text is an adequate expression of a literary-poetic text. Amos Wilder, the pioneer in this approach, sums up this central tenet briefly: "We should reckon with what we can learn about metaphorical and symbolic language from students of poetry: that it cannot really be translated, least of all into prose."[17]

Justification for the new literary approach. The most effective way to test the value of a new pair of glasses is to try them on. The best way to test the new literary method is to read some of the books and articles by scholars approaching the Bible this way and find out if indeed they provide valuable new insights. But in order to get us to give up our attachment to our old glasses, we often need reasons. What arguments can be offered to justify looking at the Bible as literature (as well as theology and history)?

Leland Ryken offers a number of criteria for identifying artistic narratives, so the more a biblical text exhibits these criteria the more literary it is. Literature focuses on human experience, not abstract thought, presented as "characters in action or concrete images and sensory descriptions." Further, "at the consciously artistic end of the narrative spectrum it is possible to discern three things: (1) a story that is carefully unified . . . , (2) a plot that has structural unity and pattern, and (3) a story that makes use of such narrative forms as foreshadowing, dramatic irony, climax, suspense, poetic justice, foils, image patterns, and symbolism." As an example of this literary form, in which the meaning is fully incarnate in the story, Ryken points to Genesis 1 – 3 and says, "in these chapters there is not a single instance of a theme stated in propositional form. All

16. Barr, *The Bible in the Modern World* (New York: Harper & Row, 1973), p. 70.
17. Wilder, *Early Christian Rhetoric: The Language of the Gospel* (Cambridge: Harvard University Press, 1971), p. 125.

of the themes and creation ordinances that we might deduce from the story have been incarnated in the actions and the dialogue."[18]

By the standards of characters in action, concrete images, unified story, use of literary techniques, and meaning incarnated in the story, there is a great deal of biblical material that can be defined as literary. This does not mean that it is not theological or historical, but it does mean that there is more to the poetry and narratives— much more— than a theological or historical approach can discern.

Ryken himself offers a superb example of this approach in action in *The Literature of the Bible*. Kenneth Gros Louis's collection, *Literary Interpretations of Biblical Narratives,* is also a noteworthy source. Dan Via's *The Parables* and the April 1971 number of *Interpretation* show the best work done on the literary dimensions of Jesus' parables, though Robert Funk's essay on "The Good Samaritan" in *Semeia* 2 is a gem, too. One other extraordinarily insightful book is Tanne-hill's *The Sword of His Mouth,* which is concerned with the forceful and imaginative language in the sayings of Jesus. Finally we should note two others works in this field, Leonard Thompson's *Introducing Biblical Literature: A More Fantastic Country* and J. P. Pritchard's *A Literary Approach to the New Testament.*

Try them, you'll like them.

A note of warning: some literary scholars have become enamored of a philosophical approach called structuralism and have begun applying it to the biblical texts. It is unbelievably jargonized, worse even than Heidegger's existentialism. After reading a number of such works, e.g. in *Semeia* 1 & 2 and *Interpretation* 28, my conclusion is the same as Perrin's: "At this point a student of the discussion begins to wonder whether the recourse to structuralist analysis in the form of actantial analysis of the narrative has helped very much."[19]

GOD'S ACCOMMODATION: METAPHOR, SYMBOLS, AND IMAGINATION

Central to all literature is the use of metaphorical language, concrete images pointing toward some deep meaning that cannot otherwise be specified. The new literary approach takes biblical metaphor, imagery, and symbolism seriously, seeing it as the window onto the great mystery.

Up until the eighteenth century, theologians recognized the Bible's central use of stories and symbols and spoke of it as God's accom-

---

18. Ryken, "Literary Criticism of the Bible," pp. 24-25.
19. Perrin, *Jesus and the Language of the Kingdom,* p. 174. An article that summarizes and advocates the structuralist hermeneutic is J. D. Crossan's "Waking the Bible: Biblical Hermeneutic and Literary Imagination," *Interpretation* 32 (1978): 269-85.

modation to our ignorance, his speaking baby-talk to us. Augustine, Aquinas, and Calvin stressed this as the essential nature of biblical God-talk.

Roland Frye decries the loss of this principle of accommodation, saying it "was apparently abandoned by theologians who tried to conform their biblical analyses more nearly to the model" of eighteenth-century science, "a one-for-one equivalence between a scientific statement and the datum to which they referred." This produced "a literalist and fundamentalist biblicism with calamitous results. The loss of accommodation from Christian theology is one of the gravest calamities in the intellectual history of Christianity."[20]

Frye is right, for most biblical scholars under the influence of philosophy and history have looked upon biblical symbolism as merely ornamental rhetoric, Bultmann being a prominent recent offender in this regard. One reason for this seems to be that theologians throughout recent church history have adopted the philosopher's assumption that clarity and precision are the marks of truth. The biblical writers, however, saw that truth is a person, a profound mystery. So they alluded to it by means of stories, poems, and symbols. As A. C. Thiselton observes, "too often in biblical interpretation exegetes have looked for exactness where the author chose vagueness."[21]

Before proceeding further we need to present a significant distinction, what C. S. Lewis called the difference between "master's metaphor" and "pupil's metaphor." The former is a metaphor used by a teacher to give a beginning understanding. For example a skier might say to a Hawaiian, "Skiing is surfing straight down a very high wave." Later, the surfer may learn to ski and no longer needs the metaphor; he has seen behind it and has come to know the reality. But there are other realms in which we are all pupils, for example, in trying to know what lies at the depths of the human heart. Then we use "pupil's metaphor," which is the only way we can speak about the mystery. All our talk about God is "pupil's metaphor."[22]

This type of metaphor, which is the only way into the mystery we seek to enter, goes beyond the merely rational. Wilder claims, echoing many other literary scholars and philosophers of language, "a true metaphor or symbol is more than a sign, it is a bearer of the

20. Frye, "A Literary Perspective for the Criticism of the Gospels," p. 204.

21. Thiselton, "Semantics and New Testament Interpretation," in *New Testament Interpretation: Essays on Principles and Methods,* ed. I. Howard Marshall (Grand Rapids: Eerdmans, 1977), p. 94.

22. C. S. Lewis, "Bluspels and Flalanspheres: A Semantic Nightmare," in *The Importance of Language,* ed. Max Black (Englewood Cliffs, N.J.: Prentice-Hall, 1962), pp. 36-50.

reality to which it refers. The hearer not only learns about that reality, he participates in it. He is invaded by it. Here lies the power and fatefulness of art. Jesus' speech had the character not of instruction and ideas but of compelling imagination, of spell, of mythical shock and transformation."[23] When Jesus spoke, people did not just argue or accept, they became enraged or delighted, made themselves enemies or found themselves born again as his followers. His language was powerful, and like all biblical language, one element of that power was its symbolism. The symbolism went through the mind to the heart — that is, to the imagination, memory, feelings, and will. That is the crucial poetic insight: symbolic speech touches and transforms the heart, while prosaic, discursive, abstract language remains largely in the head.

The centrality of imagination is apparent in this literary approach. Imagination is seen at the core of man, the place where mind, emotions, memory, and will all come together. Our whole stance is determined by how we imagine ourselves — as captains at the wheel of our destiny, as driftwood on the river, as children of a loving Father. Thus, when people are transformed, it happens first in their imaginations. "It is imaginative language which is able to meet the imagination on its own level, awaken it and turn it against its own past products. This means that the power of the Christ-event for the expansion of human being is released only as we return to the imaginative language which most richly embodies that event and acknowledge it for what it is by responding imaginatively."[24]

Now if these insights into metaphor and symbol are accurate, they lead to a conclusion similar to the one reached above concerning poetry and literary narratives: the "pupil's metaphor" cannot be adequately translated into other language, least of all into abstract, prosaic language. This does not mean that we cannot say something about the meaning of such symbols, for indeed we can. It just means, first, that we can only use other symbols to suggest the meaning, and second, that in the end nothing can totally take the place of the original symbol.

For example, we speak of God as "Our Father." When we do so our memories of our earthly fathers, our feelings about them, and our imagination of what a perfect father would be all throng together. The power of the symbol is found in that combination, and it cannot all be put into ordinary language. We can say something of what we mean; for example, as our Father, God is our guide, protector, and provider. But each of those words is also a symbol. "Guide" calls to mind the Indian guide in the wilderness, or the

23. Wilder, *Early Christian Rhetoric*, p. 84.
24. Tannehill, *The Sword of His Mouth*, pp. 22-23.

school counselor, or the museum guide, and God is not exactly like any of them. "Protector" calls to mind policemen, or the army, or a big brother, and God is not exactly like any of them. So when we interpret symbols we must use other symbols. But finally we need to return to the original and keep saying "Our Father."

This centrality and power of metaphor has been widely recognized in discussing Jesus' parables. As many have seen, a parable is a symbol in narrative form, and therefore, the power of parable is an extension and elaboration of the power of a symbol. For example "The Prodigal Son" is an expansion into narrative of the symbol "Our Father." Much has been written on the parables' symbols, but only a bare beginning has been made in reading the rest of the New Testament from this perspective.

One scholar who has made a start is Norman Perrin, who proclaims that "the extensive discussion of Kingdom of God in the teaching of Jesus has been bedeviled by the fact that scholars have thought of Kingdom of God as a conception rather than as a symbol."[25] This is a striking statement, since Perrin was one of the foremost scholars trying to pin down the exact meaning of the biblical concepts. Concepts have fairly precise meanings that can in princple be laid down. So scholars were continually asking what exactly Jesus meant by kingdom of God. But Perrin has come to see that it is not a concept or an idea but a symbol: "as a symbol, it can *represent* or *evoke* a whole range or series of conceptions or ideas."[26] In particular the symbol evokes the Old Testament imagery of God as the Ruler (King) of Israel and the universe. Many different stories (e.g., the Exodus and exile), visions (e.g., Isaiah's and Ezekiel's), and psalm-poems (e.g., Isaiah 40 and Job 38– 42) contribute to the great fund of images that Jesus evoked by speaking of the kingdom of God.

Precisely the same insight now can and must be carried over into the whole of New Testament interpretations. Paul's letters are filled with powerful symbols, for example, the Christian life as a race (1 Cor. 9:23-27), Christ's coming as the royal prince leaving his throne to become a slave (Phil. 2:5ff.), redemption as the paying of a ransom to buy back a slave (Rom. 3:24), the church as the bride of Christ (Eph. 5:23), and a thousand more. We must come to see that "Paul's language is consciously poetic."[27]

25. Perrin, *Jesus and the Language of the Kingdom*, p. 5.
26. Perrin, *Jesus and the Language of the Kingdom*, p. 23.
27. Ralph P. Martin, "Approaches to New Testament Exegesis," in *New Testament Interpretation*, p. 240.

TRANSCULTURATION

Preachers from the very beginning have taken God's self-revelation and applied it to new situations by using new language. Paul moved into the hellenistic world and took over hellenistic symbols and experiences and language in order to reach his hearers. In every age preachers have attempted to use the language and experiences of their hearers as the way to bring the gospel home to their hearts.

Over time and space there are great variations in language and culture, so there is the need for new expressions. We all know of the need to translate the Bible into our language. But now we are coming to see that we need, and have usually found a way, to transculturate the biblical message. This means to take those biblical concepts, images, and experiences that are foreign to our culture and find some way to reexpress them in concepts, images, and experiences that are present and common in our culture. Heretofore the practice of transculturation has often been good, but now a theoretical understanding of how it should be done is developing.

Though evangelicals rejected Bultmann's program of demythologizing for good reasons,[28] they have come to agree that some of what Bultmann saw was valuable. For example J. D. G. Dunn agrees that "the NT presents events critical to Christian faith in language and concepts which are often outmoded and meaningless to 20th century man. . . . Many of the NT metaphors and analogies are archaic and distasteful to modern sensibilities (e.g., blood sacrifice)."[29]

This cultural distance thus leads us to see "the need for cultural transposition between the world and the church of the New Testament and the world and the church today."[30] The crucial point of distinction separating evangelical transculturation from Bultmann's demythologizing is that "translating the gospel into present day terms . . . is very different from listing what modern man can and cannot believe."[31] Using modern language does not mean accepting modern philosophies. The gospel still stands in judgment over all modern philosophies, whether secular or religious. But it uses whatever language modern listeners will understand — even if it is also used by other "gospels." For example the language and concepts of

28. See chapter 8 of my book *The Bible in Dialogue with Modern Man.*
29. Dunn, "Demythologizing — The Problem of Myth in the New Testament," in *New Testament Interpretation*, p. 300.
30. Robin Nixon, "The Authority of the New Testament," in *New Testament Interpretation*, p. 345.
31. Robin Nixon, "The Authority of the New Testament," p. 346.

Thomas Harris's book *I'm OK, You're OK* are quite helpful for expressing the biblical understanding of sin.[32]

At the root of this development is the way linguists have come to recognize that translations can either focus on the letter of the text or on the power of it. Eugene Nida of the American Bible Society has developed this distinction in his book *Toward a Science of Translation*. In particular he emphasizes the power of some language and the necessity for a translation to reexpress that power so that modern readers will receive a similar impact to that which ancient readers received.[33]

The *Good News Bible* is the American Bible Society's contribution to transculturation, and in it examples of the practice abound. In Jeremiah 23:1-5 the symbolism of shepherd-flock-fold is reexpressed for urbanites as ruler-people-homeland. The idiom "I smote upon my thigh" (Jer. 31:19, RSV) becomes "we hung our heads in grief." "Sow the house of Israel with seed of man and beast" (Jer. 31:27) becomes "fill the land with people and animals." "Fall short of the glory of God" (Rom. 3:23) is expressed as "far away from God's saving presence." "The redemption which is in Christ Jesus" (Rom. 3:24) is translated "through Christ Jesus who sets them free." In every case the Good News translators have sought a modern symbol or image, knowing that the ancient ones lack impact.

Literary scholars have emphasized that some of the biblical imagery is provincial. Wilder notes, "as the world changes with the passage of time, nothing except things like the multiplication table can be merely repeated without translation or interpretation. Every good sermon fortunately is an interpretation. To merely reproduce the words of the New Testament is to falsify their original meaning and to defraud modern hearers of that meaning."[34]

That is a point that evangelicals have sometimes failed to grasp in their eagerness to hold on to the message of the New Testament. Now it is becoming clear that in many cases a literal expression gives the wrong impression. For example, in Jesus' parable of the Pharisee and the Publican, the original hearers took the Pharisee to be the good guy. But we in the church today know that the Pharisee is the bad guy. Therefore, if we today wish the parable to strike home, to have the same impact it did for Jesus' hearers, we must transculturate it. One way to do that could be in a story of "The Minister and the Mobster."[35]

---

32. See my article "Sin and Not-OKness," *Theological Educator* 7 (Spring 1977): 81-88.

33. Nida, *Toward a Science of Translation* (Leiden: E. J. Brill, 1964), p. 159.

34. Wilder, *Early Christian Rhetoric*, pp. 122ff.

35. See my book *The Pursuit of the Divine Snowman* (Waco, Tex.: Word Books, 1977), p. 24.

The recent gain is in our understanding of how this need for transculturation arises. Once we recognize the presence of symbols and metaphors as the basic language, we are led to see more deeply into the way the text works. Symbols call up memories and experiences. Then the imagination works to put these memories together into new vicarious experiences. For example, the parable of the Lost Sheep called Jesus' listeners to bring up memories (including feelings) of sheep-herding, of lambs running away, of life in the wilderness. But most modern readers have not had those experiences. Therefore the symbol cannot become rooted in our experience and memory and imagination as it could for Jesus' hearers. Thus, while we can get the idea of the lost being found, we miss the powerful impact that this parable once had by working on the experiences, memories, feelings, and imaginations of its hearers. Our minds may get it but our hearts do not.

For us, shepherd and lost sheep become dead images because they do not come out of our own personal experience. Many other symbols are likewise powerless, for example, king, holy one, blood sacrifice, and Samaritan. But others are still quite alive since we still have fathers, know about judges, experience storms, are dazzled by light, and feel the awesomeness of a mountain towering over our heads. Many biblical symbols are still alive and powerful and so can immediately reach many modern hearers.

The preliminary task is thus to distinguish among symbols, to know which symbols are dead (powerless), which are dormant (possibly able to be revived), and which are still alive.

But what should we do about the dead symbols? Heretofore the most common practice has been to explain them in more abstract language; for example, the Lamb of God has been explained in terms of vicarious satisfaction of justice. But the new literary approach cautions that that is only a beginning, not a finally adequate interpretation. The reason is that literary, poetic, symbolic language depends upon its form for its meaning, so when you change the form you change the meaning. Therefore when we need to interpret dead symbols, other symbols, live modern ones, are the best place to look. As Robert Funk noted, "interpretation of parables should take place . . . in parables."[36] So, the parable of the Lost Sheep may reach the hearts and imaginations of modern children if it is transculturated into:

The Lost Nursery School Boy
One spring day the four-year-old class at the Nursery School in New Wilmington went down to the lake to learn about willows and

36. Funk, *Language, Hermeneutic and Word of God* (New York: Harper & Row, 1966), p. 146.

fish and seaweed and other things that grow around and in water. They numbered themselves when they left and had fourteen, but after coming back they had one less—Johnny Redman had disappeared. Immediately the teacher asked the children to draw or play quietly and not leave the room until she got back. Half-walking and half-running she looked in the buildings along the way to the lake but found nothing. Down at the lake she called his name but got no answer. So she ran to his house and banged on the door, but no one was there. Walking back towards the school she passed the park and saw a small figure sitting forlornly on a swing. Rushing down to him she saw it was Johnny. She was so happy to see him she threw her arms around him and forgot to ask how he got there. When they arrived back at the school a few minutes later they found that some of the mothers had come to take their children home and were upset to find no teacher there. "You should have let that kid take care of himself!" one of the mothers said. But the teacher replied: "Johnny was lost; I had to find him."[37]

So far very few modern parables have made their way into print. One collection just published is John Aurelio's *Story Sunday: Christian Fairy Tales for Young and Old Alike.* These stories were all told as sermons by a parish priest and among them is a delightful Christmas story of Santa and the Christ Child. I have tried to begin creating modern parables by including twenty or so (and an allegory or two) in my book of biblical theology entitled *The Pursuit of the Divine Snowman.* In addition there are a number of excellent short movie parables produced by Paulist Productions and by Teleketics.

The advantages of stories over abstract interpretation and discussion are many. A primary one is that a good unfamiliar story holds the attention of hearers much more firmly than a discussion of ideas does. Second, a story involving human beings touches the memory, imagination, and will, whereas ideas stay just in the mind. That is why personal testimonies in story form are so valuable in evangelistic services. But most of all stories are valuable because they are closer to reality than discussions of ideas are. This is a central contention ably demonstrated by Robert Roth in *Story and Reality* where he says: stories "come alive and jump to the complexities of life . . . (for) stories acknowledge the place of mystery as a natural element in reality."[38]

CONCLUSION

The new literary approach comes as a revolutionary change in the way many scholars are reading the Bible. It does not mean that we

37. Macky, *The Pursuit of the Divine Snowman,* p. 28.
38. Roth, *Story and Reality* (Grand Rapids: Eerdmans, 1973), pp. 20ff.

will stop asking the historical question of what lies behind this text that will enable us to understand it better. It just means we will see history as preliminary. We don't stop asking the theological question either: How does this text relate to our systems of theology and ethics? It just means we will see that our theological systems are not adequate to express the full depth and power of biblical stories and symbols. Thus we will go beyond the theological-philosophical approach because it is too rational, too idea-oriented, and so does not adequately express the deeper reality the text means to communicate.

Come stand before the world's most beautiful and inspiring stained-glass window. Look at it, not at what lies behind it. Allow yourself to be caught up in the magnificent tale that is told, so it can become your story, ordering your life anew. Then perhaps you can break out of the two-dimensional world imposed upon biblical scholarship by philosophy and history. Plumb the depths, soar to the heights. You'll never go back to flatland again.

THE STRUCTURALISTS AND THE BIBLE

RICHARD JACOBSON

The French critic Tzvetan Todorov has noted that a "science does not speak of its object, but speaks itself with the help of its object." I expect this is no less true of God-centered than of man-centered studies. One wishes to know about nature but studies physics or chemistry; one wishes to study the nature of divinity and learns theology or comparative religion. In large measure, structuralism, which is not quite a science but an array of methods, is very much in the process of "speaking itself," and it is in its own elaboration that most of its energies are invested. The extent and the way in which this is so will, I hope, become clear in the exposition which follows.

A definition is in order. "Structuralism" is the application of principles derived from certain movements within linguistics to other areas of discourse. These other areas may be transphrastic — that is, units of speech greater than the sentence, such as narrative — or they may be the social discourse of ritual, kinship rules, law.[1] Structuralism is seen by its literary practitioners as part of the more global enterprise of semiology or semiotics, conceived by the classic exponent of structural linguistics, Ferdinand de Saussure, as the general science of signifying systems, of which linguistics would be a part.[2]

By way of introduction to structuralist practice on the Bible, it would be well to briefly summarize the major elements of structuralist analysis. The first key principle is the arbitrary nature of the sign. There is no necessary relation of similarity between its two parts-in-relation, the signifier and the signified. The bond between the two elements is none other than the social convention according to which, for speakers of English, the sounds /tri/ conjure up the

1. For an account of "structuralism" in such diverse disciplines as mathematics, physics, and biology, as well as linguistics and psychology, see Jean Piaget, *Structuralism* (New York: Harper & Row, 1971).
2. See Saussure, *Course in General Linguistics* (New York: McGraw-Hill, 1966), p. 16. The series Approaches to Semiology, published by Mouton, has some thirty-odd volumes dealing with narrative, costume, psychiatry, and information theory.

Reprinted from *Interpretation* 28 (1974): 146-64.

mental image of a tree. The sign is the relation arising from the two parts, one of which, the signifier, is a sound-image, the other of which, the signified, is a mental image or concept.

Many of the remaining principles are conveniently arranged in dichotomies. These are language/speaking (*langue/parole*), diachrony/synchrony, and metaphor/metonymy.

Language is everything which is social about speech. "If we could embrace the sum of word-images stored in the minds of all individuals, we could identify the social bond that constitutes language (*la langue*)."[3] *Parole*, "speaking," is all that is individual in the particular utterance. By analogy with chess, *langue* is the set of rules, *parole* each move. Recent developments in cognate fields allow for some approximate equivalents. Thus code/message in computer work, and competence/performance in transformational linguistics describe more or less the same dichotomy.

Diachrony/synchrony is the distinction between a study oriented toward change or development over time and a study of the language state at any one time. Traditional philology and etymology are of course diachronic studies. The study of the sign at any given time, or of the relations among signs in a given language-state, is synchronic.

Any utterance is constructed along the principles of selection and combination (metaphor/metonymy). For each position in the phrase, there exists a class of potential substitutes united by a principle of *similarity*, while the words so chosen are united in a linear unit governed by *contiguity*. The class of potential words is a *paradigm*, "present" in a sense, in *absentia*. The utterance as realized along the linear chain is a *syntagm*. The paradigm is united by *metaphor*, the syntagm by *metonymy*.[4]

Linguists since Saussure have added two important concepts to his; these are metalanguage and the principle of the double articulation of language.

Broadly speaking, metalanguage is any statement of a second-order language whose signified or signifier is a sign of the first-order system. Thus if I say "*moron* means 'imbecile,'" my statement is meta-linguistic in that a sign (*moron*) becomes the concept (signified) of the second-order system. If I see the formula $e = Mc^2$ on the cover of a physics textbook, the formula, itself a sign, is also the signifier of a second-order meaning, "physics" or "science." A second-order statement may be a proposition or other complex sign—for example

3. Saussure, *Course in General Linguistics*, p. 13.
4. One indication of the widespread applicability of these terms can be seen in Frazer's twofold classification of magic as "contagious" and "sympathetic." Cf. the third essay in Freud's *Totem and Taboo*.

an advertisement bearing a photograph of a well-dressed person driving one or another car may carry a second-order meaning such as "Driving a cadillac is the prosperous thing to do."

The "double articulation" of language has been most clearly stated by the linguist André Martinet.[5] Human speech is composed of two distinct levels of articulation, first into *significant units* ("monemes," or words) and these significant units into purely *differential* units (phonemes, or sounds). Phonemes have no meaning in themselves; their purpose is only to be different from one another. Meaning arises from their combination into words. But there is a related question concerning articulation which must be dealt with in any structural analysis: How is the syntagm to be divided up for the purposes of analysis, and how, indeed, is the syntagm to be separated from the larger and ultimately infinite text of all speech? There are, in effect, two parallel undifferentiated entities, one of concepts of ideas (the signified), the other of sounds (signifiers). By relating one group of sounds to an idea, a certain area is delimited which gains its value precisely from its contrast to every other such "articulation." Barthes explains this concept by an example: there exists in nature the spectrum of light, which is a continuum — there is nothing in nature to define the point where yellow merges into green. Language, through the connection of signifiers with concepts, accomplishes this articulation into discontinuous units.[6]

It was by way of the Russian formalist studies into the interrelations between language and poetic process that the possible extension of means of linguistic analysis to other kinds of discourse was first suggested. Filipp Federovic Fortunatov, one of the founders of the Moscow linguistic school, seems to be the first to have articulated the view that language is not "a means for the expression of ready-made ideas" necessarily, but primarily "an implement for thinking."[7] "In a certain respect, the phenomena of language themselves appertain to the phenomena of thought."

With the migration to the West of Russian formalists following the Russian revolution, social scientists began to appreciate the range of formalist and structuralist approaches. In particular the French anthropologist Marcel Mauss, in his *Essai sur le don*,[8] first suggested that the rules governing the structure and exchange of

5. See Martinet, "Structure and Change," in *Structuralism*, ed. Jacques Ehrmann (Garden City, N.Y.: Doubleday, 1970).

6. See Roland Barthes, *Element of Semiology* (Boston: Beacon Press, 1970), pp. 56-57, 64-65.

7. Federov, cited by Roman Jakobson in vol. 2 of *Selected Writings* (The Hague: Mouton, 1971), pp. v, vi, 527-38.

8. One English translation is *The Gift*, trans. I. Cunnison (Glencoe, Ill.: Free Press, 1954).

messages within society might be applied to other key items of exchange, such as women and goods. It was presumably from his acquaintance first with the work of Mauss, and then with the Russian linguist Roman Jakobson, that Claude Lévi-Strauss came to apply structuralist methods to the analysis of kinship system and later so fruitfully to myth.

Virtually all the structuralist analysis of the Bible harks back to Lévi-Strauss's classic essay "The Structural Study of Myth."[9] An account of this essay should give a particularly clear view of the application of the principles of structuralist analysis introduced above.

Lévi-Strauss notes "the astounding similarity between myths collected in widely differing regions," despite the fact that the restrictions of everyday reality are relaxed in myth. This bears comparison with languages, which use much the same restricted body of phonemes yet differ vastly among themselves. Just as meaning arises in language from the combination of arbitrary phonemes, so it seems likely that meaning in myth ought to arise not from the intrinsic meaning of the actions, but from their combination.

But special procedures are called for, since myth is not merely language: it is something different which begins with language. The first approximation as to this difference may be seen in the special relations between *langue* and *parole* in myth. *Langue* belongs to reversible time (i.e., its nature is synchronic), while *parole* is necessarily bound to nonreversible time. Myth belongs to both aspects at once: it unites synchrony and diachrony in that it is told in past time and yet is felt to have a real effect on the present.

Now myth is composed of *actions*, with a determined similarity to one another: "myth is the part of language where the formula *traduttore, traditore* reaches its lowest truth value." The minimal units of articulation in myth, analogous to phonemes in speech, will be simple actions and relations. The minimum significant units, analogous to words, will be "bundles of such relations." The "bundles" amount to paradigms, of which the individual relations are related to one another by a principle of similarity.

It was inevitable that Lévi-Strauss's methods of analyzing myth should be applied to the Old Testament. The first such work was carried out by the English anthropologist Edmund Leach, whose essay in two versions, "Lévi-Strauss in the Garden of Eden,"[10] and "Genesis as Myth,"[11] is an attempt to provide a structuralist anal-

9. Lévi-Strauss, "The Structural Study of Myth," in *Structural Anthropology* (Garden City, N.Y.: Doubleday, 1967).

10. Leach, "Lévi-Strauss in the Garden of Eden," *Transactions of the New York Academy of Science*, 2d ser., 23 (1961): 386-96.

11. Leach, "Genesis as Myth," in *Genesis as Myth and Other Essays* (London: Jonathan Cape, 1969).

ysis of the early chapters of Genesis. Leach goes so far as to relate this analysis, quite validly, to communications theory, singling out the elements of *redundancy* and *binary opposition*. Redundancy arises from the fact that "all important stories recur in several versions." Binarism, which is "intrinsic to the process of human thought," is the discrimination of opposing categories which are mutually exclusive. The most important such oppositions in human experience are life/death, male/female, and perhaps for myth, human/divine. The value of redundancy is the correction of errors introduced through "noise," that is, those elements of a message which are accidental to meaning. Meaningful relations are distinguished from noise by their presence in a pattern observable through all the variants of the narrative.

The major problem for myths of origin is a "childish intellectual puzzle": there are those women of our kind with whom one must not have sexual relations (due to the incest taboo) and those of the other kind who are allowed. "If our first parents were persons of two kinds, what was that other kind? But if they were both of our kind, then their relations must have been incestuous and we are all born in sin." This to Leach is the central contradiction to be resolved in the Garden of Eden story and of similar myths in other cultures.

Leach provides an elaborate diagram intended to summarize the binary distinctions and mediations of the Creation myth, which following the principle of redundancy, appears in three permutations (the two Creation stories and the Cain-Abel sequence). Genesis 1 divides into two three-day periods, the first characterized by the creation of the static or "dead" world, the second by the creation of the moving, sexual, "live" world. Just as the static triad of grass, cereals, and fruit-trees is created on the third day, the triad of domestic and wild animals and creeping things appear on the sixth, "but only the grass is allocated to the animals. Everything else, including the meat of the animals, is for Man's use." Finally, man and woman are created simultaneously and commanded to be fruitful and multiply, "but the problems of Life versus Death, and Incest versus Procreation are not faced at all."

The Garden of Eden story then takes up the very problems left at the end of the first account. The creation of Eve is analogous to that of the creeping things in that both are anomalous, the creeping things to the other animals and Eve to the man/animal opposition. The serpent, a creeping thing, is mediator between man and woman. When the first pair eat the forbidden fruit, death and the capacity for procreation enter the world together.

The Cain and Abel story repeats the earlier oppositions: Abel, the herdsman, represents the living world; and Cain, the gardener, represents the static. Cain's fratricide is a reprise of Adam's incest, which Leach believes to be demonstrated by the similarity between God's questioning and cursing of Cain and the questioning and cursing of Adam, Eve, and the Serpent (it has "the same form and sequence"). Since the latter part of 3:26 is repeated exactly (according to Leach) in 4:7, "Cain's sin was not only fratricide but also incestuous homosexuality." Just as Adam must eliminate a sister in order to acquire a wife, so Cain must eliminate a brother.

Leach's work demands scrutiny both in terms of what it says and what it fails to say. I do not wish to call into question his application of structuralist principles, with the priority of synchronic analysis, but to point up some problems.

The whole question of text is a complicated one. Granted that for Leach's purpose a single text is taken as authoritative (in this instance the "English Authorized Version," i.e., the King James Bible of 1611), Leach still fails to do it justice. His claim that meat is given to man in 1:29, for example, is a misreading. The AV says, "Behold, I have given you every herb bearing seed, which is upon the face of all the earth, and every tree, in the which *is* the fruit of a tree yielding seed; to you it shall be for meat." The phrase "for meat" translates *l^eoklah*, which can only mean "for food" in contemporary English. But even the AV, in its own idiom, clearly means that both men and animals are to be restricted to a *vegetarian* diet. This is no small error, since questions of diet are central in a number of Genesis myths (if not in the myths of many nations) and naturally call for comparison with the meat diet first expressly permitted in the Noah sequence.

Leach introduces further problematic interpretations of the plain (or corrupt) meaning of the words in the text. God's questioning of Adam and Cain are very dubiously compared. The second of these is very difficult to decipher. Oesterley and Robinson point out that "readers of *Genesis* in Hebrew will know that this is somewhat in the nature of a paraphrase of an ungrammatical and untranslateable passage."[12]

Whatever the original meaning of 4:7, an interpretation of homosexual incest between the brothers based upon it seems weak indeed. It is of course possible to reverse the order of the argument and argue for such a meaning based on a structural pattern present throughout Genesis. Such an argument has merit, but Leach does not make it.

This point does however raise the whole question of text and translation in structuralist work. These seem to be separate though related issues. An examination of Hebrew myth cannot rest upon

12. W. O. E. Oesterley and T. H. Robinson, *Hebrew Religion: Its Origin and Development* (London: S.P.C.K., 1937), p. 116.

any particular translation. Sole reliance on the AV or the Revised Version can lead to valid discussion only of the point of view of King James' translation commission or the scholarship of Oxbridge dons of the last century. The critic, whoever he is and whatever his stance, needs a clean text.

And here a further difficulty arises, for we may well be at a loss to locate the Hebrew myth at all. In the welter of primary documents and conjectured subdocuments, whatever was in fact primary and mythic may well be obscured. By itself the documentary hypothesis need not invalidate a structuralist approach, which *seeks* repetitions, parallelisms, inversions — all possible variants of a myth — in order to establish the correlations and oppositions through which the structure may be read. But awareness of the two factors of multiple documents and sacredness of text leads to suspicion of the authenticity of any given text or reading.

This is because the myths before us are both *sacred* and *text*. The various mythological materials collected in the field by anthropologists (notably, of course, by Lévi-Strauss in his four volumes of *Mythologiques*)[13] must be properly distinguished from literary material. In effect, each report from a native informant *is* the myth. But a biblical myth is so much less the thing itself by virtue of its paradoxical fixity and fluidity. Once a myth is written down, it must cease to be the product of the unconscious generative force (question, contradiction, paradox, whatever) and becomes instead the report of that force acting upon given materials at one moment — though it enters the (written) culture as the myth itself. The assumption behind a Lévi-Straussian analysis must be that the audience of the myth is aware, if "unconsciously," of the permutations and transformations of the myth because they have heard some and will yet hear others. The individual narrative element (*parole*) has the living redundancy which at whatever level of articulation is the speaking sense of the story. Once it becomes a fixed and written part of the culture, the myth (now transformed into sacred history) must inevitably sacrifice much of that structure which becomes evident in the variations of repeated telling. In effect, the competency of the culture to state the myth (*langue*) and the performance (*parole*) become identified — and the generative power and meaning of the myth must together become moribund.

And fluidity of a sort arises from the sacred character of the text as well. Despite the Deuteronomic injunction (4:2), alterations have

13. The four volumes of *Mythologiques* are *Le cru et le cuit* (Paris: Plan, 1964; ET, *The Raw and the Cooked* [New York: Harper & Row, 1969]); *Du miel aux cendres* (Paris: Plan, 1966; ET, *From Honey to Ashes*, trans. John and Doreen Weightmann [New York: Harper & Row, 1973]); *L'origine des manieres de table* (Paris: Plan, 1968); and *L'homme nu* (Paris: Plan, 1971).

occurred for a variety of reasons, such as the scribal errors of hap-lography, dittography, or a scribal practice of *lectio difficilior*.

But more significant than the alteration of written material in the hands of scribes and revisers is the work of redaction, which may transform the material either through conscious or unconscious means. A myth, by virtue of its presence in a written text, may enter into dialectical relations of a sort with other material whose conti-guity to it in scroll or codex is strictly contingent. It may also, of course, have been affected by a dialectical process with other non-preserved texts from its own culture area. The work of the redactor may advance this process by his attempt to harmonize originally disparate works reflecting etiological tales, true history, and pristine myth. He may wish to propagandize for religious doctrine, he may suppress material which is apparently contradictory on the syntag-matic plane, or he may unite conflicting material by means of new additions or suppression of old, all in the interests of one or another aesthetic end. In any case his work could well, like that of a careless archeologist, obscure or destroy what it most wishes to preserve. His intrusion of conscious material may serve to destroy the uncon-scious logic and coherence of which he is most likely unaware.

Considerations similar to these were raised in a fascinating col-loquy between Paul Ricoeur and others on the one hand and Lévi-Strauss on the other which appeared in the November 1963 issue of the French journal *Ésprit*. Here Ricoeur and Lévi-Strauss show some agreement in doubting the applicability of a structuralist analysis to the Bible. For Ricoeur, following Von Rad, the significant content of the Hexateuch is the "declaration of the great deeds of the Lord." "The method of comprehension applicable to this network of events consists in restoring the *intellectual working-out*, the result of this his-torical faith set out in a confessional framework." Consequently, in the Old Testament "we are faced with an historical interpretation of the historical. . . . The tradition corrects itself by additions, and it is these additions which themselves constitute a theological di-alectic." Lévi-Strauss, citing the early work of Leach, largely agrees "because of scruples which join with those of M. Ricoeur. First be-cause the Old Testament, which certainly does make use of mythic materials, takes them up with a view to a different end from their original one. . . . The myths have then been subjected, as M. Ricoeur well says, to an intellectual operation." Further, symbols, whose meaning is only "by position," can only be understood "by reference to the ethnographic context" which "is almost entirely lacking."

Leach discusses these matters briefly in an essay entitled "The Legitimacy of Solomon." His disagreement with Lévi-Strauss is based on the contradictory nature of Lévi-Strauss's doubts; he has no qualms, for one thing, about applying structuralist principles to

South American Indians, "peoples of whom our ethnographic evidence is sketchy to say the least."

But even in the comparative lack of other ethnographic data, the successive reinterpretations of the same material amount to an ethnographic datum par excellence. The difference is that the informants are oriented diachronically, across time rather than across space. But beyond all this, the goals of a structuralist/semiological analysis need not be the same as those of an anthropologist at work on traditional society.

For better or worse, structuralist work on the Bible starts with a text conceived as a synchronous whole. In this fact we have a definite parting of the ways with other and more traditional modes of biblical interpretation. The object of study differs: it is now to be biblical text as it entered the culture of the West. While such analysis might conceivably yield information about the prehistory of the text, such information is necessarily secondary to the kind of information provided by the text as a given whole. The object of study then changes from the textual and cultural processes, which gave to the text, to the structure of the text as it enters the cultural life of the West. It may well have been the hope and intention of biblical scholars of the past century to reveal the secrets of the text by exposing the history behind it. While such textual study has been elaborate and refined, the text still preserves a good many secrets. While I am not certain how many further secrets will be exposed by structuralist methods, I think the very conditions of the obscurity of certain texts will be explained.

For the question arises precisely where to locate the structures which a structuralist analysis brings to light. Taking the linguistic definition (one of many similar definitions) that a structure is "a whole formed of mutually dependent elements, such that each depends on the others and can only be what it is by its relationship with them,"[14] what can we say about the *source* of that structure in our biblical text, particularly in light of the heterogeneous sources of that text? Is the structure present in the first composition, or first writing? Is it a product of the mind of the first author or of his culture? If so, can we guarantee that the narrative structure of Genesis 1 will be similar to that of Genesis 2 or Genesis 4? Will the structure of Mark be that of Matthew or of Luke? Or is it something present in the mind of the reader—not then a rule of composition but a rule of reading? Or does it have yet some third kind of existence?

For Lévi-Strauss, the source of this structure seems to have changed. Early in his work on myth he seems to believe in the

---

14. Émile Benveniste, *Problems in General Linguistics*, trans. M. E. Meek (Coral Gables: University of Miami Press, 1971), p. 82.

objective presence of structure governing the elaboration of discourse: it is present in the writing, and open to decipherment in the reading.[15] But later in his work Lévi-Strauss posits an *esprit* which, according to Leach, "appears as part of an extremely involved interchange relationship in which it is the casual [*sic*; causal?] force producing myths of which its own structure is a precipitate."[16] I do not feel at the same loss which Leach claims to feel in understanding this term, but I do recognize a reasonable doubt as to its existence except at the highest reaches of abstraction, in which case it is clearly an a posteriori construct, the "mind" posited behind the total cultural product. The *esprit* of a culture may be identified with the set of implied rules which govern its discourse in all possible modes. It does seem a bit contradictory that so materially based an approach as structuralism should generate so ideal a concept. But taken as the potential formalized model of the organization of discourse, it is worth seeking—and where better to seek such a spirit than in the very interplay of successive interpretations of "the great deeds of the Lord" provided the modern world by the Bible?

Finally, we need not unduly bother about the "intellectual distortion" introduced by successive interpreters of the same mythic material. Each naive telling of the myth is equally a "distortion" because of the contingencies of individual variation—each telling will be skewed in terms of the situation which calls it forth. Even the attempt at editing need not necessarily interfere with the operation of structural rules if they are indeed the expression of the *esprit* of a culture. The editor or reviser is aware of the content of what he wishes to change in the text; he is as unconscious as the first teller of the pristine myth of the structure of his story. We ought to find the structure repeated no less in the intrusion than in the original. All we need are the analytical tools.

As noted early in this essay, structuralist methodology is still very much in the process of "speaking itself," and that rather self-consciously. One has the impression that there is a greater fascination among structuralists and semioticians with the development of the theory than with practical applications. This theoretical self-centeredness may be due to an aspiration inherited from Lévi-Strauss, the aspiration of ultimately describing the structure of mind through an account of symbolic processes. If this is so, then the goal of analysis is as much to reflect upon the development of theoretical as practical results. In any event, there has developed a kind of canonical form of structuralist exposé, somewhat along the lines of Lévi-Strauss's Oedipus essay: the methodical and theoretical con-

15. Lévi-Strauss, *Structural Anthropology*, p. 272.
16. See Leach, *Genesis as Myth and Other Essays*, p. 25.

siderations are first laid out, a morphological discussion follows, and the morphology leads to a semantic statement.

One thing is clear about the work of structuralists on the Bible that radically distinguishes it from previous scholarship: the focus of attention shifts from questions of document, composition, and *kerygma* to those of "reading" (*lecture*), text, and signification. These will be the issues of method and theory which we will see discussed by such structuralist researchers as Roland Barthes, Claude Chabrol, and Louis Marin. A glance at the footnotes will show that many of these essays appear together in a number of journals. As Chabrol points out, "plurality is a necessity for [semiotic analysis] and its reading of texts is always 'with several voices.' " The idea is to bring together a body of work by different scholars on similar texts and then advance the constitution of the theory by the observation of separate analyses based upon similar principles.

The French critic Roland Barthes occupies a position of considerable prominence in French intellectual life as the main force behind the journal *Tel Quel,* and as the author of works of cultural criticism and literary theory. His contributions to the analysis of the Bible are presented as applications of his work on theory of narrative. What is most interesting about his two essays on the Bible is the considerable distance between the claims he makes for his standpoint and the practice he carries out. This is perhaps truer of the later work "La lutte avec l'ange,"[17] a "textual" analysis of Genesis 32:23-32, which appears in a work intended to present for comparison the work of two "structuralists" and two exegetes.

Barthes introduces a refinement on the traditional structuralist analysis, introducing an approach he calls "textual" but which has little to do with traditional textual approaches. Text is defined for Barthes as "a production of significance and not at all as a philological object."[18] The text takes part in an "open network, which is the very infinitude of language." The goal of such study is not to determine where the text comes from or how it is made, but "how it undoes itself, breaks open, disseminates: according to what coded paths it *goes on its way.*"[19]

In one sense Barthes seems to be calling for most extreme arbitrariness of interpretation, and on the other hand to be suggesting no more than the inevitable consequence of a synchronic approach. Leaving aside the colorful language with which he characterizes his

17. Barthes, "La lutte avec l'ange," in *Analyse structurale et exégèse biblique,* ed. F. Bovon (Neuchâtel: Delachaux et Niestlé, 1971).

18. The original reads *"texte,* qui doit être entendu comme production de signifiance et pas du tout comme object philologique" ("La lutte avec l'ange," p. 28).

19. The original reads "comment il se défait, explose, dissémine: selon quelles avenues codées it *s'en va"* ("La lutte avec l'ange," p. 28).

method, he invites us to determine what relations the text establishes, what its rules of organization may be, how it *allows* for meaning—all of these part of the common aspiration of the structuralist school. Presumably an examination of a given text as one utterance (*parole*) governed by a code (*langue*) will lead to reflection upon the nature of those rules and consequently to the goals of structuralist analysis: formalized, exhaustive, and simple statements of the nonconscious determination of the text.

Barthes's major contribution is his pointing up of the range of ambiguity and paradox in the "struggle with the angel" story. First of all, the story of the passage over the Jabbok may be taken two ways: Jacob either crosses the ford or he does not. "If Jacob remains alone *before* having crossed the Jabbok, we are drawn toward a 'folkloristic' reading," the testing of the hero before he can cross an obstacle. If Jacob remains alone *after* having crossed over, the "passage is without structural finality, but on the other hand acquires a religious finality." Jacob is then marked by solitude. The location of the struggle is ambiguous in an equivalent way: "Passage over the Jordan would be more comprehensible than passage over the Jabbok; we find ourselves, in sum, before the passage of a neutral place." While the exegete must reach a conclusion about the intention of the text, the "textual" analyst will "relish this sort of *friction* between two ways of understanding."

In his earlier work on Acts, Barthes had suggested that "the proper narrative analyst must have a sort of imagination of the *counter-text*, an imagination of the aberration of the text, of what is scandalous in a narrative sense."[20] In connection with the struggle at the ford, Barthes carries out an imagination of such a countertext: he invites us to consider a nonparadoxical battle. If A fights B and must win at whatever cost, he may deal a low blow. In the logic of the narrative this should bring about A's victory. "The mark of which the blow is structurally the object cannot be reconciled with its ineffectiveness"—that is, it must work. But, paradoxically, the low blow fails, the adversary is not victorious; he is subject to an unannounced rule: he must depart at dawn. In two senses, then, the struggle marks one of the combatants: he is physically marked (he limps afterward), and he is also marked as the bearer of an illogical disequilibrium. This disequilibrium may be related to the disequilibrium of Jacob vis-à-vis Esau. The generational equilibrium of brothers is conventionally upset by the preference given the elder. But in the case of the sons of Isaac, it is the younger who upsets the arrangement by carrying off the ancestral blessing. In the struggle

20. Barthes, in "L'analyse structurale due récit: à propos d'Actes x-xi," *Recherches de science religieuse* 58 (1970): 17-37.

in the passage, "the conflict with Esau is *displaced* (every symbol is a *displacement*)." Barthes might have carried the pattern further and developed an extratextual correlation with other instances of such fraternal disequilibrium: Isaac/Ishmael, Ephraim/Manasseh, Zerah/Perez, Joseph/his brothers.

Barthes applies a second formal pattern to his brief narrative, the actantial model of A. J. Greimas.[21] Greimas posits six formal classes of "actants" — three pairs of narrative positions or statuses which the characters in a narrative may occupy. These are subject/object (the one who must carry out a task or quest and the goal of his action), destinator/destinee (the one who sets the task for the subject and the one for whose benefit the destinator sets the task), and adversary/helper. Note that in this scheme the parts are distributed as follows:

Subject: Jacob   *Destinator:* God   *Adversary:* God
Object: passage   *Destinee:* Jacob   *Helper:* Jacob.

There is no particular ambiguity in Jacob's having the actantial status of subject and destinee, nor even in his being his own helper. But it is extremely odd that the destinator and adversary should be the same person. Barthes sees only one kind of story which properly uses this paradoxical scheme: blackmail. He might well have added a class of stories in which the destinator *wants* the hero to succeed in the task he sets him but makes the task more difficult in order better to point up the hero's virtue.

The programmatic statements in "problèmes de la sémiologie narrative des récits bibliques"[22] show Claude Chabrol's adherence to much the same views as Barthes's. But Chabrol's reflections on the central problems raised at various points in this essay offer some progress toward a resolution, less in answering doubts than in creating a more fully coherent program. The reading (*lecture*) of a text amounts to the constitution of a new object, composed of text and reader and not identical with either one. "To read is always to destroy [*perdre*] the text and the meaning, and this definitively. In place of this destroyed text and meaning, there is constituted a 'subject wishing to know' whose quest is not an object but a desire . . . which creates this particular relation of interlocution from which the reading is taken up . . . a creation interior to the text which articulates the connection which establishes a 'textual' narrator and reader."

Meaning (*sens*) had been to Barthes, "any type of correlation,

---

21. See Griemas, *Sémantique structurale* (Paris: Larousse, 1966), pp. 172-91.
22. Chabrol, "Problèmes de la sémiologie narrative des récits bibliques," *Langages* 22 (June 1971): 3-12.

intertextual or extratextual, that is to say, any trait of a narrative which refers to another element of the narrative or to another locus of the culture necessary to read the narrative."[23] To Chabrol, meaning "is not *behind* the text; it is the system of rules which permits the engenderment of the differential interplay of oppositions which governs my reading the length of an 'infinite' text of which the text I read is only a contingent and limited — which is to say historical — actualization." There is no "hidden signified," but rather the hidden signifier, which is a "network of correlations." Instead of the notion of a "final signified" of the biblical text, there is the statement of the order which produces the infinite set of cross-references between signifiers and signifieds within and beyond the portion of text to be analyzed.

Chabrol's essay "Analyse du 'texte' de la Passion"[24] does make a major contribution to understanding the *meaning* of the biblical text, even while remaining true to the program of demonstrating the *functioning* of the text. The essay posits an "operational model" of the text, taking the three Gospel accounts of the passion as three variants of a single "meta-text." Chabrol then sets out to establish "the semantic universe which underlies the text" by comparing the three Synoptic accounts, among themselves and with the Peter and Cornelius episode in Acts. The object of the Cornelius episode is "beyond the reduction of the geographic distance, the abolition of 'distance' between Judaism and Otherness." Observe the stories of healing of the Centurion's servant and the daughter of the Canaanite woman, along with the Peter/Cornelius episode.

1. Jesus goes toward the foreign province/ /but does not enter it.
2. Jesus goes toward the foreign house/ /but does not enter it.
3. The pagan woman leaves her territory/ /and enters Galilee.
4. The Centurion leaves his house/ /and goes toward Jesus.
5. Peter goes toward the foreign province/ /and enters it.
6. Peter goes toward the foreign house/ /and enters it.
7. The Centurion does not leave his province/ /he remains in the foreign country.
8. His representatives go alone to Judea to bring Peter back.

In the case of Peter, a certain negation of the separation between the worlds of "identity" and "otherness" takes place. This is related to the various indications in the New Testament that Jesus and his followers committed *minor* infractions of the ritual prescriptions, such as eating without washing of hands, eating with sinners, not

23. Barthes, "L'analyse structurale due récit: à propos d'Actes x-xi," p. 21.
24. Chabrol, "Analyse du 'texte' de la Passion," *Langages* 22 (June 1971): 75-96.

fasting. The text thus sets up both a homology, Identity: Purity :
: Otherness : Impurity, and the beginning of the mediation of the
opposition. Jesus carries out a "nondistantiation" by approaching
the foreign territory and by healing (at a distance) the daughter of
the Canaanite. He does not affirm the opposite pole of "distantia-
tion," proximization, but he does in some way deny the distance.
Each of these semantic distinctions (purity/impurity, dis-
tance/proximity) is mediated, placing Jesus in a "neutral" position neither proximate nor distant, neither ritually pure nor impure,
and ultimately in the position of "communal indifferentiation." A
new turn is created, as expressed in Peter's declaration that "of a
truth God is no respecter of persons. But in every nation he that
feareth him . . . is accepted," and this new term must be something
like "universalism," however different from the "hierarchical" universalism of Old Testament eschatology.

   I must confess I feel myself at a loss before the work of Louis
Marin, the most subtle, rich, and complex of the struc-
turalists/semioticians who have published on the Bible. I very
much hope his work finds an adequate translator soon. The best I
can offer is a brief summary and paraphrase of a small part of his
already quite large body of analytical work.[25]

   Much of Marin's work is concerned with questions of communication as represented within the text. He has concerned himself
with parable and other forms of narrative in which questions of the
embedding of one narrative within another appear, with questions
of communications in the larger sense not only of messages but of
spirit in terms of hospitality, with the relations between locutionary
forces in language, and between silence and speech. At the same
time his methodological observations are the most extended and the
most clear.

   Since the text is defined "not in the irreversible temporality of *a*
meaning (direction and signification) but like a network of tangled
relations, with reversible orientation,"[26] it demands a *lecteur attentif*,
particularly since the biblical text makes efforts to define its own
reading (by means of the metalinguistic fragments Marin examines).
"By *'lecteur attentif'* I mean one who refuses the naivete of the simple
route of reading the thread of the text, one who interrogates the

   25. Marin's work on the Bible includes "Essai d'analyse structurale d'Actes 10,
1-11, 18," *Recherches de science religieuse* 58 (Jan.-March 1970); "Essai de'analyse structurale d'um récit-parabole: Matthieu 13, 1-23," *Etudes Theologigues et Réligieuses* 46
(1971); "En guise de conclusion," *Langages* 22 (1971); "Les femmes au tombeau,"
Langages 22 (1971); "Du corps au texte," *Esprit* (April 1973); and, with Claude
Chabrol, *Le récit évangelique* (Paris: BSR, 1973).
   26. See Marin, "Essai de'analyse structurale d'um recitparabole: Matthieu 13,
1-23," p. 40.

text, which is to say rereads it, and in this rereading, works it out—
makes it work—who consequently accepts the task of listening to
the relations and the multiple echoes which guide him to the depths
where, it seems, what he had read the first time is dismembered and
rebuilt without ever being resolved." "Still, the reading is a construction of the object, and as such, is at the same time regressive
and progressive—constitutive."[27] A text "*provokes* correlations between elements and totality, (and) this provocation, at the level of
each text, unveils its rules of reading." But at the same time the
text's *infinitization,* its relentless intertextuality, defines the principle
of incertitude of reading. "As much as reading [*lecture*] adds signified
by an articulation of the signifier of the text different from that which
the text lays claims to, by just so much the text harbors signified at
another point on its surface. Incertitude means the impossibility of
stopping this movement between signified and signifier, a movement
which *is* the reading, and whose exemplary form the text gives us
in the parable."

In his essay "The Women at the Tomb,"[28] Marin offers a structural analysis based on the Greimas "actantial model." The overall
model for the Passion may be diagrammed as follows:

Destinator: God ⟶ *Object:* The Gospel ⟵ *Destinee:* Mankind
                              Life Eternal
                                  ↑
Adversaries: High Priests, ⟶ *Subject:* Jesus ⟵ *Helpers:* Disciples,
       Elders, Judas   Women

What is significant is that the recognition of Jesus as risen is only
effective when performed by the community. All the recognitions by
individuals fail or are incomplete. When the women come to the
tomb, their actantial "object," the focus of their desire, is the body
of the crucified Jesus. But in place of the object they seek they find
the Angel, the bearer of the message "Jesus is risen." The women
intend to look after a dead body; their relation with the hero is
individual and passive. This double relation is opposed to (1) the
recognition that the hero is indeed alive and (2) the recognition of
the hero in the community of disciples. "This double opposition is
a modulation of the two great profound semic categories: life/death,
individual/society."

At the tomb, they find the annulment of their desire and its satisfaction in one. It is the verification of the earlier prophetic utterance of Jesus: "He is not here, for he is risen, as he said." "The
prophetic word, recalled and verified in the form of a quotation by

27. Marin, "En guise de conclusion," p. 120.
28. Marin, "Les femmes au tombeau," pp. 39-50.

the angel, makes disappear the body of the crucified." When the angel tells the women, "tell his disciples that he is risen from the dead: and behold, he goeth before you into Galilee: there shall you see him," his statement is both *factum* and *dictum*. Just as the fact of the absent body becomes something said ("I tell you I shall rise"), this second statement, by the speech-act of the angel, becomes fact ("You shall see him").

Thus there is, within a narrative centered on an occurrence, a discourse which speaks of a *thing*, there appears another discourse "centered upon itself and its texture . . . upon its own communication, its own transmission. It is that exceptional moment in the narrative where things, the referent, the body, are effaced and absent, and where, in their place, there appears words, messages — in brief, where words become things."

THE INTERPRETED WORD: REFLECTIONS ON CONTEXTUAL HERMENEUTICS

C. RENÉ PADILLA

The Word of God was given to bring the lives of God's people into conformity with the will of God. Between the written word and its appropriation by believers lies the process of interpretation, or *hermeneutics*. For each of us, the process of arriving at the meaning of Scripture is not only highly shaped by who we are as individuals but also by various social forces, patterns, and ideals of our particular culture and our particular historical situation. (*Culture* is used in this paper in a comprehensive way to include not only technical skills, lifestyle, attitudes, and values of people, but also their thought patterns, cognitive processes, and ways of learning, all of which ultimately express a religious commitment.)

One of the most common approaches to interpretation is what may be called the *intuitive* approach. This approach, with its emphasis on immediate personal application, is found in many of the older commentaries and in contemporary popular preaching and devotional literature.

In contrast to this is the *scientific* approach, which employs the tools of literary criticism, historical and anthropological studies, linguistics, and the like. It is adopted by a large majority of biblical scholars, and by Christians interested in serious Bible study. It appreciates the need for understanding the original context. But like the intuitive approach, it may not be sensitive to contemporary social, economic, and political factors and cultural forces that affect the interpretive process.

A third approach is the *contextual* approach. Combining the strengths of the intuitive and scientific methods, it recognizes both the role of the ancient world in shaping the original text and the role of today's world in conditioning the way contemporary readers are likely to "hear" and understand the text.

The Word of God originated in a particular historical context—

Reprinted from *Themelios*, September 1981, pp. 18-23.

the Hebrew and Greco-Roman world. Indeed, the Word can be understood and appropriated only as it becomes "flesh" in a specific historical situation with all its particular cultural forms. The challenge of hermeneutics is to transpose the message from its original historical context into the context of present-day readers so as to produce the same kind of impact on their lives as it did on the original hearers or readers.

Thus, hermeneutics and the historical context are strongly linked. Without a sufficient awareness of the historical factors, the faith of the hearers of the gospel will tend to degenerate into a "culture-Christianity" which serves unredeemed cultural forces rather than the living God. The confusion of the gospel with "culture-Christianity" has been frequent in Western-based missionary work and is one of the greatest problems affecting the worldwide church today. The solution can come only through a recognition of the role that the historical context plays in both the understanding and communication of the biblical message.

TRADITIONAL HERMENEUTICS

The unspoken assumption of the *intuitive model* is that the situation of the contemporary reader largely coincides with the situation represented by the original text. The process of interpretation is thought to be rather straightforward and direct (see Diagram 1).

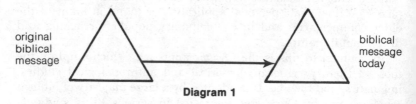

original
biblical
message

biblical
message
today

Diagram 1

This approach brings out three elements essential to sound biblical hermeneutics. First, it clearly assumes that Scripture is meant for ordinary people and is not the domain of trained theologians only. (Was it not the rediscovery of this truth that led the sixteenth-century reformers to translate and circulate the Bible in the vernacular?) Second, it highlights the role of the Holy Spirit in illuminating the meaning of the Scripture for the believer. Third, it emphasizes that the purpose of Scripture is not merely to lead readers to an intellectual apprehension of truth but to elicit a conscious submission to the Word of God speaking in Scripture. These elements are of particular importance at a time when, as Robert J. Blaikie protests, "only as mediated through the scholarly priesthood of 'Biblical

Critics' can ordinary people receive the truth of God's Word from
the Bible."[1]

On the other hand, the intuitive approach can easily lead to
allegorizations in which the original meaning of the text is lost.
Someone has said that allegory is the son of piety. The fantastic
interpretations by such reputable theologians as Origen and Augustine, Luther and Calvin, are more or less sophisticated illustrations of a piety-inspired approach to the Bible. The question to be
posed to this approach is whether the appropriation of the biblical
message is possible without doing violence to the text.

The *scientific approach* also has its merits and defects. Anyone with
even a superficial understanding of the role of history in shaping the
biblical revelation will appreciate the importance of linguistic and
historical studies for the interpretation of Scripture. The raw material of theology is not abstract, timeless concepts which may be
simply lifted out of Scripture but rather a message embedded in
historical events and the linguistic and cultural backgrounds of the
biblical authors. One of the basic tasks of interpretation therefore
is the construction of a bridge between the modern readers or hearers and the biblical authors by means of the historical method. Thus,
the *Sitz im Leben* of the biblical authors can be reconstructed, and
the interpreters, by means of grammatico-historical exegesis, can
extract those normative (though not exhaustive) and universal elements which the ancient text conveys. This view of the interpretive
process is represented in Diagram 2.

This approach throws into relief the historical nature of biblical
revelation. In a way, it widens the gulf between the Bible and modern readers or hearers. In so doing, however, it witnesses to the fact
that the Word of God today has to do with the Word of God which
was spoken in ancient times by the prophets and apostles. Unless

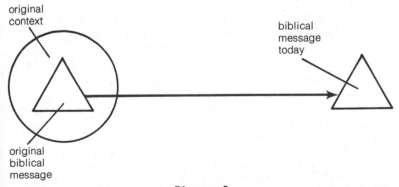

Diagram 2

modern interpreters allow the text to speak out of its original situation, they have no basis for claiming that their message is continuous with the message recorded in Scripture.

The problem with the scientific approach is, first, that it assumes that the hermeneutical task can be limited to defining the original meaning of the text, leaving to others its present application. Second, it assumes that the interpreters can achieve an "objectivity" which is in fact neither possible nor desirable. It is not possible, because contemporary interpreters are stamped with the imprint of their particular time and place as surely as is the ancient text, and therefore they inevitably come to the text with historically conditioned presuppositions that color their exegesis. It is not desirable, because the Bible can be properly understood only as it is read with a *participatory involvement* and allowed to speak into one's own situation. Ultimately, if the text written in the past does not strike home in the present, it has not been understood.

THE CONTEXTUAL APPROACH AND THE HERMENEUTICAL CIRCLE

How can the chasm between the past and the present be bridged? An answer is found in the *contextual approach*, which combines insights derived from classical hermeneutics with insights derived from the modern hermeneutical debate.

In the contextual approach both the context of the ancient text and the context of the modern reader are given due weight (see Diagram 3).

The diagram emphasizes the importance of culture to the biblical message in both its original and contemporary forms. That is, there is no such thing as a biblical message detached from a particular cultural context.

However, contrary to the diagram, the interpretive process is not a simple one-way process. For whenever interpreters approach a particular biblical text they can do so only from their own perspective. This gives rise to a complex, dynamic two-way interpretive process depicted as a "hermeneutical circle," in which interpreters and text are mutually engaged. The dynamic interplay will be seen more clearly if we first examine the four elements of the circle: (1) the interpreter's historical situation; (2) the interpreter's world-and-life view; (3) Scripture; and (4) theology.

1. Blaikie, *Secular Christianity and the God Who Acts* (London: Hodder & Stoughton, 1970), p. 27.

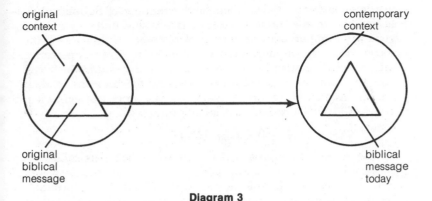

Diagram 3

1. The Interpreter's Historical Situation

Interpreters do not live in a vacuum. They live in concrete historical situations, in particular cultures. From their cultures they derive not only their language but also patterns of thought and conduct, methods of learning, emotional reactions, values, interests, and goals. If God's Word is to reach them, it must do so in terms of their own culture or not at all.

This is clear from the Incarnation itself. God did not reveal himself by shouting from heaven but by speaking from within a concrete human situation: he became present as a man among men in Jesus, a first-century Jew! This unmistakably demonstrates God's intention to make his Word known from within a concrete human situation. No culture as a whole reflects the purpose of God; in all cultures there are elements which conspire against the understanding of God's Word. If this is recognized, it follows that every interpretation is subject to correction and refinement; there is always a need for safeguards against syncretism—that is, cultural distortions of the Word of God. Syncretism occurs whenever there is accommodation of the gospel to premises or values prevalent in the culture which are incongruent with the biblical message.

On the other hand, every culture possesses positive elements, favorable to the understanding of the gospel. This makes possible a certain approach to Scripture which brings to light certain aspects of the message which in other cultures remain less visible or even hidden. The same cultural differences that hinder intercultural communication turn out to be an asset to the understanding of the many-sided wisdom of God; they serve as channels to aspects of God's Word which can be best seen from within a particular context.

Thus, the hermeneutical task requires an understanding of the concrete situation as much as an understanding of Scripture. No transposition of the biblical message is possible unless the interpreters are familiar with the frame of reference within which the message is to become meaningful. There is, therefore, a place for auxiliary sciences such as sociology and anthropology which can enable interpreters to define more precisely the horizons of their situation, even as linguistics, literature, and history can help them in their study of the text and its original context.

2. The Interpreter's World-and-Life View

Interpreters tend to approach Scripture from their particular perspectives. They have their own world-and-life view, their own way of apprehending reality. This imposes certain limits but also enables them to see reality as a coherent whole. Whether or not they are conscious of it, this world-and-life view, which is religiously determined, lies behind all their activities and colors their understanding of reality in a definite way. We can extend this observation to biblical hermeneutics and say that every interpretation of the text implies a world-and-life view.

Western theology generally has been unaware of the extent to which it is affected by the materialistic and mechanistic world-and-life view. It is only natural, for instance, that those who accept the modern "scientific" view — which assumes a closed universe where everything can be explained on the basis of natural causes — will have difficulty taking the Bible at face value whenever it points to a spirit world or to miracles. Western theology, therefore, greatly needs the corrective provided by Scripture in its emphasis on a personal Creator who acts purposefully in and through history; on creation as totally dependent upon God; on man as the "image of God," affected by sin and redemption. Such elements are the substance of the biblical world-and-life view apart from which there can be no proper understanding either of reality or of Scripture. It may well be that what prevents Westerners from entering into the "strange world of the Bible" is not its obsolete world-and-life view but their own secularistic and unwarranted assumption with regard to the powers of reason!

3. Scripture

Hermeneutics has to do with a dialogue between Scripture and the contemporary historical context. Its purpose is to transpose the biblical message from its original context into a particular twentieth-century situation. Its basic assumption is that the God who spoke in the past and whose Word was recorded in the Bible continues to speak today to all mankind in Scripture.

Although the illumination of the Spirit is indispensable in the

interpretive process, from one point of view the Bible must be read
"like any other book." This means that the interpreters have to take
seriously that they face an ancient text with its own historical horizons. Their task is to let the text speak, whether they agree with
it or not, and this demands that they understand what the text
meant in its original situation. In James Smart's words,

> All interpretation must have as its first step the hearing of the text
> with exactly the shade of meaning that it had when it was first spoken
> or written. First the words must be allowed to have the distinctive
> meaning that their author placed upon them, being read within the
> context of his other words. Then each word has to be studied in the
> context of the time in order to determine . . . what meaning it would
> have for those to whom it was addressed. . . . The religious, cultural
> and social background is of the greatest importance in penetrating
> through the words to the mind of the author. . . . The omission of any
> of these disciplines is a sign of lack of respect not only for the text
> and its author, but also for the subject matter with which it deals.[2]

It has been argued, however, that the approach described in this
quotation, known as the grammatico-historical approach, is itself
typically Western and consequently not binding upon non-Western
cultures. What are we to say to this?

First, no interpreters, regardless of their culture, are free to make
the text say whatever they want it to say. Their task is to let the
text speak for itself, and to that end they inevitably have to engage
with the horizons of the text via literary context, grammar, history,
and so on.

Second, Western theology has not been characterized by a consistent use of the grammatico-historical approach in order to let the
Bible speak. Rather a dogmatic approach has been the dominating
factor, by which competing theological systems have muted Scripture. Abstract conceptualization patterned on Greek philosophy has
gone hand in hand with allegorizations and typologies. Even sophisticated theologians, losing sight of the historical nature of revelation, have produced capricious literary or homiletical exercises.

Third, some point to the New Testament use of the Old as legi-
timizing intuitive approaches and minimizing the importance of the
grammatico-historical approach. But it can hardly be claimed that
the New Testament writers were not interested in the natural sense
of Old Testament Scripture. There is little basis for the idea that
the New Testament specializes in highly imaginative exegesis, similar to that of rabbinic Judaism. Even in Paul's case, despite his

2. Smart, *The Interpretation of Scripture* (London: SCM Press, 1961), p. 33.

rabbinic training, there is great restraint in the use of allegory. As James Smart has put it, "The removal of all instances of allegory from his [Paul's] writings would not change the structure of his theology. This surely is the decisive test."[3]

The effort to let Scripture speak without imposing on it a ready-made interpretation is a hermeneutical task binding upon all inter-preters, whatever their culture. Unless objectivity is set as a goal, the whole interpretive process is condemned to failure from the start.

Objectivity, however, must not be confused with neutrality. To read the Bible "like any other book" is not only to take seriously the literary and historical aspects of Scripture but also to read it from the perspective of faith. Since the Bible was written that God may speak in and through it, it follows that the Bible should be read with an attitude of openness to God's Word, with a view to conscientious response. The understanding and appropriation of the biblical message are two aspects of an indivisible whole — the *comprehension* of the Word of God.

4. Theology

Theology cannot be reduced to the repetition of doctrinal formu-lations borrowed from other latitudes. To be valid and appropriate, it must reflect the merging of the horizons of the historical situation and the horizons of the text. It will be relevant to the extent that it is expressed in symbols and thought forms which are part of the culture to which it is addressed, and to the extent that it responds to the questions and concerns with are raised in that context. It will be faithful to the Word of God to the extent that it is based on Scripture and demonstrates the Spirit-given power to accomplish God's purpose. The same Spirit who inspired Scripture in the past is active today to make it God's personal Word in a concrete his-torical situation.

Daniel von Allmen has suggested that the pages of the New Tes-tament itself bear witness to this process, as the early Christians, dispersed by persecution from Palestine, "undertook the work of evangelism and tackled the Greeks on their own ground. It was they who, on the one hand, began to adapt into Greek the tradition that gave birth to the Gospels, and who, on the other hand, preached the good news for the first time in Greek."[4] They did not consciously set out to "do theology" but simply to faithfully transcribe the gospel into pagan contexts. Greek-speaking Christian poets then gave

3. Smart, *The Interpretation of Scripture*, p. 30.
4. Von Allmen, "The Birth of Theology," *International Review of Mission*, January 1975.

expression to the faith received not in a systematically worked theology but by singing the work which God had done for them. According to von Allmen, this is the origin of a number of hymns quoted by the New Testament writers, particularly the one in Philippians 2:6-11. The theologians ensured that this new way of expressing the faith corresponded to apostolic doctrine and showed that all theological statements must be set in relation to the heart of the Christian faith — that is, the universal lordship of Jesus Christ.

In other words, the driving force in the contextualization of the gospel in apostolic times was the primitive church's obedience to God's call to mission. What is needed today, says von Allmen, is missionaries like the hellenists, who "did not set out with a theological intention," and poets like the authors of the hymns quoted in the New Testament, who "were not deliberately looking for an original expression of their faith," and theologians like Paul, who did not set out to "do theology." Von Allmen concludes, "the only object of research which is allowed, and indeed commended, is the kingdom of God in Jesus Christ (cf. Mt. 6:33). And theology, with all other things, will be added unto us."

I would also add that neither the proclamation of the gospel nor the worship of God is possible without "theology," however unsystematic and implicit it may be. In other words, the hellenistic missionaries and poets were *also theologians* — certainly not dogmaticians, but proclaimers and singers of a living theology through which they expressed the Word of God in a new cultural context. With this qualification, von Allmen's conclusion stands: the way in which Christianity was communicated in the first century sets the pattern for producing contextualized theology today.

DYNAMICS OF THE HERMENEUTICAL CIRCLE

The aim of the interpretive process is the transformation of the people of God within their concrete situation. Now a change in the situation of the interpreters (including their culture) brings about a change in their comprehension of Scripture, while a change in their comprehension of Scripture in turn reverberates in their situation. Thus, the contextual approach to the interpretation of Scripture involves a dialogue between the historical situation and Scripture, a dialogue in which the interpreters approach Scripture with a particular perspective (their world-and-life view) and approach their situation with a particular comprehension of the Word of God (their theology), as indicated in Diagram 4.

We begin the hermeneutical process by analyzing our situation, listening to the questions raised within it. Then we come to Scripture asking, "What does God say through Scripture regarding this

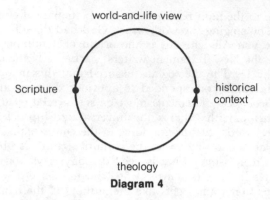

Diagram 4

particular problem?" The way we formulate our question will depend, of course, on our world-and-life view — that is, the historical situation can only approach Scripture through the current world-and-life view of the interpreters. Lack of a good understanding of the real issues involved will be reflected in inadequate or misdirected questions, and this will hinder our understanding of the relevance of the biblical message to that situation. Scripture does not readily answer questions which are not posed to it. Asking the wrong or peripheral questions will result in a theology focused on questions no one is asking, while the issues that urgently need biblical direction are ignored.

On the other hand, the better our understanding of the real issues in our context, the better will be the questions which we address to Scripture. This makes possible new readings of Scripture in which the implications of its message for our situation will be more fully uncovered. If it is true that Scripture illuminates life, it is also true that life illuminates Scripture.

As the answers of Scripture come to light, the initial questions which arose in our concrete situation may have to be reformulated to reflect the biblical perspective more adequately. The context of theology, therefore, includes not only answers to specific questions raised by the situation but also questions which the text itself poses to the situation.

The deeper and richer our comprehension of the biblical text, the deeper and richer will be our understanding of the historical context (including the issues that have yet to be faced) and of the meaning of Christian obedience in that particular context. The possibility is thus open for changes in our world-and-life view and consequently for a more adequate understanding and appropriation of the biblical message. For the biblical text, approached from a more congenial world-and-life view, and addressed with deeper and richer questions, will be found to speak more plainly and fully. Our theology, in turn, will be more relevant and responsive to the burning issues which we have to face in our concrete situation.

THE CONTEXTUALIZATION OF THE GOSPEL

The present situation of the church in many nations provides plenty of evidence to show that all too often the attempt has been made to evangelize without seriously facing the hermeneutical task. Western missionaries have often assumed that their task is simply to extract the message directly from the biblical text and to transmit it to their hearers in the "mission field" with no consideration of the role of the historical context in the whole interpretive process. This follows a simplistic pattern which does not fit reality (see Diagram 5).

This simplistic approach to evangelism has frequently gone hand in hand with a Western view of Christianity which combines biblical elements with elements of Greek philosophy and of the European-American heritage and places an unbalanced emphasis on the numerical growth of the church. As a result, in many parts of the world Christianity is regarded as an ethnic religion — the white man's religion. The gospel has a foreign sound, or no sound at all, in relation to many of the dreams and anxieties, problems and questions, values and customs of people. The Word of God is reduced to a message that touches life only on a tangent.

It would be easy to illustrate the theological dependence of the younger churches on the older churches, which is as real and as damaging as the economic dependence that characterizes the "underdeveloped" countries! An amazing quantity of Christian literature published in these countries consists of translations from English (ranging from "eschatology fiction" to how-to-enjoy-sex manuals) and in a number of theological institutions the curriculum is a photocopy of the curriculum used at similar institutions in the West.

The urgent need everywhere is for a new reading of the gospel *from within each particular historical situation,* under the guidance of the

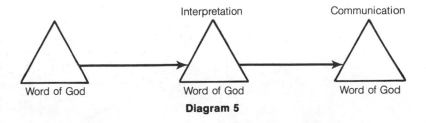

Diagram 5

Holy Spirit. The contextualization of the gospel can only be the result of a new, open-ended reading of Scripture with a hermeneutic in which gospel and situation become mutually engaged in a dialogue whose purpose is to place the church under the lordship of Jesus Christ.

It is only as the Word of God becomes "flesh" in the people of God that the gospel takes shape within history. According to God's purpose the gospel is never to be merely a message in words but a message incarnate in his church and, through it, in history. The contextualization of the gospel demands the contextualization of the church, which is God's hermeneutical community for the manifestation of Christ's presence among the nations of the earth.

SUPRACULTURAL MEANINGS VIA CULTURAL FORMS

CHARLES H. KRAFT

ANTHROPOLOGICALLY INFORMED THEOLOGY

In an early attempt to deal with God and culture from what I am labeling a Christian ethnotheological position, William A. Smalley and Marie Fetzer (now Reyburn) coined the terms *superculture* and *supercultural* to refer to God's transcendent relationship to culture.[1] Smalley later developed this concept in the pages of the journal *Practical Anthropology* in an article entitled "Culture and Superculture."[2] His article was prompted by a letter published in that journal the previous year, the author of which betrayed a high degree of confusion as to just what roles theology and anthropology should play in our attempts to discover what is absolute and what is relative.

The author of the letter contended that "one should not establish an episcopal church government simply because the society is characterized by strong kings and subordinate lords" since "the question of church government is not an anthropological but a theological one."[3] Rather, the missionary should go into the situation convinced through a study of theology "that either the congregational or the episcopal or some other form of church government is the kind Jesus Christ meant for every society, all over the world and at all times." He continues,

> this procedure — first the theological and then the anthropological — must be applied to a myriad of problems . . . such as theft, polygamy, premarital sexual relations, lying, lay and/or clerical marriages, etc. . . .

1. Smalley and Kraft, "A Christian View of Anthropology," in *Modern Science and Christian Faith,* ed. F. A. Everest (Wheaton, Ill.: Van Kampen Press, 1948).

2. Smalley, "Culture and Superculture," *Practical Anthropology* 2 (1955): 58-71.

3. Since the author of the letter has now totally changed his views, I think it best to refrain from referring to him by name. The position he espoused is so common and well articulated, however, that it is helpful to cite the letter directly.

Reprinted from *Christianity in Culture: A Study in Dynamic Biblical Theologizing in Cross-Cultural Perspective* (Maryknoll, N.Y.: Orbis Books, 1979), pp. 116-46.

An anthropologist *describes* but a Christian *prescribes*. He believes that God has revealed a system which is *absolutely* right, valid for every society during every epoch. [Italics mine]

The writer of that letter was seeking to dichotomize the theological and the anthropological evaluations of the situation. He says, "it is one thing to be a Christian and another to be an anthropologist." One may look at the situation anthropologically, he contends, only in order to obtain information about the customs of the people one seeks to reach. One should have already made up one's mind on the theological issues. Thus, in applying his theological conclusions to the indigenous situation, the writer says, "I must 'play God' " and "prescribe" the system that God has revealed to me through my study of theology as "absolutely right, valid for every society during every epoch."

The writer is undoubtedly right when he says, "The anthropology minded Christian missionary . . . *must not be so enchanted by his science that he fails to pursue the consummation of his goal*: the establishment of a truly Christian but, nevertheless, indigenous Church" (italics mine).

The author's desire to discover absolute models before approaching the indigenous system and his feeling that it is to theology that we should turn for understanding of these models are likewise commendable. Unfortunately, his position appears deficient at two crucial points: (1) he does not see the contradiction between the imposition from outside of an "absolutely right" system that will be the same in cultural *form* (not merely in function or meaning) "for every society during every epoch" and the necessity that a truly indigenous church spring from the employment by Christianity of indigenous cultural forms, and (2) he fails to take account of the extreme limitation that the monoculturalness of most Western theology imposes upon its ability to deal with these issues in a cross-culturally valid way.

What cross-cultural witnesses need is not a continuation of the current dichotomization of the theological and the anthropological perspectives but a single perspective in which the insights of each specialization are taken seriously *at the same level*. For both are human-made disciplines (in spite of the sacredness of the subject matter of the one). And both disciplines suffer from the kind of myopia that all specialization leads to. For when we specialize *into* anything we automatically specialize *out of* everything else. In attempting to understand this or any other aspect of the relationships between Christianity and culture, therefore, we cannot afford to be "enchanted" with *either* discipline. For each discipline is too limited by itself to handle the specialization of the other adequately. Our model 4b postulates that *theology (as well as anthropology) is human-*

made and culture-bound.[4] Our theology, therefore, must be informed by anthropology and our anthropology informed by theology.

From an anthropologically informed theology, then, we propose model 4c: *Christianness lies primarily in the "supracultural"* (see below) *functions and meanings* expressed in culture rather than in the mere forms of any given culture. What God desires is not a single *form* of church government "absolutely right, valid for every society and during every epoch," but the employment of the large number of diverse cultural forms of government with a single *function* — to glorify God by facilitating the smooth, well-ordered, and in-culturally intelligible operation of the organizations that bear his name.

To assume that this point of view endorses an abandonment of theological absolutes (or constants) is to miss the point in the other direction. Yet this is a natural overreaction, since theological understandings (especially at the popular level) have so often focused strongly on particular cultural *forms* such as the wording of creeds, the modes (rather than the meanings) of baptism and the Lord's Supper, the supposed sacredness of monologic preaching, the merits of one or another form of church government, refraining from smoking and drinking, and the like—as if these were absolute understandings of God's absolute models. Seldom have arguments over such matters dealt with anything but the *forms* of belief or practice.

Neither the Reformation nor any subsequent church split, for example, has centered around *whether* the church should be governed (i.e., the necessity or non-necessity of the governing function). That churches *should be* governed has always been assumed, since Christian things are to be done "decently and in order" (1 Cor. 14:40). Church splits have, rather, focused on the *type* of church government—a matter of form, not of function. Nor have arguments concerning doctrine generally focused on whether or not, for example, God has provided for human redemption, inspired the Scriptures, invited human beings to respond in faith, worked in history, or the like. They have nearly always dealt with the *forms* these doctrines

4. EDITOR'S NOTE: This essay is excerpted from a larger discussion in which Kraft proposes various models that have been advanced concerning God's relationship to culture. He presents several broadly defined categories of relationships (including God *against* culture, God *in* culture, and God *above* culture), paying special attention to what he calls the "God-above-but-through-culture position," which in the context of the larger discussion is labeled "model 4a" (see *Christianity in Culture: A Study in Dynamic Biblical Theologizing in Cross-Cultural Perspective* [Maryknoll, N.Y.: Orbis Books, 1979], pp. 113-15).

Having introduced this model of an essentially transcendent God who uses culture to effect his purposes, Kraft is now turning to a consideration of the relationships between Christian meanings and the cultural forms into which they are fitted. He maintains that these considerations call for the development of an anthropologically informed theology—and it is at this point that we join his argument here.

should take. They have ordinarily centered on theories of how they are to be understood and formulated rather than on the fact that God has provided for these very important functions.

An anthropologically informed approach, however, identifies as the constants of Christianity the functions and meanings behind such forms rather than any given set of doctrinal or behavioral forms. It would leave the cultural forms in which these constant functions are expressed largely negotiable in terms of the cultural matrix of those with whom God is dealing at the time. In what follows, then, I will argue that it is the *meaning conveyed* by a particular doctrine (e.g., consumption of alcoholic beverages, baptism) that is of primary concern of God. There is, I believe, no absoluteness to the human formulation of the doctrine, the historical accuracy of the way in which the ritual is performed, or the rigidity with which one abides by one's behavorial rules.

This is the point at which Jesus scored the Pharisees. For they, in their strict adherence to the forms of their orthodox doctrines, rituals, and behavior, had ignored the fact that these forms had changed their meanings. The way they used the forms had come to signify oppression rather than concern, self-interest rather than divine interest, rejection rather than acceptance, God against human beings rather than God with them. That is, as the culture changed, the meanings of the forms that once adequately conveyed God's message changed, along with the rest of the culture. And those whose responsibility it was to see to it that the message of God continued to be understood became primarily concerned with perpetuating and elaborating on the cultural forms in which the message came to them. They became legalistic concerning the traditional forms. But according to Jesus, godliness lies in the motives behind the meanings conveyed by the forms of belief and behavior, not simply in adherence to the beliefs and practices as traditionally observed. The beliefs and practices are simply the cultural vehicles (the forms) through which God-motivated concern, interest, and acceptance are to be expressed. And these forms must be continually watched and altered to make sure that they are fulfilling their proper function — the transmission of the eternal message of God. As culture changes, these forms of belief and behavior must be updated in order to preserve the eternal message.

Perhaps it is this focus on function and meaning rather than on cultural form that led John to refer to Christ as the *logos*, the expression of God (John 1:1, JBP). Perhaps more clearly than with other cultural forms, linguistic forms such as words are seen to be important only insofar as their function is important. In John's prologue, Christ the Word, the Expression of God, is presented functioning as creator and sustainer, as the light of the world, and, latterly, as a human embodiment of God. The focus is continually on his functioning on behalf of God, on his expressing God with respect to the human context. The form that he took to communicate these functions is mentioned but never elaborated upon because it is so subsidiary to his function of expressing God.

This is not to deny the importance of cultural forms — whether they be words, rituals, behavior, beliefs, or the physical body in which the Son of God lived on earth. The forms are extremely important because only through the forms does the communication take place. Even though it may be said that the water is more important to a river than the riverbed in which it flows, it is still the riverbed that determines what the destination of the water will be (except in a flood). So it is that the forms (like the riverbed) through which the meanings of language and culture flow determine the destination of those meanings. In communication, however, as in irrigating a garden, it is of crucial importance that would-be communicators (or irrigators) choose the proper channel (set of forms). They must then direct their message (water) into that channel rather than into another one if they are to reach those whom they seek to reach. Intelligent irrigators do not choose last year's channels simply because they have become attached to them, having learned to regard them reverently because the channels served them so well last year. Rather, they decide where they want the water to go and adapt last year's channels or create new ones to reach this year's crops. Even so, the effective communicator (human or God) chooses, adapts, or creates cultural forms (channels) specifically appropriate to the task of getting his or her meaning (the "water") across to the present hearers. In this way the forms he or she chooses are very important, but only as means, never as ends in themselves.

THE SUPRACULTURAL AND THE CULTURAL (MODEL 4d)

In the development of an ethnotheological understanding of the relationship between God and culture, Smalley's reply to the letter mentioned previously was a truly significant contribution. I will here build upon that approach, though with two major and several minor modifications. The first of these is to change Smalley's term *supercultural* to *supracultural* and to reject noun forms such as *super-culture* or *supraculture* as unusable.[5] Since I contend that there is no

5. Smalley's original term *supercultural* was developed by analogy with *supernatural*. Perhaps because of such widespread terms as *superman, superbowl, superstar,* and the like, the prefix *super-* makes a word to which it is appended particularly prone to be used as a noun. The use of the prefix *supra-* is not nearly so likely to result in a noun. I understand that Smalley himself now prefers the term *supracultural*.

such thing as an absolute set of cultural forms, terms such as *super-culture* or *supraculture* that would seem to imply the existence of some sort of absolute cultural structure (i.e., some set of absolute cultural forms) are so misleading that they must be abandoned.

The adjective *supracultural*, however, serves a very useful purpose in signifying the transcendence of God with respect to culture. That is, God, being completely unbound by any culture (except as he chooses to operate within or in terms of culture) is *supra*cultural (i.e., above and outside culture). Likewise, any absolute principles or functions proceeding from God's nature, attributes, or activities may be labeled *supracultural*. For they, too, transcend and are not bound by any specific culture, except when they are expressed within a culture.

The second major modification of Smalley's scheme, though noted here, will not be developed in detail here. It divides the outside-of-culture realm (the supracultural) into two compartments in order to show the place of angels, demons, and Satan in relationship to God, human beings, and culture. And this leads to a distinction between *supracultural* and *absolute* that Smalley did not seem to envision. That is, though God is supracultural, standing outside culture, so are angels, demons, and Satan. The latter, however, are not absolute, as God is. Smalley dealt with only two categories — the cultural, which is relative (i.e., nonabsolute) and the supracultural, which is absolute. The present treatment, however, assumes three categories: the supracultural absolute God, the supracultural non-absolute beings (angels, demons, Satan), and the relative cultural context (see Figure 1).

As Smalley states (in a rather Pauline sentence),

> The whole question might well be phrased in the following form: Granted that there is a God above and beyond all human culture, that He has revealed Himself to man in several cultural forms (notably the Holy Scriptures and the life of His Son, lived as a man partaking fully of the life of a particular human culture), and that He has taken an active interest in parts of man's cultural behavior through time, proscribing and prescribing at various times and places; granted also that most (if not all) culture has developed through time by natural processes of development in different times and places, that particular forms in one place may have a completely different meaning in terms of function than what nearly identical forms do in another place, that God has at various historical periods proscribed certain forms of behavior which he has not proscribed at other times, that He has emphasized as highly desirable certain forms of behavior which He has not prescribed at other times, and that the heavy emotional attachment which people normally have for the familiar pattern (i.e., ethnocentrism) colors and distorts judgment; granted all this, what in human experience is God's absolute, unchanging,

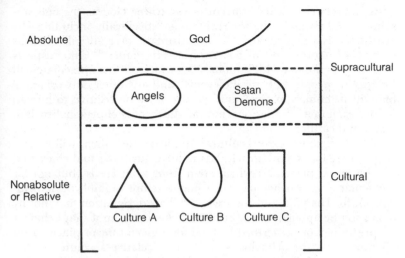

Fig. 1. The cultural, supracultural, absolute, and relative.

permanent will, and what is His will for particular times and places, and what is neutral?[6]

In approaching an answer to this question, E. A. Nida states categorically that "the only absolute in Christianity is the triune God."[7] If finite, limited humans are involved, Nida continues, the thing under consideration must of necessity be limited and therefore relative. Nida is clearly correct with respect to God as the only absolute *being* in the universe. Christian theology has always strongly asserted this. One might contend, in fact, that if the universe and all in it has been created, it is logically impossible to have more than one absolute related to it. Only that One who has brought the universe into being and who stands outside it can be said to be unlimited by it (as far as we know). All else that we know is somehow limited by the universe or, in the case of angels, demons, and Satan, by God directly, and is therefore relative to either or both God and the universe. For relativity is simply "the state of being dependent for existence on or determined in nature, value or quality by relation to something else."

One might qualify Nida's categorical statement by suggesting that the absolute God has, in his manifold activities, manifested attributes and operated in terms of principles that are constant. These also look like absolutes from our vantage point. Smalley sug-

6. Smalley, "Culture and Superculture," pp. 58-59.
7. Nida, *Customs and Cultures* (New York: Harper & Row, 1954), pp. 282 n.22.

gests, therefore, that the concept of the triune God as the only absolute in Christianity be interpreted as "specifically including His attributes, His nature, and His . . . ultimate, over-all will which is part of His nature and which stems from His nature."[8] Other aspects of God's interaction with human beings such as "his immediate will for specific people and specific events" and any other outworking of his will in human affairs "must of necessity be relative to human finiteness, human limitations, human differences of personality, language and culture."[9]

The designation "supracultural and absolute," then, will be employed here for "God Himself, His nature, attributes and character, for the moral principles which stem from what He is (but not for particular acts of behavior which may attempt to fulfill those principles), for His plan and total will."[10] This designation may not by definition be applied to any cultural behavior, even if that behavior is "prescribed or proscribed by God for a given time or place, or for all time" or if the behavior is "a kind of 'relative absolute' in that a Christian is not allowed a choice in his particular situation, [for] the behavior is still cultural."[11] Christian behavior, therefore, and the specific interactions between God and humans that resulted in it are always cultural, even though God is supracultural and the principles on which the behavior is based are constants of the human condition.

But can we know these principles and can we trust our understanding of God and his will? That is, can we know supracultural truth? The answer is Yes because of God's revelation of himself. But our understanding can never be absolute or infallible, since it is only partial. Our culture-bound perspectives allow us to see even revealed truth only "like the dim image in a mirror" (1 Cor. 13:12 TEV). The Christian does, however, "know something, at least, of the nature of the [supracultural], but does not know all, and what he does know is colored by the cultural screen through which he must know anything he does know."[12]

The writer of the letter raises another difficult question. He suggests the possibility that this view of God may portray him as extremely fickle, since he seems always to be "changing the arithmetic so that poor Jack [can] understand it." Can it be that the God whom Scripture contends is "the same yesterday, today and forever" (Heb. 13:8) has such a variety of standards that we cannot, through the

8. Nida, "Are We Really Monotheists?" *Practical Anthropology* 6 (1959): 59.
9. Smalley, "Culture and Superculture," pp. 59-60.
10. Smalley, "Culture and Superculture," p. 60.
11. Smalley, "Culture and Superculture," p. 60.
12. Smalley, "Culture and Superculture," p. 60.

study of the Scriptures, ascertain a trustworthy answer to any problem of Christian belief or behavior?

The answer to such queries lies in a redefinition of our understanding of God's consistency. I believe the Scriptures show God to
be marvelously consistent, operating always in terms of the same
principles. But one of these principles (a constant) is that he adapts
his approach to human beings to the cultural, sociological, and psychological limitations in which humans exist. The apostle Paul, following God's principle, endeavored to be a Hebrew to Hebrews and
a Greek to Greeks (1 Cor. 9:19-23). God did not deal with Moses
as if he were a Greek or with the Athenians (Acts 17) as if they were
Hebrews. A culturally perceptive understanding of the Scriptures
leads to the conviction that

> one of the supreme characteristics of God's grace to man [is] the fact
> that God changed the arithmetic repeatedly so that Jack could under-
> stand it. The very fact that the Revelation came through language,
> a finite cultural medium, limits the Revelation, and limitation is a
> change. The fact that Revelation came through the life of Jesus Christ
> . . . living out a typical world culture modifies the Revelation, for it
> gives it the cast and hue of a particular finite culture at a particular
> period of time.
>
> When Jesus said, "Ye have heard that it hath been said by them
> of old time . . . but I say unto you . . ." God was changing the arith-
> metic so that Jack could know more about it than Jack's grandparents
> knew. All church history records the changes in the cultural super-
> structure of Christianity. This does not mean that the [supracultural]
> has changed. The [supracultural] is God, His personality, His over-
> all will, His principles. The cultural manifestations of the [supracul-
> tural] change, and are relative to the particular situation.[13]

We see, therefore, that what from one point of view looks like
inconsistency on God's part is actually the outworking of a greater
consistency. For God in his mercy has decided consistently to adapt
his approach to human beings in *their* cultural contexts. Many, however (with the author of the letter cited above), will find such a view
threatening. Among these will be closed conservatives who regard
their particular culturally conditioned understandings of God's revelation as well-nigh absolute and their culturally molded behavior
in response to his revelation as the only behavior acceptable to God.
Such persons, under the tutelage of ethnocentric theological traditions, fail to make the distinction between the inspiration of the
scriptural data and the fallibility of their understanding of God and

13. Smalley, "Culture and Superculture," pp. 61-62.

his works. They therefore look on any deviation from their understandings as a deviation from orthodoxy.[14]

The perspective presented here is not a deviation from orthodoxy. It is, rather, an attempt to modify the understanding and expression of orthodoxy in such a way that (1) it will be more useful to cross-cultural witnesses and (2) it will not have to be abandoned by anyone who recognizes that a good bit of the insight of the behavioral sciences into the relativities of human existence simply cannot be dismissed. From this point of view we are forced to recognize "that much of what [certain ethnocentric theologies have] decreed to be absolute is not, that much theological difference of view arises out of the ethnocentrism of theologians and their followers, and that God is not culture-bound."[15] For the human-made discipline known as theology has developed into "the philosophical study of almost anything identified with Christianity," including in a major way the behavior of humans and God within the cultural milieu. Theologies, therefore, concern themselves with culture—but often without the preciseness that anthropological study has developed in this area.[16] Since theological study is (largely for historical reasons) often limited in its understanding of culture, its insights need to be supplemented with the insights into culture of other human-made disciplines such as anthropology. Only then can theological understandings of the relationships between supracultural truth and culture-bound expressions of that truth be both maximally useful to cross-cultural witnesses and relevant and attractive to contemporary Westerners, who often know more about culture than do those trained in traditional conservative theology.

BIBLICAL CULTURAL RELATIVISM (MODEL 4e)

As we have suggested elsewhere,[17] we cannot go all the way with those anthropologists (a decreasing number, by the way) who might be labeled "absolute cultural relativists." We can sympathize with the motivation to combat the evolutionary hypothesis of cultural development that, by evaluating all cultures by European technological criteria, ethnocentrically saw our culture as superior to all others. And I believe we must continue to oppose such a misinformed point of view whenever we find it (especially among Christians). But the proper alternative is not absolute relativism if by

14. See Harold Lindsell, *The Battle for the Bible* (Grand Rapids: Zondervan, 1976), and Francis Schaeffer, *How Should We Then Live?* (Old Tappan, N.J.: Revell, 1976).

15. Smalley, "Culture and Superculture," p. 69.

16. See Smalley, "Culture and Superculture," p. 62.

17. See *Christianity in Culture*, pp. 81-99.

this we mean that it is never permissible to evaluate cultural behavior. For Christians (and, indeed, non-Christians) are never completely neutral toward cultural behavior, whether their own or that of others. We constantly monitor and evaluate the behavior of ourselves and of others.

The difficulty is that too often when we evaluate the behavior of others we do not first seek to understand the behavior from the point of view of that person and of that culture (i.e., in its cultural context). We simply judge the behavior as if it were a part of our own system. Yet the meaning of that behavior is derived *entirely* from within the other's system, never from ours or from some "cosmic pool" of universal meanings. And when we evaluate our own behavior we frequently ignore the fact that our actions make sense *only* within the total pattern of life in which we are involved. We cannot assume that the behavior which we hold so dear and which we may feel to be so superior can simply be grafted into someone else's culture as it is and prove to be superior within that system.

We must adopt a sufficiently relativistic stance to help us toward understanding and appreciation (rather than judgmental condemnation) of another's activity within that person's cultural system. But we must reject emphatically the absolute relativism that simply says, "Live and let live without ever attempting to influence anyone else in the direction of one's own values since there are no absolute standards and, therefore, his system is just as good as ours."[18]

Rather, as Christians we may find helpful a model or perspective that Nida calls "relative cultural relativism."[19] This model asserts the presence of absolutes (supracultural truths) but relates them all to God, who stands outside of culture, rather than to any cultural expression, description, or exemplification of a God-human relationship (be it American, Greek, or Hebrew). Nida and other Christian ethnotheologians see this "biblical cultural relativism" as "an obligatory feature of our incarnational religion," asserting that "without it we would either absolutize human institutions" (as ethnocentric positions do) or, going to the opposite extreme (as absolute relativists do), we would "relativize God."[20] In his excellent discussion of this topic, Nida points out that the Bible

> clearly recognizes that different cultures have different standards and that these differences are recognized by God as having different values. The relativism of the Bible is relative to three principal factors:

18. For illustrations of certain disturbing results of this kind of principle, see Donald A. McGavran, *The Clash between Christianity and Cultures* (Washington: Canon Press, 1974), pp. 2-6.
19. Nida, *Customs and Cultures*, p. 50.
20. Nida, *Customs and Cultures*, p. 282.

(1) the endowment and opportunities of people, (2) the extent of revelation, and (3) the cultural patterns of the society in question.[21]

1. God conditions his expectations of human beings, in the first place, by making allowance for differences in the endowment and opportunities of the people with whom he is dealing. In the parable of the Talents (Matt. 25:14-30) and again in the parable of the Pounds (Luke 19:12-27), Jesus teaches a modified relativism. For in God's interaction with people, "rewards and judgment are relative to people's endowments, for the one who receives five talents and gains five additional talents receives not only the commendation of his master but an additional talent" — the one taken from the servant who refused to use (and risk) that which was entrusted to him.[22] Likewise, the one to whom two talents were given was commended because he also had used what he had to gain more. Though the main point of the passage has to do with the importance of people using what is given them for the sake of their master, it is clear that the parable also implies (a) that there is relativity (i.e., difference) in what each human being starts with, (b) that God therefore expects relatively more from those who have started with relatively more, and (c) that his judgment of people is relative both to what they have been given and to what they do with it.

This is not an absolute relativity, since the principle in terms of which the master makes his judgments is constant and universally applicable. Note that the servant who received relatively less than the others was not condemned because he started with less, nor even because he finished with less (these are both relative), but because he refused to operate by a supracultural principle of accountability. This principle is articulated clearly in Luke 12:48: "The man to whom much is given, of him much is required; the man to whom more is given, of him much more is required" (TEV). Thus we are here dealing with a relative relativity rather than with absolute relativity, which would allow no standard of evaluation whatsoever.

2. In the second place (and partially overlapping with the first), we see in the Bible a relativism with respect to the extent of the revelational information available to given culture-bound human beings. Jesus points clearly to this fact time and time again when he compares his superior revelation of God to previous (Old Testament) revelations of God. To the Hebrews of Moses' time God allowed and even endorsed their cultural principle of "an eye for an eye and a tooth for a tooth" (Lev. 24:20). But Jesus spoke differently to Moses' descendants who, several hundred years later, had an understanding of God based on the accumulation of considerably

21. Nida, *Customs and Cultures*, p. 50.
22. Nida, *Customs and Cultures*, p. 50.

more revealed information than was available to their ancestors. To them he said:

> You have heard that it was said, "An eye for an eye, and a tooth for a tooth." But now I tell you: do not take revenge on someone who does you wrong. If anyone slaps you on the right cheek, let him slap your left cheek too. (Matt. 5:38-39 TEV)

When Jesus "changed the arithmetic" from "retaliate" to "love your enemies" (Matt. 5:44), his hearers and all of us who have come after them (i.e., who are "informationally A.D.")[23] became accountable for a higher standard than was expected of the Hebrews of Moses' day. This higher standard is also illustrated in the matter of murder (i.e., hate now equals murder — Matt. 5:21-22) and with reference to adultery (i.e., lust equals adultery — Matt. 5:27-28). Perhaps the lowest revelational standard available to people is that referred to by Paul in Romans 2:14-16:

> When Gentiles who do not possess the law carry out its precepts by the light of nature [culture?], then, although they have no law, they are their own law, for they display the effect of the law inscribed on their hearts. Their conscience is called as witness, and their own thoughts argue the case on either side, against them or even for them, on the day when God judges the secrets of human hearts through Christ Jesus. So my gospel declares. (NEB)

It is clear, then, that human accountability before God is relative to the extent of revelation that human beings have received. And we end up with respect to revelation at the same point at which we ended vis-à-vis endowment — at a degree of accountability determined according to a supraculturally controlled given that differs from person to person and from group to group. Thus,

> the servant who knew his master's wishes, yet made no attempt to carry them out, will be flogged severely. But one who did not know them and earned a beating will be flogged less severely. Where a man has been given much, much will be expected of him; and the more a man has had entrusted to him the more he will be required to repay. (Luke 12:47-48 NEB)

3. A third aspect of biblical relativism (again partially overlapping with the other two) is the fact that God takes into account the cultures of the peoples with whom he deals. That is, God conditions his expectations for each society to take account of the cultural patterns in terms of which their lives are lived. True, God works with people for culture change. But he starts by accepting and even endorsing customs practiced by Old Testament peoples that he con-

---

23. See *Christianity in Culture*, pp. 239-57.

demns or at least does not endorse in his dealings with Greco-Roman peoples. God's approach, then, is relative to the human cultures of the Bible. We assume that he deals with contemporary cultures in terms of the same principle.[24]

Leviticus 25:39-46, for example, sanctions the enslaving of Gentiles by Jews (though not of Jews by Jews). This was undoubtedly the prevalent custom. But God chose to work *with it* on the surface, while at the same time advocating other principles that would eventually do away with the custom. It seems to have died out by New Testament times. He seems to have chosen to refrain from making a big issue of such nonideal customs, probably to keep from diverting attention from more important aspects of his interaction with the Hebrews. He treated polygamy (see 2 Sam. 12:7-8) including levirate marriage (Deut. 25:5-6), trial by ordeal (Num. 5:11-28), and numerous other Hebrew customs similarly. In dealing with divorce, Jesus makes explicit the reason why God chose to allow and endorse such less-than-ideal customs — it was because of the "hardness of their hearts" or, as the New English Bible translates it, "because [their] minds were closed" (Mark 10:5) and God was patient (2 Pet. 3:9).

The most significant New Testament indication of biblical endorsement of a relativistic attitude toward culture, however, lies in Paul's statement that he attempted to be "all things to all men." This statement is buttressed by several illustrations of his application of this principle. In 1 Corinthians 9:20-22, for example, he indicates his movement back and forth over the cultural barrier separating Jews from Greeks:

> To Jews I became like a Jew, to win Jews; as they are subject to the Law of Moses, I put myself under that law to win them, although I am not myself subject to it. To win Gentiles, who are outside the Law, I made myself like one of them, although I am not in truth outside God's law, being under the law of Christ. . . . Indeed, I have become everything in turn to men of every sort, so that in one way or another I may save some. (NEB)

This principle of approaching each situation in terms of its own special cultural circumstances is a constant supracultural principle of God's interaction with people. The principle, therefore, is not relative, but its application in the relative context of human culture illustrates once again the correctness of the "biblical relativity" understanding of God's approach to people. Both the supracultural principle and this understanding of biblical relativity enable us to

---

24. For a good contemporary illustration of this approach, see G. Linwood Barney, "The Meo — An Incipient Church," *Practical Anthropology* 4 (1957): 31-50.

explain a large number of apparent discrepancies in the working of God in the human context. The relative application of God's supracultural principle explains, for example, how Paul could object strenuously to Peter's compromising in a Gentile context under pressure from the Judaizers (Gal. 2:11-14). Yet, later, he himself, when in a wholly Jewish context, went through Hebrew rites of purification to demonstrate to them that he had not abandoned Judaism (Acts 21:20-26). Likewise, Paul could circumcise Timothy, who had a Greek father but a Jewish mother, in order to give him an "in" with the Jews (Acts 16:3), yet not compel Titus, whose parentage allowed him no such "in" with the Jews, to go the same route (Gal. 2:3).

Nida helpfully summarizes this perspective by stating,

> biblical relativism is not a matter of inconsistency but a recognition of the different cultural factors which influence standards and actions. While the Koran attempts to fix for all time the behavior of Muslims, *the Bible clearly establishes the principle of relative relativism, which permits growth, adaptation, and freedom, under the Lordship of Jesus Christ.* The Bible presents realistically the facts of culture and the plan of God, by which He continues to work in the hearts of men "till we all come in the unity of the faith, and of the knowledge of the Son of God, unto a perfect man, unto the measure of the stature of the fulness of Christ" (Eph. 4:13). *The Christian position is not one of static conformance to dead rules, but of dynamic obedience to a living God.*[25]

Far from being a threat to a Christian perspective (even a conservative one), the development of an understanding of biblical cultural relativism should be regarded as a part of the leading "into all truth" (John 16:13), which is one of the important functions of the Holy Spirit today.

ADEQUATE, THOUGH NEVER ABSOLUTE, HUMAN PERCEPTION OF SUPRACULTURAL TRUTH (MODEL 5a)

Perhaps the most basic problem in this whole area is the reliability of our perception of supracultural truth. Can we trust what we think we understand? If sincere specialists such as theologians are not exempt from cultural limitations in their understandings of supracultural truth, where does that leave the rest of us? Furthermore, if we adopt the position here advocated and open ourselves up to the validity of a diversity of culturally conditioned interpretations, can we be certain that any supracultural truth will survive at all? The answers lie in (1) coming to better understand how the Holy Spirit

25. Nida, *Customs and Cultures*, p. 52; italics mine.

goes about leading culture-bound human beings "into all truth" and (2) accepting the sufficiency of an adequate, though nonabsolute, understanding of supracultural truth.

The Spirit leads "into all truth" via the human perception of those to whom he speaks. Since the channel is culture-bound human perception, the receptors do not understand supracultural truth absolutely. Indeed, we are limited by at least five factors:

1. The limitations of the revelations (including "illuminations"). God has seen fit to reveal only certain things concerning himself, his plans, and his purposes. That which he has not yet revealed we cannot know.

2. Our finiteness. We are limited in our understanding of even that which has been revealed. We all study the same Scriptures, but there are a multitude of differing interpretations of the meaning of much of what is there revealed.

3. Our sinfulness. Our perception and ability to understand and respond to God's revelation is, like every other aspect of our lives, affected at every point by sin. For this reason our motives are never completely pure nor our vision completely lucid.

4. Our cultural conditioning. The fact that we are totally immersed in a given culture conditions us to perceive all of reality, including God's revelation, in terms of that culture.

5. Our individual psychological and experiential conditioning. Even within shared cultural boundaries, the life experience of every individual is unique. This likewise conditions one's perception of the revelation.

The assumption here is that supracultural truth exists (with God) above and beyond any cultural perception or expressions of it. God reveals to us glimpses of this truth via the human languages and cultures of the Scriptures. Our perception of the various aspects of this truth may be barely acceptable to God at the start but may, during the course of our maturing as Christians, develop into a much more ideal understanding. This may eventually approach, though never quite reach, the supracultural ideal that lies outside culture and therefore beyond our grasp.

As receptors who are limited in these ways, we interpret the Word and other (e.g., experiential) data at our disposal in terms of culturally organized models that incorporate and exhibit these limitations. Though we are not totally unable to see beyond what such cultural structuring channels us into, our tendency is to gravitate toward and most readily understand those portions of supracultural truth that connect most closely with life as we already perceive it. How the faces of Africans light up as they hear that God endorsed levirate (Deut. 25:5-10), polygamous (2 Sam. 12:7-9), arranged marriages (Gen. 24:50-51; 34:10-12) and many other customs similar to theirs. But none of these Hebrew perceptions of God excited Luther, for German culture is related to and has been influenced by Greek culture. So it was those portions of Scripture couched in Greek thought patterns that caught Luther's attention. The Spirit, then, spoke most clearly to Luther via those portions.

In the original revelation of biblical materials, God also worked in terms of culturally conditioned human perception. For each biblical writing participates completely in the context to which it is addressed. And the topics treated are dealt with, under the leading of the Spirit, in categories culturally and linguistically appropriate to the way a particular culturally and psychologically conditioned participant perceives of that situation and its needs.

It is not at all strange that large portions of the New Testament are phrased in terms of *Greek* conceptual categories (rather than in supracultural categories). For God wanted his message contextualized within the human frame of reference in such a way that it would be maximally intelligible to those within that frame of reference. So he led Paul and others to write about those things that they noticed and perceived to be important both to God and to their hearers. There are many questions that we twentieth-century Euro-Americans wish Paul had written about (e.g., race relations, the place of women, the relative importance of evangelism, and "social action"). But he, in his cultural setting, did not see the importance of providing a word from God on such issues. God will have to provide that word through people today whom he leads to be as concerned about these issues as Paul was about the issues he faced.

Nor is it strange that the writings of the Old Testament and those portions of the New Testament written to Hebrews show other authors dealing under the leading of God with other issues. Apparently it has always been God's plan to lead people via their concerns. What might be considered surprising is that so many very specific issues in both the Old Testament and the New Testament are of such wide general relevance to peoples of many other cultures, and are dealt with within Hebrew and Greek cultural matrices in such a way that people today can benefit from the scriptural treatments. Beyond the divine factors involved, we can point to two human conditions that God has exploited. The first is the high degree of basic similarity between peoples of different cultures. So much of the Bible deals with basic issues of life that its relevance is assured at this level. The second of the human conditions is the great similarity between the cultures of the Bible and contemporary cultures. This is especially true of Hebrew culture throughout most of the world and of Greek culture and European cultures. Most of the Bible is couched in Hebrew thought patterns. Though those portions of the Scriptures are often less compelling for Europeans, the

Spirit frequently speaks clearly through them to other peoples of the world.

The Scriptures are like the ocean and supracultural truth like the icebergs that float in it. Many icebergs show at least a bit of themselves above the surface, though some lie entirely beneath the surface. Much of God's revelation of himself in the Scriptures is at least partially visible to nearly anyone who is willing to see it—though belief must precede "seeing" (John 5:39). But much lies beneath the surface, visible only to those who search to discover what supracultural truth lies beneath the specific cultural applications in Scripture.

"PLAIN MEANINGS" AND "INTERPRETATIONAL REFLEXES"

Searching beneath the surface involves the process of interpretation (technically called *hermeneutics*). The fact that we are in a different culture from that in which the original events occurred causes problems, for our perception and our interpretation are affected by that different culture. We learn as part of our cultural conditioning a set of "interpretational reflexes"—a set of habits in terms of which we automatically interpret whatever happens. We don't think things through before we interpret in these ways. Our responses are reflexive in the same way that most of our muscular responses are reflexive. We need to develop hermeneutical techniques for getting beyond these reflexive interpretations into as close an approximation as possible to the perception of the original participants. What follows is but a preliminary presentation of an approach to biblical interpretation.

Those unaware of the pervasive influence of their own culture on their interpretations often slip unconsciously into the assumption that arriving at most supracultural truth is simply a matter of accepting the "clear" or "plain meanings" of Scripture. A typical statement of this view says, "The plain meaning of the Bible is the true meaning."[26] Harold Lindsell condemns those who disagree with his point of view by accusing them of developing "interpretations of Scripture *at variance with the plain reading* of the texts."[27]

A plain-meaning position assumes that our interpretation corresponds with that of the authors of Scripture. There is, however, a major problem here, stemming from the fact that those who agree on large areas of cultural experience seldom discuss (or make explicit in other ways) these areas of agreement. What everyone in a given context assumes (i.e., agrees on) is not mentioned. People

26. McGavran, *The Clash between Christianity and Cultures*, p. 65.
27. Lindsell, *The Battle for the Bible*, p. 39; italics mine.

conditioned by the same culture agree on, and therefore seldom if ever discuss, thousands of interpretationally (hermeneutically) significant understandings and perspectives. Hebrews, for example, assumed that God exists. The author of Genesis, as a Hebrew writing to other Hebrews, did not have to prove God's existence. Jesus could rightfully assume that his hearers understood what a mustard bush and its seeds looked like, that those who sowed seeds scattered them "broadcast" (rather than, say, putting each seed in a separate hole), that sheep could be *led* (rather than driven) by a shepherd, and so on.

The interpretational reflexes of Jesus' hearers were conditioned by the same culture as his were, and so they did not need explanation of the assumptions and agreements underlying his words and actions. Our interpretational reflexes are conditioned by quite a different culture. Thus we are likely to find that any given portion of Scripture falls into one or the other of the following categories characteristic of any communicational situation that involves the crossing of a cultural border.

1. We, as readers, may not understand major portions of what is going on at all, since we don't know the cultural agreements. In the story of the Woman at the Well, for example, we are likely to miss entirely the significance of such things as Jesus' going through Samaria, his talking to a woman, the fact that the woman was at the well at midday, the necessity that she go back to get her supposed husband before she could make a decision, and so on. For us to understand such things we need large doses of explanation by those who study the cultural background. We cannot simply trust our culturally conditioned interpretational reflexes. For the Scriptures are specific to the cultural settings of the original events. Sheep, mustard seeds and bushes, broadcast sowing, levirate marriage, and many other aspects of the life of biblical cultures fit into this category.

2. A much bigger problem of interpretation lies in those areas where the Scriptures use cultural symbols that are familiar to us but for which our cultural agreements are different. We are tempted to interpret according to what seems to be the "plain meaning" — as if we could get the proper meaning of Scripture as we would from a document originally written in English. To avoid this pitfall, many translation theorists are now contending that a faithful translation of the Scriptures must involve enough interpretation to protect the reader from being seriously misled at points such as these. Our interpretational reflexes tell us, for example, that a fox is sly and cunning. So, when Jesus refers to Herod as a fox (Luke 13:32), we misinterpret the symbol to mean sly when, in fact, on the basis of the Hebrew cultural agreement, it was intended to signify treachery. Our cultural reflexes tell us that plural marriage is primarily a

sexual matter, though in non-Western cultures it seldom is. Our cultural reflexes tell us that Jesus was impolite to his mother when he addressed her the way he did in the temple and at the wedding feast. Our culturally conditioned interpretational reflexes lead us to understand "the faith once for all delivered to the saints" (Jude 3) to be a system of doctrine rather than a relationship to God, and the "by faith" of Hebrews 11 to signify something somewhat less than behavioral obedience (faith=faithfulness or obedience in Hebrew categories). The culturally conditioned interpretational reflexes of the Nigerians I worked among misled them into thinking that Psalm 23 presented Jesus as insane, since in their culture only young boys and insane men tend sheep. The interpretational reflexes of the Sawi of New Guinea misled them into admiring the treacherous Judas even more than Jesus,[28] and those of the Chinese to regarding positively the dragon of Revelation.

The point is that, for cultural reasons, we who are not a part of the biblical cultures cannot *trust* our interpretational reflexes to give us the meanings that the original authors intended. What are to us the "plain meanings" are almost certain to be the wrong meanings unless the statements are very general. Therefore, we must engage in exegesis to discover what the original utterances meant to those whose interpretational reflexes were the same as those of the authors.

With respect to interpretational reflexes, there seem to be four principles:

1. If the culture of the original is at any given point very similar to ours, our reflexes are going to serve us fairly well. In these instances the interpretational principle that says "the plain meaning is the true meaning" is a valid principle. Such a situation is rarely the case between Euro-American culture and the Hebrew and Aramaic portions of the Scripture. Certain Greek customs do, however, seem to be similar enough to Euro-American customs that our interpretational reflexes will give us the correct meaning. I think in this regard of the language of the track meet that Paul uses in Philippians 3. The same may be true of the language of economics that Paul uses earlier in that same chapter. The amount of biblical material where there is such close cultural similarity to our agreements is, however, distressingly small, and the fact that we cannot trust our interpretational reflexes in most places means that *we can never be sure of them unless we have independent evidence* that this is a place where their custom is close to ours.

2. If the scriptural statement is *a cultural universal*, however, our interpretational reflexes will enable us to get close to the intended meaning. Statements that exist, as far as we know, in every one of

28. See Don Richardson, *The Peace Child* (Glendale, Cal.: Regal Books, 1974).

the world's cultures (e.g., the concepts in the Ten Commandments) are easy to interpret relatively accurately. There is a slight problem in the fact that each culture defines murder, adultery, and so on in its own way. But the fact that such commands occur in all cultures means that these statements are elevated out of the most difficult interpretational category—that of the culturally specific. Other parts of Scripture, such as those dealing with eating together, injunctions like "Love your neighbor," and many of the proverbs, are also in the cultural-universal category.

3. Similarly, if a scriptural statement relates to *experiences that are common to all humankind,* our culturally conditioned interpretational reflexes can be of considerable help. When the Scriptures say "go," "come," "trust," "be patient," and the like, they are dealing with experiences that are common to all human beings and readily interpretable. Likewise with respect to illness and death, childbirth and rearing, obtaining and preparing food, and the like.

4. But, as indicated above, much of the biblical material is presented in cultural forms that are *very specific to cultural practices quite different from ours.* Because of their specificity to the cultural agreements of the original hearers, these materials communicated with maximum impact to them. This is a major part of the genius of God and of his Word—that he speaks specifically to people where they are and in terms of the culture in which they are immersed. At the same time, this fact enormously complicates the task of the person immersed in another culture who seeks to interpret the Scriptures.

The fact that our interpretational reflexes are so limited when dealing with biblical materials argues strongly for the application of the sharpest tools available to the study of the cultural matrices through which God revealed his Word. The harnessing of the perspectives of anthropology and linguistics to this end of the interpretational task (as well as to the communication end) could be a real boon to the exegete. One important result of such harnessing is the development of faithful dynamic equivalence translations and highly interpretive "transculturations" of God's Word.[29] These aim to communicate God's message as specifically as possible in today's languages and cultures so that the members of these cultures will be able to trust their interpretational reflexes when they study the Scriptures.

BEYOND GRAMMATICO-HISTORICAL TO ETHNOLINGUISTIC INTERPRETATION (MODEL 5b)

The statement of model 5b does not differ in essence from the ordinary hermeneutical principle of biblical theology that states that

29. See *Christianity in Culture,* pp. 261-90.

biblical passages are to be interpreted in their original contexts.[30]
The method employed is often referred to by some such label as
"the grammatico-historical method."[31]

The hermeneutical concern is for "extracting" or decoding from
biblical texts the meanings that their authors encoded in those texts.
The problem of biblical hermeneutics is thus the same problem as
that faced by the receptor of any message in any context. It is therefore likely that the insights of contemporary studies into the nature
of the ethnolinguistic setting in which communication takes place
and into the nature and process of communication itself will be most
helpful. Such insights enable us to go beyond the grammatico-historical model as previously developed to at least two points: (1) the
extent to which the linguistic (grammatical) and cultural (historical)
facts are taken into account, and (2) the attempt to focus both on
the central biblical message in the original linguistic and cultural
vehicles (as that approach does) and on certain other important
aspects of supracultural truth — especially those related to the processes God uses to convey that truth.

This approach attempts to see more deeply into language and
culture both at the biblical end and with respect to their influence
on the interpreter himself. We may refer to this approach as "ethnolinguistic" (i.e., "culturo-linguistic") hermeneutics or even as
"ethnohermeneutics."[32] The "context" of which we speak is not simply the literary or even the linguistic context in which an utterance
occurs;[33] *it is the total cultural context* (including both literary and
extraliterary components). And we focus not only on the central
message of the Scriptures as expressed in the original linguistic and
cultural vehicles (as important as that is), but also on the total
process by means of which God seeks to communicate that and
numerous other messages (both then and now) via language and
culture. This approach, in keeping with the aims of biblical theol-

30. See, for example, Bernard Ramm, *Protestant Biblical Interpretation*, 3d rev. ed.
(Grand Rapids: Baker Book, 1970), pp. 138ff. For a critique of certain of the methods
of interpretation traditionally used by biblical theologians, see James Barr, *The Semantics of Biblical Language* (London: Oxford University Press, 1961).

31. See Ramm, *Protestant Biblical Interpretation*, p. 114; A. Berkeley Mickelsen, *Interpreting the Bible* (Grand Rapids: Eerdmans, 1963), p. 159; and Daniel P. Fuller,
"Hermeneutics," unpublished syllabus in use at Fuller Theological Seminary, Pas-
adena, California, in 1969, chapter 11.

32. I am indebted to Mr. Phillip Leung, a Chinese student at the School of World
Mission, 1976-78, for suggesting this term.

33. For an elaboration of this point, see Ramm, *Protestant Biblical Interpretation*,
pp. 138-39; and Nida, *Toward a Science of Translating* (Leiden: E. J. Brill, 1964), and
"Implications of Contemporary Linguistics for Biblical Scholarship," *Journal of Biblical Literature* 91 (1971): 84-87.

ogy, emphasizes the pervasive importance of the cultural context but adds considerations of process to those related to the product (the Scriptures).

At this point it is important to define, in at least a preliminary way, several of the key concepts that will be employed below. The complex relationships between information, message, context, and meaning will be in primary focus. By *information* we designate the raw materials from which messages and meanings are constructed. A *message* consists of the structuring of a body of information in a way appropriate to the ethnolinguistic context within which it is transmitted. The *context* is the structured and structuring matrix within which and according to the rules of which information is organized into messages that may then be reliably encoded, transmitted, and decoded to provide people with meanings. *Meaning* is the structuring of information in the minds of persons. It is frequently encoded into messages that are transmitted by communicators to receptors who decode the messages and, under the stimulus of those messages, restructure meanings in their own minds.

The fact seems to be that messages and, by implication, the information they contain require structured contexts in order to be interpretable (i.e., to be transformed into meanings in the mind of the receptor of the message). As Edward T. Hall states, "Information taken out of context is meaningless and cannot be reliably interpreted. . . . [The] separation of information from context, as though the two were unrelated, is an artifact of Western science and Western thought."[34] And, as David Hunter and Mary Ann Foley suggest, "information, context, and meaning are inseparably and dynamically linked to one another."[35] Figure 2, similar to one provided by Hunter and Foley,[36] is an attempt to depict this dynamic relationship.

If this perspective is correct, there is no possibility of a message (a structured body of information) making sense (i.e., taking on meaning) to a receptor without participating in *some* context. Two questions arise, however: (1) Which is the essential context, that of the originator of the communication, or that of the receptor? and (2) In the interaction between the message and the context, what does each contribute to the resultant meaning?

Model 5b holds that it is the interaction between the message and the *original* context that determines the correct meaning — the meaning that the interpreter seeks to ferret out. As discussed above,

34. Hall, *Handbook for Proxemic Analysis* (Washington: Society for the Anthropology of Visual Communication, 1974), p. 21.

35. Hunter and Foley, *Doing Anthropology* (New York: Harper & Row, 1976), p. 45.

36. Hunter and Foley, *Doing Anthropology*, p. 46.

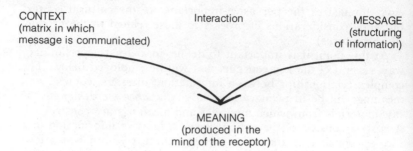

CONTEXT	Interaction	MESSAGE
(matrix in which		(structuring
message is communicated)		of information)

MEANING
(produced in the
mind of the receptor)

Fig. 2. The dynamic relationship between context, message, and meaning. Read: In a given situation information is structured into a Message and communicated within a Context to produce signals that a receptor transforms into Meanings.

the biblical interpreter is hindered in this process by interpretational reflexes conditioned to derive meanings immediately from messages interacting with a different cultural context. Such an interpreter, to transcend this disability, needs to probe to discover the answer to the second question.

The context contributes that part of the meaning deriving from the culture-specific nature of an event. A certain amount of information implicit in the context is a part of this contribution. The fact that a given event occurred in the first century rather than in the twentieth, in Palestine rather than in America, and in Hebrew culture rather than in American culture is extremely significant to the meanings of that event at every point. The context must, therefore, be taken as seriously and analyzed as thoroughly as the message if the meaning of the message is to be understood either for its own time or for ours. The fallacy of the plain-meaning concept lies in the fact that it advocates simply extracting the message as if it would mean the same in interaction with a contemporary context *in that same form*. Such extracted messages "cannot be reliably interpreted."[37]

Nida points in this regard to the unsatisfactory way in which words are traditionally dealt with by biblical scholars. He points to three fallacies (we shall cite only two of these) that stem from certain deficiencies in the philological and historical models commonly employed by such scholars:

In the first place, there has been the tendency to regard the "true meaning" of a word as somehow related to some central core of meaning which is said to exist, either implicitly or explicitly, in each of the different meanings of such a word or lexical unit. It is from this

37. Hall, *Handbook for Proxemic Analysis*, p. 21.

central core of meaning that all the different meanings are supposed to be derivable.[38]

Words are, therefore, regarded by many as *bearing meaning* independently of their contexts. But words, like all information-bearing vehicles within culture, derive their meanings *from* their interaction with the contexts in which they participate. Nida goes on:

> In the second place, a common mistake has been to regard the presumed historical development of meaning as reflecting the "true meaning" of a word. . . . The so-called etymology of a word is supposed to contain the key to the proper understanding of all its meanings.[39]

The historical development of a word or other cultural form is occasionally relevant to its meaning in the same way that a person's genealogy is occasionally relevant to his or her "meaning" (the nature of his or her participation) in a given context. But again, it is the relevance of this aspect of the cultural form to and in interaction with the context in which it occurs that determines its meaning. *A cultural form does not have inherent meaning, only perceived meaning —and this is context-specific.* "Valid lexicography must depend in the ultimate analysis upon patterns of co-occurrence in actual discourse" — in actual situations.[40]

As an example of the kind of contextual analysis here recommended, we may choose two scriptural commands that ought to be treated the same according to the plain-meaning dictum (though in practice they seldom are). The problem is how to explain the difference between the command against stealing (Exod. 20:15) and the command that a woman cover (veil) her head when praying in public (1 Cor. 11:10). In America I have heard the one strongly advocated as it stands, while the other is explained away as "merely cultural." This approach is very unsatisfactory. The problem of the differential interpretation of these commands was vividly brought home to me by one of the Nigerian church leaders whom I was assisting. He pointed out to me that the Bible commands both that we not steal and that we not allow women to pray with their heads uncovered. He then asked why we missionaries teach that the one command be obeyed and the other ignored. Are we using a different Bible?

The fact is that both commands are expressed in cultural terms —

38. Nida, "Implications of Contemporary Linguistics for Biblical Scholarship," p. 84.

39. Nida, "Implications of Contemporary Linguistics for Biblical Scholarship," p. 85.

40. Nida, "Implications of Contemporary Linguistics for Biblical Scholarship," p. 85. For further elaboration of this point, see *Christianity in Culture*, pp. 345-59.

that is, via cultural and linguistic forms or symbols. So both are cultural messages. But, since nothing in the Bible is "merely" cultural, we need to look beyond each command to discover how the word and custom symbols were understood by the authors and those to whom they were originally written. That is, we need to look for the supracultural meaning in each by getting beyond our own cultural conditioning (with its "plain meanings") to the interpretation of each within its original cultural context.

At this point we are in danger of being put off by the fact that our culture has a rule against stealing. We may, therefore, simply employ our interpretational reflexes and assume that we know what the command against stealing meant in its Hebrew context on the basis of what similar word symbols mean in our culture. We are wrong, however, since no cultural symbols have exactly the same meanings in any two cultures, owing to the differences in the contexts with which the symbols interact. Yet, since those words do have a meaning in our culture and that meaning is consonant with Christianity, most accept the meaning assigned to those words (that message) in our culture as the plain meaning of Scripture. They see no need to go into Hebrew culture to discover their original meaning.

With respect to the headcovering command, however, many take an opposite point of view—and appear to some to be "explaining away" the command. Since those word symbols and the whole context in which they occur have no plain meaning that seems to bear Christian truth in our culture, most American Christians feel compelled to study the Greek cultural background to discover the original meaning. Some groups, of course, are consistent at this point and interpret the headcovering command in terms of the meaning of those word forms within our culture. These groups make their women wear headcoverings.

We infer that the stealing command already existed in Hebrew culture (as, from cross-cultural data, we learn it does in every culture). It had specific reference, however, only to what the Hebrews of that time considered to be the unwarranted appropriation of certain of those things considered to be the property of another. In that kind of strongly kinship-oriented society it is unlikely that it would be considered stealing if a person appropriated his brother's goods without asking. Nor is it likely that a starving person who "helped himself" to someone else's food could be accused of stealing (see Matt. 12:1-4).

By interpreting in terms of the Hebrew cultural context, we find this command to differ only slightly from our own cultural understanding of it. This fact illustrates that, due to human commonality, meanings derived from the interaction of certain (general) messages with any cultural context are appropriate even in quite diverse cultures. The relative importance of context and message, however, varies from situation to situation. In situations such as this where the significance of the context in the determination of the meaning is less, the possibility is increased for transferring the message from one cultural situation to another in roughly its original form with *most* (never all) of its meaning intact. Truly "propositional" statements in Scripture such as "God is love" illustrate this point.[41] For this reason, even plain-meaning interpretations are fairly accurate for such statements.

When, however, the contribution to the meaning of implicit contextual information is high (as, for example, with the genealogies or the headcovering issue), it is necessary to interpret at a much deeper level of abstraction (see model 5c below) to ferret out the more general transferable meanings. Ethnolinguistic insight into the cultural and linguistic factors involved is especially valuable at this point. For there is much more meaning that God seeks to communicate through his Word than the surface level, context-specific messages so often in focus.

As for the headcovering command, analysis of the meaning of the custom in its cultural context does not lead simply to an alternative understanding of the same command. It leads, rather, to a *meaning* that demands *expression via a different cultural form* if it is to be understood in English. In the Greek culture of that day, apparently, the cultural form "female praying in public without headcovering" would have been interpreted to mean "this female is immoral," or, at least, "she is not showing proper respect to men" (see commentaries on 1 Cor. 11:10-12). Since that meaning was not consonant with the witness that Christians ought to make, Paul commands against the use of the head-uncovered symbol in favor of its opposite, the head-covered symbol. For only this latter symbol conveyed the proper Christian meaning in that culture—that Christian women were not immoral and were properly subject to their men. The theological truth then—a truth just as relevant today as in the first century— is that Christian women should not behave in such a way that people judge them to be "out of line" (whether morally or with respect to authority).[42]

DIFFERING LEVELS OF ABSTRACTION (MODEL 5c)

Such cross-cultural analysis of the two passages shows that in comparing the two commands we are not comparing sames. For the

41. For an enlightened discussion of the pros and cons of using the term *proposition* as a designation for that which God has revealed, see Ronald H. Nash, "Truth by Any Other Name," *Christianity Today* 22 (1977): 15-17, 19.

42. For a useful discussion of this issue, see Robert C. Sproul, "Controversy at Culture Gap," *Eternity* 27 (1976): 13-15, 40.

commands are given at different levels of abstraction. That is, the relative importance of the specific cultural context to the meaning of the utterances differs. Those utterances that relate most specifically to their particular cultural contexts are at what is here termed the "surface" or "cultural-specific" level of abstraction. For correct understanding (interpretation) these depend greatly on implicit information embedded in the context with which the given custom interacts. Those utterances in which the specific context is less important to the meaning, and which, therefore, relate to pancultural human commonality, are at what may be termed a "deeper" or "general-principle" level of abstraction. These utterances are not so dependent on information implicit to their original contexts for interpretation. That the stealing command is at a deeper level of abstraction is evident from the fact that it does not refer to a specific cultural act but to a *category* of cultural behavior. The command is general rather than specific. Note, by way of contrast, the specificity of the tenth command. That command is at the surface level of abstraction (like the headcovering command) in that it specifies the proscribed cultural *acts* rather than (until the final phrase) generalizing them into an *overall principle* as we do when we refer to that command as a general command against "covetousness." Note the wording:

> Do not desire another man's house; do not desire his wife, his slaves, his cattle, his donkeys, or anything else that he owns. (Exod. 20:17 TEV)

The headcovering command is at this more specific level, where the embedded information in that particular cultural context is very important to the meaning. A corresponding specific stealing command would be something like "Don't take your neighbor's donkey without his permission." A headcovering command at the same level of generality as the stealing command would be something like "Don't appear out of line with respect to immorality or authority." Thus we see a specific cultural form/symbol level with the original context contributing relatively more to the meaning, and a deeper general-principle level in which the original context contributes relatively less. These two possibilities are illustrated in Figure 3.

There seems, however, to be a yet deeper level of abstraction in Scripture. This is made explicit by Jesus when he summarizes the teaching of the law and the prophets in two statements:

> "Love the Lord your God with all your heart, with all your soul, and with all your mind." This is the greatest and the most important commandment. The second most important commandment is like it: "Love your neighbor as you love yourself." The whole Law of Moses and the teachings of the prophets depend on these two command-

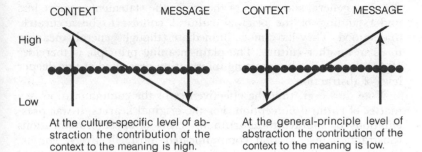

At the culture-specific level of abstraction the contribution of the context to the meaning is high.

At the general-principle level of abstraction the contribution of the context to the meaning is low.

Fig. 3. "Seesaw" diagrams illustrating the relationship between the context-message interaction concept and the levels of abstraction concept.

ments (Matt. 22:37-40 TEV; cf. Deut. 6:5; Mark 12:29-31; Luke 10:27).

These three levels correspond to some extent with the three levels charted in Figure 4: the level of specific customs, the level of world-view values, and the deep level of human universals. The universals apply to every person in every culture at all times. These may be regarded as transcultural or even supracultural ideals. The general principles (such as the Ten Commandments) seem, likewise, to apply universally. If these are seen as corresponding with the cultural worldview level, it is with the recognition that values such as these occur in the worldviews of every culture. At the level of specific custom, though, there is a considerable range of diversity expressive of the general principles.

There are occasional problems as to which of the levels to assign certain of the general statements of Scripture. We may advance Figure 5 as a step in the direction of developing this model more precisely. Note that a complete chart would show (even more than this one does) the fact that there are fewer categories at the Basic Ideal Level, more at the General Principle Level, and an enormous number at the Specific Cultural Form/Symbol Level.

In such expositions as the Ten Commandments (especially as Jesus summarizes them in Matt. 22:37-40), the Sermon on the Mount, the listing of the fruits of the Spirit (Gal. 5:22-23), and many similar statements, the Scriptures seem to us to come closest to a clear statement of a portion of the supracultural will of God for human conduct. The reason for the apparent clarity of these portions is that they are phrased at a level of abstraction that largely extricates them from specific application to the original cultures in which they were uttered. As one moves from specific cultural applications of supra-cultural truth (as with the headcovering command) back toward the most general statements of the truth, the statements require less understanding of the original cultural context to be accurately understood. They have more immediate (though general) meaning to us in another culture. The plain-meaning principle is therefore often adequate for interpreting information presented at this deeper level of abstraction.

Note, however, that the effectiveness of the communication is a matter of cultural perception. For the original hearers, it was presentations of supracultural truth in terms of specific applications (abstraction level 3) that communicated most effectively. For us, likewise, specific applications of scriptural generalizations would most effectively communicate. But, since the Scriptures were written in terms of cultures other than ours, we are denied enscripturated applications of supracultural truth in our culture. The general statements, therefore, make more sense to us than the specific cultural forms through which these principles were applied in biblical cultures. And the more specific applications in the Scriptures are often the most confusing to us.

Throughout the Scriptures we are provided with glimpses of the

Customs A	Customs B	Customs C	Customs D	Customs E
Worldview A	Worldview B	Worldview C	Worldview D	Worldview E

UNIVERSAL CULTURAL FUNCTIONS			
Obtaining and maintaining biological necessities —food, shelter, health, sex, air, excretion	Obtaining and maintaining psychological necessities —meaning in life, personal security, a measure of freedom	Obtaining and maintaining socio-cultural necessities —language, family, education, social control	Obtaining and maintaining spiritual necessities —mythology, ritual
Food, shelter, air, sex, excretion, health	Meaning, maintenance of individual psyche	Communication, provide for children, transmission of culture, maintenance of social system	Understanding of and relationships to supracultural beings and factors
BIOLOGICAL	PSYCHOLOGICAL	SOCIO-CULTURAL	SPIRITUAL
UNIVERSAL HUMAN NEEDS			

Fig. 4. Human commonality and cultural diversity.

1. BASIC IDEAL LEVEL	2. GENERAL PRINCIPLE LEVEL	3. SPECIFIC CULTURAL FORM/ SYMBOL LEVEL
◄---- More General ◄----►		More Specific ------►
A. Love your neighbor as you love yourself (Matt. 22:39)	1. Don't steal (Exod. 20:15)	a. Don't take your neighbor's donkey (Hebrew) b. Don't take your employer's money (U.S.A.)
	2. Don't covet	a. Don't desire another man's house . . . (Exod. 20:17) b. Same for U.S.A.
	3. Be free from partiality (1 Tim. 5:21; Jas. 3:17)	a. Treat Gentiles/blacks/ women as human beings b. Rebuke whoever needs it (1 Tim. 5:20)
B. Love the Lord your God with all your heart . . . (Matt. 22:37)	1. Worship no God but me (Exod. 20:3)	a. Don't bow down to any idol or worship it (Exod. 20:5) b. Don't pledge primary allegiance to material wealth (U.S.A.)
	2. Seek by all means to save people (1 Cor. 9:22)	a. Live as a Jew to win Jews (1 Cor. 9:20) b. Live as a Gentile to win Gentiles (1 Cor. 9:21) c. Live as an African to win Africans
C. Everything must be done in a proper and orderly way (1 Cor. 14:40)	1. Leaders should be beyond reproach (1 Tim. 3:2; Tit. 1:6)	a. They must be self-controlled, etc. (1 Tim. 3:2)
	2. Christian women should not appear out of line	a. They should cover their heads when praying in Greek culture (1 Cor. 11:10) b. They should not wear their clothes too tight (U.S.A.)
	3. Christians should live according to the rules of the culture (as long as they don't conflict with Christian principles)	a. Women should learn in silence in Greek culture (1 Tim. 2:11) b. Women may speak up in mixed groups in U.S.A. c. Pay the government what belongs to it (Matt. 22:21) d. Obey governmental authorities (Rom. 13:1) e. Wives submit to their husbands in Greek and many segments of U.S.A. culture (Eph. 5:22; Col. 3:18; etc.) f. Wives and husbands work coordinately in many segments of U.S.A. culture.

D. Other ideals?

Fig. 5. Illustrative chart of differing levels of abstraction model (5c).

supracultural, clothed in specific events taking place within specific cultures at specific times. Frequently, as with statements at the general-principle or basic-ideal level, we get the impression that we are looking at supracultural truth with a minimum of cultural conditioning. More frequently, however, we are exposed to supracultural truth applied in a specific situation in a specific biblical culture. The record of this comes to us only in translation, so that we see such truth as "puzzling reflections in a mirror" (1 Cor. 13:12 JBP). Among these "reflections," Smalley feels that

> those parts of Scripture which give us evaluations of human motives and emotions, human attitudes and personalities, give us the deepest insight into God's ultimate will, and that to understand the revelation in terms of God's will for our behavior we will have to learn to look behind the cultural facade to see as much as we can of what the Word indicates about those questions. The cultural examples given us are thereby not lost. They provide most valuable examples of the way in which God's will was performed in another cultural setting to help us see how we may perform it in ours.[43]

In this way it is possible for Christians to learn something of supracultural truth even though this, like all human knowledge, is perceived by us in terms of the cultural grid in which we operate. Though often puzzling and never total or absolute, such knowledge is adequate for God's purposes — the salvation and spiritual growth of all who give themselves to him in faith.[44] We may then, under the leading of the Spirit, come to know something of how the Spirit desires us to live out these truths in terms of our cultural forms.

"TWO-CULTURE DIALOGIC" INTERPRETATION (MODEL 5d)

As amply indicated in the foregoing, we are dealing with both the interpreter's culture and the ethnolinguistics of the biblical contexts when we interpret. Any model of hermeneutics that ignores the influence of the interpreter's culture on that person's attempts to understand the Scriptures is seriously deficient. Many who seek to employ grammatico-historical methodology are severely hampered by a failure to grasp the full significance of the culture-boundness of themselves and of their methodology.

The plain-meaning approach, though providing reasonably accurate interpretations at the most general levels of abstraction, is flawed by its simplistic approach to the original contexts. In reaction against that approach the grammatico-historical approach digs deeply

---

43. Smalley, "Culture and Superculture," p. 66.
44. See Mickelsen, *Interpreting the Bible*, p. 353.

into the original contexts. But it tends to overestimate the possibility of objectivity on the part of the contemporary scholarly interpreter. We have attempted, by means of the application of anthropological, linguistic, and communicational insights, to increase our ability to maximize the strengths of these approaches (especially the latter) while minimizing their deficiencies. It remains to deal explicitly with the dialogical nature of the interaction between the messages of Scripture in their contexts and the concerns of the interpreters in their contexts.

A concern for the contextualization of biblical messages is a concern that scriptural meanings get all the way across what might be pictured as a "hermeneutical bridge" into the real-life contexts of ordinary people. In a perceptive article dealing with hermeneutics from the perspective of one deeply committed to the contextualization of Christianity, C. René Padilla says,

> hermeneutics has to do with a dialogue between Scripture and a contemporary culture. Its purpose is to transpose the biblical message from its original context into a particular twentieth-century situation. Its basic assumption is that the God who spoke in the past and whose Word was recorded in the Bible continues to speak today in Scripture.[45]

If interpretation is done naively, as in the plain-meaning approach, meaningful dialogue between past revelation and present need is often prevented, owing to a premature application of hastily and superficially derived meanings. Scholarly approaches to interpretation, on the other hand, have prevented such dialogue by considering the biblical message in its original context in such a way that its meanings remain in "a world which is definitely not our world." A balanced approach takes both contexts seriously and gives both due weight. "The aim is that the horizon of the receptor culture is merged with the horizon of the text in such a way that the message proclaimed in the receptor culture may be a dynamic equivalent of the message proclaimed in the original context."[46]

The hermeneutical process, then, involves a dynamic interaction or dialogue between an interpreter deeply enmeshed in his or her own culture and worldview (including theological biases) and the Scriptures. The interpreter has needs, some of which he or she formulates into questions, "asking" these questions of the Scriptures and finding certain of them answered. Other questions remain unanswered, since "there is a large number of topics on which Scripture says nothing or very little."[47] Still other questions are stimulated

45. Padilla, "Hermeneutics and Culture," paper presented at the Willowbank Consultation on the Gospel and Culture, January 1978, p. 11.
46. Padilla, "Hermeneutics and Culture," pp. 5, 6. For a detailed treatment of the concept of dynamic equivalency, see *Christianity in Culture*, pp. 261-344.
47. Padilla, "Hermeneutics and Culture," p. 17.

in the mind of the interpreter as a result of the person's interaction with Scripture. Meanwhile, in attempting to live life in a particular context, the interpreter's interaction with that context also stimulates new questions.

> The richer and deeper the questions brought by the interpreter from the receptor culture, the richer and deeper the answers provided by Scripture. It follows that without a good understanding of the real issues involved in living in a particular situation there cannot be an adequate understanding of the relevance of the biblical message to that situation. Each new formulation of the questions based on a more refined understanding of the situation makes possible a new reading of Scripture and consequently the discovery of new implications of its message. If it is true that Scripture illuminates life, it is also true that life illuminates Scripture.[48]

Hermeneutics is not, therefore, merely an academic game to be played by supposedly objective scholars. It is a dynamic process that properly demands deep subjective involvement on the part of Christian interpreters operating within the Christian community (which includes scholars) both with the Scriptures and with the life of the world around them in which they live. Hermeneutics is thus a kind of three-way conversation, proceeding according to the rules of communication,[49] under the guidance of the Holy Spirit, issuing in what might be pictured as an upward "spiraling" of understanding of Scriptures, of self, of the world, and of the proper, God-guided interactions between the three at *this* time and in *this* setting. At the beginning of the "spiral" the interpreter goes with certain felt needs to the Scriptures under the guidance of God and with the assistance of the Christian community (in person or via published materials). Within the community, then, the interpreter moves from needs to Scripture, to application in the living of his or her life, to needs (some of which are newly perceived and at a deeper level), to Scripture (some of which he or she sees with "new eyes"), to deeper-level application in the living of his or her life, and so on.

The life context with which the interpreter is interacting is critical to the whole process. If the life context to which the applications are made is merely an academic context, the nature of the insights derived from Scripture and their usability outside that context are vitally affected. This is what makes much of what goes on in academic institutions and scholarly writings unusable in life contexts other than the classroom. One of the damaging effects of such academicization of biblical interpretation has been the excessive infor-

---

48. Padilla, "Hermeneutics and Culture," p. 17.
49. On this, see Charles R. Taber, "Hermeneutics and Culture," paper presented at the Willowbank Consultation on the Gospel and Culture, January 1978, pp. 9ff.

mationalizing of revelation.[50] Given the "down-to-earth" nature of the Scriptures, it is often the unschooled interpreter who can best interpret them, in spite of the difficulty that one may have in understanding the more culture-specific passages. For the Scriptures are *life*-related, not merely "religious discourse . . . couched in technical language," as Western exegetes have tended to assume.[51]

This dialogical approach to hermeneutics is more serious than previous approaches in the place it gives to the interpreter and the receptor group in their respective contexts. It does not assume either unbiased interpreters or the universality for all times and places of the answers arrived at by previous interpreters in their times and places. It places real people with real needs in real-life contexts at the center of the hermeneutical process. It questions the ultimacy of academic, scholarly interpretation outside academic, scholarly contexts. Dialogical hermeneutics draws its

> concern for context from the Bible itself. And it recognizes in the multi-leveled character of biblical context the multi-leveled character of context in the process of understanding itself. What was that original context addressed by Jesus Christ when he called, "Repent, for the kingdom of heaven is at hand" (Matt. 4:17)? What was that context to which Matthew spoke as interpreter of Jesus when he used the words, "kingdom of heaven"? How was it different from the context of Mark who summarizes the same message of Jesus in terms of the "kingdom of God" (Mark 1:15)? What was the context Paul addressed as the re-encoder of the kingdom message at Rome, transposing "preaching the kingdom of God" into "teaching concerning the Lord Jesus Christ" (Acts 28:23, 31)?
>
> A process of this kind can be liberating as the man of God wrestles with biblical context, his own, and those to whom he speaks and before whom he lives. Charles Taber writes that such an appeal to Scripture "can free indigenous theology from the bondage of Western categories and methodologies."[52]

The concern for the importance of the contexts of interpreter and receptor must not diminish our concern for Scriptures as our "tether" and "yardstick." For the hermeneutical process is an interactional process with the Bible as the necessary point with which all else is to interact.

50. On this, see *Christianity in Culture*, pp. 169-93.
51. See Taber, "Hermeneutics and Culture," p. 12.
52. Harvie M. Conn, "Contextualization: A New Dimension For Cross-Cultural Hermeneutic," *Evangelical Missions Quarterly* 14 (1978): 45. Conn's citation of Taber is taken from "The Limits of Indigenization in Theology," *Missiology* 6 (1978): 71.

HERMENEUTICS, TRUTH, AND PRAXIS
JOSÉ MIGUEZ BONINO

The new theological consciousness is not without opposition inside Latin America. Serious objections have also been expressed outside our continent. "Our language is so new," writes Juan Luis Segundo, "that to some it looks like a travesty of the gospel."[1] While the new Latin American theology is deeply polemical, it is not isolationist. Its spokesmen are aware of the problems raised by this new way of doing theology and are willing to discuss them. But they will refuse to be subject to the academic theology of the West as a sort of *norma normans* to which all theology is accountable. And they will reject a theological debate which proceeds as if abstracted from the total situation in which reflection takes place. We shall explore some of the questions raised in the theological dialogue which begins to develop across the chasm that divides the rich and the poor. We shall simply try to locate the questions and suggest lines along which they can be pursued. Obviously, they will be approached from the perspective of our own—Latin American—location. But hopefully it will be possible to suggest their correspondence with old and fundamental theological questions and motifs.

The "ideologization" of the gospel is perhaps the charge most frequently brought against this theology. In an acid criticism of the thought of Iglesia y Sociedad en America Latina (ISAL = Church and Society in Latin America), the Peruvian evangelical Pedro Arana concludes that "in the ideology of ISAL, God is translated by revolution, the people of God by the revolutionary hosts, and the Word of God by the revolutionary writings. Nobody will fail to see that all of this is Marxist humanism."[2] The ghost of "German Chris-

1. Segundo, *De la Sociedad a la Teología* (Buenos Aires: Editorial Carlos Lohle, 1970), p. 7.
2. Arana, in "The Authority of the Bible," paper presented at the meeting of the Asociación Teológica Evangélica Latinoamericana, Cochabamba, Bolivia, December 1971. It is interesting to note, however, that Arana has increasingly come to express a concern with a genuinely evangelical and engaged approach to the social and political questions. See, for instance, his essay "Ordenes de la creación y responsabilidad social," in *Fe cristiana y Latinoamerica hoy,* ed. C. René Padilla (Buenos Aires: Ediciones Certeza, 1974), pp. 169-84; and, more especially, "La Liberación," a series of outlines for Bible study reproduced in *Pasos,* 4 June 1973.

Reprinted from *Doing Theology in a Revolutionary Situation* (Philadelphia: Fortress Press, 1975), pp. 86-105.

tians" and their monstrous accommodation to Nazi ideology are frequently conjured in order to anathematize the theology of liberation. The problem is serious. It is not simply a question of some unfortunate or risky formulations of avant-garde or scandal-loving theologians, but of the very basis of the method of interpretation and the structure of theological reflection used in this theology. It appears as the hopeless prisoner of a hermeneutical circle, the spell of which it cannot break. The text of Scripture and tradition is forced into the Procrustean bed of ideology, and the theologian who has fallen prey to this procedure is forever condemned to listen only to the echo of his own ideology. There is no redemption for this theology, because it has muzzled the Word of God in its transcendence and freedom.

This criticism is not without significance. In fact, it seems to me that our Latin American theology of liberation has not yet become sufficiently aware of the weight of this risk and consequently has not yet developed adequate safeguards against it. But before we undertake such a task it seems important to put the question in the right way, which, if I understand things correctly, is not primarily the cognitive level of understanding and interpretation, but the *historical* level of praxis and obedience; or, to put it more precisely, the mutual relation and the unity of the two.

I shall try to indicate the problem by means of a brief story.[3] A young Puerto Rican professor of theology spent some time in prison for political reasons—demonstration against U.S. military experiments in his land. As he was trying to explain to other (non-Christian) fellow prisoners how his participation in this action was anchored in his Christian faith, one of them cut him short: "Listen, your faith does not mean a thing, because you can justify your political course of action and the man who put you in prison can do the same, appealing to the same truth." How can this objection be answered? There are two possible answers that we want to exclude. The first one would be: "This is the way I feel," "This is the way I decide," or "This is what Christianity means to me." There is no need to spend much time on this answer: it clearly places us in the quicksands of subjectivism and voluntarism, in which all objective historical contents either in Christianity or of the present are vacated. For this reason, most people would veer to a second answer: "There is an absolute Christian truth, or Christian principles, somehow enshrined in Scripture and/or in the pronouncements of the church. But then, there are more or less imperfect *applications* of that truth." This answer expresses what could be called the classical

---

3. The story was told by Professor Luis N. Rivera Pagán, from the Seminario Unido of Río Piedras, Puerto Rico, at a meeting on liberation and theology in Buenos Aires in June 1971.

conception of the relationship between truth and practice. Truth belongs, for this view, to a world of truth, a universe complete in itself, which is copied or reproduced in "correct" propositions, in a theory (i.e., a contemplation of this universe) which corresponds to this truth. Then, in a second moment, as a later step, comes the application in a particular historical situation. Truth is therefore preexistent to and independent of its historical effectiveness. Its legitimacy has to be tested in relation to this abstract "heaven of truth," quite apart from its historicization.

It is this conception of truth that has come to a crisis in the theology which we are discussing. When Hugo Assmann speaks of the rejection of "any *logos* which is not the *logos* of a *praxis*"[4] or Gustavo Gutiérrez writes about an "epistemological split,"[5] they are not merely saying that truth must be applied, or even that truth is related to its application. They are saying, in fact, that there is no truth outside or beyond the concrete historical events in which men are involved as agents. There is, therefore, no knowledge except in action itself, in the process of transforming the world through participation in history. As soon as such a formulation is presented, objections will be raised that (1) biblical truth is reduced to ethical action—the classical heresy of several forms of humanism, (2) the vertical dimension is swallowed in the horizontal, (3) this is the Marxist view of knowledge.

Before arriving at such judgments, we should raise at least two questions concerning the classical view. The first one is whether it corresponds to the biblical concept of truth. In this respect it will suffice to mention several converging lines in biblical scholarship and interpretation. Whatever corrections may be needed, there is scarcely any doubt that God's Word is not understood in the Old Testament as a conceptual communication but as a creative event, a history-making pronouncement. Its truth does not consist in some correspondence to an idea but in its efficacy in carrying out God's promise or fulfilling his judgment. Correspondingly, what is required of Israel is not an ethical inference but an obedient participation—whether in action or in suffering—in God's active righteousness and mercy. Faith is always a concrete obedience which relies on God's promise and is vindicated in the act of obedience: Abraham offering his only son, Moses stepping into the Red Sea. There is no question of arriving at or possessing previously some theoretical clue. There is no name of God to call forth—or to exe-

4. Assman, *Opresión-Liberación: Desafío a los cristianos* (Montevideo: Tierra Nueva, 1971), p. 87.

5. Gutiérrez, *Praxis de Liberación y Fe Cristiana* (Lima: Centro de Documentación MIEI-JECI, 1973), p. 16.

gete — except as he himself is present in his power (i.e., his powerful acts). Again, the faith of Israel is consistently portrayed not as a *gnosis* but as a *way*, a particular way of acting, of relating inside and outside the nation, of ordering life at every conceivable level, which corresponds to God's own way with Israel. This background, so well attested in the Psalms, for instance, may explain Jesus' use of the word *way* to refer to himself. The motif, on the other hand, appears in parenetic contexts in Pauline literature. Faith is a "walking." It is unnecessary to point out that even the idea of knowledge and knowing has this active and participatory content.

This way of conceiving truth finds explicit confirmation in the Johannine emphasis on "*doing* the truth." God's Word (his *Logos*) is an incarnate word, a human flesh which has pitched its tent in history. Knowledge of such Logos is fellowship, participation in this new "life" which has been made available in the midst of the old "world." It is "a new birth." There is no way to this understanding through the mere exegetical exercise of the new teaching: "Why do you not understand what I say [*lalia*]? It is because you cannot bear to hear my word [*Logos*]" (John 8:43). One must be ready to enter actively into this relation, this life: only he who *does* the word will know the doctrine. The Johannine epistles work out the same theme relating the knowledge of God to the love of the brother. God is unknown unless man participates in his concrete life through love. There is here no minimizing of the historical revelation in Jesus Christ; quite the contrary, this is a critical test for the author. But this revelation is not an abstract theoretical knowledge but a concrete existence: the existence in love.[6]

The point could be elaborated further in relation to other blocks of biblical writings. It seems clear enough that the classical conception can claim no biblical basis for its conceptual understanding of truth or for its distinction between a theoretical knowledge of truth and a practical application of it. Correct knowledge is contingent on right doing. Or rather, the knowledge is disclosed in the doing. Wrongdoing is ignorance. But, on the other hand, we can also ask whether this classical distinction is phenomenologically true. Is there, in fact, a theoretical knowledge prior to its application? It seems that both Scripture and social analysis yield the same answer: there is no such neutral knowledge. The sociology of knowledge makes abundantly clear that we think always out of a definite context of relations and action, out of a given praxis. What Bultmann has so

---

6. The Mexican Jesuit J.-L. Miranda has published a very penetrating exegetical study of this concept in Johannine literature, *El ser y el Mesías* (Salamanca: Ediciones Sígueme, 1973). See also the work of the Spanish biblicist José M. Diez Alegría *Yo creo en la esperanza* (Bilbao: Desclée de Brouwer, 1972), pp. 68-87.

convincingly argued concerning a *preunderstanding* which every man brings to his interpretation of the text must be deepened and made more concrete, not in the abstract philosophical analysis of existence but in the concrete conditions of men who belong to a certain time, people, and class, who are engaged in certain courses of action, even of Christian action, and who reflect and read the texts within and outside of these conditions.

If these observations concerning the biblical understanding of truth and of the conditions of knowing are correct, as the phenomenological analysis also indicates from another perspective, several basic points emerge in relation to the question of hermeneutics. We indicate some of these points, which demand a careful examination.[7]

Every interpretation of the texts which is offered to us (whether as exegesis or as systematic or as ethical interpretation) must be investigated in relation to the praxis out of which it comes. At this point the instruments created by the two modern masters in the art of "suspecting"—namely, Freud and Marx—are of great significance. Very concretely, we cannot receive the theological interpretation coming from the rich world without suspecting it and, therefore, asking what kind of praxis it supports, reflects, or legitimizes. Why is it, for instance, that the obvious political motifs and undertones in the life of Jesus have remained so hidden to liberal interpreters until very recently? Is this merely a regrettable oversight on the part of these scholars or is it—mostly unconscious, to be sure—the expression of the liberal ideological distinction of levels or spheres which relegates religion to the area of subjectivity and individual privacy? In a similar vein, Juan Luis Segundo finds the clue to the common image of a timeless and impersonal God not only in the speculative, philosophical influences which went into its creation but also in a view of a split life where man works and produces in an external, public, material area in order to "emerge to a zone identified as 'privacy'" in which he is supposed to realize his humanity. Is it not therefore quite understandable that God will be identified with this area, or even more, made the guarantor of it, and consequently held to be distant from the world of outward, material history?[8] When Freud and Marx denounce such a God as an ideological projection through which we disguise our inability to deal with our own human historical and material reality, they are providing the tools for a purification of our theological hermeneutics.

7. For some further observations and illustration in this area, see my essay "Marxist Critical Tools: Are They Helpful?" *Movement*, May 1974.

8. See Segundo, *Our Idea of God*, trans. John Drury, Artisans of a New Humanity Series, vol. 3 (Maryknoll, N.Y.: Orbis Books, 1974), pp. 66ff.

This, in turn, opens the door to a reconception of the theological heritage.

Even more important is the question of the verifiability of Christianity—or of the interpretation of Christianity as it operates historically. The problem of verifiability cannot be evaded; it has always confronted Christianity. But since the second century it has been approached apologetically as the question of the rationality of the Christian faith. Theological systems have changed according to the changes in the philosophical systems which at a given time offered the framework for the explanation of ultimate reality. It was crucial to show that the Christian faith made sense in terms of such frameworks of interpretation. Three facts, at least, force us today out of this type of verification. First, the demise of metaphysics has made all reference to this transreality of human and worldly things largely irrelevant. We can no longer find in such a world a valid correlate for our theological language. Second, we have now the instruments for assessing and analyzing the historical impact of the Christian faith. Since socioanalytical sciences have uncovered the concrete historical dynamics of Christianity (i.e., the relation of Protestantism to capitalism, the relation of social *anomie* to the growth of sects, and so on) and since structural analysis permits us to expose the ideological functions of religious language, we can no longer measure the proclamation and witness of the church in terms of the conceptual contents of its doctrine, disclaiming as "spurious" or "incidental" the so-called consequences of such doctrine. The meaning of Christianity cannot be abstracted from its historical significance. Words—whatever the speaker may intend—communicate in relation to a code that is historically defined, and this code has been created not out of ideas but out of the total experience of a given time and people—an experience which incorporates the actual historical impact of the Christian faith. Third, the biblical witness itself will not let us find refuge in such a conceptual firmament. Its references are always time- and place-bound. It speaks of events that took place, take place, and will take place in history, in the world of men, events that can be dated in relation to Pharaoh, Nebuchadnezzar, or Augustus. God himself is, to be sure, the main actor in these events. But there is no attempt to infer God's action from some previously ascertainable project or idea. Rather, his character is to be known in his acts (which, to be sure, are not without their "word," but a word verified in the act).

Finally, both the criticism and the introduction of the criterion of historical verifiability introduce into the hermeneutical task new areas and instruments. We are not concerned with establishing through deduction the consequences of conceptual truths but with analyzing a historical praxis which claims to be Christian. This critical analysis includes a number of operations which are totally unknown to classical theology. Historical praxis overflows the area of the subjective and private. If we are dealing with acts and not merely with ideas, feelings, or intentions, we plunge immediately into the area of politics, understood now in its broad sense of public or social. Billy Graham, the South African Reformed Church, Martin Luther King, Jr., and "Christians for Socialism" do not confront us primarily as systems of ideas or theological positions but as historical agents acting in certain directions and with certain effects which are objectively possible to determine. The area of research is the total society in which these agents are performing; economic, political, and cultural facts are as relevant to a knowledge of these praxes as the exegesis of their pronouncements and publications. Their Christianity must be verified in relation to such questions as imperialism, apartheid, integration, self-determination, and many other sociopolitical magnitudes.

It is obvious that such an analysis brings with it the tools of sociopolitical sciences. A recent study of Chilean Pentecostalism, for instance, researches the mechanisms of authority and control operative in these communities in relation to secular models prevailing in the society: the *caudillo* (leader), the paternalistic landowner, the democratic model. It compares the behavior of the Pentecostal groups with the normal class behavior of Chilean society (of the same classes). It assesses attitudes toward money, work, and politics with reference to classic Protestant models. Out of these data a picture emerges of an interpretation of the gospel *as it really* works itself out in history in this particular time and place. The result of this research, though, does not leave us simply with a sum of facts; it discloses a (more or less coherent, or partially modified) unified perception of the world — an ideology.[9] Hermeneutics in this new context entails an identification of the ideological frameworks of interpretation implicit in a given religious praxis. It is important to point out, in this respect, that such discernment of an ideology implicit in a theological or religious praxis does not necessarily imply the intention of the person or group in question to uphold or promote such ideology. One could even venture to say that, in most cases, people are themselves unaware of it. Their words and actions may intend something else. But in the context of a given situation they may in *fact* be supporting and buttressing a certain political and/or economic line and, therefore, functioning, in the wider context of the total society, as ideological justification of such lines. It is important to make this distinction, because it has to do with the

9. On this, see Christian Lalive d'Epinay, *Haven of the Masses: A Study of the Pentecostal Movement in Chile* (London: Lutterworth Press, 1969).

concrete historical character of Christian acts and pronouncements. This makes it possible—and this is nothing new in the area of doctrinal development—that a position taken at one point in history may acquire in a different setting an ideological connotation.

In the same context, it is important to recognize that this identification of the ideology implicit in a given historical praxis does not as such disqualify it. Any course of action which keeps a certain coherence implies a unified perspective on reality, an explicit or implicit project. Ideology, in this sense, has also a positive meaning: it is the instrument through which our Christian obedience gains coherence and unity. It is so, though, provided that it be always brought to consciousness and critically examined both in terms of the gospel and of the scientific analysis of reality. As soon as we make such a formulation, we are faced with several problems, which it is now necessary to broach.

If it be true that every form of praxis articulates—consciously or unconsciously—a view of reality and a projection of it, an analysis and an ideology, this means that reflection on this praxis must necessarily raise the question of the rightness or inadequacy of such analysis and ideology. This is a complex problem to which we cannot expect to find an unobjectionable answer. But the question is unavoidable. It is at this point that the theology of the most history-conscious European and American theologians seems to us to fail. They grant that faith emerges as a historical praxis. Moreover, they grant the political (i.e., public) character of this praxis. But then, they want to remain at some neutral or intermediate level in which there is no need to opt for this or that concrete political praxis— that is, to assume a particular analysis and a particular ideological projection. We have already seen that such an attempt is self-deceptive. The opposite position, which we adopt, brings with it a particular risk. Nobody will claim, in fact, that his analysis of social, political, and economic reality is more than a rational exercise, open to revision, correction, or rejection. It is in this sense that we incorporate the Marxist analysis of society. The point is of great importance and the source of many misunderstandings. Our assumption of Marxism has nothing to do with a supposedly abstract or eternal theory or with dogmatic formulae—a view which is not absent in certain Marxist circles—but with a scientific analysis and a number of verifiable hypotheses in relation to conditions obtaining in certain historical moments and places and which, properly modified, corrected, and supplemented, provide an adequate means to grasp our own historical situation (insofar, moreover, as it is closely related and significantly shaped by the model originally analyzed).

It seems to me that there is no small confusion in Christian revolutionary circles because of an ambivalence or oscillation in the

Marxist self-understanding. Dialectical materialism and historic materialism are conceived by some as a metaphysical theory, an absolute philosophical formulation. As such, it seems to enter immediately in conflict with the Christian faith in God. There are, therefore, a number of Christians who, while unreservedly taking up the cause of the oppressed, refuse (or at least take with great reticence) elements of the Marxist analysis such as the class struggle, the role of the proletariat, and other elements. The problem is that instead they usually assert "ethical principles" which, lacking a rigorous historical mediation, not infrequently end up in frustration, inability to act, or different forms of reformism. On the other extreme, and falling prey to the same error, not a few Christians have embraced Marxist ideology—understood in the absolute terms indicated above—with a sort of religious fervor. This, in turn, results in a total loss of faith or in the surrender of the historical contents of the Christian gospel. There can be no doubt as to the sincerity of many of these people. They may in fact be much closer to the kingdom than most of their orthodox opponents. But it seems that neither alternative is satisfactory: we cannot accept the either/or of political naivete and inefficacy or the surrender of Christian identity.

A third and difficult way seems to be open. It begins by recognizing that a concrete and specific form of analysis of reality is necessary for Christian obedience (not only in general but in specific and particular political, social, and economic terms). It further recognizes that such an analysis cannot be neutral, uncommitted (supposedly objective), because such so-called descriptive views (witness sociological functionalism) take present reality as normative and consequently are simply tools for the preservation of the status quo. A really objective view of historical reality requires significant hypotheses relating to "constancies" or (with all necessary caveats) "laws" to direct our action in history. For some of us Marxism can be assumed at this level. It is an analysis of the way in which socioeconomic-political reality functioned at a certain point in history (the stage of capitalism which Marx observed). This analysis was significantly projected into a hypothesis concerning the relation of human history (and all its achievements) to the process of producing material goods. As a hypothesis it has been tested against our knowledge of the past and against conditions obtaining later on and in different situations. It has been refined, supplemented, and developed. But it seems to many of us that it has proved, and still proves to be, the best instrument available for an effective and rational realization of human possibilities in historical life. A Marxist praxis is both the verification and the source of possible correction of the hypothesis.

Admittedly, Marxism does not behave as the cool rational entity we have described. It is frequently possessed by an apostolic zeal, a dogmatic certainty, and a messianic fervor the causes of which we cannot discuss here. We have here a particular form of the old problem of the relation of the Christian faith to the form of rationality in and through which it shapes its obedience and reflection. Philosophical systems used in the past seemed to be somewhat removed from actual practice and confined to speculation, while Marxism proposes a form of action as the rationality corresponding to history. We have already seen that this distinction is superficial both in terms of the ideological contents of metaphysical speculation and the historical demand of the Christian faith. When we speak of assuming Marxist analysis and ideology at this point, there is therefore no sacralization of an ideology, no desire to "theologize" sociological, economic, or political categories. We move totally and solely in the area of human rationality—in the realm where God has invited man to be *on his own*. The only legitimate question is therefore whether this analysis and this projection do in fact correspond to the facts of human history. If they do, or to the extent that they do, they become *the unavoidable historical mediation* of Christian obedience.

Once we have located the sociopolitical and even (to some extent) ideological problems at this rational, historical level, the question remains whether this dimension is, so to speak, autonomous or somehow related to or "overdetermined" by other considerations. Posed in this way, the question might lead to misunderstanding, as if we would fall again into the scheme of some supratemporal moral or religious truth which then is applied through a rational, scientific method. The desire to eradicate this fatal mistake has led many Latin American theologians to neglect this question or to dismiss it rather summarily. The problem, nevertheless, will not rest. Christian obedience, understood to be sure as a historical praxis and therefore incarnate in a historical (rational, concrete) mediation does, nevertheless, incorporate a dimension which, using christological language, can never be separated from—or confused with—the historical mediation. In other terms, how are the original events (or the "germinal" events as it would perhaps be more accurate to call them)—namely, God's dealings with Israel; the birth, life, death, and resurrection of Jesus; the hope of the kingdom—how are they determinative in this single, synthetical fact that we call the historical praxis of a Christian? If we are condemned to remain silent on this point, we are really resigning any attempt to speak of such praxis as *Christian* obedience.

We are just at the beginning of the historical praxis of Christian obedience that will help us to reflect on this problem. We will know as we do. Some considerations can, nevertheless, be advanced on the basis of the experience we already have, both in our own situation and in the tradition of the Christian community. The first remark is that this question is closely connected with the revolutionary need to criticize one's own praxis from within in order to reproject it in a deeper, more significant, and more effective way. Such criticism must be done from within in a double sense. On the one hand, it must be done in the context of active engagement, in relation to the real questions which are posed in the praxis itself. On the other hand, it should deepen and push further the theory which is incorporated in such praxis. This means in the context of our discussion at least two things. Negatively, it means that theology cannot claim to have some "pure kerygmatic truths or events," unengaged or uncompromised in a concrete historical praxis, from which we can judge the concrete Christian obedience of a person or a community. All we have today in Latin America are reactionary, reformist, and revolutionary engagements, and therefore reactionary, reformist, and revolutionary readings of what we have called "germinal events of the Christian faith." Significant and fruitful self-criticism and dialogue can only take place when we consciously assume our own praxis and reflect from within it—or are converted to another. We cannot, therefore, take too seriously the frequent warnings and admonitions coming from European and (to a lesser extent) American theologians against our "ideological biases" as if they were speaking from some sort of ideologically aseptic environment.

But there is also a positive consequence of the same fact. Within the historical mediation of our Christian obedience, that is, the struggle for liberation in the terms that have been defined, there is an ideological projection (now in a positive sense) which provides the terms for a significant criticism of our praxis. The social (collective) appropriation of the means of production, the suppression of a classist society, the de-alienation of work, the suppression of a slave consciousness, and the reinstallation of man as agent of his own history are the theoretical hypotheses on the basis of which revolutionary praxis is predicated. They become, therefore, *intrinsic tests* for such praxis. A consistent engagement demands a constant criticism in these terms.

It is not for us to say whether a Christian is in a better position to exercise that engaged criticism. This will be seen concretely in experience or not at all. But it is possible to say, I think, that a Christian is called to do it, at least on two accounts. The first is the nature of the Christian kerygma itself. The second is the fact that, as a Christian, he has no self-image to preserve, no need to be justified by the blamelessness of his action, no value to attach to achievement beyond its significance for the neighbor, no claim to make on the basis of rightness. A Christian can offer his praxis to the fire of criticism totally and unreservedly on the trust of free grace just as he can offer his body totally and unreservedly in the hope of the resurrection. That so many nonbelievers do these things and so many Christians do not belongs to the mystery of grace and the mystery of evil. But the fact that this freedom is offered to faith at every moment is the very center of the gospel.

The mention of the Christian kerygma brings us to a final point which deserves our attention. We have said that there are only engaged readings of the Scripture, the kerygma, the story of the founding and generative events of the faith. But are they *readings* or only arbitrary *inventions*? The question is by no means academic for a Christian whose faith is rooted in Jesus Christ, who "has come in the flesh" and not in some gnostic myth which can be reinvented at every new occasion. It is therefore decisive for an obedience that claims to be Christian obedience, the discipleship of that Christ, and not a new law or man-made ordinance.

The Scripture itself offers illustrative instances of engaged readings of the germinal events, for example, from the contexts in which the Lord's resurrection is presented in the New Testament. A careful and cautious exegete like the Swiss P. Bonnard indicates that "when the New Testament speaks of the resurrection of Jesus . . . it does not merely say that he has risen: it says a *number of things* which can be grouped . . . around six subjects." He then proceeds to indicate these various things that are said: "all will rise!"; "Christ is risen for our justification"; "we have risen with him"; "powers and dominations have been defeated"; "the risen one is the one who died"; "the Lord is present." In every case, as Bonnard himself indicates, these texts "are bearers of a present word." A careful study of the texts shows that "present word" is not understood merely as a consequence of the resurrection, a deduction from it, far less "an application" of the truth of the resurrection. In every case, it is the historical fact of the resurrection itself which is present and active in the second term of the message. In other words, the resurrection of Jesus *is* itself (and not merely means or causes) our resurrection, our justification, the defeat of the powers, the power of his death, the general resurrection, the active presence of Christ.[10] Is it altogether absurd to reread the resurrection today as the death of the monopolies, the liberation from hunger, or a solidary form of ownership?

Whether a reading of such events as the resurrection is arbitrary or not cannot be a purely subjective or situational judgment. When we say that, for the New Testament, the resurrection is read as one

10. Bonnard, "Quelques récits évangéliques relatifs au Réssuscité," *Foi et Vie*, January-February 1970, pp. 29-59.

of several things, it is important to remark that we are really talking about the resurrection. At this point, with Barth, and contrary to Bultmann, we must reject any reduction to an "Easter faith" (or the equivalent in relation to other events). These events, and consequently the kerygma in which they come to us, are present in our reading in the full weight of their objective historicity as well as in the full efficacy of their dynamism. For this reason, theological hermeneutics cannot forgo the effort to gain access to the text by means of the critical (historical, literary, traditio-historical, linguistic) instruments which the sciences of interpretation have created. In this respect our theology must battle on two fronts. One—about which our theologians are very perceptive—is the criticism of the ideological premises of the Western sciences of interpretation. Even a cursory reading of the history of interpretation in European theology since the eighteenth century leaves little doubt in this respect. "Scientific," "historical," or "objective" exegesis reveals itself as full of ideological presuppositions. On the other hand, this battle of interpretations is not without a positive balance insofar as it has unmasked previous ideological readings and has helped us to liberate the text for a new and creative obedience. While the more significant Latin American theologians avail themselves continually of such study, they tend to minimize its theological significance. Their insistence on "present obedience" as the only legitimate reading of the biblical text is certainly quite justified. It is the first and most important thing that must be said. But we should not overlook the fact that the text opens itself for this present reading not in spite of its concrete, local, and *dated* historicity but because of it. To be sure, this affirmation opens the question of a double location of the texts and the threat of a new dualism. We must insist that the penetration of the original historicity of the biblical events is basic for its present demand and efficacy. Consequently, however questionable and imperfect, the critical use of the instruments that help us to reach a better understanding of this historicity is indispensable for a reflection on our Christian obedience today. Through these means we reach what Professor Casalis has called "a hermeneutical circulation" (over against the famous "hermeneutical circle" of the Bultmannians) between the text in its historicity and our own historical reading of it in obedience.[11]

Is the path of this circulation in any way verifiable? In other words, can the correlation between the text in its own historicity and our own historical reading of it be in any way controlled, ver-

11. Perhaps the best discussion of this hermeneutical method can be found in José Severino Croatto's *Liberción y Libertad: Pautas Hermenéuticas* (Buenos Aires: Ediciones Mundo Nuevo, 1973).

ified, or falsified? The problem is as old as interpretation itself and can be clearly illustrated from the New Testament history of tradition itself. There is no point here in rehearsing the different forms in which such correlation has been found throughout history. But it seems important to define at least the limits within which a legitimate answer may be found. In the first place, let us underline again the fact that this reading is always a synthetic act, or, as the New Testament puts it, "a discernment in the Spirit," which has been promised to the faithful community. Obedience is not found as the conclusion of a syllogism but in the prophetic word of discernment received in faith. This prophecy is only partially justified theologically or even historically. Its final justification is eschatological, as the New Testament makes abundantly clear. Second, we cannot expect a direct historical correspondence, either in the form of law — witness the miscarriage of the Calvinist attempt at Geneva or the "enthusiasts" throughout history — or as precedent. This is the reason why, significant as they are, the attempts to derive direct political conclusions (either revolutionary or pacifist) from the ambivalent relation of Jesus to the Zealots, seems to me a dangerous shortcut.

In order to avoid these shortcuts we can rely on two mediations. One is the reading of the direction of the biblical text, particularly of the witness of the basic, germinal events of the faith. They seem, in fact, to point, in their integrity and coherence, to certain directions which such concepts as liberation, righteousness, shalom, the poor, and love help us to define. The scope of these mediating concepts must always be searched in the historical elucidation, the progressive historicization, and the mutual complementation of the biblical text. The other mediation, on which we have already commented, is the determination of the historical conditions and possibilities of our present situation, as discovered through rational analysis. The correlation of the historical and conceptual mediations can offer us, not certainly a foolproof key to Christian obedience, but a significant framework for it.

On the basis of such an understanding of faithfulness to the revelation, a man in the situation we described at the beginning of this essay can say not "My enemies and myself draw different possible conclusions from the same truth" or "This is the way I feel" but "This is Christian obedience" and consequently "Repression and imperialism are disobedience and heresy." This is certainly a dangerous answer. But every confessing decision that the church has dared throughout history has been dangerous. Obedience is always a risk.

TOWARD A FEMINIST BIBLICAL HERMENEUTICS: BIBLICAL INTERPRETATION AND LIBERATION THEOLOGY

ELISABETH SCHÜSSLER FIORENZA

To discuss the relationship between liberation theology and biblical interpretation in general, and to ask for the function of the Bible in the struggle of women for liberation in particular, is to enter an intellectual and emotional minefield. One must detect and lay bare the contradictions between historical exegesis and systematic theology, between value-neutral scientific inquiry and "advocacy" scholarship, between universal-objectivist preconceptions of academic theology and the critical partiality of liberation theologies. To attempt this in a short essay entails, by necessity, a simplification and typologization of a complex set of theological problems.

To raise the issue of the contemporary meaning and authority of the Bible from a feminist theological perspective, and to do this from the marginalized position of a woman in the academy,[1] is to expose oneself to triple jeopardy. Establishment academic theologians and exegetes will reject such an endeavor as unscientific, biased, overly conditioned by contemporary questions, and therefore unhistorical, or they will refuse to accept it as a serious exegetical or theological question because the issue is raised by a woman. Liberation and political theologians will at best consider such a feminist theological endeavor as one problem among others, or at worst label it "middle class" and peripheral to the struggle of oppressed people. After all, how can middle-class white women worry about the ERA or the sex of God when people die of starvation, are tortured in prisons, and vegetate below poverty level in the black and Hispanic ghettos of

1. See Adrienne Rich, "Towards a Woman-Centered University," in *Women and the Power to Change*, ed. Florence Howe, Carnegie Commission on Higher Education Series (New York: McGraw-Hill, 1975); see also my analysis in "Towards a Liberating and Liberated Theology: Women Theologians and Feminist Theology in the U.S.A.," *Concilium* 115 (1979): 22-32.

Reprinted from *The Challenge of Liberation Theology: A First World Response,* ed. Brian Mahan and C. Dale Richesin (Maryknoll, N.Y.: Orbis Books, 1981), pp. 91-112.

American cities? However, such an objection against feminist theology and the women's movement overlooks the fact that more than half of the poor and hungry in the world are women and children dependent on women.[2] Not only do women and children represent the majority of the "oppressed," but poor and Third World women suffer the triple oppression of sexism, racism, and classism. If liberation theologians make the "option for the oppressed" the key to their theological endeavors, then they must become conscious of the fact that "the oppressed" are women.

Feminist theology, therefore, not only challenges academic theology to take its own intellectual presuppositions seriously, but it also asks other liberation theologies to concretize their option for the oppressed. Finally, the feminist theologian challenges not only the supposedly neutral and objective stance of the academic theologian, but she also must qualify the definition of the advocacy stance of liberation theology as "option for the oppressed." Her involvement in liberation theology is not "altruistic," but it is based on the acknowledgment and analysis of her own oppression as a woman in sexist, cultural, and theological institutions. Having acknowledged the dimensions of her own oppression, she can no longer advocate the value-neutral, detached stance of the academician. In other words, the feminist theologian's experience of oppression is different from that of Latin American theologians, for instance, who often do not belong to the poor but have made the cause of the oppressed their own.[3] Such an emphasis on the differences in the approaches of different liberation theologies is important. Robert McAfee Brown has pointed out that "what we see depends on where we are standing."[4]

2. See, for example, Lisa Leghorn and M. Roodkowsky, *Who Really Starves? Women and World Hunger* (New York: Friendship Press, 1977); *Crimes against Women: Proceedings of the International Tribunal*, ed. Diane E. Nichole Russel and N. Van de Ven (Millbrae, Cal.: Les Femmes, 1976); and Susan Hill Lindley, "Feminist Theology in a Global Perspective," *Christian Century* 96 (1979): 465-69.

3. Gustavo Gutiérrez, for example, states that "a spirituality of liberation will center on a *conversion* to the neighbor, the oppressed person, the exploited social class, the despised race, the dominated country. Our conversion to the Lord implies this conversion to the neighbor" (*A Theology of Liberation* [Maryknoll, N.Y.: Orbis Books, 1973], pp. 204-5). Compare the description of feminist conversion by Judith Plaskow: "the women who, having seen the non-being of social structures, feels herself a whole person, is called upon to become the person she is in that movement. . . . The experience of grace is not the experience of the sole activity of God, but the experience of the emergence of the 'I' as co-creator. . . . Relatedness to God is expressed through the never-ending journey toward self-creation within community, and through the creation of ever wider communities, including both other human beings and the world" (*Sex, Sin, and Grace: Women's Experience and the Theologies of Reinhold Niebuhr and Paul Tillich* [Washington: University Press of America, 1980], pp. 171-72).

4. Brown, *Theology in a New Key: Responding to Liberation Themes* (Philadelphia: Westminster Press, 1978), p. 82.

Moreover, the Native American theologian Vine Deloria has cautioned that one way of co-opting liberation theology is to classify all minorities as oppressed and in need of liberation.[5] Christian theologians often add to this that we are all under sin and therefore all equally oppressed: male and female, black, white, and red. In co-opting the term *oppression* and generalizing it so much that it becomes meaningless, the liberal establishment successfully neutralizes specific analyses of oppression and prohibits oppressed groups from formulating their own goals and strategies for liberation. Therefore, it seems to be methodologically inappropriate to speak in generalized terms about oppression or about liberation theology in the singular.

THE "ADVOCACY" STANCE OF LIBERATION THEOLOGIES

This insight has far-reaching consequences for the methodological approach of this essay. Instead of asking for the scriptural *loci* of liberation theology in general, or critically evaluating their approach from a "superior" methodological historical-critical point of view, I have decided to concentrate on one specific issue of contention between so-called academic theology and all forms of liberation theology. The basic insight of liberation theologies and their methodological starting point is the insight that all theology knowingly or not is by definition always engaged for or against the oppressed. Intellectual neutrality is not possible in a historical world of exploitation and oppression. If this is the case, then theology cannot talk about human existence in general, or about biblical theology in particular, without identifying whose human existence is meant and about whose God biblical symbols and texts speak.

This avowed "advocacy" stance of all liberation theologies seems to be the major point of contention between academic historical-critical or liberal-systematic theology on the one side and liberation theology on the other side. For instance, in many exegetical and theological circles a feminist interpretation of the Bible or the reconstruction of early Christianity is not the proper substantive historical and theological subject matter for serious academic theology. Since such a feminist interpretation is sparked by the women's movement and openly confesses its allegiance to it, academic theologians consider it to be a "fad" and judge it not to be a serious historical-

5. Deloria, "A Native American Perspective on Liberation," in *Mission Trends No. 4: Liberation Theologies,* ed. Gerald H. Anderson and Thomas F. Stransky (New York: Paulist Press, 1979), pp. 261-70.

theological problem for historical-critical scholarship.[6] Since this interpretative approach is already prejudiced by the explicit advocacy position of the inquiring scholar, no value-neutral scientific inquiry is possible. Therefore, no one publicly identified with the "feminist cause" in theology and society can be considered to be a "serious" scholar. Or as one of my colleagues remarked about a professor who wrote a rather moderate article on women in the Old Testament: "It's a shame! In writing this article she may have ruined her whole scholarly career."

The ideal of historical-critical studies that all exegetical inquiry should be a value-neutral and objective historical description of the past overlooks the fact that biblical studies as "*canonical*" studies are already "engaged," insofar as the Bible is not just a document of past history but functions as holy Scripture in Christian communities today.[7] The *biblical* exegete and theologian, in distinction from the historian of antiquity, never searches solely for the historical meaning of a passage but also raises the question of the Bible's meaning and authority for today. The argument that the "hermeneutical privilege of the oppressed"[8] or the feminist interest in the role of women in the New Testament is too engaged or biased pertains, therefore, to all biblical inquiry qua biblical inquiry, and not only to the study and use of the Bible by liberation theologians. Insofar as biblical studies are "canonical" studies, they are related to and inspired by their *Sitz im Leben* in the Christian church of the past and the present. The feminist analysis of the Bible is just one example of such an ecclesial contextuality and of the theological commitment of biblical studies in general.

This fact is recognized by Schubert Ogden, who nevertheless objects to the "advocacy" stance of liberation theology. He argues that all existing liberation theologies are in danger of becoming ideologies in the Marxist sense insofar as they, like other traditional theological enterprises, are "the rationalization of positions already taken."[9] Rather than engaging in a critical reflection on their own positions, liberation theologies rationalize, with the help of the Bible,

6. See my essay "Women in Early Christianity: Methodological Considerations," in *Critical History and Biblical Faith in New Testament Perspectives*, ed. T. J. Ryan (Villanova, Pa.: Catholic Theology Society Annual Publications, 1979), pp. 30-58.

7. For a more extensive discussion of the literature, see my essay "For the Sake of Our Salvation . . . Biblical Interpretation as Theological Task," in *Sin, Salvation, and the Spirit*, ed. Daniel Durken (Collegeville, Minn.: Liturgical Press, 1979), pp. 21-39.

8. See Lee Cormie, "The Hermeneutical Privilege of the Oppressed: Liberation Theologies, Biblical Faith, and Marxist Sociology of Knowledge," *Proceedings of the Catholic Theological Society of America* 32 (1977); see also D. Lockhead, "Hermeneutics and Ideology," *The Ecumenist* 15 (1977): 81-84.

9. Ogden, *Faith and Freedom: Toward a Theology of Liberation* (Nashville: Abingdon Press, 1979), p. 116.

the positions of the oppressed instead of those of the oppressors. Insofar as they attempt to rationalize the prior claims of Christian faith and their own option for the oppressed, they are not theologizing but witnessing. Theology as a "second act" exists according to Latin American liberation theologians, not "for its own sake," but for the sake of the church's witness, its liberating praxis.

One must, however, question whether this statement adequately characterizes the "advocacy" stance of liberation theologians. Ogden suggests that the only way theology—be it academic or liberation theology—can become emancipated is by conceiving its task as that of a critical reflection on its own position. He then proceeds to work out a "still more adequate theology of liberation than any of them has as yet achieved."[10] However, he not only fails to reflect critically on the political standpoint and implications of his own process theology, but he also goes on to talk about "women's theology" and to explore the "being of God in himself" as if he had never studied feminist theology.

While Ogden accuses liberation theologians of too "provincial an understanding of bondage," James Cone insists to the contrary that the option for the oppressed should become the starting point of all theology: "If Christian theology is an explication of the meaning of the gospel for our time, must not theology itself have liberation as its starting point or run the risk of being, at best, idle talk, and at worst blasphemy?"[11] Such a provocative formulation should not, however, be classified as mere "rhetoric,"[12] but must be seen as an indicator of serious theological differences in the understanding of the task and function of theology.

This disagreement about the function and goal of theology has serious implications for the way theologians understand the task of biblical interpretation. As a feminist theologian, I have taken the "advocacy" position but do not think that this option excludes "critical reflection" on my own feminist position. Such a critical reflection must not only be applied to the "advocacy" position of liberation theologies but must also be extended to the ways exegetes and theologians have construed the relationship between the biblical past and its meanings and have explicated the claim of Christian theology that the Bible has authority and significance for Christians today.

Such a critical reflection indicates *first* that biblical and theological interpretation has always taken an advocacy position without

10. Ogden, *Faith and Freedom*, p. 32.
11. Cone, *God of the Oppressed* (New York: Seabury Press, 1975), pp. 51-52.
12. See Charles H. Strain, "Ideology and Alienation: Theses on the Interpretation and Evaluation of Theologies of Liberation," *Journal of the American Academy of Religion* 45 (1977): 474.

clearly reflecting upon it. Such an advocacy position is not unique to liberation theologies.

Second, in order to reflect critically on the function of liberation theologians' explicit advocacy position in the process of biblical theological interpretation, I have chosen to discuss two concrete examples of liberation theological hermeneutics. This is necessary because it is methodologically incorrect to reduce every advocacy stance and every analysis of concrete structures of oppression by liberation theologies to one common level. I will argue that liberation theologies, because of their option for a specific group of oppressed people (e.g., women or Native Americans) must develop, within the overall interpretative approach of a critical theology of liberation, more adequate heuristic interpretative models appropriate to specific forms of oppression. In short, the biblical interpretation of liberation theologians must become more concrete, or more "provincial," before an "interstructuring" of different interpretative models and a more universal formulation of the task of a critical theology of liberation can be attempted.

T. S. Kuhn's categories of scientific paradigms and heuristic models, which evolved in the methodological discussions of the natural sciences, provide a conceptual theoretical framework that allows for the advocacy stance of liberation theologies, as well as for their distinctive interpretative approaches. According to Kuhn, a paradigm represents a coherent research tradition, and creates a scientific community.[13] Since paradigms determine how scientists see the world and how they conceive of theoretical problems, a shift in paradigm also means a transformation of the scientific imagination and thus demands an "intellectual conversion" which allows the community of scientists to see old "data" in a completely new perspective. For a period of time different paradigms may be competing for the allegiance of the scientific community until one paradigm replaces the other or gives way to a third.

The usefulness of this theory for biblical and theological studies in general and for our discussion here is obvious. It shows the conditioned nature of all scientific investigation, and maintains that no neutral observation language or value-free standpoint is possible inasmuch as all scientific investigations demand commitment to a particular research approach and are carried out by a community of scholars dedicated to such a theoretical perspective. Moreover, this theory helps us to understand that theological approaches, like all other scientific theories, are not falsified but replaced, not be-

13. See Kuhn, *The Structure of Scientific Revolutions* (Chicago: University of Chicago Press, 1962); see also Ian G. Barbour, *Myths, Models, and Paradigms* (New York: Harper & Row, 1974).

cause we find new "data" but because we find new ways of looking at old data and problems. Research paradigms are therefore not necessarily exclusive of each other. They can exist alongside each other until they are finally replaced by a new paradigm.

PARADIGMS IN BIBLICAL INTERPRETATION

The debate around the "advocacy" stance of liberation theology and the "value-neutral" stance of academic theology appears to reflect such a shift in theological paradigms. Since the Bible as holy Scripture is a historical book but at the same time claims to have significance and authority for Christians today, theological scholarship has developed different paradigms to resolve this tension between the historical and theological claims of the Bible.[14]

The *first* paradigm, which I will call the "doctrinal paradigm," understands the Bible in terms of divine revelation and canonical authority. This paradigm is concerned with the truth-claims, authority, and meaning of the Bible for Christian faith today. It conceives of biblical authority in ahistorical, dogmatic terms. In its most consistent form it insists on the verbal inspiration and literary inerrancy of biblical writings. In this understanding the Bible does not just *communicate* the Word of God but it *is* the Word of God. It is not simply a record of revelation but revelation itself. As such, it functions as proof-text, "first principle," or *norma normans non normata*. The tension between the historical and contemporary meaning of the Bible can be dissolved by means of allegory, typology, or the distinction between the literal sense and the spiritual sense of Scripture.

The most widely used method is proof-texting, which provides the ultimate theological arguments or rationalizations for a position already taken. The general formula is "Scripture says, therefore . . ." or "This argument is also borne out by Scripture." The proof-texting method presupposes that the Bible reveals eternal truth and timeless principles which can be separated from their historical expression. Biblical writings are only important for theology insofar as they are a source of "proof-texts" or "principles" which can be taken out of their historical context. Biblical texts function as theological justification for the moral, doctrinal, or institutional interests of the Christian community. Insofar as liberation theology too exclusively and abstractly focuses on certain biblical texts (e.g., the

---

14. For the development of these paradigms, see my essay "For the Sake of Our Salvation." On the general paradigm shift in biblical studies, see Walter Wink, *The Bible in Human Transformation: Toward a New Paradigm for Biblical Studies* (Philadelphia: Fortress Press, 1973).

Exodus-texts,[15] certain prophetic indictments against the rich in Luke 4:16-30, or the Last Judgment in Matthew 25:31-45), it could be in danger of submitting to the "proof-texting" or the allegorical method.

The *second* paradigm of historical-critical exegesis was developed in confrontation with the dogmatic use of Scripture and the doctrinal authority of the church. It linked its attack on the doctrinal paradigm with an understanding of exegesis and history that is objective, value-free, rationalist, and scientific. Modeled after the natural sciences, historical-critical exegesis seeks to achieve a purely objective reading of the texts and a scientific presentation of the historical facts. As objective, scientific exegesis, it identifies theological truth with historical facticity. According to James Barr, in this paradigm "a biblical account of some event is approached and evaluated primarily not in terms of significance but in terms of correspondence with external reality. Veracity as correspondence with empirical actuality has precedence over veracity as significance."[16]

Although academic historical criticism has become suspicious of the objectivist-factual understanding of biblical texts, it still adheres to the dogma of value-neutral, detached interpretation. Academic historical-critical scholarship reconstructs as accurately as possible the historical meaning of the Bible, but on methodological grounds it refuses to discuss the significance of biblical texts for the contemporary community of faith. Therefore, academic biblical exegesis must limit itself to historical and literary inquiry, but strictly speaking it is not a theological endeavor.

It is obvious that liberation theologians must distance themselves from such an understanding of biblical interpretation since they focus on the significance of the Bible for the liberation struggle. However, it is interesting to note that José Miranda, the prolific biblical exegete among the Latin American liberation theologians, adheres to this paradigm.[17] He insists that the historical-critical method is in itself objective, scientific, and controllable. When Western exegetes frequently miss the true meaning of the text, this is not due to the exegetical method but to the Greek thought which Western exegesis has adopted — and which it must abandon in favor of

15. See, for example, G. Sauter, " 'Exodus' und 'Befreiung' als theologische Metaphern: Ein Beispiel zur Kritik von Allegorese und missverstandenen Analogien in der Ethik," *Evangelische Theologie* 38 (1978): 538-59, although one suspects that his criticism leads to a totally depoliticized interpretation.

16. Barr, *Fundamentalism* (Philadelphia: Westminster Press, 1978), p. 49.

17. See Miranda, *Marx and the Bible* (Maryknoll, N.Y.: Orbis Books, 1974). See also J. A. Kirk, "The Bible in Latin American Liberation Theology," in *The Bible and Liberation*, ed. Norman K. Gottwald and Antoinette C. Wire (Berkeley: Radical Religion, 1976), p. 161.

a Marxist reading of the Bible. However, it is questionable whether Miranda's distinction between Greek and biblical thought can still be maintained, and whether liberation theology can adopt the value-neutral stance of historical criticism.

The *third* paradigm of biblical interpretation takes seriously the methodological insights of historical-critical scholarship, and at the same time radically questions how it conceives of its interpretative task. This paradigm is justified by two developments in biblical scholarship: the methods of form and redaction criticism have demonstrated how much biblical writings are theological responses to pastoral-practical situations and problems, while the hermeneutic discussions have elaborated how biblical texts can have meaning today.

First, form and redaction critical studies have highlighted the fact that the biblical tradition understands itself not as a doctrinal, exegetical, or historical tradition but as a living tradition.[18] In order to understand biblical texts, it is important not only to translate and interpret a text in its immediate context but also to know and determine the situation and the community to whom the text is addressed.

The New Testament authors rewrote their traditions in the form of letters, gospels, or apocalypses because they felt theologically compelled to illuminate or to censure the beliefs and praxis of their communities. The biblical books are thus written with the intention of serving the needs of the community of faith and not of revealing timeless principles or of transmitting historically accurate records. They, therefore, do not locate revelation only in the past, but also in their own present, thereby revealing a dialectical understanding between present and past. On the one hand, the past is significant because revelation happened decisively in Jesus of Nazareth. On the other hand, the writers of the New Testament can exercise freedom with respect to the Jesus traditions because they believe that the Jesus who spoke, speaks now to his followers through the Holy Spirit.

However, form and redaction critical studies can be criticized for conceptualizing the situation of early Christian communities too readily in terms of a confessional struggle between different theologies and church groups. Such a reconstruction often reads like the history of the European Reformation in the sixteenth century or a description of a small town in America where five or six churches

18. See Norman Perrin, *What Is Redaction Criticism?* (Philadelphia: Fortress Press, 1969); see also Werner G. Kümmel, *Das Neue Testament im 20 Jahrhundert* (Stuttgart: KBW, 1970).

of different Christian persuasions are built within walking distance of one another.

The studies of the social world of Israel[19] and early Christianity[20] emphasize the fact that it is not sufficient merely to reconstruct the ecclesial setting. Christian faith and revelations are always intertwined within cultural, political, and societal contexts. It does not suffice merely to understand biblical texts as expressions of religious-theological ideas or ecclesial disputes. What is necessary is to analyze their societal-political contexts and functions. For instance, it does not suffice merely to recognize the literary form of the household code, or its theological imperative in the post-Pauline community tradition if one does not also ask why these communities appropriated this particular form in their societal-political environment.[21] While the doctrinal paradigm understands miracles as proofs of the divinity of Jesus, the historical-contextual paradigm discusses whether they actually could have happened as they are told, and the form and redaction paradigm debates whether they are a religious expression of the time or a genuine expression of Christian faith, the contextual paradigm points out that miracle-faith was widespread in lower classes who did not have money for medical treatment. Miracle-faith in Jesus is best understood as protest against bodily and political suffering. It gives courage to resist the life-destroying powers of one's society.[22]

Second, the hermeneutical discussion is concerned with the meaning of biblical texts. While one direction of hermeneutics seeks to discover the synchronic ontological, atemporal, ideal, noematic meaning of written texts by separating it from the diachronic, temporal, communicative, personal, and referential speech-event, another direction does not concentrate so much on the linguisticality

19. See especially Norman K. Gottwald, *The Tribes of Yahweh: A Sociology of the Religion of Liberated Israel, 1250-1050 B.C.E.* (Maryknoll, N.Y.: Orbis Books, 1979).

20. See, for example, Leander E. Keck, "On the Ethos of Early Christians," *Journal of the American Academy of Religion* 42 (1974): 435-52; John C. Gager, *Kingdom and Community* (Englewood Cliffs, N.J.: Prentice-Hall, 1975); Gerd Theissen, *Sociology of Early Palestinian Christianity* (Philadelphia: Fortress Press, 1978); Wayne A. Meeks, "The Social World of Early Christianity," *CRS Bulletin* 6 (1975): 1, 4-5; and Willy Schottroff and Wolfgang Stegemann, *Der Gott der kleinen Leute: Sozialgeschichtliche Auslegungen,* vol. 2, *Neues Testament* (Munich: Kaiser, 1979).

21. See my essay "Word, Spirit, and Power: Women in Early Christian Communities," in *Women of Spirit,* ed. Rosemary Radford Reuther and Eleanor McLaughlin (New York: Simon & Schuster, 1979), pp. 29-70; see also David Balch, *"Let Wives Be Submissive . . ."* (Ann Arbor: University Microfilms International, 1978).

22. See Theissen, "Synoptische Wundergeschichten im Lichte unseres Sprachverhältnisses," *Wissenschaft und Praxis in Kirche und Gesellschaft* 65 (1976): 289-308. For the interrelation between poverty, violence, and exploitation, see Luise Schottroff and Wolfgang Stegemann, *Jesus von Nazareth: Hofnung der Armen* (Stuttgart: Kohlhammer, 1978).

of the text as on the involvement of the interpreter with the text. The interpreter always approaches the text with specific ways of raising questions, and thus with a certain understanding of the subject matter with which the text is concerned.[23]

The hermeneutic circle conceives of the relationship between the contemporary interpreter and the historical text as a continuous dialogue that corrects the presuppositions of the interpreter and works out the true meaning of the text. At this point, it becomes clear that in this third paradigm dialogical interpretation is the governing model. While form and redaction criticism show that early Christian communities and "authors" were in constant dialogue with the tradition and the living Lord authorizing this tradition, the hermeneutic circle continues this dialogic endeavor in the act of interpretation. Therefore, this hermeneutic understanding can be combined with the neo-orthodox theological enterprise. Or as Schillebeeckx points out, "the apparent point of departure is the presupposition that what is handed down in tradition and especially the Christian tradition, is always meaningful, and that its meaning must only be deciphered hermeneutically and made actual."[24]

In conclusion, all three paradigms of biblical interpretation espouse a definite stance and allegiance to a research perspective and community. The doctrinal paradigm clearly has its allegiance to the church and its teachings. The norm by which it evaluates different texts and their truth claims is the *regula fidei*. The scientific paradigm of historical-critical exegesis shares in the objectivist-scientific worldview, and espouses the critical rationality and value-free inquiry of academic scholarship. The hermeneutic-contextual paradigm is interested in the "continuation" of the tradition, and therefore advocates a position in line with neo-orthodox theology, a "hermeneutics of consent."[25] It would be interesting to explore which political interests each of these paradigms serves, but this would go far beyond the task and aim of this essay. The explicit advocacy position, however, of liberation theologies threatens to uncover the hidden political interests of existing biblical interpretative paradigms. This may be one of the main reasons why established the-

23. See T. Peters, "The Nature and Role of Presupposition: An Inquiry into Contemporary Hermeneutics," *International Philosophical Quarterly* 14 (1974): 209-22; see also Frederick Herzog, "Liberation Hermeneutic as Ideology Critique," *Interpretation* 27 (1974): 387-403.

24. Edward Schillebeeckx, *The Understanding of Faith* (New York: Seabury Press, 1974), p. 130.

25. See especially Peter Stuhlmacher, *Historical Criticism and Theological Interpretation of Scripture: Toward a Hermeneutics of Consent* (Philadelphia: Fortress Press, 1977), pp. 83ff.

ology refuses to reflect critically on its own societal-ecclesial interests and political functions.

LIBERATION THEOLOGY AND BIBLICAL INTERPRETATION

The second part of this essay will attempt to explore critically the position of a theology of liberation within the existing paradigms of biblical interpretation. I will do this by discussing two different hermeneutical approaches of liberation theologies. As case studies, I have chosen the hermeneutical model of Juan Luis Segundo as one of the more sophisticated proposals in contemporary theology, and have placed in contrast to it Elizabeth Cady Stanton's approach in proposing the *Woman's Bible*. Both examples indicate that liberation theologies have worked out a distinctive approach to biblical interpretation which leads to a redefinition of the criteria for public theological discourse. Instead of asking whether an approach is appropriate to the Scriptures and adequate to the human condition,[26] one needs to test whether a theological model of biblical interpretation is *adequate* to the historical-literary methods of contemporary interpretation and *appropriate* to the struggle of the oppressed for liberation.

The Interpretative Model of Juan Luis Segundo[27]

While the hermeneutic-contextual approach advocates the elimination of all presuppositions and preunderstandings for the sake of objective-descriptive exegesis, existential hermeneutics defines preunderstanding as the common existential ground between the interpreter and the author of the text. Political theologians have challenged this choice of existential philosophy, while liberation theologians maintain a hermeneutics of engagement instead of a hermeneutics of detachment. Since no complete detachment or value-neutrality is possible, the interpreter must make her/his stance explicit and take an advocacy position in favor of the oppressed. To truly understand the Bible is to read it through the eyes of the oppressed, since the God who speaks in the Bible is the God of the oppressed. For a correct interpretation of the Bible, it is necessary to acknowledge the "hermeneutical privilege of the oppressed" and to develop a hermeneutics "from below."

26. For these criteria, see Ogden, *Faith and Freedom*, p. 26, and especially David Tracy, *Blessed Rage for Order: The New Pluralism in Theology* (New York: Seabury Press, 1975), pp. 72-79.

27. This whole section is based on an analysis of Juan Luis Segundo, *The Liberation of Theology* (Maryknoll, N.Y.: Orbis Books, 1976).

Since theology is explicitly or implicitly intertwined with the existing social situation, according to Segundo the hermeneutic circle must begin with an experience or analysis of the social reality that leads to suspicion about our real situation. In a second step we apply our ideological suspicion to theology and to all other ideological superstructures. At a third level we experience theological reality in a different way, which in turn leads us to the suspicion that "the prevailing interpretation of the Bible has not taken important pieces of data into account."[28] At a last stage we bring these insights to bear upon the interpretation of Scripture. However, only active commitment to the oppressed and active involvement in their struggle for liberation enable us to see our society and our world differently, and give us a new perspective for looking at the world. This perspective is also taught in the New Testament if the latter is interpreted correctly.

Segundo acknowledges that James Cone has elaborated such a liberation theological interpretation for the black community. He admits his indebtedness to Bultmann, but he reformulates the hermeneutic circle to include action: "the circular nature of this interpretation stems from the fact that each new reality obliges us to interpret the Word of God afresh, to *change* reality accordingly, and then go back and reinterpret the Word of God again and so on."[29] It is apparent that Segundo cannot be accused of rationalizing a previously taken position. He does not operate within the interpretative tradition of the doctrinal paradigm. He also clearly distinguishes his own theological interpretation from that of academic historical-critical scholarship by rejecting the biblical revelation-contemporary application model. According to him, biblical interpretation must reconstruct the second-level learning process of biblical faith. Faith is identical with the total process of learning in and through ideologies, whereas the faith responses vis-à-vis certain historical situations are ideologies. Therefore, faith should not be defined as content or *depositum fidei*, but as an educational process throughout biblical and Christian history. Faith expresses the continuity and permanency of divine revelation, whereas ideologies document the historical character of faith and revelation. "Faith then is a liberative process. It is converted into freedom for history, which means freedom *for ideologies*."[30] It is obvious that Segundo does not

28. Segundo, *The Liberation of Theology*, p. 9. See also José Miguez Bonino, *Doing Theology in a Revolutionary Situation* (Philadelphia: Fortress Press, 1975), pp. 86-105; Miguez Bonino accepts Professor Casalis's reformulation of the "hermeneutical circle" as "hermeneutical circulation" (p. 102).

29. Segundo, *The Liberation of Theology*, p. 8; italics mine.

30. Segundo, *The Liberation of Theology*, p. 110.

understand ideology as "false" consciousness but as historical-societal expression.

According to him, Christian faith is also not to be defined as content, doctrine, or principle but as an educational process to which we willingly entrust ourselves. "In the case of . . . the Bible we learn to learn by entrusting our life and its meaning to the historical process that is reflected in the expressions embodied in that particular tradition."[31] It is thus clear that Segundo does not work within the overall approach of either the doctrinal or historical value-free paradigms but proposes an interpretative model within the hermeneutic-contextual paradigm. He shares with neo-orthodoxy the hermeneutical presupposition that scriptural traditions are meaningful, and that they can therefore claim our obedience and demand a "hermeneutics of consent." In distinction from neo-orthodox theology, Segundo does not claim that it is the content of Scripture that is reflected in the Bible as meaningful and liberative. It is, rather, in the process of learning how to learn that meaning and liberation are seen.

However, this assumption does not take into account the fact that not only the content of Scripture but also this second-level learning process can be distorted. Segundo must, therefore, either demonstrate that this is not the case, or formalize this learning process to such a degree that the "advocacy" becomes an abstract principle not applicable to the contents of the Bible. In other words, Segundo's model does not allow for a critical theological evaluation of biblical ideologies as "false consciousness." One must question whether historical content and hermeneutic learning can be separated. Such a proposal also does not allow us to judge whether a text or interpretation is appropriate and helpful to the struggle of the oppressed for liberation. The failure to bring a critical evaluation to bear upon the biblical texts and upon the process of interpretation within Scripture and tradition is one of the reasons [the biblical interpretation of] liberation theologians often comes close to "proof texting." To avoid such an impression, liberation hermeneutics must reflect on the fact that the process of interpretation of Scripture is not necessarily liberative.

The Hermeneutics of the Woman's Bible

While liberation theologians affirm the Bible as a weapon in the struggle of liberation and claim that the God of the Bible is a God of the oppressed, feminist writers since the inauguration of the women's movement in the last century have maintained, to the contrary, that the Bible and Christian theology are inherently sexist

31. Segundo, *The Liberation of Theology*, p. 179.

and thereby destructive of women's consciousness. A revisionist interpretation of Scripture and theology, therefore, will either subvert women's struggle for liberation from all sexist oppression and violence or it will be forced to reinterpret Christian tradition and theology in such a way that nothing "Christian" will remain.

Feminist theology as a critical theology of liberation must defend itself against two sides: while liberation theologians are reluctant to acknowledge that women are exploited and oppressed, radical feminist thinkers claim that feminist consciousness and Christian faith are contradictions in terms. When our daughter Christina was born we announced her baptism with the following statement:

> She is born into a world of oppression
> She is born into a society of discrimination
> She is reborn into a church of inequality. . . .

The reaction of our friends to this announcement illustrates these objections to Christian feminist theology. Some colleagues and students in theology shook their heads and asked whether we had planned a Marxist initiation rite. Or in indignation they pointed to the privileged status of a girl born to middle-class professional parents. However, a very bright college student (who felt suffocated by the patriarchal environment of Notre Dame and was later hospitalized with a nervous breakdown) challenged me on the street saying, "How can you do this to her? She will never be able to be a consciousness-raised woman and a committed Christian. Christian faith and the church are destructive of women-persons who struggle against sexism and for liberation."

The question which feminist theologians must face squarely is thus a foundational theological problem: Is being a woman and being a Christian a primary contradiction which must be resolved in favor of one to the exclusion of the other? Or can both be kept in creative tension so that my being a Christian supports my struggle for liberation as a woman, while my being a feminist enhances and deepens my commitment to live as a Christian?[32] Insofar as feminist theology as a Christian theology is bound to its charter documents in Scripture, it must formulate this problem also with reference to the Bible and biblical revelation. Since the Bible was and is used against women's demand for equality and liberation from societal, cultural, and ecclesial sexism, it must conceive of this task first in critical terms before it can attempt to formulate a hermeneutics of liberation. While the danger of liberation theology is

---

32. See my essay "Feminist Spirituality, Christian Identity and the Catholic Vision," in *Womanspirit Rising: A Feminist Reader in Religion,* ed. Carol P. Christ and Judith Plaskow (New York: Harper & Row, 1979), pp. 136-48.

"proof texting," the pitfall to be avoided by feminist theology is apologetics, since such an apologetics does not take the political implications of scriptural interpretation seriously.

The debate surrounding the *Woman's Bible*, which appeared in 1895 and 1898, may serve here as a case-study for the *political* conditions and implications of feminist biblical interpretation as well as for the radical critical impact of feminist theology for the interpretative task.[33] In her introduction to the *Woman's Bible* Elizabeth Cady Stanton, the initiator of the project, outlined two critical insights for a feminist theological hermeneutics. The Bible is not a "neutral" book, but it is a political weapon against women's struggle for liberation. This is so because the Bible bears the imprint of men who never saw or talked with God.

First, Elizabeth Cady Stanton conceived of biblical interpretation as a political act. The following episode characterizes her own personal conviction of the negative impact of Christian religion on women's situation. She refused to attend a prayer meeting of suffragists that was opened by the singing of the hymn "Guide Us, O Thou Great Jehovah" by Isabella Beecher Hooker. Her reason was that Jehovah had "never taken any active part in the suffrage movement."[34] Because of her experience that Yahweh was not on the side of the oppressed, she realized the great political influence of the Bible. She therefore proposed to prepare a revision of the Bible which would collect and interpret (with the help of "higher criticism") all statements referring to women in the Bible. She conceded, however, that she was not very successful in soliciting the help of women scholars because they were "afraid that their high reputation and scholarly attainments might be compromised by taking part in an enterprise that for a time may prove very unpopular. Hence we may not be able to get help from that class."[35] And indeed, the project of the *Woman's Bible* proved to be very unpopular because of political implications. Not only did some of the suffragists argue that such a project was either not necessary or politically unwise but the National American Woman's Suffrage Association formally rejected it as a political mistake. In the second volume, which appeared in 1898, Cady Stanton sums up this opposition: "Both friend and foe object to the title" and then replies with biting wit to the accusation of a clergyman that the *Woman's Bible* is "the work of women and the devil":

33. Elizabeth Cady Stanton, *The Woman's Bible* (1895; rpt., New York: Arno Press, 1974).

34. Barbara Welter, "Something Remains to Dare: Introduction to the Woman's Bible," in *The Original Feminist Attack on the Bible (The Woman's Bible)*, by E. Cady Stanton, facsimile edition (New York: Arno Press, 1974), p. xxii.

35. Cady Stanton, *The Woman's Bible*, 1: 9.

This is a grave mistake. His Satanic Majesty was not to join the Revising Committee which consists of women alone. Moreover, he has been so busy of late years attending Synods, General Assemblies and Conferences, to prevent the recognition of women delegates, that he has no time to study the languages and "higher criticism."[36]

Although the methods and theological presuppositions of the "higher criticism" of the time are rather outdated today, the political arguments and objectives of a feminist biblical interpretation remain valid. They are outlined by Cady Stanton in her introduction to the first volume. She gives three reasons why such an objective scientific feminist revision and interpretation of the Bible is politically necessary:

1. Throughout history and especially today the Bible is used to keep women in subjection and to hinder their emancipation.

2. Not only men but especially women are the most faithful believers in the Bible as the Word of God. Not only for men but also for women the Bible has a numinous authority.

3. No reform is possible in one area of society if it is not advanced also in all other areas. One cannot reform the law and other cultural institutions without also reforming biblical religion which claims the Bible as holy Scripture. Since "all reforms are interdependent," a critical feminist interpretation is a necessary political endeavor, though perhaps not opportune. If feminists think they can neglect the revision of the Bible because there are more pressing political issues, then they do not recognize the political impact of Scripture upon the churches and society, and also upon the lives of women.

Second, Elizabeth Cady Stanton advocated such a revision of the Bible in terms of "higher criticism." Her insights, therefore, correspond with the results of historical biblical studies of her time. Over and against the doctrinal understanding of the Bible as Word of God, she stresses that the Bible is written by men and reflects patriarchal male interests. "The only point in which I differ from all ecclesiastical teaching is that I do not believe that any man ever saw or talked with God."[37] While the churches teach that such degrading ideas about patriarchal injunctions against women come from God, Cady Stanton maintains that all these degrading texts and ideas emanated from the heads of men. By treating the Bible as a human work and not as a magic fetish, and by denying divine inspiration to the negative biblical statements about women, she claims that her committee has shown more reverence and respect for God than does the clergy or the church. She concedes that some teachings of the Bible, such as the love command and the golden

36. Cady Stanton, *The Woman's Bible*, 2: 7-8.
37. Cady Stanton, *The Woman's Bible*, 1: 12.

rule, are still valid today. Since the teachings and lessons of the Bible differ from each other, the Bible cannot be accepted or rejected as a whole. Therefore, every passage on women must be carefully analyzed and evaluated for its impact on the struggle for the liberation of women.

In conclusion, although the idea of a *Woman's Bible* consisting only of the biblical texts on women must be rejected today on methodological grounds,[38] biblical scholarship on the whole has proven accurate Cady Stanton's contention that the Bible must be studied as a human work and that biblical interpretation is influenced by the theological mindset and interests of the interpreter. Contemporary feminist interpreters, like some of Cady Stanton's suffragist friends, either reject biblical interpretation as a hopeless feminist endeavor because the Bible is totally sexist or they attempt to defend the Bible in the face of its radical feminist critics. In doing so, they follow Frances Willard, who argued against the radical critique of the *Woman's Bible* that not the biblical message but only its patriarchal contemporary interpretation preaches the subjugation of women: "I think that men have read their own selfish theories into the book, that theologians have not in the past sufficiently recognized the progressive quality of its revelation nor adequately discriminated between its records as history and its principles of ethics and religion."[39]

The insight that scholarly biblical interpretations need to be "depatriarchalized" is an important one. However, this critical insight should not be misunderstood as an apologetic defense of the nonpatriarchal character of the Bible's teachings on ethics and religion. It was exactly Elizabeth Cady Stanton's critical insight that the Bible is not just misunderstood but that its contents and perspectives can be used in the political struggle against women. What Gustavo Gutiérrez says about human historiography in general must also be applied to the writing of the Bible:

Human history has been written by a white hand, a male hand from the dominating social class. The perspective of the defeated in history is different. Attempts have been made to wipe from their minds the memory of their struggles. This is to deprive them of a source of energy, of an historical will to rebellion.[40]

If we compare Cady Stanton's hermeneutical stance with that of

38. For a contemporary application, however, see Marie Fortune and Joann Haugerud, *Study Guide to the Woman's Bible* (Seattle: Coalition Task Force on Women and Religion, 1975). And for a discussion following basically the same principle, see Leonard Swidler, *Biblical Affirmations of Woman* (Philadelphia: Westminster Press, 1979).

39. Willard, cited by Cady Stanton in *The Woman's Bible*, 2: 200.

40. Gustavo Gutiérrez, "Where Hunger Is, God Is Not," *The Witness* 59 (April 1976): 6.

Segundo, then we see that she could not accept his understanding of a liberative second-level learning process within Christian history precisely because she shares his "advocacy stance for the oppressed." Cady Stanton cannot begin with the affirmation that the Bible and the God of the Bible are on the side of the oppressed because her experience of the Bible's use as a political weapon against women's struggle for suffrage tells her otherwise.

The subsequent reaction to the *Woman's Bible* also warns liberation theologians that a biblical interpretation that resorts too quickly to the defense of the Bible could misconstrue its advocacy stance for the oppressed. The task of liberation theologians is not to prove that the Bible or the church can be defended against feminist or socialist attacks. Only when we critically comprehend how the Bible functions in the oppression of women or the poor can we prevent its misuse for further oppression. Otherwise, liberation theology is in danger of succumbing to proof-texting. The advocacy stance of liberation theology can only be construed as a rationalization of preconceived ecclesial or dogmatic positions if it does not fully explore the oppressive aspects of biblical traditions. Because of their advocacy stance for the oppressed, feminist theologians must insist that theological-critical analysis of Christian tradition should not only begin with the time of Constantine but must also apply itself to the Christian charter documents themselves.

Because of its allegiance to the "defeated in history," a feminist critical theology maintains that a "hermeneutics of consent" which understands itself as the "actualizing continuation of the Christian history of interpretation" does not suffice. Such a hermeneutics overlooks the fact that Christian Scripture and tradition are not only a source of truth but also of untruth, repression, and domination. Since the hermeneutic-contextual paradigm seeks only to *understand* biblical texts, it cannot adequately take into account the fact that the Christian past, as well as its interpretations, has victimized women. A critical theology of liberation, therefore, must work out a new interpretative paradigm that can take seriously the claim of liberation theologians that God is on the side of the oppressed.[41] Such a paradigm must also accept the claim of feminist theologians that God has never "taken an active part in the suffrage movement" and that the Bible can therefore function as a male weapon in the political struggle against women's liberation.

41. For the conceptualization of feminist theology as a critical theology of liberation, see my essay "Feminist Theology as a Critical Theology of Liberation," in *Woman: New Dimensions,* ed. Walter Burkhardt (New York: Paulist Press, 1977), pp. 19-50.

TOWARD A FEMINIST INTERPRETIVE PARADIGM OF EMANCIPATORY PRAXIS[42]

A critical theology of liberation cannot avoid raising the question of the truth-content of the Bible for Christians today. If, for instance, feminist theologians take fully into account the androcentric language, misogynist contents, and patriarchal interests of biblical texts, then we cannot avoid the question of the "canon," or the criterion that allows us to reject oppressive traditions and to detect liberative traditions within biblical texts and history.

First, such a need for a critical evaluation of the various biblical texts and traditions has always been recognized in the church. While the doctrinal paradigm insisted that Scripture must be judged by the *regula fidei* and can only be properly interpreted by the teaching office of the church, the historical-critical paradigm evaluated the theological truth of biblical texts according to their historicity. The hermeneutic-contextual paradigm has not only established the canon as the pluriform root-model of the Christian community but has also underlined the fact that the Bible often includes various contradictory responses to the historical situation of the Israelite or Christian community.

Since not all these responses can equally express Christian revelation, biblical scholarship has attempted to formulate theological criteria to evaluate different biblical traditions. Such a "canon within the canon" can be formulated along philosophical-dogmatic or historical-factual lines. Some theologians distinguish between revelatory essence and historical expression, timeless truth and culturally conditioned language, or constant Christian tradition and changing traditions. When such a canon is formulated along the lines of the hermeneutic-contextual paradigm, scholars juxtapose Jesus and Paul, Pauline theology and early Catholicism, the historical Jesus and the kerygmatic Christ, or Hebrew and Greek thought. Whereas, for example, Ogden accepts as such a canon the Jesus-traditions of Marxsen,[43] Sobrino emphasizes the Jesus of history as the criterion for liberation theology. Segundo, on the other hand, is methodologically most consistent when he insists that no contextual biblical statement can be singled out as such a criterion because all historical expression of faith is ideological. In line with the hermeneutic-contextual paradigm, he insists that not the content but the process of

---

42. See Francis Schüssler Fiorenza's groundbreaking essay "Critical Social Theology and Christology: Toward an Understanding of Atonement and Redemption as an Emancipatory Solidarity," *Proceedings of the Catholic Theological Society of America* 30 (1975): 63-110.

43. Ogden, *Faith and Freedom,* pp. 44ff.; see also his essay "The Authority of the Scripture for Theology," *Interpretation* 30 (1976): 242-61.

interpretation within the Bible and Christian history should be normative for liberation theology. Yet such a proposal does not allow for the insight that this process of expressing faith in a historical situation can also be falsified and serve oppressive interests.

Therefore, a critical theology of liberation cannot take the Bible or the biblical faith defined as the total process of learning in and through ideologies as *norma normans non normata*[44] but must understand them as sources alongside other sources. This point was already made by James Cone, who pointed out that the sources of theology are the Bible as well as our own political situation and experience. However, the norm for black theology is *"Jesus as the Black Christ who provides the necessary soul for black liberation. . . . He is the essence of the Christian gospel."*[45]

I would be hesitant to postulate that Jesus as the feminist Christ is the canonical norm, since we cannot spell out concretely who this feminist Christ is if we do not want to make Christ a formalized *chiffre* or resort to mysticism. This is the argument of Jon Sobrino, who in turn postulates that the historical Jesus is the norm of truth since *"access to the Christ of faith comes through our following of the historical Jesus."*[46] However, such a formulation of the canonical norm for Christian faith presupposes that we can know the historical Jesus and that we can imitate him, since an actual following of Jesus is not possible for us. Moreover, a feminist theologian must question whether the historical man Jesus of Nazareth can be a role model for contemporary women, since feminist psychological liberation means exactly the struggle of women to free themselves from all male internalized norms and models.

Second, I would suggest that the canon and norm for evaluating biblical traditions and their subsequent interpretations cannot be derived from the Bible or the biblical process of learning within and through ideologies but can only be formulated within and through the struggle for the liberation of women and all oppressed people. It cannot be "universal," but it must be specific and derived from a particular experience of oppression and liberation. The "advocacy stance" of liberation theologies must be sustained at the point of the critical evaluation of biblical texts and traditions. The personally and politically reflected experience of oppression and liberation must become the criterion of "appropriateness" for biblical interpretation.

A hermeneutical understanding which is not only oriented toward

44. For a discussion of this expression, see David Tracy, "Theological Classics in Contemporary Theology," *Theology Digest* 25 (1977): 347-55.

45. Cone, *Liberation: A Black Theology of Liberation* (Philadelphia: Lippincott, 1970), p. 80.

46. Sobrino, "The Historical Jesus and the Christ of Faith," *Cross Currents* 27 (1977/78): 460.

an actualizing continuation of biblical history but also toward a critical evaluation of it must uncover and denounce biblical traditions and theologies that perpetuate violence, alienation, and oppression. At the same time, such a critical hermeneutics also must delineate those biblical traditions that bring forward the liberating experiences and visions of the people of God. Such a hermeneutics points to the eschatological vision of freedom and salvation and maintains that such a vision must be historically realized in the community of faith.

A feminist theological interpretation of the Bible that has as its canon the liberation of women from oppressive sexist structures, institutions, and internalized values must, therefore, maintain that only the nonsexist and nonandrocentric traditions of the Bible and the nonoppressive traditions of biblical interpretation have the theological authority of revelation if the Bible is not to continue as a tool for the oppression of women. The "advocacy stance" demands that oppressive and destructive biblical traditions cannot be accorded any truth and authority claim today.[47] Nor did they have such a claim at any point in history. Such a critical hermeneutic must be applied to *all* biblical texts and their historical contexts. It should also be applied to their subsequent history of interpretation in order to determine *how* much these traditions and interpretations have contributed to the patriarchal oppression of women. In the same vein, such a critical feminist hermeneutics must rediscover those biblical traditions and interpretations that have transcended their oppressive cultural contexts even though they are embedded in patriarchal culture. These texts and traditions should not be understood as abstract theological ideals or norms but as faith-responses to concrete historical situations of oppression. For instance, throughout the centuries Christian feminism has claimed Galatians 3:28 as its magna charta, while the patriarchal church has used 1 Corinthians 14 or 1 Timothy 2 for the cultural and ecclesial oppression of women.[48]

Third, the insight that the Bible is not only a source of truth and revelation but also a source of violence and domination is basic for liberation theologies. This insight demands a new paradigm of bib-

47. Such a proposal should not be misunderstood in the sense of the *Woman's Bible* approach that has singled out for discussion biblical texts on women. The criterion has to be applied to all biblical texts insofar as they claim authority for today. Such a theological evaluation must also be distinguished from a reconstruction of early Christian history in a feminist perspective. While a feminist reconstruction of early Christian history asks for women's history and heritage, a feminist biblical hermeneutics evaluates the truth-claims of biblical texts for today. Thus both approaches are interdependent but quite distinct.

48. See my analysis in "Word, Spirit, and Power."

lical interpretation that does not understand the Bible as archetype, but as prototype.

> A dictionary definition reveals the significant distinction between the words. While both archetype and prototype "denote original models," an archtype is "usually construed as an ideal form that establishes an unchanging pattern. . . ." However, . . . a prototype is not a binding, timeless pattern, but one critically open to the possibility, even the necessity of its own transformation. Thinking in terms of prototypes historicizes myth.[49]

Since the hermeneutic-contextual paradigm has as a goal the appropriation of biblical truth and history but not its ideological critique, liberation theologians must develop a new critical paradigm of biblical interpretation. T. S. Kuhn has pointed out that such a new scientific paradigm must also create a new scientific ethos and community.

The hermeneutic-contextual historical paradigm allows for the "advocacy stance" within the hermeneutical circle as a presupposition from which to raise questions but objects to it as a conviction or definite standpoint. However, a new critical paradigm must reject such a theory as ideological. It must, in turn, insist that all theologians and interpreters of the Bible stand publicly accountable for their own position. It should become methodologically *mandatory* that *all* scholars explicitly discuss their own presuppositions, allegiances, and functions within a theological-political context, and especially those scholars who in critiques of liberation theology resort to an artificially construed value-neutrality. Scholars no longer can pretend that what they do is completely "detached" from all political interests. Since we always interpret the Bible and Christian faith from a position within history, scholarly detachment and neutrality must be unmasked as a "fiction" or "false consciousness" that serves definite political interests. Further, theological interpretation must also critically reflect on the political presuppositions and implications of theological "classics" and dogmatic or ethical systems. In other words, not only the content and traditioning process within the Bible but the whole of Christian tradition should be scrutinized and judged as to whether or not it functions to oppress or liberate people.

Finally, the "advocacy stance" as a criterion or norm for evaluating biblical texts and their political functions should not be mistaken as an abstract, formalized principle. The different forms of a critical theology of liberation must construct specific heuristic models

---

49. Rachel Blau DuPlessis, "The Critique of Consciousness and Myth in Levertov, Rich, and Rukeyser," *Feminist Studies* 3 (1975): 219.

that adequately analyze the mechanisms and structures of contemporary oppression and movements for liberation. On the one hand, too generalized an understanding of oppression and liberation serves the interests of the oppressive systems which cannot tolerate a critical analysis of their dehumanizing mechanisms and structures. At the same time, it prevents the formulation of very specific goals and strategies for the liberation struggle. On the other hand, too particularized an understanding of oppression and liberation prevents an active solidarity among oppressed groups, who can be played out against each other by the established systems. The "advocacy stance" as the criterion or norm for biblical interpretation must, therefore, develop a critical theology of liberation that promotes the solidarity of all oppressed peoples, and at the same time has room enough to develop specific heuristic theological models of oppression and liberation.[50]

In conclusion, liberation theologians must abandon the hermeneutic-contextual paradigm of biblical interpretation, and construct within the context of a critical theology of liberation, a new interpretative paradigm that has as its aim emancipatory praxis. Such a paradigm of political praxis has as a research perspective the critical relationship between theory and practice, between biblical texts and contemporary liberation-movements. This new paradigm of emancipatory praxis must generate new heuristic models of interpretation that can interpret and evaluate biblical traditions and their political function in history in terms of their own canons of liberation.

50. Rosemary Radford Reuther has called for an "interstructuring" of various models of alienation/liberation (see *New Woman/New Earth: Sexist Ideologies and Human Liberation* [New York: Seabury Press, 1975], pp. 115-32).

INDEX